"Douglas Valentine writes books that rip th
criminal enterprise known as the US gover
he combines incredibly in-depth research, i
style of prose that exposes the dark truth al
national security state. *The CIA as Organized Crime* continues that
tradition and is an important and crucial text. Its publication would
be timely at any moment in recent history, yet its publication in late
2016 seems even more so given the recent campaign season and the
accompanying destruction of any semblance of a fair electoral process
in the United States."

—RON JACOBS, Counterpunch

"...connecting the CIA's geopolitical relativism to even more current
affairs, Valentine explores the recent failed support of the rebels in
Bashar al-Assad's Syria. Valentine emphasizes that 'Iran publicly
backs Assad, as does Russia, and that Iran seeks to help Assad defeat
the rebels, many of whom are foreign mercenaries trained and financed
by the CIA, Israel, Jordan, Turkey and Saudi Arabia.' Never have CIA
loyalties been more confused and counterintuitive, Valentine asserts,
than in a world where factions of our sworn enemies al-Qaeda and ISIS
aid us in our failed attempt to depose Assad."

—BRAD SCHREIBER, *Huffington Post*

"...in Valentine's view, the CIA is the hit team for the worst elements
of American business and those elements have their ideological hopes
pinned to the man in the Oval Office. So much for an intelligence
counter-revolution in response to the Trump revolution, responds
Valentine. Far more likely, in his view, that CIA provides the means
and modes of repression to keep those most likely to overturn the
domestic political applecart well in hand. Why? Because, Valentine
argues, this is precisely the CIA's operational stock-in-trade: the
brutalization of local politics as phase one; blackmail and murder as
phase two (already, he says, institutionalized in the Phoenix program
expertise and refined to a near-clinical degree post 9/11 with the
rendition/black sites program globally); and an American Phoenix
program, ready and waiting in the wings, he says, to be operationalized
against those on US soil who oppose the status quo."

—The Daily Kos

"Taking on the CIA as a subject is a monumental task, as its tentacles delve into myriad facets of empire and society. The CIA operates as a mafioso on a grand scale, an imperial scale. Valentine's depth of knowledge on the subject is very apparent. The CIA is known as a surveillance and information gathering apparatus of the USA that engages in various international intrigues. That view of the CIA is superficial. *The CIA as Organized Crime* presents the CIA as much more and in decidedly more sinister shades."

—KIM PETERSEN, Dissident Voice

"[W]hat the author has to say is important, and his analysis opens us to a clearer understanding of the Big Picture. Interlocked with the State Department and the military, not to mention all the other intelligence agencies with vast funds at their command, the CIA has increasingly applied social science to the plan for "controlling the natives" of every contested land. Operation Phoenix, which we understand to be a mass murder project of the 1960s in South Vietnam, failed at pacification but not at setting out a blueprint still central to operations. Specialists of all kinds, most emphatically working in universities as well as think tanks, are naturally central...Thanks to extensive interviews, he has an almost intimate feel for the operating mentality of the agency, why they operate the way they do—not only their bloody-minded ruthlessness or their rationalizations, important and interesting as these are—and why they are unbothered by such distinctions as Republican or Democratic presidents."

—PAUL BUHLE, Portside

"Valentine, a warrior of astute knowledge from his wanderings in the CIA's labyrinth, has reemerged with his new guidebook to the Minotaur's deadly ways. *The CIA As Organized Crime* is a tour de force, a counterpuncher's no-holds-barred passionate battle to reverse "the terrible truth . . . that a Cult of Death rules America and is hell-bent on world domination." Unlike many writers, he holds back nothing. He names names. He is adamantine in his accusations against those he considers accomplices—in particular, "the compatible left"—"liberals and pseudo-intellectual status seekers who are easily influenced"—in the CIA/media/elite's efforts at domination and mind-control."

—Prof. EDWARD CURTIN, The Intrepid Report

THE CIA
AS ORGANIZED
CRIME

How Illegal Operations
Corrupt America and the World

by

Douglas Valentine

Clarity Press, Inc

© 2017 Douglas Valentine

ISBN: 978-0-9972870-1-1

EBOOK ISBN: 978-0-9972870-2-8

In-house editor: Diana G. Collier

Cover: R. Jordan P. Santos

Photo Douglas Valentine: Michael S. Gordon, *The Republican*

Library of Congress Cataloging-in-Publication Data

Names: Valentine, Douglas, 1949- author.
Title: The CIA as organized crime : how illegal operations corrupt
America
  and the world / by Douglas Valentine.
Description: Atlanta, GA : Clarity Press, Inc., 2017. | Includes
  bibliographical references and index.
Identifiers: LCCN 2016035980 (print) | LCCN 2016046335 (ebook) |
ISBN
  9780997287011 (alk. paper) | ISBN 9780997287028
Subjects: LCSH: United States. Central Intelligence Agency--Corrupt
  practices. | Phoenix Program (Counterinsurgency program : Vietnam) |
  Organized crime. | Drug traffic.
Classification: LCC JK486.I6 V35 2017 (print) | LCC JK486.I6 (ebook)
| DDC
  327.1273--dc23
LC record available at https://lccn.loc.gov/2016035980

Clarity Press, Inc.
2625 Piedmont Rd. NE, Ste. 56
Atlanta, GA. 30324 , USA
http://www.claritypress.com

TABLE OF CONTENTS

"Personal violence is for the amateur in dominance, structural violence is the tool of the professional. The amateur who wants to dominate uses guns; the professional uses social structure."
—Johan Galtung

ACKNOWLEDGMENTS

I've taken many liberties with the interview transcripts and articles, expounding and updating for relevance, editing out and consolidating information to avoid repetition. Though a compilation, the material is arranged in narrative form to entertain, hopefully, as well as educate.

I'd like to thank my interviewers for indulging me:

Ryan Dawson is Webmaster and host for www.ANCreport.com which features podcasts on politics and economics with professionals from around the world.

Guillermo Jimenez is the owner and editor of Traces of Reality and a regular columnist for the Pan American Post. He is based in South Texas, deep within the DHS "constitution-free zone."

Ken McCarthy is an American activist, educator, entrepreneur and Internet commercialization pioneer. Brasscheck TV features videos on a wide range of contemporary topics, available via e-mail subscription.

Lew Rockwell is an American libertarian author and editor, self-professed anarcho-capitalist promoter of the Austrian School of economics, and founder and chairman of the Ludwig von Mises Institute.

James Tracy is the author of numerous scholarly publications. His weekly interview program, Real Politik, has been carried on TruthFrequencyRadio.com since 2014, and is published as a podcast on his website, MemoryHoleBlog.com.

Kourosh Ziabari is an award-winning Iranian journalist, writer and media correspondent writing for newspapers and journals across the world.

My co-author of the "War Crimes as Policy" article, Nicolas J. S. Davies, is the author of *Blood on Our Hands: the American Invasion and Destruction of Iraq* (Nimble Books: 2010).

I'd like to say thanks to Diana Collier for envisioning this book; Thomas Wilkinson, Adam Engel and Kara Zugman Dellacioppa for rounding out my thoughts; John Prados for preserving my work at the National Security Archive; and Mark Crispin Miller for giving *The Phoenix Program* new life at Open Road. Special thanks to Robert Parry at Consortium News, and the late Alex Cockburn and Jeff St. Clair at Counterpunch for publishing my articles.

Most of all, thanks to Alice.

Douglas Valentine
1 August 2016

Credit for prior publication should go to the following:

Chapter 1: How William Colby Gave Me the Keys to the CIA Kingdom (adapted from a July 2015 interview with Professor James Tracy at Real Politic, originally titled "Interview 56: Douglas Valentine").

Chapter 2: One Thing Leads to Another: My Rare Access in Investigating the War on Drugs (adapted from a January 2015 interview with Ryan Dawson at ANC Report, originally titled "Cops, the CIA, Drugs and the Mafia").

Chapter 3: The Vietnam War's Silver Lining: A Bureaucratic Model for Population Control Emerges (adapted from a May 2015 article at Dissident Voice, originally titled "Inside the CIA's Use of Terror During the Vietnam War").

Chapter 4: The Systematic Gathering of Intelligence (adapted from a May 2004 article at Counterpunch, originally titled "ABCs of American Interrogation Methods").

Chapter 5: What We Really Learned From Vietnam: A War Crimes Model for Afghanistan and Elsewhere (adapted from a November 2009 article at Consortium News, originally titled "Learning the Wrong Vietnam Lessons").

Chapter 6: The Afghan 'Dirty War' Escalates (adapted from a January 2010 article at Consortium News).

Chapter 7: Vietnam Replay on Afghan Defectors (adapted from a February 2010 article at Consortium News).

Chapter 8: Disrupting the Accommodation: CIA Killings Spell Victory in Afghanistan and Defeat in America (adapted from a January 2010 article at Dissident Voice, originally titled "Disrupting the Accommodation: CIA Killings Spell Defeat in Afghanistan").

Chapter 9: The CIA in Ukraine (adapted from an interview with Ryan Dawson in May 2014, originally titled "Doug Valentine on the CIA and NGOs in Ukraine, date was May 2014.

Chapter 10: War Crimes as Policy (adapted from a May 2013 article with Nicolas Davies at Counterpunch) pp. 95 – 101.

Chapter 11: New Games, Same Aims: CIA Organizational Changes (adapted from a November 2014 interview with Guillermo Jimenez originally titled "The CIA Has Become the Phoenix").

Chapter 12: Creating a Crime: How the CIA Commandeered the DEA (adapted from a September 2015 article at Counterpunch).

INTRODUCTION

Chapter 1

HOW WILLIAM COLBY GAVE ME THE KEYS TO THE CIA KINGDOM

JAMES TRACY: You've been doing historical research for close to 40 years and I wanted to ask how you orient yourself toward a project. How you know where to look for information that's pertinent to a given story.

VALENTINE: It's complicated, and my experience was different from other writers and researchers I've spoken with about it. From the time I started college back in 1967, I wanted to be a writer. And since then my philosophy of life has been based on the study of language and literary criticism. I have a very broad approach. I started out studying Greek and Roman literature, reading the Norton anthologies of English and American literature, taking courses in classical myth and the Bible. Very early in my studies I was introduced to literary criticism, to people like Robert Graves, poet and author of *The White Goddess*, and Sir James Fraser who wrote *The Golden Bough*. Fraser brought a socio-anthropological way of looking at the world of literature. That led me to Carl Jung, Eric Newman, Northrop Frye and a few other people who approached literature from a variety of different perspectives – psychological, political, anthropological, sociological, historical, philosophical. All those things were of interest to me. When I look at a subject I look at it comprehensively from all those different points of view.

Literary criticism teaches the power of symbolic transformation, of processing experience into ideas, into meaning. To be a Madison

Avenue adman, one must understand how to use symbols and myths to sell commodities. Admen use logos and slogans, and so do political propagandists. Left or right; doesn't matter. The left is as adept at branding as the right. To be a speech writer or public relations consultant one must, above all, understand the archetypal power of the myth of the hero. That way you can transform, through words, Joe the Plumber or even a mass murderer, into a national hero.

When I decided to research and write about the CIA's Phoenix program,[1] that was how I went at it. I went directly to William Colby, who'd been Director of the Central Intelligence Agency. Colby was the person most associated with Phoenix, the controversial CIA "assassination" program that resulted in the death of tens of thousands of civilians during the Vietnam War. No one had written a book about it, so I wrote Colby a letter and sent him my first book, *The Hotel Tacloban*. I told him I wanted to write a book that would de-mystify the Phoenix program, and he was all for that. Colby liked my approach – to look at it from all these different points of view – so he got behind me and started introducing me to a lot of senior CIA people. And that gave me access from the inside. After that it was pretty easy. I have good interview skills. I was able to persuade a lot of these CIA people to talk about Phoenix.

But I also approached it from an organizational point of view, which is absolutely essential when writing about bureaucracies like the CIA or the DEA. You really have to understand them as a bureaucracy, that they have an historical arc. They begin somewhere, they have a Congressional mandate, they have a purpose, and organizational and management structures. And in that regard I really lucked out. One of the first people I interviewed was the CIA officer, Nelson Brickham, who actually organized the Phoenix program. Brickham graduated magna cum laude from Yale and was something of an organizational genius. He explained to me how he organized Phoenix. He also explained the different divisions and branches of the CIA so I'd be able to understand it.

So I lucked out. Through Colby I had access to the people in the CIA who created the Phoenix program, and I was able to find out what was on their minds and why they did what they did. That never would have happened if I had gone to the Columbia School of Journalism, or if I'd been involved with journalism for many years. I'd have had a much narrower way of going at the thing. But the CIA officers I spoke with loved the broad view that I was bringing to the subject. They liked me asking them about their philosophy. It enabled me to understand the subject comprehensively.

TRACY: There's an associate of William Colby's whom you discuss and write about, also a CIA officer, Evan Parker. You were able to get a great many names from him and then you asked these people for interviews. The interview subjects, many of whom were CIA personnel, would go back to Colby or Parker and ask if it was okay to speak to you. Correct?

VALENTINE: That's right. Once I had Colby's approbation, many CIA officers thought I was in the CIA. No one had heard of me. I wasn't Morley Safer or Seymour Hersh or someone who'd been a celebrity reporter in Vietnam. I was a Nobody, in the Eduardo Galeano sense of the word. I'd published a book about my father's experiences in World War Two which some of these guys would read. Those who did read *The Hotel Tacloban* tended to like it, because it was sympathetic to soldiers and showed I understood what it means to be a soldier. Most CIA officers consider themselves to be soldiers. The CIA is set up as a military organization with a chain of command. Somebody tells you what to do, and you salute and do it.

Evan Parker had that feeling about me – that I would understand him personally, why he did the things he did, because I'd written this sympathetic book about my father as a soldier, and because Colby sent me to him. I had an interesting experience with him. He invited me to his house for an interview and when I arrived, he invited me upstairs to his little den, which was stacked with bookshelves full of Welsh history and poetry books. Parker is a Welsh name. Because of my background in literature, I was able to talk to him about things like *The Mabinogion*, which is a book about Welsh mythology. I had this broad knowledge that helped me relate to people like him. I put him at ease.

Also, for a year before I started interviewing people, I'd read everything I could find about Vietnam and the CIA. I was knowledgeable, plus I looked like a good Methodist. I wore a suit and a tie. We spoke for an hour and Parker got to like me. I hadn't asked him anything about the CIA. We were just getting to know each other. But he had a stack of official-looking documents on his coffee table. He glanced at the documents and politely said he was going down to get us some tea and cookies. "It'll take about fifteen minutes. I'll be back." He winked and went downstairs.

I opened the top folder. It was a roster of everybody in the Phoenix Directorate from when Parker started it in the summer of 1967. I started furiously writing their names and ranks and the position they held in the program. Fifteen minutes later as I'm writing the last name, he yells from downstairs: "Doug, the tea is ready. I'm coming up." I closed the file and put my notebook away. He came up with a tray with tea and cookies on it. He winked, and sat down, and I started to ask him about Phoenix.

We never got to the documents on his desk. But he liked me and he referred me to people. That's the way it went with most of the CIA people I met. They cooperated because Colby had sent me to them. Like Parker said, "(Colby) was the Director and we still consider him to be the Director. If he says you're okay, we believe it."

He didn't say, "Now I can waive my secrecy oath." But that's what they did.

I talked to members of almost every branch of the CIA and I approached my interviews organizationally. What kind of a budget did you have? Who was your boss and how did you report to him? Who worked for you and what jobs did you give them? I had a big organizational chart in my den and I'd fill in names and positions. I never asked anyone, "Did you kill anybody? Did you do this kind of illegal thing?" And because I approached it in that benign way, they were confident I was de-mystifying the program and just sticking to the facts. It had the effect of reverse psychology. They trusted me because I didn't ask them their secrets — so they told me their secrets.

They didn't like it in the end because I exposed all the secrets. I talked to so many people that eventually they all started thinking that I was CIA. Because the CIA compartmentalizes itself, I ended up knowing more about the program than any individual in the CIA. I got a rat-a-tat going and pitted them against each other. They started telling me secrets about their rivals. They all want to be the hero in their myth.

TRACY: The interviews you conducted and the multitude of conversations you documented were placed alongside actual documentation which you had to acquire through a considerable amount of research.

VALENTINE: In the interviews, people were giving me original documents to confirm their assertions. Nelson Brickham was the CIA's head of Foreign Intelligence Field Operations in Saigon (1965-1967).

Brickham managed the liaison officers the CIA placed in the provinces to work with the South Vietnamese Police Special Branch, which is an organization like our FBI. The CIA created and funded the Special Police and sent them after the Viet Cong's civilian leadership, and anyone else trying to undermine the American puppet government. Phoenix is political warfare. He managed the staff that ran all those operations in the provinces.

In late 1966 the CIA station chief in Saigon, John Hart, was working on improving operations against the VC's leadership with a CIA officer in Washington, Robert Komer. Komer was Lyndon Johnson's personal aide on pacification in Vietnam, what was called "the other war". Anyway, Hart gave Brickham the task of creating a general staff for pacification, at which point Brickham went to work for Komer. In creating a general staff for pacification, Brickham cobbled together the Phoenix program. And Brickham gave me, over the course of several interviews, copies of all the original documents he wrote for Komer and Hart. These were the enabling documents of the Phoenix program.

That happened a lot. I'd ask a guy if he had any documents to back up what he was saying and if he did he'd give me copies of what he kept in his library. Everyone thought because Colby had sent me that somehow this was all going to be okay. I wasn't going to reveal all this stuff or that Colby had decided it was okay to reveal all of it.

The documents Brickham gave me showed in his own words what he was thinking when he created the Phoenix program. I posted all those documents online at Cryptocomb, along with the taped interviews with Brickham, Colby, Parker and several other CIA and military officers. They are part of the collection titled *The CIA Speaks*. I put them online so my critics can't challenge me on the facts, other than by making up things, which they do all the time. I just quoted from these documents and my interviews. So it's accurate reporting.[2]

TRACY: There is a Douglas Valentine Collection at the National Security Archives at George Washington University.

VALENTINE: Yes, the collection contains my interview notes with close to 100 CIA officers and military officers involved in the Phoenix program. People kept referring me to people, and I made some great connections. I met a guy named Tullius Acampora who recently passed away; he was in his nineties. He'd been an army counterintelligence officer and worked for General Douglas MacArthur in Shanghai after World War Two. When the CIA was formed, Tully, like many army counterintelligence officers, started working with the counterintelligence staff at the CIA. He was detailed to the CIA. Although he kept his military rank, Tully was a CIA officer for many years. He went to Italy in 1958 and met and worked closely with Bureau of Narcotics agents in Rome. In the 50s and 60s, federal narcotic agents spent half their time doing favors for the CIA, and in exchange the CIA gave them intelligence on the mobsters they were going after.

Tully was sent to Vietnam in 1966 and was involved in one of the "anti-infrastructure" programs that Phoenix was based upon. Tully's program was called Cong Tac IV and, like Phoenix, it targeted civilians who were functioning as secret agents for the Viet Cong. When the CIA and military created Phoenix, Evan Parker moved into Tully's office. Tully knew the top Vietnamese officials and CIA officers in Vietnam, and he also knew the Italian Americans who were prominent in the Bureau of Narcotics and later the DEA. Tully and I became personal friends and he introduced me to senior people from the Bureau of Narcotics and the DEA.

The same way I had entrée through Colby into the CIA, I had an entrée through Tully into federal drug law enforcement at a high level. I met historically important people and got historically important documents, most of it new history. I haven't gotten around to digitizing the tapes of the federal drug law enforcement officers I interviewed, but there are separate collections at the National Security Archive, for both my CIA/Phoenix program materials and my federal drug law enforcement materials.

TRACY: I'm wondering how the former governor of Pennsylvania and Bush administration officer, Tom Ridge, fits into all this. Was he not involved in Operation Phoenix?

VALENTINE: I'm not sure about Ridge. He was in an infantry unit in Vietnam from late 1969 into 1970. He worked in a team with four Americans and seven Vietnamese soldiers going after insurgents, not North Vietnamese regulars. So he was part of the pacification program. He got a bronze star for killing a young man carrying a sack of potatoes. He may have been a sniper and he may have been involved in one of the programs Phoenix coordinated, but it doesn't seem like he was a Phoenix advisor.

Ridge had been a governor and had executive management experience when he was appointed to run the Office of Homeland Security and later the Department of Homeland Security (DHS). He was a political cadre who could be trusted to implement Republican Party policy.

At the same time, the Department of Homeland Security was based on the Phoenix program model Nelson Brickham developed in Vietnam. Ridge may have had some related pacification experience, which is what homeland security is; but he certainly understood how to manage organizations. The key word is coordination. When the National Security Establishment wanted to centralize the War on Terror here in the United States, through the DHS, they copied how Phoenix had coordinated multiple agencies in order to streamline and bureaucratize the war against the Viet Cong Infrastructure (VCI).

Phoenix proved an incredibly successful model for pacification in South Vietnam. It was the silver lining in the Vietnam War. Politically the war was a disaster, but bureaucratically the Phoenix program succeeded. It became the model for CIA operations in Central America – the Salvador Option.

The Phoenix program established Intelligence Operations and Coordinating Centers in the provinces and districts (PIOCCs and DIOCCs) of South Vietnam. Similarly, the Department of Homeland Security has created "fusion centers" in every state and major city across the country. The fusion centers coordinate all the agencies in an area exactly like IOCCs did in Vietnam; systematized and computerized, they coordinate contributing intelligence analysts and operating units. It's the same highly bureaucratized system for dispensing with anything and anyone who can't be assimilated.

TRACY: That's an ominous set of observations for someone who has studied the Phoenix program in such great depth. You are saying the Phoenix template is something that has been grafted onto the American homeland.

VALENTINE: Absolutely. And I'm not the only one that talks about it. David Kilcullen was a counterinsurgency advisor to the Bush and Obama administrations and in 2004 he called for a global Phoenix operation.[3]

Tom Hayden described Kilcullen as the "chief advisor on counterinsurgency operations" to General David Petraeus "in planning the 2007 US troop surge (in Iraq). He also served as chief strategist in the State Department's counterterrorism office in 2005 and 2006, and has been employed in Iraq, Pakistan, Afghanistan, the Horn of Africa and Southeast Asia. In the section titled 'A Global Phoenix Program' in his 2004 article, Kilcullen describes the Vietnam Phoenix program as 'unfairly maligned' and 'highly effective.' Dismissing CIA sponsorship and torture allegations as 'popular mythology,' Kilcullen calls Phoenix a misunderstood 'civilian aid and development program' that was supported by 'pacification' operations to disrupt the Vietcong, whose infrastructure ruled vast swaths of rural South Vietnam. A 'global Phoenix program,' he wrote, would provide a starting point for dismantling the worldwide jihadist infrastructure today."[4]

TRACY: How did Kilcullen want to see a Phoenix program imposed upon the world?

VALENTINE: If he understood it correctly, he'd know that the strength of the Phoenix program was in the IOCC centers, which allowed for political control. Through a network of Phoenix centers, management is able to control targeting and messaging. I imagine Kilcullen wanted such highly bureaucratized centers set up in or near nations in which the CIA and military are hunting terrorists. Such centers would allow the White House to direct the CIA to direct the military to target the right terrorists. Leave ours alone.

Seymour Hersh is always looked to for insight into the CIA. In December 2003 he wrote an article in *The New Yorker* in which he said the Special Operations people in the military were going to use Phoenix as a model in Iraq.[5] True to his high-toned style, Hersh focused on the sensational "death squad" aspect of Phoenix, not the revealing organizational aspect. He keeps the focus narrow.

Phoenix is greater than the sum of its parts because it has symbolic meaning. But its lurid aspects – like the death squads Hersh emphasizes – grab everyone's attention. In Iraq, the CIA handed out decks of "playing" cards featuring pictures of "High Value" Sunni officials in the Saddam Hussein government. That psywar gimmick and jargon was right out of the Phoenix program.

The purpose of the Phoenix program was to "neutralize" the civilian members of the underground revolutionary government in South Vietnam. Neutralize was a broad term that included a number of measures.

The first step was to identity a suspected subversive. After that, Nelson Brickham, the CIA officer who created Phoenix in 1967, explained the process to me as follows: "My motto was to recruit them; if you can't recruit them, defect them (that's Chieu Hoi); if you can't defect them, capture them; if you can't capture them, kill them. That was my attitude toward high-level VCI."

VCI was the acronym for Viet Cong Infrastructure – the name the CIA gave to the members of the revolutionaries' underground government and guerrilla support system.

As part of its Congressional mandate, the CIA has the job of counter-subversion outside the United States. Thus, when the US is waging a counterinsurgency in a nation like Iraq or Afghanistan, the CIA pursues a political order of battle, while the US armed forces pursue a military order of battle. In practice, however, counter-subversion during a counterinsurgency is a paramilitary police function. Thus, in South Vietnam, the US military supported the CIA's Phoenix program with troops and equipment.

In 1969, the CIA ostensibly turned the Phoenix program over to the US military, at which point soldiers first began to pursue a political order of battle and conduct systematic counter-subversive operations against foreign civilians. The creation of Phoenix was a watershed. Prior to it, military people were only allowed to target civilians if they were secret agents or guerrillas attacking military bases or personnel. But in its fanatical pursuit of victory in Vietnam, the military deliberately blurred the lines between subversives and innocent civilians, and killed anyone who got in the way, including children, like it did at My Lai and a thousand other places.

Following its ignoble defeat in Vietnam, America was driven by a reactionary impulse to reassert its global dominance. The justifications used to rationalize Phoenix were institutionalized as policy, as became evident after 9/11 and the initiation of the War on Terror. Since then the CIA and US military have been conducting joint Phoenix-style operations worldwide without any compunctions, most prominently in Afghanistan and Iraq.

Also evolving was the relationship between the CIA, the military and the media. In Vietnam, there was more press freedom and the carnage was filmed and shown on TV every night. But the CIA and military felt those images turned the public against the war, so by the time America invaded Iraq in 2003, reporters were embedded in military units. The media became a PR unit of the military and the CIA, with the Orwellian result that the public did not see images of the mangled bodies. The public was denied access to the truth of what its government was actually doing, and when Chelsea Manning leaked the Collateral Murder video to Wikileaks, she was summarily tried and imprisoned.[6]

When I was doing my interviews for *The Phoenix Program*, certain CIA people would tell me how a particular correspondent from CBS or *The New York Times* would come into their offices and ask about the programs they managed. The CIA officers would talk openly about their operations, but the Vietnam-era correspondents wouldn't publish the details, because their editors had a gentlemen's agreement with the CIA not to reveal the secrets. They could know the secrets and as long as they didn't reveal them, they could continue to have access.

While I was researching Phoenix, I went to people like Seymour Hersh and Gloria Emerson but they wouldn't talk to me. I had a harder time getting reporters to talk to me than I did CIA people, because as soon as they expressed any knowledge about Phoenix, the follow up question was: Why weren't you writing about it? Then they'd have to reveal this gentlemen's agreement with the CIA.

The "old boy" network existed in Vietnam but it's gotten a lot worse; it's impossible now for anyone to interview mid-level CIA people on the record and reveal the facts. Since Iran Contra, the bureaucracies have instituted incredible obstacles that make it impossible for people to see what's going on inside their private club. The public is totally reliant now on whistle-blowers like Chelsea Manning and Edward Snowden, who are then vilified, imprisoned, and/or chased into exile.

TRACY: We see what, for example, happened to Gary Webb in the mid-1990s. He had some people who had divulged significant information to him and yet the CIA denied it, and that more or less cost him his career. He had no one, no colleagues of his, who actually went to bat for him to any significant degree to keep him in the industry because what he was doing is what investigative journalists and historians, such as you, should be doing.

VALENTINE: Yes. Gary Webb was an investigative journalist whose "Dark Alliance" series in 1996 exposed the link between the CIA's "Contras" in Central America and a crack cocaine dealer in Los Angeles. The story rattled the CIA. Members of the black community were up in arms. Then the CIA's old boy network sprang into action and Webb was nit-picked to death by fellow journalists for minor inaccuracies in his work. But his real sin was revealing the CIA's criminal involvement in systematic racial oppression through the war on drugs.

Webb committed suicide in 2004. But he wasn't the first American citizen to be attacked for telling the truth about the CIA's central role in drug trafficking. In his 1972 book *The Politics in Heroin in Southeast Asia*, Al McCoy detailed much of the CIA's drug network in Vietnam and the Golden Triangle region of Laos, Burma and Thailand. When the CIA found out what McCoy was doing, one of its most senior executives, Cord Meyer, tried to get McCoy's publisher to suppress the book. When that didn't work, the CIA tapped McCoy's phone and the IRS audited his income tax. Behind the scenes, the CIA forced McCoy's sources to recant. The famous Church Committee, which exposed a lot of the CIA's secrets, investigated McCoy's allegations and found the CIA innocent of any involvement in drug trafficking. McCoy moved to Australia and didn't return to America for eleven years.

The CIA's control of international drug trafficking is America's darkest secret, and after the Webb scandal, the old boy network imposed even more restrictions on the media. The pressures the CIA imposes on the media amount to political warfare directed against the American public. It's no different than how the CIA mounts counter-subversion operations overseas.

Nowadays, the only way you can discern what's going on is by studying and understanding the historical arc of these bureaucracies. Where did the CIA come from? Where is it going? If you look at it historically, you can see beyond the spin and it becomes de-mystified. And that is not a happy story. As power gets more concentrated in the security services, the media is no longer simply compliant, it's functioning as their public relations arm. It simply ignores anything that contradicts the official line.

TRACY: There is almost a complete blackout of Jade Helm in the mainstream media. It is only getting coverage and discussion and analysis in the alternative media.

VALENTINE: Yes. Jade Helm was a military training exercise in Texas, Arizona, Florida, Louisiana, Mississippi, New Mexico and Utah. Military and local officials set up Phoenix-style coordination centers, as a way of giving Special Operations and "Civil Affairs" personnel experience working with para-militarized police forces in what was called a realistic "war experience" in domestic counterinsurgency operations. The media blackout was an essential part of the plan. The censorship was symbolic of how, as a function of the concentration of capital, the communications/media industry has been centralized and is now part of the political warfare apparatus. The media industry has been reduced to a few huge corporations that control most of the outlets. Control of information has become the key to the oligarchy's success. Very few independent news organizations are able to compete with the giants, or get information out across the country, so people really have to search for facts on the Internet

TRACY: Even some of the alternative progressive left media that were good twenty or so years ago are increasingly dependent upon foundation money that comes with strings attached, and they're not as inclined to push the envelope as I think they once were.

VALENTINE: Sure. As a person who is interested in how the CIA uses language and mythology to control political and social movements, I see this development as ominous. People like Glenn Greenwald who take money from billionaires insist it has no editorial influence on them. But media people who are taking money from billionaires and CIA-connected foundations must realize that their sugar daddies can sink their operations in a moment because of something they write, and that knowledge surely impacts what they are willing to do and say.

Taking money from a billionaire also has tremendous symbolic meaning. It means the person taking the money approves of one person having eight billion dollars when three billion people barely survive. Through their example, celebrity media figures like Greenwald are telling their followers that they support the exploitation and imperialism their benefactors engage in.

As all advertising people know, symbolic messages don't have to be articulated, they're understood subliminally. Greenwald's followers like it that way. It means they don't have to consciously confront their tacit support for an unjust system. That self-censorship allows celebrity journalists like Greenwald and his sidekick Jeremy Scahill to promote themselves as heroic adversaries of the system. And they'll continue to get away with the double game until their followers start challenging their own basic assumptions. The system will never change until people climb out of their comfortable darkness and start rejecting the system's inequalities, instead of just feeding off of them.

TRACY: You mention Greenwald. There are other prominent figures on the left who fashion themselves as freedom fighters in the informational sphere, where that's arguably not the case. This is something that I think goes back over forty years to Daniel Ellsberg. The most important case in freedom of the press in the twentieth century, if not the country's history, was the Pentagon Papers, and yet Ellsberg himself was a member of the CIA.

VALENTINE: Well, Greenwald and Ellsberg certainly aren't "left", and Ellsberg was not a fully integrated, back-stopped employee of the CIA. But for a period of time in 1965 and 1966, he did work for the CIA's station chief in Saigon, John Hart (whom I mentioned earlier as having initiated the Phoenix program), gathering intelligence on what prominent South Vietnamese politicians and officials were thinking. I was told that Ellsberg could recall conversations verbatim, and that he was introduced to these important political people at social events and then reported to Hart about their thoughts. He was also working at a high level in the pacification programs upon which Phoenix was based. Ellsberg worked with CIA officers Edward Lansdale and Lucien Conein, and US Information Service officer Frank Scotton, about whom more remains to be said.

The problem is that Ellsberg presented himself in his autobiography as having been working with the State Department. That was his cover. And in the movie about him, he's pictured in an army uniform on patrol. He misrepresented himself. He wasn't honest. All of his work with the CIA is absent. Why?

It goes back to the fact that Ellsberg was a full-fledged hawk who turned against the Vietnam War. But after he leaked the Pentagon Papers, the left adopted him as a symbol of someone who saw the light. The left takes credit for ending the war, and Ellsberg is a central character in its narrative. So the anti-war movement in particular and the left (whatever that is) in general goes along with the cover story.

But people can't understand the significance of the Pentagon Papers, or the true nature of the Vietnam War, without understanding Ellsberg's work for the CIA. His worldview was defined by his intimate relationships with his mentor, Ed Lansdale,[7] and the other political warfare people he worked with in Vietnam, especially Frank Scotton. Ellsberg, Scotton, and a handful of other experts prepared America's organizational blueprint for pacifying South Vietnam's civilian population in the seminal "Roles and Missions" report in August 1966. That study sets the stage for the Phoenix program.

All this loops back to the issue of access. I didn't know who Scotton was until Colby referred me to him in 1986. Like the other people Colby referred me to, Scotton thought I was CIA-approved. He tried to impress me, and when I interviewed him at his home in McLean, Virginia, he said "we" (which could only have meant him and Colby) had instructed Ellsberg to release the Pentagon Papers. Scotton has since written an autobiography in which he denies having told Ellsberg to do it. He now says Ellsberg merely showed him the Pentagon Paper documents in 1970.

All this also loops back to CIA drug trafficking. A moment ago I mentioned that Al McCoy's sources had recanted. Chief among McCoy's sources who recanted was Dan Ellsberg's former comrade, Lou Conein. When McCoy spoke to him in the summer of 1971, Conein confessed to having arranged a truce between the CIA and Corsican drug traffickers in 1965, at the same time he was working with Ellsberg.

The summer of 1971 was a busy time as well. Colby was due to testify to Congress about the Phoenix program in July, but a larger event grabbed the headlines. On June 13, 1971, *The New York Times* began printing lengthy excerpts from the Pentagon Papers – that painstakingly edited stack of documents that, even by name, deflected attention away from the CIA. Consequently, little public attention was paid when, on July 15, 1971, the *Times* reported: "Previously classified information read into the record of a House Government Operations subcommittee today disclosed that 26,843 non-military Vietcong insurgents and sympathizers were neutralized in 14 months through Operation Phoenix."

All these threads weave together to create the myths Americans believe about the CIA; and Ellsberg's cover story is part of the fictionalized tale.

TRACY: The reluctance of certain editors to publish what you've researched and revealed about Ellsberg, do you think in part that has to do with just a wish to sustain the legend of Ellsberg, the symbol of what he's become?

VALENTINE: Sure. They're part of the same network of management level media people the CIA influences; what CIA officer Cord Meyer dubbed "the Compatible Left".

Let me tell you about my experience with the Compatible Left. William Morrow & Company published *The Phoenix Program* in 1990, but before it hit the bookstands, *The New York Times* gave it a terrible review. After that, the media wouldn't touch it with a ten-foot pole. As far as the left was concerned, the book presented new material they couldn't digest. I guess it threatened their proprietary claim on Vietnam War history.

The militant Right was never going to acknowledge it anyway. But the left's leadership is part of the CIA's old boy network and like all American intellectuals, they look to the *Times* for direction and validation. So the word went out to ignore the book, not just because it revealed CIA secrets, but because it identified the media, and the *Times* in particular, as the reason why the public can't see the CIA clearly for what it is: a criminal conspiracy on behalf of wealthy capitalists.

I had also noted that the release of the Pentagon Papers distracted attention from Congressional hearings into Phoenix. In subsequent books I added that it distracted attention from reports on CIA drug trafficking as well.

In any event, all my access to the CIA was meaningless. The CIA through its friends in the media was able to "neutralize" me. Only a handful of people recognized the book's historical value – people like Al McCoy, who called the book "the definitive account" in a blurb for the iUniverse edition.

But my supporters all had the same response: I'd crossed the line and would never get another book published in the United States. So I learned the hard way that the CIA has a strategic intelligence network of management level people in the information industry who know, through instruments like the Times Book Review section, what books and authors to marginalize.

Peter Dale Scott had also been marginalized as a result of his 1972 book, *The War Conspiracy*, and his 1993 book, *Deep Politics and the Death of JFK*. Peter supported me, and a few years after the Phoenix book was published, I mentioned to him that I was writing an article, based on my interviews with Scotton and Conein, about Ellsberg's deep political association with the CIA. Peter is Ellsberg's friend, and even though the article had the potential to embarrass Ellsberg, he arranged for me to interview him. Peter gave me Ellsberg's number and I called at a pre-arranged time. And the first thing Ellsberg said to me was, "You can't possibly understand me because you're not a celebrity."

If you want to understand the critical role celebrities play in determining what society accepts as real and valuable, read Guy Debord's books *The Society of the Spectacle* and its sequel, *Comments*. Debord explains the symbolic role celebrities play (at times inadvertently) in maintaining the illusions we confuse with reality.

Debord cites the German philosopher Ludwig Feuerbach, who famously said: "But certainly for the present age, which prefers the sign to the thing signified, the copy to the original, representation to reality, the appearance to the essence... illusion only is sacred, truth profane. Nay, sacredness is held to be enhanced in proportion as truth decreases and illusion increases, so that the highest degree of illusion comes to be the highest degree of sacredness."

When Ellsberg told me he was a celebrity, he was saying that he underwent a symbolic transformation the moment he leaked the Pentagon Papers, and landed in a social realm that alienated him from non-celebrities like me. He became an icon, and nobody on the left is about to say, "Oh, my god! Valentine had this revelation about Ellsberg. Let's rethink everything we believe is true."

Like its doppelgangers on the right, the management class on the left is invested in celebrity heroes who represent their business interests. They focus on the symbol and ignore any contradictory but essential facts, the way Greenwald and Scahill ignore Pierre Omidyar's funding of the Center for the United Action in Kiev, which was a Phoenix-style coordination center for covert political action.[8]

If the owners of a symbol are forced to talk about an embarrassing fact that undermines their business interests, they interpret the fact narrowly. This is one of the methodologies the political parties and their compatible media outlets employ: they summarize and misrepresent a problematic subject in nine seconds and then repeat the summary over and over again. They don't take the approach of a literary critic; they don't look honestly at what the government's carefully chosen words mean. They don't look for what's not said. In fact, they play the same game. Their methods are identical.

I experienced the same thing when I wrote my article about Ellsberg. No one on the American left would publish it. Eventually Robin Ramsay published it in *Lobster* magazine in Great Britain. The article was titled "The Clash of the Icons" and demonstrated that Ellsberg and Al McCoy held contradictory positions about the CIA's relationship with drug traffickers in Vietnam.[9] McCoy accused CIA officers Ed Lansdale and Lou Conein of collaborating with Corsican drug smugglers in 1965, at the same time Ellsberg was working closely with them. But when I interviewed him, Ellsberg insisted that these CIA officers were not involved in the drug traffic, despite overwhelming evidence to the contrary.[10]

Several years later Alex Cockburn and Jeff St. Clair published my Ellsberg article in Counterpunch. They were having fun ridiculing whacky left assumptions and sacred cows, like Israel. They loved my Phoenix program book and my article on Ellsberg, which we renamed "Will the Real Daniel Ellsberg Please Stand Up."[11] They featured it in Counterpunch, and of course everyone on the left ignored it.

Maintaining Ellsberg's image is mostly a business decision, because Ellsberg is what the Mafia calls "a money-maker." If one of these Compatible Left media outlets has Ellsberg talk at a peace conference it's sponsoring, a hundred fans will pay cash to see him. The Compatible Left is a business venture that's dependent on the capitalist society within which it operates. At the same time, Ellsberg is a symbol of the illusion that change is possible within the system. He calls for reform, yes, and like the Compatible Left, he backs many important progressive programs. But more importantly, by covering up his own CIA connections, he's reassuring the bourgeoisie that subscribes to these media outlets that everything they assume about their leaders is right. And that's how symbolic heroes mislead the way.

This is Ellsberg's symbolic function; as a certified hero who has achieved celebrity status, he proves the system works. He leaked the Pentagon Papers and stopped the war. And he suffered for it. President Nixon wanted to put him on trial for treason. Nixon's staff pulled all sorts of dirty tricks to intimidate and discredit him, but he soldiered on. That's the myth of the hero.

But there are no heroes, and the system doesn't work for everyone, like it rewards Amy Goodman at Democracy Now! Or like it rewards Greenwald and Scahill.

If Ellsberg were to reveal the CIA's secrets, he would no longer have the same reassuring effect on the liberal bourgeoisie. So his sponsors never mention that he had an affair with the mistress of a Corsican drug smuggler in Saigon. That's not in the book or the movie. He denies his

CIA buddies were involved in the drug trade, even though they were. He won't talk about the CIA war crimes he witnessed or the contradictions of capitalism. Like Seymour Hersh and other liberal media icons, he avoids naming CIA officers or detailing the CIA's class functions. He's an expert who tells the bourgeoisie it's all under control. He serves this symbolic function and he's been doing it for forty years. And if, like me, you violate his sanctity by revealing the truth, you'll never get published by the Compatible Left. You lose access.

TRACY: A recent incarnation of Daniel Ellsberg might be Jeremy Scahill. You mentioned Democracy Now! a moment ago. He was a correspondent for them in the early 2000s when the Iraq war was ramping up along with the War on Terror.

VALENTINE: Ellsberg was never a reporter or media mogul like Scahill, but they are both celebrities; Ellsberg with the older generation, Scahill with naïve millennials. They are also similar in that Scahill made a grandiose documentary film about himself, in which he characterized himself as a hero. He barely mentioned the CIA in the film, and his publication, The Intercept, avoids any analysis of the CIA as an instrument of capitalism and imperialism.

Scahill and Greenwald have the same pacifying effect on the liberal bourgeoisie as Ellsberg. They rile them up a bit with recycled exposés, but symbolically they're part of the system. They style themselves as alternative, but they're not about to engage in self-criticism or risk revealing the critical evidence that would indict individual CIA officers.

It's a Catch-22. Until the media stops covering for the CIA, people will never understand how illegal, covert operations systematically distort our basic assumptions about everything. Meanwhile, these media celebrities perpetuate all the myths upon which the class system is based. Greenwald and Scahill are too busy grabbing for the candy and portraying themselves as heroes and winners who made it big.

TRACY: The War on Drugs, as you chronicle in your books, fundamentally changes in the late 1960s and early 1970s. Can you provide us an overview of the CIA's increased involvement up to the present?

VALENTINE: The Bureau of Narcotics was removed from Treasury and recreated as the Bureau of Narcotics and Dangerous Drugs in the Justice Department in 1968, because it had gathered indisputable evidence that the CIA was running the Golden Triangle narcotics business. The heroin being sold to American soldiers in Vietnam was coming from the CIA's clients in Laos. Al McCoy wrote about this back in 1972. The CIA was protecting the major opium producers in the Golden Triangle, just like they've been protecting the major drug dealers in Afghanistan for the last fifteen years. They were funneling heroin and opium to their warlords in South Vietnam as a payoff for advancing the US policies that were detrimental to their own country. The CIA bought their services by allowing them to deal narcotics, and a lot of the dope made its way back to the homeland through enterprising soldiers and various criminal organizations. It was a criminal conspiracy of the highest order.

The National Security Establishment realized the conspiracy was on the verge of being exposed in 1968, so it pulled various executive management, enforcement and intelligence functions out of the BNDD and gave them to the CIA, so the CIA could protect its drug smuggling assets around the world. At that point federal drug law enforcement became an adjunct of national security.

TRACY: So this firewall that theoretically exists between the CIA operations abroad and in the United States has been by-passed in the war on drugs.

VALENTINE: Yes. And by studying the relationship between the CIA and federal drug law enforcement, you can see why I refer to the CIA as the organized crime branch of the US government. Nowhere is that more evident than in how it controls international drug networks. If you're a general in Bolivia and you're assassinating leftists, the CIA will allow you to deal drugs.[12] If you're Manuel Noriega and you're providing intelligence on revolutionaries in Central America, you're allowed to deal drugs. If you're a South Vietnamese general or an Afghan warlord, you're allowed to deal drugs because you're furthering the national security interests of the United States, which means its corporate, as well as political and social interests.

In order for this to happen, two things are important: the CIA has to control certain branches of the DEA, and it has to control the media. And it has systematized its control over these institutions.

Chapter 2

ONE THING LEADS TO ANOTHER: MY RARE ACCESS IN INVESTIGATING THE WAR ON DRUGS

RYAN DAWSON: Let's discuss the relationship between crime and law enforcement. You talked about this in an article about an experience you had growing up in New York.[1] Let's start off with what you learned in your young adulthood, and do tell about the relationship between crime and law enforcement, if there can even be a line.

VALENTINE: What I learned is that there isn't a line. The story I'm going to tell about my experience is allegorical. It's a microcosm of the way the world works, how propaganda and Madison Avenue advertising convince people that there are forces of good fighting forces of evil. But if people saw through the propaganda, they'd have different attitudes and our country would be structured differently. But the law-making branch of our government is in the hands of professional criminals. Everything they do is in the service of crime, of holding down or stealing from the poor and protecting or giving to the rich. I came to realize all this as a young person, thanks to my father.

The lesson my father taught me occurred in 1968, just 23 years after World War Two. It's almost fifty years since then, so the experience I had was contextually closer to the "good" war than the "bad" Vietnam

War. Adult men in 1968 viewed America as having saved the world for democracy. It was easier to be rebellious back then, when millions of middle class white males had to re-educate themselves and support one another in order to avoid being killed for Dow Chemical and Dow Jones in Vietnam.

My father worked in the Post Office in the village where he'd lived as a child. He worked the graveyard shift and I worked for a tree company in town. I was home from college for the summer and I worked for the Coggeshall Tree Company, climbing trees.

My father and I didn't get along. But I ate breakfast in the same diner where my father had a cup of coffee after getting off the graveyard shift. These were the days of the "generation gap". He sat on one side of the diner by the kitchen door with the cops and the older blue collar workers. They'd talk about how much they hated Muhammed Ali, who'd refused to go to Vietnam, and Joe Willy Namath. My friends and I had long hair and resisted the war. We were smoking dope and taking acid, and our girlfriends were young and pretty and sexually liberated thanks to the pill, so they hated us too.

One day my father and I met at the cash register. He was waiting for me when I got outside. "I want you to meet me tomorrow at the bank," he said. "There's something I want to show you. Come about an hour early."

We didn't get along, but he was my father so I did what he said.

The bank was at the other end of Wheeler Avenue, but not far from the diner. My great Uncle Tom Colligan worked there as a security guard. Tom had been a cop in town for many years. My father's father had been a cop in town too, during Prohibition.

Anyway, we met at the bank the next morning and walked down Wheeler Avenue toward the diner. The sun was just coming up and nobody was on the street. We got to the corner store at the end of Wheeler Avenue and turned right up Manville Road. The diner was a few steps up the street and I could see the bread delivery truck parked in front of it. Another car was parked beside it. I knew who the car belonged to.

My father walked into the street with me following behind. He stood behind the delivery truck, flung the back doors open, and said to me: "Take a good look. This is the true relationship between crime and law enforcement."

Inside was the bakery truck driver, the Mafia representative who picked up the money and slips from the local bookie. The bookie worked at the diner and was sitting beside the bread truck driver. In the back of the truck were three village cops. I'd known them all my life. I went to school with their kids. I knew their names.

They'd been caught red-handed and their mouths were hanging open. When they started muttering curses, my father abruptly closed the doors. He walked away and went about his business. Me too.

The next day I was back in the diner and nobody said a word. It was like I'd been initiated into a secret society. Most of the people in town had no idea this was going on. They thought the cops give you a speeding ticket. They don't see the cops associating with professional criminals and making money in the process. They believe that when a guy puts on a uniform – a guy who was a bully in school and didn't develop the skills to be a plumber or go to college – he becomes virtuous. But the guys who go into law enforcement relate more to the crooks they associate with on a daily basis than the citizens they're supposed to protect and serve. They're corrupted.

The CIA is populated with the same kind of people. Nelson Brickham, whom I mentioned in the previous chapter as the CIA officer who created the Phoenix program, told me this about his colleagues: "I have described the intelligence service as a socially acceptable way of expressing criminal tendencies. A guy who has strong criminal tendencies but is too much of a coward to be one, would wind up in a place like the CIA if he had the education." Brickham described CIA officers as mercenaries "who found a socially acceptable way of doing these things and, I might add, getting very well paid for it."

Occasionally the cops have to arrest criminals and put them in jail, but it's generally the ones who aren't in the Mafia or Mafia guys who broke some agreement. If you're black or a minority, you're rarely going to benefit from this accommodation the cops have with organized crime.

What I witnessed was mind-boggling, and being 18 years old, I wasn't ready to think about it then. But I did think about it over the ensuing twenty years. And as I started researching and writing, that experience, and some similar ones I had, got me interested in the underworld; things like the Mafia's involvement in the Kennedy assassination. I wanted to learn about those things.

In 1981 my father gave me the lesson that got me writing. We hadn't spoken in ten years. But he'd just gotten out of the hospital after his second open heart surgery, and his defenses were down. He called me up and said, "I understand you want to be a writer. Come on home. I've got a story to tell you."

Turns out he'd been a prisoner of war in World War Two. He hadn't told anyone, but he'd been a POW in the Philippines in a camp with around 120 Australian and 40 English soldiers. My father was the only American and aligned with the Aussies. The camp commandant, a major in the British army, made a deal with the Japanese; in exchange for having control over discipline in the camp, he would ensure that there would be no escape attempts.

The Australians didn't care what this English major said, and four of them tried to escape. But the major found out and informed on them. The four Australians were brought back to camp and beheaded on Christmas Day 1943.

A couple of days later, two Australians, along with my father, murdered this English major in retaliation. Nothing happened until the camp was liberated in October 1944, at which point the existence of the camp was covered up. The military gave my father a new military record and warned him that if he ever told anyone about the camp, he'd be prosecuted for his role in the murder of the English major.

I wrote about that in my first book, *The Hotel Tacloban.*[2]

I'd seen the true relationship between crime and law enforcement and after my father told me his story about the prison camp, I knew the military can rewrite history. It can coerce someone into a silence so deep and damaging it causes heart disease. That was a turning point for me. I realized how deeply entrenched the corruption is, and I began to observe the forms it takes in our society, including racism. The double standard associated with racism allows one group to get away with breaking the laws, and unfairly punishes another group for breaking the same laws. That's corruption. It's organized crime.

Meanwhile the CIA, the military and the cops are covering their collective asses through their propaganda outlets. They're corrupting our understanding of the world by controlling the information we receive. They create the myths we believe. If we were allowed to understand the CIA, we'd realize it's a criminal organization that is corrupting governments and societies around the world. It's murdering civilians who haven't done anything wrong. The military does the same thing in a more violent way. Cops too.

The Vietnam War had greatly affected my generation, and I wanted to find what sort of secret things the CIA did in Vietnam. As a first step I spoke to the director of a veteran's organization in New Hampshire, where I was living at the time. I asked if there was any facet of the war that hadn't been written about. Without hesitation he said the Phoenix program.

So I decided to write about Phoenix. I sent a copy of *Tacloban* to William Colby, who'd been director of the CIA and was closely associated with Phoenix. Colby read *Tacloban* and liked it. His reaction was, "Well, you have a basis to understand what happened in Vietnam." We did two interviews and he introduced me to some senior CIA people who were involved in facets of the Phoenix program.

It was incredibly eye-opening for me. I wrote about all that in *The Phoenix Program*.

In the course of investigating the CIA in Vietnam, I learned that huge amounts of narcotic drugs were flowing from the Golden Triangle area in Burma, Thailand and Laos. The network began after World War Two, when the CIA had set up a Kuomintang army in Burma. The Kuomintang was the ruling party of the Nationalist Chinese who'd been chased out of China by the Communists in 1947.

The CIA watched while the Nationalist Chinese massacred about 30,000 people in Taiwan in 1947. The Kuomintang had fantasies of reconquering China and the CIA played on those fantasies; it established a Kuomintang army in Burma and used it to attack China. At the same time the CIA was conspiring with the Thai government, which was up to its eyeballs in drug trafficking. Opium trafficking wasn't frowned upon in that part of the world, the way it is here, and the press here took little notice.

By the 1960s the CIA also had a secret army in Laos under Vang Pao, the leader of the Hmong tribe, who supported themselves by growing opium, with considerable CIA assistance. The Hmong were looked down upon by the ruling ethnic Laotians, who ran a CIA-protected heroin processing operation. The CIA worked with the Hmong and Laotians just like the cops and the Mafia ran that bookie operation in suburban New York.

Opium from the Kuomintang army in Burma was moved by mule caravan to Houei Sai, Laos, next to the CIA's 118A base at Nam Yu, and from Houei Sai it was flown to Taiwanese middlemen who worked with the Mafia. Opium from the Hmong was converted into heroin in Vientiane. The CIA controlled the operation and made sure that some of the heroin and opium got to Saigon. Top generals in Vietnam controlled various provinces and regions like warlords. The CIA made sure the drugs got to these generals. They each had a distribution franchise and they'd sell the drugs in their area and make huge profits off it; which is why they supported American policy and gave the CIA a free hand.

By the late 1960s, most of the drugs were going to American soldiers. By 1970 the Nixon administration was aware that thousands of soldiers were addicts and that the problem was affecting the course of the war. Veterans returned to America with their habits, and the CIA was underwriting the whole thing.

I was curious about how US drug law enforcement dealt with the fact that American soldiers were being addicted and that tons of drugs were pouring into the US thanks to the CIA. The DEA had to be involved in this CIA drug smuggling operation, and I was determined to write a book about that.

My next two books, *The Strength of the Wolf* and *The Strength of the Pack*, focus on the corruption the CIA fosters within US law enforcement.[3] Those books are about the role the federal drug agencies play in protecting the CIA and its drug smuggling assets. I did interviews with agents and I provide a lot of documentation. Most of that material is archived at the National Security Arcives.[4] The books also show how the drug law enforcement agencies make sure drugs get to despised minorities, people our rulers want to see in prison and politically disenfranchised. I show how drug law enforcement serves the national security function of making sure the right people get the drugs.

Essential to this arrangement is the CIA's accommodation with organized crime. The gangsters are allowed to import and distribute the drugs in the major cities, in exchange for telling drug agents which street dealers they're supplying. The hoods get rich by informing, and when the CIA has no more use for them, they're discarded like the generals in Vietnam.

DAWSON: Let's talk about plausible deniability.

VALENTINE: The CIA doesn't do anything it can't deny. A senior CIA officer named Tom Donohue told me about this. Colby introduced me to Donohue and he was very forthcoming. Some of the guys Colby referred me to were hoping for the opportunity to tell their stories. It has to do with grandiosity; there's no point doing dangerous things unless the guys talk about your heroics in saloons. They saw me as a chance to memorialize themselves as heroes. But in the process they had to explain a bit about how the CIA works – if not sources, at least its methods.

Donohue was a prime example. He'd studied Comparative Religion at Columbia University and understood symbolic transformation. He was a product and practitioner of Cook County politics who joined the CIA after World War Two when he perceived the Cold War as "a growth industry." He'd been the CIA's station chief in the Philippines at the end of his career and when I spoke to him, he was in business with a former Filipino Defense Minister. He was putting his contacts to good use, which is par for the course. It's how corruption works for senior bureaucrats.

Donohue said the CIA doesn't do anything unless it meets two criteria. The first criterion is "intelligence potential." The program must benefit the CIA; maybe it tells them how to overthrow a government, or how to blackmail an official, or where the report is hidden, or how to get an agent across a border. The euphemism "intelligence potential" means it has some use for the CIA. The second criterion is that it can be denied. If they can't find a way to set it up so they can deny it, they won't do it.

Most everything the CIA does is deniable. It's part of their Congressional mandate. Congress doesn't want to be held accountable for the criminal things the CIA does. The only time something the CIA does becomes public knowledge – other than the occasional accident or whistleblower – is when Congress or the President think it's helpful for propaganda reasons to let people know the CIA is doing this.

Torture is a good example. After 9/11, and up until and through the invasion of Iraq, the American people wanted revenge. They wanted to see Muslim blood flowing. So the Bush administration let it leak that they were torturing evil doers. They played it cute and called it "enhanced interrogation," but everyone understood symbolically.

DAWSON: They may have tortured people for four years.

VALENTINE: They've always tortured people. Look at slavery. In America the bosses cover it up, which goes back to what I was telling you in the beginning. If you visit Thomas Jefferson's estate at Monticello, you won't see the slave quarters. It's a cover up, like *The Hotel Tacloban*. But, unfortunately, many people like it that way; they prefer not to know. They prefer a poster with a happy cliché on it – if we all join hands and drink Pepsi there will be peace in the world. Like any other kind of advertising, propaganda is meant to delude not inform. But it's better to face the facts.

While I was researching Phoenix, I found out about the CIA's involvement in drug trafficking. I also learned that as the Vietnam War was winding down, the CIA started reducing the number of officers serving in Laos and Vietnam. The CIA felt it had the situation under control there and was looking for new homes for those guys. I discovered that over one hundred officers were funneled into the BNDD and DEA. These recycled CIA officers had been involved in Phoenix and associated programs, and I wondered, "Why are they going into the DEA, and who are they really working for?"

One of my CIA contacts was a fascinating man named Tully Acampora. Tully was a World War Two veteran who started working for the CIA in Korea and ended up being detached to the CIA for most of his career. In Vietnam, starting in 1966, he was General Nguyen Ngoc Loan's advisor. Loan was famous as the guy who was photographed shooting a VC guerrilla in the head during the Tet offensive in 1968.

Al McCoy described Loan at length in *The Politics of Heroin*. Loan, McCoy explained, was Air Marshall Nguyen Cao Ky's deputy. After Ky was appointed Premier in July 1965, he appointed Loan to head the National Police, the Military Security Service, and the Central Intelligence Organization. Loan established and managed Ky's political machine by "using systematic corruption to combat urban guerrilla warfare." Corruption financed cash rewards for agents. Loan "systematized the corruption, regulating how much each particular agency would collect, how much each officer would skim off for his personal use, and what percentage would be turned over to Ky's political machine."[5]

As McCoy noted, "the opium traffic was undeniably the most important source of illicit revenue." And my friend Tully was Loan's CIA advisor until 1968, until the CIA decided to replace Ky's political machine with one under President Nguyen Van Thieu.

Tully was one of the people that started funneling CIA officers into the DEA in the early 1970s. I don't want to bore you with details, but it's important to know why he was in position to do that. From 1958 until 1965, Tully worked for the CIA in Italy, and while he was there he became close friends with three federal narcotic agents stationed in Rome. They were agents in the Federal Bureau of Narcotics (FBN). They were Italian-Americans like Tully, and were making cases on the Mafia and its associates throughout Europe and the Middle East.

Tully formed friendships with FBN agents Charlie Siragusa,

Hank Manfredi, and Andy Tartaglino. Siragusa was the boss. He's been in the OSS and had worked with James Jesus Angleton in Italy during World War Two. As chief of counterintelligence in the CIA, Angleton became dependent on Siragusa for his Mafia contacts. You might have wondered how it is that the CIA can reach into the underworld and compel mobsters to do its dirty work (like the assassination attempts on Castro); well, the CIA often does it through senior law enforcement officials like Charlie Siragusa.

According to Tully, Angleton "kissed Siragusa's ass in Macy's window at noon."

Hank Manfredi had been in the Army CID in World War Two and was actually a CIA officer working under FBN cover. He spent his entire career in Italy until 1968, when he had a crippling heart attack and returned to the US. The FBN had been reformed as the BNDD by then, and Andy Tartaglino was one of its deputy directors. Tartaglino arranged for Manfredi to join the BNDD first as an inspector and later as a manager in its foreign operations division.

Siragusa and Manfredi were no longer alive when I started researching the CIA and the DEA, but Tartaglino was. I told Tully that I want to learn about the CIA's involvement in drug trafficking, and he sent me to Andy.

Andy became the DEA's Deputy Director of Administration when the organization was formed in 1973. He was one of the most knowledgeable guys about how the CIA corrupted federal law enforcement. So meeting Andy was like meeting Colby; I now had an entrée into the highest levels of the DEA.

Tully sent me to Andy and Andy said, "Okay, I'll talk to you as a favor for Tully, but first you have to start at the beginning with the Bureau of Narcotics. Spend a year, talk to as many people as you can, and then come back and I'll talk to you."

That's what I did and it was amazing what I found out. Tartaglino had led a corruption investigation that lasted from 1965 to 1968. It resulted in 32 agents having to resign for committing all manner of crimes. Twenty-seven informants had been murdered, allegedly by FBN agents. None of the agents were prosecuted for those murders, but the ones who were suspected were allowed to resign – it was a cover up like happened at the Hotel Tacloban POW camp. Four or five agents were indicted for other crimes, and in 1968 the Bureau of Narcotics was taken out of Treasury and put in the Justice Department. It was merged with other agencies and reorganized as the Bureau of Narcotics and Dangerous Drugs (BNDD) as a result of Tartaglino investigation into corruption, mostly in New York City.

The media loves to talk about corruption in foreign countries, but if you want to understand corruption, you have to study the relationship between crime and law enforcement in New York City. Siragusa, Manfredi and Acampora were from New York. I'm from the suburbs, but my mother and her Italian-American family are from the city.

Frank Serpico was a cop who exposed corruption in the NYPD in the early 1970s. He was a narcotics detective and was shot in the face by fellow cops. He survived and went to the Knapp Commission and revealed the extent of corruption within the NYPD. It was tied into what happened within the FBN, and Tartaglino was involved in that investigation too. It uncovered rampant corruption among judges, prosecutors and politicians, but they covered most of that up too. Because everyone involved in law enforcement depends on corruption so they can send their kids to college, move to the suburbs, and take vacations in Mexico. They don't get paid enough otherwise. But I'm getting ahead of myself.

As you're probably aware, opiates were legal until 1914 when Congress passed the Harrison Narcotic Act and the federal government started to regulate opium and cocaine. The Act was a tax revenue measure; people who were importing opium and cocoa leaves into the US had to report how much they were importing so they could be taxed and the government could make some money. The government regulated how much they brought in and which companies could manufacture it. This explains how it was that the Bureau of Narcotics was first set up in the Treasury Department!

Within a few years, Congress decided that it should be a law enforcement issue. It was a way of giving doctors, drug manufacturers and pharmaceutical companies a monopoly and sending anyone else who used or sold regulated drugs to jail. They created a narcotics law enforcement agency to find out who the addicts and their suppliers were, and to put them in prison. They gave narcotics agents guns. This is during Prohibition and anyone who knows anything about Prohibition knows that a lot of booze was coming into the country in police vans, and that cops were out on the beaches protecting the gangsters unloading the ships and making sure the police chief got the best bottle of scotch.

Prohibition was the genius invention of Congress that allowed crime to become organized under the direction of law enforcement in the United States.

DAWSON: They made it the biggest black market ever.

VALENTINE: All of a sudden crime becomes as big an industry as the oil industry. As Meyer Lansky famously said, "We're bigger than General Motors!"

DAWSON: The same thing happened in Russia when they had Prohibition.

VALENTINE: The demand was huge. So illegal drugs became a big money-making facet of our business society and the guys smuggling booze and dope became politically powerful. People like Arnold Rothstein, the Jewish mobster who bankrolled most of the bookie operations in America. Rothstein was extorting labor organizations in New York City. He controlled the booze coming in from Canada and by ship from Europe and Asia. He had the alcohol smuggling infrastructure so he controlled narcotics too. He had a network of Jewish gangsters working for him out of Eastern Europe and as far away as Shanghai. The first international drug smuggling network consisted of Jews who'd been relegated to certain illegal occupations, like smuggling, through discrimination. They got pushed into this business and excelled at it.

Rothstein's organization ended in 1928, when the Mafia and a group of younger Jewish mobsters got upset because he had a monopoly. Lucky Luciano joined forces with Meyer Lansky and they bumped off Rothstein and divvied up his empire. They incorporated crime and started dealing with the Kuomintang Chinese.[6] That's the original syndicate. Before there was a CIA, the US government was protecting the Nationalist Chinese because they were fighting Communists. The government protected Kuomintang opium and heroin routes into Mexico and the US West Coast, which was another boon for this drug smuggling syndicate run by the Mafia.

Luciano and Lansky organized crime on the totalitarian corporate model. They set up banks and created shell companies and paid off the cops at every step of the way. That's their plausible deniability. The CIA hired some of these drug traffickers in World War Two for their expertise at creating false identities, crossing borders with contraband, and eluding policemen. The Mafia also controlled many unions the ruling class wanted to subvert and use for its own purposes. Hiring drug traffickers was no big deal when you consider that the military and CIA recycled a slew of Nazis, like Werner Von Braun and Reinhard Gehlen, and used them in the secret war against the Soviets after World War Two.

DAWSON: They consolidated power too. They had Bugsy Siegel kick off a couple of Dons. It really became a syndicate, La Cosa Nostra. Like you said, it became a real corporate enterprise. They consolidated Mafia power.

VALENTINE: Believe me it's not actually called La Cosa Nostra. That's an FBI invention. Nobody had heard the phrase until the FBI told Joe Valachi to introduce it to the public during Congressional hearings in 1963. La Cosa Nostra means The Our Thing. That's the literal translation of La Cosa Nostra: The Our Thing.

I'll try to explain how corruption evolves. When Rothstein was assassinated, the cops ran to his office. He lived in a suite at the Park Central Hotel, but had an office elsewhere. Unfortunately, someone else got there first and grabbed Rothstein's accounting books. Maybe that's one of the reasons he was killed? Anyway, panic ensued in New York because everyone was on his payroll. The state Republicans started an investigation that tracked back to Tammany Democrats. Republicans were running for Congress saying, "My opponent was on Rothstein's payroll and here are the documents."

Eventually it tracked back to Republicans as well. The scandal also tracked back to the top federal narcotics agents in New York City, and to Colonel Levi Nutt, who had been appointed in 1920 to run the Narcotics Division of the IRS Prohibition Unit. The Prohibition Unit was notoriously corrupt. It was in the Treasury Department and Levi Nutt was in charge of its narcotics unit, and his agents were famous for being more corrupt than the Prohibition agents. The investigation of Rothstein ended up showing that narcotics investigator Levi Nutt's son-in-law was Rothstein's tax attorney.

Village cops running the numbers racket with a Mafia hood in the back of a bread truck is Corruption 101. The PhD level course is the son-in-law of the chief of the Narcotics Division writing tax returns for the world's biggest drug smuggler. One narcotics agent told me there wasn't a drug deal that went down in Chicago in the '40s and '50s that didn't go through the cops to the politicians. That's still the case today, except they've gotten better at disguising it. They're able to hide the CIA's fifty billion dollar budget. They're better at fooling the public too, so you'd never in your wildest dreams think that your protectors are dealing with the people preying upon you. But that is a fact, and that accommodation between crime and law enforcement is the glue that holds the system together.

Their most egregious crime is the systematic falsification of history. What starts out as an agent padding reports becomes, when all those reports are assembled, the myth of the cop or soldier or CIA agent as hero.

FBN Agent Frankie Waters explained it to me. "One of my talents was testifying in court," Waters said. "It was a situation that terrified me at first, but then I did it a few times and realized I liked it, because it fueled all the grandiose ideas I had about myself. And I was good at it. I could testify about a case made in Chicago!" Waters smiled exuberantly. "They called us pinch hitters."

It didn't matter that some agents couldn't testify well, Waters added, especially in big cases where 20 agents were involved. "Say agent Joe Blow seizes the most crucial piece of evidence, a note that's essential for the jury to understand the case. Joe's a great agent but he freezes if he has to speak in front of a crowd. A block away is his articulate partner. I'm the case agent, to whom they both submit their memos. So when I write up the final report, guess who seized the note?"

As a way of justifying the systematic falsification of reports, Waters evoked the myth of the seasoned investigator who must bend the rules to get the bad guys. "There's a bigger picture you've got to see," he stressed. "There was a war between good and evil, and we were losing it, and it seemed that when justice triumphed, it was by accident. So let me tell you about integrity. On the one hand you had the critics who couldn't make cases for moral reasons or because they were inept. On the other hand were the case-makers, who knew we had to be the superior force, because the only thing that kept the criminals from over-running us was that they knew that our goon squad would wipe out their neighborhood if they tried."

To show success to the politicians who control their budgets, top managers in every bureaucracy rely on fictionalized reporting. The essential fictions, like the need to bend the rules, are taught to new agents.

The agents must learn them by heart to advance. Over time the agents come to believe the fictions, which reinforce all their false assumptions about society and their role in it. For example, black agents in the FBN weren't allowed to supervise whites. The bosses said the blacks couldn't write well enough, because in their reports they didn't ascribe to the fiction of white supremacy.

Not until 1968 was a black agent made a group leader in the FBN. The organization, like American society in general and its security services in particular, accepted white superiority as gospel, and compulsory belief in that gospel paved the way for the political cadre at the top of the organizations to propagate other myths, like the myth that the *Communist* Chinese were pushing drugs on Americans as a kind of psychological warfare, and the myth that pot was as dangerous as heroin.

The most important fiction of all is the need for secrecy to preserve our national security. From time to time that is true, but far more often officials use secrecy to conceal their corruption and crimes.

So, Levi Nutt was shuffled off to Buffalo and given a sinecure job in upstate New York. And then the political bosses hired Harry Anslinger to run the Bureau of Narcotics, which was formed in 1930.

Anslinger became the Commissioner of the FBN when it was created. His job was to clean up corruption and one way he did it was to limit the inspections staff. There were approximately 300 agents in the FBN around the country and Anslinger had only two Inspectors on his staff; one for agents east of the Mississippi River, and one for agents west of it. Periodically they hopped on a train and visited offices around the country and made sure nobody was getting exposed in the newspapers for being corrupt. The corruption, obviously, continued apace.

I met agents who had been in the FBN in the late 1930s. Most of the FBN agents I interviewed had joined after World War Two. These were the people Andy Tartaglino introduced me to – old agents who knew how things really worked. If anyone out there wants to know all the details, read my books *The Strength of the Wolf* and *The Strength of the Pack*.

Tartaglino, however, only introduced me to the "straight" agents who had worked with him trying to root out corruption. I soon realized that was not how I was going to get the story. But through Tartaglino and his clique I knew who the corrupt agents were, so I went to them and presented them with a deal. These were the "case-making" agents Frankie Waters talked about, the guys who brought down the Mafia and its French connection.[7] These guys had no fear and no ethics and that's why the first book is called *The Strength of the Wolf.*

I went to this group of agents, maybe ten of them, and told them individually what I wanted to do. I told them the story about my father and the bread truck, and what I knew about the CIA. I promised I wouldn't link them to any murders or felonies. And on that basis they agreed to talk to me. They talked about how they went about making cases. So if you want to understand the situation from their point of view, read the books. I can't explain it all to you in an hour. But I'll try to summarize it.

Narcotics agents are agent provocateurs. They "create a crime" by setting up a series of undercover buys, which they do largely through informants who get paid or otherwise compensated for buying or selling drugs to people the agents bust. The best undercover agents would shoot heroin so they could pose as addicts and traffickers. These guys would do anything. But they had to provide heroin to their informants. An agent wasn't looking to cure an addict. He was looking to use an addict as an informant and sustain his habit while working "up the ladder" to his or her supplier. So the agents became suppliers of heroin. They became an instrumental part of the problem at the basic level. And that's still the case today but on a grander scale: agents are in the illicit narcotic business, in both an official and unofficial capacity.[8]

Within the old FBN, a certain amount of illicit drug distribution was officially allowed. But behind the scenes, the case-making agents were competing with each other to make cases. In New York City there were five groups of agents, maybe ten agents in a group, and they were all trying to get promoted so they didn't have to be street agents forever, so they could become the bosses. Ideally, an ambitious agent latched onto an informant who could make a big case on a member of the Mafia. Doing that guaranteed a successful career. But the competition was fierce and sometimes an ambitious agent in one group would intentionally arrest another agent's informant for dealing junk. One case-making agent would subvert another case-making agent, and now you have life and death conflict between wolves.

This is how informants ended up getting killed. The agents started bumping off each other's informants, and then each other. They killed each other. This was what got Andy Tartaglino so upset; agents were giving other agents "hot shots". They'd slip heroin into someone's beer or tie him down and give him an injection of heroin and kill him.

There were instances of this happening. So that's the level of corruption that permeated drug law enforcement. Without centralized control, it was a Hobbesian War.

To make big cases, case-making agents needed to acquire heroin unofficially. They knew where the big dealers kept their stash, so they would burglarize an apartment and steal the drugs. They would cut the dope and resell it through their informants, share the profits, and make more cases. If they didn't get caught, they got promoted and became the bosses.

Agents were raping women. A lot of addict informants were prostitutes and the corrupt agents would force them to have sex to avoid going to jail. Agents were stealing money from floating crap games and gamblers. They were ripping off everybody left and right. They were murdering people. So the FBN was dissolved in 1968 and reformed as the BNDD in the Justice Department.

John Ingersoll, who had been chief of the Charlotte, North Carolina police department, became the director of the BNDD. The Johnson administration charged him with eliminating corruption and the first thing Ingersoll did was ask CIA Director Richard Helms for help. Ingersoll told Helms that the senior managers of the BNDD, most of whom were former FBN agents, were still up to their eyeballs in corruption. The BNDD had 16 regional offices and most were headed by a former FBN agent, and Ingersoll was worried they were spreading corruption throughout this new organization.

Helms exploited the situation. He wanted to take over federal drug law enforcement, so he slipped a group of CIA officers into the BNDD ostensibly to investigate the corrupt bosses. This actually made it into the 1975 Rockefeller Commission Report about illegal domestic CIA operations. It's worth reading the two pages they devoted to this.

I wrote an article about it called Operation Twofold.[9] The CIA infiltrated around 20 officers into the BNDD. Each one of these guys was given a job in a region. They were put in proximity to the regional boss and told to spy on him. Ingersoll thought the CIA was doing him a favor, which was very naïve, because the CIA used this secret program for its own nefarious purposes. You know the old adage about the camel that put its nose in the tent; pretty soon the whole camel is inside. That applies here, and pretty soon the CIA had taken over certain facets of the BNDD.

It was 1970 and people like Al McCoy were becoming aware of the CIA's drug connections in Southeast Asia. The CIA had to protect its drug smuggling operations in Vietnam, or risk losing the war. It was not like the '50s and '60s. Press people were flying all over the world. They weren't taking boats anymore. They could communicate faster and learn things they didn't know before. Suddenly the monstrous things the CIA had done for twenty years were in danger of being exposed. For twenty years the CIA had been working with the criminal underworlds in every nation, doing exactly what the old narcotic agents did – creating crimes and covering them up.

That's why the CIA wanted to commandeer federal drug law enforcement. Through Operation Twofold, the CIA infiltrated the BNDD's inspections staff and intelligence division. It created and staffed the BNDD's office of special operations. It took over the BNDD's foreign operations and executive management staffs, and it still runs them today within the DEA.

DAWSON: The US was getting opium from Afghanistan?

VALENTINE: When the United State took over drug law enforcement in Afghanistan, opium production increased dramatically. All of a sudden Afghan heroin is flooding the US and Europe. It still is. You can say it's a coincidence, except all the opium warlords are on the CIA payroll. The DEA sends six hundred agents to Afghanistan to make sure that nobody knows about it.

DAWSON: It's important to show what the money finances. It's more than personal profit. They use that black-market money from the drugs to get into other shenanigans, supporting rent-a-terrorist groups.

VALENTINE: The CIA is the most corrupting influence in the United States. It corrupted the Customs Bureau the same way it corrupted the DEA. It corrupts the State Department and the military. It has infiltrated civil organizations and the media to make sure that none of its illegal operations are exposed. Many CIA officers spent their careers posing as federal narcotics agents.

DAWSON: They're the managerial arm of the cartel.

VALENTINE: It's the untold part of the Gary Webb story – where the hell was the DEA? Well, the DEA was making sure no one made a case against CIA drug dealers. They make sure the drugs go to the black and Latino communities. In my opinion, that's the National Security Establishment's deepest, darkest secret. Exposing it was what got Webb in trouble, not a few inaccuracies in his reporting.

The media's job is to bury stories about corruption, whether it's in Congress, law enforcement or the CIA. It sticks to the fictionalized script and spreads disinformation about how things are organized and how they operate. They do it by telling the story in a certain way, just like Frankie Waters described how the FBN group leaders wrote reports. The DEA has a public affairs branch staffed by creative writers who filter out anything bad and tell you only what the bosses want you to know. The media echoes what the DEA and CIA PR people say. But it's a big lie and it's pervasive.

PART I

THE CIA'S PHOENIX PROGRAM IN VIETNAM: A TEMPLATE FOR SYSTEMIC DOMINATION

"The secret dominates this world, and first and foremost as the secret of domination."

Guy Debord, Comments on the Society of the Spectacle*

* http://libcom.org.libcom.org/files/Comments%20on%20the%20Society%20of%20the%20Spectacle.pdf

THE VIETNAM WAR'S SILVER LINING: A BUREAUCRATIC MODEL FOR POPULATION CONTROL EMERGES

The CIA's Phoenix program changed how America fights its wars and how the public views this new type of political and psychological warfare, in which civilian casualties are an explicit objective.[1]

The CIA created Phoenix in Saigon in 1967 to "neutralize" the leaders and supporters of the Communist-led insurgency in South Vietnam. Referred to by the CIA as the Viet Cong Infrastructure (VCI), the targets were civilians who were working at regular jobs while secretly engaged in administrative and support functions for the armed guerrillas. These people were patriots resisting foreign aggression and seeking to take back their country, but they were considered spies and terrorists. American officials wrote laws that allowed US military forces to detain, torture, and kill them by every means possible, including B-52 raids, battalion-sized "cordon and search" operations, and death squads.

Phoenix was originally called ICEX-SIDE, for Intelligence Coordination and Exploitation – Screening, Interrogation and Detention of the Enemy. But the name was quickly changed for symbolic purposes. In time, the mere mention of Phoenix, the omnipotent bird of prey with a blacklist in one claw and a snake in the other, was enough to terrorize not only targeted members of the VCI, but the entire civilian population.

Phoenix evolved from a 'rifle-shot" approach to neutralize enemy leaders into a program of systematic repression for the political control of the South Vietnamese people. It sought to accomplish this through a highly bureaucratized system of disposing of people who could not be ideologically assimilated.

The CIA found a legal basis for the program in "emergency decrees" and "administrative detention" laws that enabled American "advisors" to detain, torture, and kill "national security offenders" (as the VCI were legally referred to) without due process. The program was implemented over the objections of Government of Vietnam (GVN) officials who understood that it undermined their national sovereignty.

Within this extra-legal judicial system, with its Stalinist security committees, a member of the VCI was anyone who didn't actively support the government. To be neutral or advocate for peace was viewed as supporting terrorism. Proof wasn't required, just the word of an anonymous informer.

The psychological warfare aspect of Phoenix was so pervasive that people had to watch every word they said. Advocating peace with the Communists was punishable by imprisonment without trial for two years or even death under the administrative detention laws. And the threat of being detained was a boondoggle for corrupt officials and professional criminals on the CIA payroll. Persons arrested as VCI suspects or sympathizers were released only when their families scraped together enough money to bribe the local Security Committee members.

As a result, CIA officer Lucien Conein described Phoenix as "the greatest blackmail scheme ever invented: If you don't do what I want, you're VC."

Modeled by its creator, Nelson Brickham, on Ford Motor Company's "command post" structure, Phoenix concentrated power in a chief executive officer and an operating committee at the top of the Embassy's organizational chart. The chief executive position – the Deputy for Civil Operations and Revolutionary Development – oversaw the Phoenix Directorate in Saigon. The Directorate was headed by a CIA officer supported by a statistical reporting unit, which assigned a quota of 1800 neutralizations a month to the Phoenix "coordinators" who ran the program in the field.

But Phoenix was a CIA program and deniability was one of its main objectives, so the CIA left gaping holes in its safety net in order to facilitate the systematic corruption that ensured the program's true but unstated objective of terrifying the entire civilian population into submission.

As CIA officer Frank Snepp wrote in *Decent Interval*, "the

Phoenix strike teams opted for a scattershot approach, picking up anyone who might be a suspect, and eventually, when the jails were packed to overflowing, they began simply taking the law, such as it was, into their own hands."[2]

The program existed in relative secrecy until June 1969, when numerous South Vietnamese legislators complained in open session about Phoenix abuses. Everyone knew that thousands of innocent people were being extorted, jailed and killed, but the complicit American press corps never reported it. And in the absence of any objection by the American public, the CIA had no reason to relent. It was not until late 1970, when a handful of anti-war Phoenix veterans exposed the program's many abuses, that Congress finally launched an investigation.

But even then, thanks to skillful dissembling on the part of William Colby, the erstwhile Deputy for Civil Operations and Revolutionary Development in charge of Phoenix, the CIA was able to shirk any responsibility. At Congressional Hearings into Phoenix in 1971, Representative Ogden Reid (D-NY) asked Colby: "Do you state categorically that Phoenix has never perpetrated the premeditated killing of a civilian in a noncombat situation?"

Conflating stated policy with operational reality, the master of "Double-Speak" replied: "Phoenix as a program has never done that. Individual members of it may have done it. But as a program it is not designed to do that."[3]

Colby, to put it mildly, lied. In actuality the Phoenix program was designed to be mismanaged, to open the door to and incentivize bribery, corruption and terror as an unstated policy lever for ensuring domination over the Vietnamese population.

The Other Side of the Story

Censorship of opposing narratives is one of the main mechanisms for controlling information. Americans rarely get to hear the other side of the story, especially during a war. But in late 1970 and early 1971, a Vietnamese reporter named Dinh Tuong An wrote a series of articles titled "The Truth About Phoenix" for the newspaper *Tin Sang* (*Morning News*).[4] *Tin Sang* was published in Saigon by Ngo Cong Duc, a member of the Vietnamese legislature. Half of *Tin Sang*'s issues about Phoenix were confiscated by the secret police on orders from the minister of information, Truong Buu Diem, a CIA asset.

An knew from personal experience what he was writing about; he'd been a translator for Major Oscar L. Jenkins, one of the CIA's Special Police advisors running Phoenix operations in the Mekong Delta in 1968 and 1969.

"Phoenix," wrote An, "is a series of big continuous operations which, because of the bombing, destroy the countryside and put innocent people to death. In the sky are armed helicopters, but on the ground are the black uniforms, doing what they want where the helicopters and B-52s do not reach. Americans in black uniforms," according to An, "are the most terrible."[5]

The "black uniforms" were members of American "hunter-killer" teams. The hunter team was a four-man unit, usually all Americans, sometimes with one or two Vietnamese, Cambodian, or Chinese mercenaries called counterterrorists, CTs for short. According to An, the CIA would send the hunter teams into a village the day before a Phoenix cordon-search operation to map out the village and capture people targeted for interrogation. The next day the CTs would return in black choppers with the killer team, usually 12-25 South Vietnamese Special Forces or Rangers led by Green Berets.

"When they go back to their base," An said, "they bring people's bleeding ears. But are these the ears of the VC?"

CIA officials like Colby did their best to narrowly define Phoenix as a perfectly legal program targeting specific individuals. But like Snepp explained, and as An alluded to above, everyone was caught up in the dragnet, including and especially those who were perfectly innocent.

The original purpose of Phoenix, An said, was "to avenge what the VC did during Tet, which is why President Thieu did not hesitate to sign Phoenix into law. But," he added, "local officials (including the legislators who complained in 1969) knew nothing about the program except the decree. The central government didn't explain anything. Furthermore, the CIA and their assistants had a hard time trying to explain to province chiefs about operations to pacify the countryside and destroy the VC."

Indeed, bombing villages and spraying fields with the toxic defoliant Agent Orange served only to kill, maim and impoverish rural villagers. And despite the avalanche of American propaganda telling the villagers such operations were done for their protection, the rural population understood that such indiscriminate attacks were directed at them, not at a few specific VCI.

By 1969, they also understood that American money and bribes prolonged the war as a means of preventing any coalition government being formed with the Communists. They knew from firsthand experience that powerful South Vietnamese officials profited from the carnage; that corrupt province chiefs reported the damage to their American advisors, ostensibly to get compensation for those hurt in the attacks, but kept the money for themselves.

The Americans knew their counterpart officials in the Government of Vietnam (GVN) were keeping the blood money, but they wanted it that way. The Americans used those officials as straw dogs and blamed them for the problems they had created. It's the same patronage system that America imposes on any nation it wishes to control. In Vietnam, the patronage system enabled the CIA to maintain the illusion, pushed upon the American public by the complicit press corps, that it cared for the Vietnamese people and wanted to protect them, while assuring, through massive corruption, its freedom to pound them into submission – and, of course, traffic in narcotics.

The result was a total lack of trust in the GVN, not in the VCI. As An noted, the rural Vietnamese wondered how Phoenix could turn things around – the same way average Syrians, Iraqis and Afghanis wonder how relentless US bombing and death squad operations are helping them, as opposed to helping the corrupt warlords and government officials on the CIA payroll that authorize the bombings and death squads.

Behind closed doors, CIA officials like An's American boss, the aforementioned Major Jenkins, argued that Phoenix was needed because B-52 strikes and defoliation "dustings" did not destroy "the VCI's lower structure." This unstated policy was proof that the CIA could not reach the VCI leadership, and instead opted for genocide - wiping out grass roots support for the insurgency through the blanket application of terror.

In the process, An emphasized, Phoenix dragged everyone into its trap. For example, as more and more fields were destroyed by Agent Orange, people had no choice but to buy rice from Chinese merchants and smugglers. The CIA-advised Special Police knew this and accused them of collaborating with the VC. Naturally, the merchants and smugglers were then forced to bribe the police to keep from being arrested.

This is how the CIA's patronage system of corruption turned into the greatest blackmail scheme ever invented. Anyone – including cops and soldiers – who visited family members in VC-controlled areas was put on the Phoenix blacklist and extorted by government security forces. They were surveilled, harassed, and forced to become informants in order to protect their family members from CIA "hunter-killer" teams and US military assaults.

The CIA relied heavily on false accusations to terrorize the Vietnamese. An told of five teachers working for a Catholic priest in Vinh Long Province. The women refused to attend a VC indoctrination session. When the group of actual VC were captured, they named these five teachers as VC cadres. The teachers were jailed without trial or evidence.

"That's why people feared Phoenix," An explained. "The biggest fear is being falsely accused, from which there is no protection. That's why Phoenix doesn't bring peace or security."

Adding to the terror of being falsely accused, detained, tortured and even killed, was the fact that the CIA rewarded security officials who extorted the people. "The CIA," An wrote, "spends money like water."

"Many agents from the different police in IV Corps receive money from the CIA," An reported, "in the form of merit pay." Money was spent bribing cops on the CIA payroll with telephones, generators, air conditioners, Lambrettas, and Xerox machines. Pretty secretaries and cash awards were lavished on officials sitting on the Stalinist security committees the CIA created to prosecute national security offenders. "Conveniences" given to committee members, wrote An, made it easier for them "to explore information from agents," leading to the arrest of more suspects and, consequently, more bribes.

The corrupting effect of massive infusions of CIA money was no secret. In an interview for *The Phoenix Program*, CIA officer Warren Milberg told me: "I had virtually unlimited resources to develop agent operations, to pay for a staff that translated and produced intelligence reports."

Milberg had more secret CIA money, he claimed, than what the official province budget was. While he saw this as "creating economic stability," the incentive to sell false information served only to further destabilize Vietnamese society. The CIA had no way of corroborating the information it bought, but the accusations were nevertheless used to build cases against VCI suspects, in order to meet neutralization quotas imposed by the Phoenix Directorate. It was a perfectly deniable facet of population control.

An stressed that CIA officers took no disciplinary action against officials who took bribes, because the payoffs were often a vehicle for agent penetration operations into the VCI. As An explained, "The CIA works to keep some Communist areas intact so they can get information."

These types of covert intelligence operations were in direct opposition to the stated Phoenix mission of protecting the people from terrorism. Such covert operations were many and varied. An noted that South Vietnamese CIA agents often posed as pharmacists or doctors. These agents would smuggle CIA-supplied medicines to VC hideouts in Cambodia in exchange for information.

"Phoenix," explained An, "was watching and talking to the VC while at the same time working to prevent the National Liberation Front from reorganizing the VCI."

All of the above, and more, led An to conclude that America was never interested in ending the war. The goal was total victory, "even if many lives must be lost." Phoenix, for An, was a mechanism to extend the war indefinitely with a minimum of American casualties. It was a cynical ploy used to pit the Vietnamese against each other and undermine their efforts to negotiate a peaceful settlement by fueling the conflict with money, lies and psychological operations designed to destabilize the society.

Phoenix Is Gone But the Method Lingers On

Ironically, before Phoenix was adopted as the model for policing the American empire, many US military commanders in Vietnam resisted the Phoenix strategy of targeting civilians with Einsatzgruppen-style "special forces" and Gestapo-style secret police. They resented the fact that military officers were being involuntarily assigned to the program. "People in uniform who are pledged to abide by the Geneva Conventions," General Bruce Palmer said in letter to me, "should not be put in the position of having to break those laws of warfare."

Unfortunately, the current "stab-in-the-back" generation of military officers, government officials and reporters was forged on the anvil of defeat in Vietnam. This generation, which staffs the burgeoning number of Phoenix-style committees in the public and private sectors, carries the burden of restoring America's reputation for invincibility. This ruling class within the National Security Establishment, represented most perfectly by Hillary Clinton, knows that its enemies, foreign and domestic, must be suppressed ideologically as well as militarily. Thus they have embraced the Phoenix concept of employing implicit and explicit terror to control, organize and pacify societies.

Phoenix was always understood as the silver lining in the Vietnam debacle. The aforementioned CIA officer, Warren Milberg, wrote a thesis in 1974 titled, "The Future Applicability of the Phoenix Program."[6] Many of the CIA and military officers I interviewed wrote similar papers extolling Phoenix.

As I'll explain in greater detail in this book, Phoenix fulfilled its destiny in the wake of 9/11 and became the template for policing the empire and fighting its eternal War on Terror. So successful were Phoenix operations in overthrowing the Ba'athist Party regime in Iraq that David Kilcullen, one of the US government's top terrorism advisors in 2004, called for a "global Phoenix program."

The threat of a global Phoenix program is that it will become fully activated in the United States. If the CIA and military are successful at politically and psychologically neutralizing suspected terrorists, what is to stop them applying the full systematic extent of Phoenix-style operations to include political dissidents, immigrants and despised minorities in America, just as they did in Vietnam?

As Dinh Tuong An noted above, the program's stated policy – consumer safety – is contradicted by its operational reality – buyer beware. This is nothing to take lightly. Security officials are adept at using double-speak to hide repressive "covert actions" within "intelligence" operations, and they are using the exact same advertising campaign they used in Vietnam: when the Phoenix first arrived in America in the form of Homeland Security, it was advertised as "protecting the people from terrorism," just as it was in Vietnam.

Any domestic Phoenix-style organization or operation depends on double-speak and deniability, as well as official secrecy and media self-censorship. The overarching need for total control of information requires media complicity. This was one of the great lessons defeat in Vietnam taught our leaders. The highly indoctrinated and well rewarded managers who run the government will never again allow the public to see the carnage they inflict upon foreign civilians. Americans never will see the mutilated Iraqi, Afghani, Libyan and Syrian children killed by marauding US forces and their cluster bombs.

On the other hand, falsified portrayals of CIA kidnappings, torture, and assassinations are glorified on TV and in movies. Telling the proper story is absolutely essential.

Thanks to media complicity, Phoenix has already become the template for providing internal political security for America's leaders.

The process began immediately after 9/11 with the repressive Patriot Act and a series of Presidential executive orders that have since legalized the administrative detention and murder of American citizens said to be involved in terrorism – like Kamal Derwish, killed by a drone strike in 2002, and cleric Anwar al-Awlaki, killed by CIA drone strikes in 2009.

Since then, the government has steadily sought to expand its powers to target Americans. In an editorial correction to an article written in 2010 by Dana Priest, the *Washington Post* said: "The military's Joint Special Operations Command maintains a target list that includes several Americans. In recent weeks, U.S. officials have said that the government is prepared to kill U.S. citizens who are believed to be involved in terrorist activities that threaten Americans."[7]

The list of targeted individuals is growing too, and the intent to kill them is there. As part of the National Defense Authorization Act of 2012, the military (no mention is ever made of the CIA) was given the right to administratively detain and assassinate US citizens without due process. Right now the authorization is ostensibly limited to extraordinary circumstances. But the public is being prepared for the worst. In 2013, Attorney General Eric Holder announced that President Obama "has authority to use drone strikes to kill Americans on US soil."[8]

The bureaucratic groundwork is being laid as well. Just as Phoenix "Intelligence Operations and Coordination Centers" were established in every province and district in South Vietnam, the Department of Homeland Security has now established fusion centers, and the FBI has established Joint Terrorism Task Forces, to coordinate representatives from every police, security, military *and civic organization* in every state and major city.

The fascistic merging of government and corporate forces against the public interest is the most insidious facet of Phoenix in American society. And it is done with the full cooperation of the corporate media, which exploits each and every mass murder we endure, whether it is a terrorist attack or not – like the gay attacker's assault on the gay nightclub in Orlando – to terrorize the public into consenting to greater restrictions on civil liberties and more wars overseas.

The success of the Phoenix doctrine is most evident in the ability of its advocates in the ruling class to corrupt Congress and force it to divert massive amounts of public money into the militarization of foreign and domestic policy. The constant barrage of propaganda about looming terrorist threats, and the lurid human rights violations of straw dog enemies abroad, serves only to justify heavily armed police officers and National Guardsmen patrolling in paramilitary formations in our airports and train stations. Implicitly, the public knows those weapons can be used against them.

Now that the corrupt and corrupting Phoenix institutional structure is firmly in place in America, it is only a matter of time until we enter the next Phoenix phase of explicit terror here at home.

Chapter 4

THE SYSTEMATIC GATHERING OF INTELLIGENCE

"A census, if properly made and exploited, is a basic source of intelligence. It would show, for instance, who is related to whom, an important piece of information in counterinsurgency warfare because insurgent recruiting at the village level is generally based initially on family ties. "[1] David Galula

As counterinsurgency expert Galula noted over 50 years ago – long before the Internet made it easy for governments and internet corporations like Google to amass and manipulate private information about individuals – an old-fashioned, door-to-door census was an effective basis for the political control of large numbers of persons.

So it was in South Vietnam, where in 1962 the CIA implemented its Family Census program.

The Family Census program was the brainchild of Robert Thompson, a British counterinsurgency expert the CIA hired in 1961 to advise it on population control in South Vietnam. The CIA was still learning the ropes of modern neo-colonial repression and it looked to Brits like Thompson for guidance. Based on his success in suppressing a Communist uprising in Malaya, Thompson proposed a three-pronged approach that coordinated military, intelligence and police agencies in a concerted attack on the underground Communist resistance to American rule.

Managed by the National Police, the census meant compiling a dossier on every family in South Vietnam. Along with everyone's name and a portrait of the family, the dossier included each person's political affiliation, fingerprints, income, savings, and other relevant information, such as who owned property or had relatives outside the village and thus a legitimate reason to travel. By 1965 there were 7,453 registered families, primarily in Saigon and major cities.

The Family Census dossiers also helped the CIA discover the names of secret Communist Party cell members in GVN-controlled villages. Apprehending these political cadres was then a matter of arresting their associates and "softening them up" until they informed. The idea was to weaken the insurgency by forcing its political cadres to flee to guerrilla units in rural areas, thus depriving the VCI of leadership in GVN-controlled areas. This was critical to winning the war, for as South Vietnam's President Nguyen Van Thieu once observed, "Ho Chi Minh values his two cadres in every hamlet more highly than ten military divisions."[2]

Thompson's three-pronged method was successful, but only up to a point, for many political cadres were not terrorists. As Galula wrote, many were "men whose motivations, even if the counterinsurgent disapproves of them, may be perfectly honorable. They do not participate directly, as a rule, in direct terrorism or guerrilla action and, technically, have no blood on their hands."[3]

Indeed, Thompson's systematic approach created little love for the GVN, as noted in the previous chapter, in so far as innocent people were routinely tortured or extorted by crooked cops. On other occasions, double agents tricked security forces into arresting people hostile to the insurgency.

Recognizing these weaknesses, Thompson persuaded the CIA to organize a "Special Police" force (Cảnh-Sát Đặc-Biệt), later known as the Special Branch, within the National Police. The Special Police was to be composed, theoretically, of highly trained interrogators and carefully selected case officers – plain-clothed professionals who, like FBI agents, could not be confused with regular cops. Many were trained at the Central Intelligence Organization (CIO) school the CIA established in 1961.

The CIA used the same sophisticated method to recruit staff for the South Vietnamese Special Police and South Vietnam's version of the CIA, the Central Intelligence Organization (the CIO) that it used for recruiting cadres for the Korean CIA.

As John Marks revealed in *The Search for the Manchurian Candidate*, the CIA sent its top psychologist, John Winne, to Seoul to "select the initial cadre" using a psychological assessment test. "I set up an office with two translators," Winne told Marks, "and used a Korean version of the Wechsler." CIA psychologists gave the personality assessment test to 25 to 30 military and police officers, "and then wrote up a half-page report on each, listing their strengths and weaknesses. Winne wanted to know about each candidate's ability to follow orders, creativity, lack of personality disorders, motivation – why he wanted out of his current job. It was mostly for the money, especially with the civilians."[4]

In this way the CIA recruits secret police forces as assets in every country where it operates, including occupied Iraq. In Latin America, Marks wrote, "The CIA...found the assessment process most useful for showing how to train the anti-terrorist section. According to results, these men were shown to have very dependent psychologies and needed strong direction."[5]

That "direction" came from the CIA. Marks quoted one assessor as saying, "Anytime the Company spent money for training a foreigner, the object was that he would ultimately serve our purposes." CIA officers "were not content simply to work closely with these foreign intelligence agencies; they insisted on penetrating them, and the Personality Assessment System provided a useful aid."[6]

By 1964, plans were made to center the Special Police in Province Intelligence Coordinating Committees (PICCs) in South Vietnam's 44 provinces. But first the government had to secure Saigon, and in July 1964, 2500 regular policemen were introduced into seven provinces surrounding Saigon. By December, 13,000 policemen were participating, of whom 7000 were manning 700 checkpoints, and ABC-TV had done a documentary on the program.

Motivational Indoctrination

At the same time as the CIA was forming special police units to identify, capture, interrogate and kill secret Communist cadres and their sympathizers in GVN-controlled villages, it was also developing paramilitary "counterterror" teams to locate, capture and kill cadres in rural areas. To this end, the CIA in 1964 formed experimental counter-terror teams in seven districts surrounding Saigon. The CIA provided money and supplies, while US military intelligence and Special Forces provided training and advisors. Lists of defectors, criminals, and other potential recruits came from Special Police files.

Key to staffing the counterterror teams was the "motivational indoctrination" training program designed by US Information Service officer Frank Scotton. As Scotton explained it to me when we met at his home in McClean, Virginia, the idea was to "develop improved combat skills and increased commitment to close combat for South Vietnamese. This is not psywar against civilians or VC," he emphasized. It meant finding the most highly motivated people, saying they deserted from the army, typing up a contract, and using them in these units. "Our problem," Scotton said, "was finding smart Vietnamese and Cambodians who were willing to die."

Volunteers for Scotton's paramilitary program tended to be overly aggressive mercenaries. Many were recruited from South Vietnamese Special Forces units based along South Vietnam's borders with Laos and Cambodia. On a portable typewriter, Scotton would type a single-page contract, which each recruit signed, acknowledging that although listed as a deserter, he was employed by the CIA in "a sensitive project" for which he received substantially higher pay than before.

The most valuable quality possessed by people serving in "sensitive" CIA paramilitary projects like Scotton's was their expendability. Deserters, deranged desperados and hardened criminals facing lengthy prison terms or execution were placed in special reconnaissance teams, outfitted with captured enemy equipment and clothing, and given a "one-way ticket to Cambodia" to locate enemy sanctuaries. When they radioed back their position and that of the enemy encampment, the CIA would bomb them along with the target.

Minds capable of such scenarios were not averse to exploiting American soldiers who'd committed war crimes. Rather than serve hard time in military stockades, they would volunteer for and be accepted to do reprehensible jobs for the CIA's paramilitary Special Operations Group.

The CIA trained and treated its secret policemen differently than its mercenaries, but they were both CIA creations, and the CIA could plausibly deny them when necessary. And in each case it got exactly what it wanted. Indeed, the counterterror teams and secret policemen were the twin pillars upon which the Phoenix program would be founded in 1967.

About the death squads he developed, Scotton said, "For us, these programs were all part of the same thing. We did not think of things in terms of little packages." That "thing" of course was a grand scheme to win the war, at the base of which were Province Interrogation Centers (PICs).

PICs and the Systematic Gathering of Intelligence

John Patrick Muldoon, "Picadoon" to the folks who knew him in Vietnam, was the first director of the CIA's Province Interrogation Center (PIC) program in Vietnam. Standing six four and weighing well over 200 pounds, Muldoon was a college dropout who, thanks to family connections, joined the CIA in 1958. He did his first tour in Germany and the next in South Korea. "I worked interrogation in Seoul," Muldoon recalled. "I'd never been involved in interrogation before. Ray Valentine was my boss. There was a joint KCIA-CIA interrogation center in Yon Don Tho, outside Seoul."

Muldoon was assigned to South Vietnam in November 1964. "I was brought down to the National Interrogation Center [NIC] and told, 'This is where you're going to work. You're going to advise X number of interrogators. They'll bring you their initial debriefing of the guy they're working on, then you'll give them additional CIA requirements'."

The CIA had its own requirements, Muldoon explained, because "the South Vietnamese wanted information they could turn around and use in their battle against the Viet Cong in the South. We were interested in information about things in the North that the South Vietnamese couldn't care less about. And that's where the American advisors would come in – to tell them, 'You've got to ask this, too.'

"We had standard requirements depending on where a guy was from. A lot of VC had been trained in North Vietnam and had come back down as volunteers. They weren't regular North Vietnamese Army. So if a guy came from the North, we wanted to know where he was from, what unit he was with, how they were organized, where they were trained. If a guy had been up North for any length of time, we wanted to know if he'd traveled on a train. What kind of identification papers did he need? Anything about foreign weapons or foreigners advising them. That sort of thing."

Built in 1964, the NIC was where the CIA coordinated strategic civilian, police, and military intelligence. "It was located down on the

Saigon River," Muldoon recalled, "as part of a great big naval compound. On the left was a wing of offices where the American military chief, an Air Force major, was located. In that same wing were the chief of the CIO, his deputy, and the CIA advisors."

The same CIA interrogators were still at the NIC two years later when Muldoon departed for Thailand in 1966. There were four interrogators when he arrived. Three were Air Force enlisted men serving under an Army captain. Muldoon's boss, Ian "Sammy" Sammers, was the CIA chief of the NIC and worked under the station's senior liaison officer, Sam Hopler.

"There was a conference in Nha Trang in April 1965," Muldoon continued. "They were putting together an interrogation center in an existing building and asked for help from the NIC. I was sent up there with the Army captain to look at the place, figure out what kind of staff we needed, and how we were going to train them. And while we were up there trying to break these guys in, the CIA liaison officer in Nha Trang, Tony Bartolomucci, asked Sammy if he could keep me there for this conference, at which all of our people were going to meet Jack 'Red' Stent, who was taking over from Paul Hodges as chief of foreign intelligence. Bartolomucci wanted to show off his new interrogation center to all the big shots.

"The military people from the NIC had done their job," Muldoon continued, "so they left. But I stayed around. Then Tucker Gougelmann and Red showed up for this conference. Tucker was chief of Special Branch field operations, and things were just starting to get off the ground with the PICs. A few were already under way, and Tucker told me, 'We're going to build, build, build, and I need someone to oversee the whole operation. I want you to do it.'

"So we had this big conference, and they packed the interrogation center full of prisoners. Bartolomucci wanted to show off, so he got his police buddies to bring in a bunch of prostitutes and what have you and put them in the cells. I don't think they had one VC in the place. After the conference they all went back to the regular jail, and I went to work for Tucker.

"It's funny," Muldoon recalled," but me and Tucker used to talk about the PICs. He said something like 'John, if we lose this war one day, we could end up in these god-dammed things if we get caught.'

"'Well,' I asked, 'what would you do if you were in there?'

"He said he thought he'd kill himself rather than go through interrogation." Muldoon laughed. "Tucker wanted to turn the PICs into whorehouses. The interrogation rooms had two-way mirrors.

"Tucker was a hero in the Marine Corps in World War Two," Muldoon added. "He joined the Agency right after and worked in Korea running operations behind the lines. He was in Afghanistan and worked in training. He got to Vietnam in 1962 and was base chief in Da Nang running everything that had to do with intelligence and paramilitary operations. When I arrived in Saigon he was trying to set up the Province Intelligence Coordination Committees with Jack Barlow, a British guy from MI Six. Barlow had been in Malaya with Robert Thompson, and they were the experts."

Thompson's proposed Province Intelligence Coordination Committee (PICC) program was designed to extend CIO operations into the provinces. Theoretically, the CIO officer assigned to run a PICC would guide, supervise, and coordinate all military, police and civilian operations in a province. But the US military refused to go along with Thompson's PICC plan, so (and please don't be confused by the similar acronyms) the CIA settled on its unilateral Province Interrogation Center (PIC) program.

Starting in late 1964, the PICs became the places where the CIA hoped to coordinate its paramilitary and intelligence operations at the province level. The Special Police officers assigned to a PIC would interrogate suspects and then tell the CIA who and where the VCI were. The CIA liaison officer assigned to the PIC would share the information with the CIA's paramilitary officer in the province, and the paramilitary officer would then send a counterterror team to kidnap or kill the VCI. This was the one-two punch of the counterinsurgency; through the PICs, the CIA learned the identity and structure of the VCI in each province; and through the CTs, it eliminated VCI cadres and destroyed their organization.

The problem with the PIC in Nha Trang was that it had been built within an existing structure, so the CIA logistics staff hired Pacific Architects and Engineers (PA&E) to design a standardized facility that was strictly functional, minimizing cost while maximizing security. The CIA's logistics staff scouted out suitable locations and then, through PA&E, hired local Vietnamese contractors to build an interrogation center in each of South Vietnam's 44 provinces. Funds and staff salaries came from the CIA through the Special Police budget.[7]

After it was built, the CIA bought the PIC then donated it to the National Police, at which point it became a National Police facility under the direction of the Special Police. The four region capitals also had interrogation centers. The difference was that region interrogation centers were larger and held, according to Muldoon, 200-300 prisoners each.

It was the job of the CIA's liaison officer to convince the province chief and his CIO counterpart to find a spot near the provincial capital to build a PIC. Once it was built, the liaison officer became its advisor and Muldoon helped him recruit its staff. Most PICs were built or under construction by the time Muldoon was transferred to Thailand to build the CIA's huge interrogation center in Udorn.

Inside a PIC

One storey high, fashioned from concrete blocks, poured cement and wood in the shape of a hollow square, a PIC consisted of four buildings with tin roofs linked around a courtyard. In the center of the yard was a combination lookout-water tower with an electric generator under it.

"You couldn't get the guards to stay out there at night without lights," Muldoon explained. "So we had spotlights on the corners, along the walls, and on the tower shooting out all around. We also bulldozed around it so there were no trees or bushes. Anybody coming at it could be seen crossing the open area."

People entered and exited the PIC through green, steel-plated gates, "Which were wide open every time I visited," said Muldoon, who visited the PICs only during the day. "You didn't want to visit at night when attacks occurred." PICs were located on the outskirts of town, away from residential areas, so as not to endanger people living nearby, as well as to discourage rubbernecking. "These were self-contained places," Muldoon emphasized.

Telephone lines to the PICs were tapped by the CIA.

On the left side were interrogation rooms and the cellblock; depending on the size of the PIC, 20 to 60 solitary confinement cells the size of closets. Men and women were not segregated. "You could walk right down the corridor," according to Muldoon. "It was an empty hallway with cells on both sides. Each cell had a steel door and a panel at the bottom where you could slip the food in, and a slot at the top where you could look in and see what the guy was doing."

There were no toilets, just holes to squat over. "They didn't have them in their homes." Muldoon laughed. "Why should we put them in their cells?"

Prisoners slept on concrete slabs. "Depending on how cooperative they were, you'd give them a straw mat or a blanket. It could get very cold at night in the Highlands." A system of rewards and punishments was part of the treatment. "There were little things you could give them and take away from them, not a lot, but every little bit they got they were grateful for."

Depending on the amount of VCI activity in a province and the personality of the PIC chief, some were always full while others always empty. In either case, "We didn't want them sitting there talking to each other," Muldoon said, so "we would build up the cells gradually, until we had to put them next to each other. They were completely isolated. They didn't get time to go out and walk around the yard. They sat in their cells when they weren't being interrogated. After that they were sent to the local jail or turned back over to the military, where they were put in POW camps or taken out and shot. That part I never got involved in," he said, adding gratuitously that political prisoners "were treated better in the PICs than in the local jails for common criminals. Public Safety was advising the jails with the National Police.[8] Sometimes they had sixty to seventy people in a cell that shouldn't have had more than ten. But they didn't care. If you're a criminal, you suffer. If you don't like it, too bad; don't be a criminal."

Interrogation

According to Muldoon, the CIA interrogation process worked like this. "As we brought prisoners in, the first thing we did was run them through the shower. That's on the left as you come in. After that they were checked by the doctor or nurse. That was an absolute necessity because god knows what diseases they might be carrying with them. They might need medication. They wouldn't do you much good if they died the first day they were there and you never got a chance to interrogate them. That's why the medical office was right inside the main gate. In most PICs," Muldoon noted, "the medical staff was usually a local South Vietnamese army medic who would come out and check the prisoners coming in that day."

After the prisoner was cleaned, examined, repaired, weighed, photographed and fingerprinted, his or her biography was taken by a Special Police officer in the debriefing room. This initial interrogation extracted "hot" information that could be acted upon immediately – the whereabouts of an ongoing Communist Party committee meeting, for example, and other basic information needed to come up with requirements for the series of interrogations that followed. Then the prisoner was stuck in a cell.

The interrogation rooms were at the back of the PIC. Some had two-way mirrors and polygraph machines, although sophisticated equipment was usually reserved for region interrogation centers where expert CIA staff interrogators could put them to better use. Most CIA liaison officers were not trained interrogators. "They didn't have to be," according to Muldoon. "They were there to collect intelligence, and they had a list of what they needed in their own province. All they had to do was to make sure that whoever was running the PIC followed their orders. All they had to say was: 'This is the requirement I want.' Then they read the initial reports and went back and gave the Special Police interrogators additional requirements, just like we did at the NIC."

The guards lived in the PIC. As they returned from duty, they stacked their weapons in the first room on the right. The next room was the PIC chief's office, with a safe for classified documents, handguns, and a bottle of scotch. The PIC chief's job was to help "turn" captured VCI into agents and maintain informant networks in the hamlets and villages. Farther down the corridor were offices for interrogators, collation and report writers, translator-interpreters, and clerical and kitchen staff. There were file rooms with locked cabinets and map rooms for tracking the whereabouts of VCI. And there was a room where defectors were encouraged to become counterterrorists.

Once an interrogation center had been constructed and a staff assigned, Muldoon summoned the training team from the NIC. Each member was a specialist. The Army captain trained the guards. One Air Force sergeant taught the staff how to write proper reports. There were standard formats for tactical as opposed to strategic intelligence, as well as for agent reports. To compile a finished report, an interrogator's notes were reviewed by the chief interrogator, then collated, typed, copied and sent to the Special Police, CIO and CIA. Translations were never considered accurate unless read and confirmed in the original language by the same person, which rarely happened. Likewise, interrogations conducted through interpreters were never considered totally reliable, given that significant information was generally lost or misrepresented.

A second Air Force sergeant taught interrogators how to take notes and ask questions during an interrogation. "You don't just sit down with ten questions, get ten answers, and then walk away," Muldoon said. "Some of these guys, if you gave them ten questions, would get ten answers for you, and that's it. They had to learn that you don't drop a line of questioning just because you got the answer. The answer, if it's the right one, should lead to sixty more questions.

"For example," Muldoon said, "Question one was: 'Were you ever trained in North Vietnam?' Question two was, 'Were you ever trained by people other than Vietnamese?' Well, lots of times the answer to question two is so interesting and gives you so much information you keep going for an hour and never get to question three: 'When did you come to South Vietnam'?"

Special Police officers in region interrogation centers were sent to a special interrogation training program conducted at the NIC by experts from the CIA's Support Services Branch, most of whom worked on Russian defectors and were brought out from Washington to handle important cases. Training of administrative personnel was conducted at region headquarters by professional female secretaries, who taught their students how to type, file and use phones.

According to Muldoon, the Special Police employed "the old French methods." That means interrogation that included torture. "All this had to be stopped by the Agency," he said. "They had to be re-taught with more sophisticated techniques."

The Vietnamese, however, did not change "their" ways. It's also important to note that "they" did not conceive the PIC gulag archipelago; the Special Police were the stepchildren of Robert Thompson, whose aristocratic Norman-English ancestors perfected torture in dingy castle dungeons, on the rack and in the Iron Lady, with thumbscrews and branding irons.

As for the American role: according to Muldoon, "You can't have an American there all the time watching these things."

"These things" included rape, gang rape, rape using eels, snakes or hard objects, and rape followed by murder; "the Bell Telephone Hour" rendered by attaching wires to the genitals or other sensitive parts of the body; waterboarding; "the airplane," in which a prisoner's arms were tied behind the back and the rope looped over a hook on the ceiling suspending the prisoner in midair while he or she was beaten;

beatings with rubber hoses and whips; and the use of police dogs to maul prisoners. All this and more occurred in PICs, one of which was run by former Congressman Rob Simmons (R-CT) while he was a CIA officer running the PIC in Phú Yên Province in 1972.[9]

"The PIC advisor's job was to keep the region officer informed about real operations mounted in the capital city or against big shots in the field," Muldoon said, adding that advisors who wanted to do a good job ran the PICs themselves, while the lazy ones hired contractors who were paid by the CIA but worked for themselves, doing a dirty job in exchange for an inside track to the black market.

Apart from serving as torture chambers, PICs were faulted for only producing information on low-level VCI. Whenever a VCI cadre with strategic information (for example, a cadre in Hue who knew what was happening in the Delta) was captured, he was immediately grabbed by the region bosses or the NIC where expert CIA interrogators could produce quality reports for Washington. The lack of feedback to the PIC for its own operations resulted in a revolving door syndrome, wherein the PIC was reduced to picking up the same low-level people month after month.

"A lot of PICs didn't produce anything because the CIA advisors in the provinces didn't push them," Muldoon said. "Some of them said, 'It's not that we didn't try; it's just that it was a dumb idea in the first place, because we couldn't get the military, who were the ones capturing prisoners, to turn them over. The military weren't going to turn them over to us until they were finished with them, and by then they were washed out.'

"This," Muldoon conceded, "was part of the overall plan: let the military get the tactical intelligence first. Obviously that's the most important thing in a war. But after the military got what they could use tomorrow or next week, then CIA should talk to this guy. That was the idea of having the Province Intelligence Coordination Committees and why the PICs became part of them, so we could work this stuff back and forth. And in provinces where our guys went out of their way to work with the MACV sector advisor, they were able to get something done."

As of August 2016, one can assume that similar CIA networks of secret interrogation centers have been built to updated PIC specifications in every nation the US engages militarily – Afghanistan, Iraq, Syria, and Libya, etc. The "black sites" the CIA establishes in other nations, by corrupting that nation's security forces, will also conform to the updated, computerized PIC design.

Last but not least, the CIA's interrogation methods remain unchanged, though the organization is now more perfectly able to punish people by driving them insane.

The Military's Side of the Story

The military's side of the story was presented by Major General Joseph McChristian in his book *The Role of Military Intelligence 1965-1967.* [10]

McChristian arrived in Saigon in July 1965 as the military's intelligence chief. He recognized the threat posed by the VCI and, in order to destroy it, proposed "a large countrywide counterintelligence effort involved in counter sabotage, counter subversion and counterespionage activities." In structuring this attack against the VCI, McChristian assigned military intelligence detachments to each US Army brigade, division and field force, as well as to each Army of the Republic of Vietnam (ARVN) division and corps. He created combined centers for intelligence, document exploitation and interrogation, and directed the centers to support and coordinate allied units in the field. He also ordered the construction of military interrogation centers in each sector, division, and corps.

McChristian conceded the primacy of the CIA-advised Special Police in anti-VCI operations. He admitted that the military did not have the CIA's sophisticated agent nets, and that military advisors focused on acquiring tactical intelligence needed to mount offensive operations. But he was upset when the CIA, "without coordination with MACV, took over control of the files on the infrastructure located" in the PICs. He got an even bigger shock when he "was refused permission to see the infrastructure file by a member of the [CIA]." [11]

Everyone was competing for success. As a result, some CIA officers prevented military personnel from entering their PICs, and in retaliation the military refused to send its prisoners to those PICs. As a result, anti-VCI operations were often poorly coordinated at province level.

The US military assigned intelligence teams to the provinces to form agent nets with the ARVN's Military Security Service (MSS). These advisory teams sent reports to the *political order of battle* section in the Combined Intelligence Center, which "produced complete and timely intelligence on the boundaries, location, structure, strengths, personalities and activities of the Communist political organization, or infrastructure." Information filtering into the Combined Intelligence Center was placed in an automatic database, which enabled analysts to compare known VCI offenders with known aliases. Agent reports and special intelligence collection programs provided information on low-level VCI, while information on high-level VCI came from the Combined Military Interrogation Center, which, according to McChristian, was "the focal point of tactical and strategic exploitation of selected human sources."[12]

By mid-1966, US military intelligence employed about a thousand agents in South Vietnam, all of whom were paid through the 525th Military Intelligence Group's Intelligence Contingency Fund.

The 525th had a headquarters unit, a battalion placed in each corps, and a battalion working with third countries. Like the CIA, it also had unilateral teams working without the knowledge or approval of the GVN. Operational teams consisted of five enlisted men reporting to an officer who served as team chief. Each enlisted man functioned as an agent handler. Some agent handlers worked undercover as State Department Foreign Service officers or employees of private American companies like PA&E. They kept their military IDs for access to classified information, areas and resources.

Upon arriving in South Vietnam, an agent handler was assigned a Principal Agent (PA), who usually had a functioning agent network in place. Some of the nets had been set up by the French decades earlier. Each PA had several subagents working in cells. Like most spies, subagents were in it for the money; in many cases the war had destroyed their businesses and left them no alternative.

Agent handlers worked with PAs through interpreters and couriers. In theory, an agent handler never met the PA's subagents; instead, each cell had a cell leader who secretly met with the PA to exchange information and receive instructions, which were passed along to the other subagents. Some subagents were political specialists; others attended to military concerns. Posing as woodcutters or rice farmers or secretaries or auto mechanics, subagents infiltrated VC-controlled villages and businesses, and reported on VCI cadres and the GVN's criminal undertakings, as well as on the size and whereabouts of VC and NVA combat units.

Agent handlers managing political "accounts" were given requirements by their team leaders for information on individual VCI.

The cell leader would report on a particular VCI to his PA, who would pass the information back to the agent handler using standard tradecraft methods, such as a cryptic mark on a wall or telephone pole that his handler would periodically look for. Upon seeing the mark, the agent handler would send a courier to retrieve the report from the PA's courier at a prearranged time and place. The agent handler would then pass the information to his team leader as well as other "customers," including the CIA liaison officer at "The Embassy House," as CIA headquarters in a province or major city was called.

The finished products of positive and counterintelligence operations were called Army Information Reports. AIRs and agents were rated on the basis of accuracy, but insofar as most agents were in it for money, accuracy was hard to judge. An agent might implicate a person who owed him money or a rival in love, business or politics. Many agents were in fact working for the insurgency, and as a result all agents were periodically given lie detector tests. They were also given code names. They were paid through the Military Intelligence Contingency Fund, but not well enough to survive, so most dabbled in the black market too.

The final stage of the intelligence cycle was the termination of agents, usually by paying them off, swearing them to secrecy and saying goodbye. Another option was termination with prejudice, which meant ordering an agent out of an area and placing his or her name on a blacklist so they could never work for the US again. Third was termination with extreme prejudice, a euphemism meaning "to kill" which applied when the mere existence of an agent threatened the security of an operation or other agents.

Military Intelligence officers were taught in off-the-record sessions how to terminate their agents with extreme prejudice. CIA officers received similar instruction.

These methods still apply today but on a grander scale; military intelligence groups operate agent nets in the "camp-follower" communities that surround the military's hundreds of overseas bases. Agent handlers conduct much of their business in the brothels and night clubs that sprout up around the bases and provide sex and drugs to military personnel. These cottage industries provide what Warren Milberg cynically characterized in the previous chapter as "economic stability." The agent handlers also spread money around, ostensibly for information, but actually as the preferred methods of bribing local officials to follow American policy at the expense of their own nation's best interests. Like missionaries of old, they preach the gospel and pave the way for capitalist investment.

The end result is billions of unaccounted for tax dollars.[13]

Case Studies: Ed Murphy and Sid Towle

Sergeant Ed Murphy was trained as a counterintelligence specialist at Fort Holabird, then sent to the Defense Language Institute in Texas for Vietnamese language training. From Texas he was assigned to Fort Lewis. "On the plane from Fort Lewis to Cam Ranh Bay," Murphy recalled, "I was given an article to read. It was a study by the American Medical Association on interrogation methods used in the Soviet Union. It showed how to do things without laying a hand on a person, how you could torture a person just by having them stand there."

Upon his arrival in Vietnam in May 1968, Murphy was assigned to 4th Infantry Division headquarters at Camp Enari outside Pleiku City, where his understanding of counterinsurgency warfare rapidly evolved from theory to reality. There were five enlisted men in his counterintelligence team, each with a sector, each sector having around ten agents. The main function of the agents was to uncover VC plans to attack and sabotage Camp Enari. Murphy's agents, furnished by the MSS, acted as day workers on the base. He also ran a team of agents eleven miles away in Pleiku City.[14]

Sometimes the agents got tips about a suspected VCI, and when that happened, Murphy took the name and information to the local Phoenix coordinator.

"Phoenix," Murphy said, "was a bounty-hunting program, an attempt to eliminate the opposition, by which I mean the opposition to us, the Americans, getting what we wanted, which was to control the Vietnamese through our clients – the Diems, the Kys, the Thieus."

For Murphy, all other definitions of Phoenix are "intellectual jargon."

Once a week Murphy went to the CIA's Embassy House where he and the other civilian and military intelligence people in the area submitted the names of VCI suspects their agents had fingered. The names were sent to the Phoenix Committee, which decided how to handle each case.

Surrounded by a concrete wall, its gate manned by a Montagnard PRU team,[15] the CIA compound was located in a remote corner of Pleiku.

Inside it was a barbed-wire cage for prisoners. The cage was too small for prisoners to stand up in. Murphy was not permitted into the PIC, which "sat on a hill and looked like a U-shaped school."

"I would never see a North Vietnamese or Vietcong soldier," Murphy stressed. "This is post-Tet and those people are dead. We're talking civilian infrastructure people supporting the NVA and VC. It could be anybody. It could be somebody who works in a movie theater, somebody sweeping up."

When asked what kind of information he needed before he could have a suspect arrested, Murphy answered, "None. Whatever you wanted."

When asked what sort of criteria he used to classify VCI suspects, Murphy replied, "Nothing. One of my agents says somebody's a spy. If I had reason to believe he's telling the truth, and if I wanted to bring somebody in for interrogation, I could do it. It was that easy. I had an agreement with the team leader that I could do anything I wanted. I wore civilian clothes. My cover identity was as a construction worker with Pacific Architects and Engineers."

Murphy called his agents "hustlers and entrepreneurs making money off intelligence." After noting the difficulty of verifying information submitted at Phoenix Committee meetings, "the lack of files and things like that," Murphy told how one female suspect was raped and tortured simply because she refused to sleep with an agent.

"Phoenix," Murphy said, "was far worse than the things attributed to it. It was heinous, but no worse than the bombing. And I don't apologize. But it was a watershed for me. It focused things. I realized it wasn't just a war; but that based on the assumption that nothing is worse than communism, the Government of Vietnam, backed by the US, felt justified in suppressing all opposition while extending its control throughout the country."

That control, Murphy explained, served an economic purpose. "An employee at Pacific Architects and Engineers told me about two million dollars in materiel and cash being unaccounted for; that goods being sold on the black market didn't come from the Vietnamese, but from the Americans.

"In order to get into military intelligence school," Murphy continued, "I had to write an essay on the debate about the Vietnam War. The thrust of my paper was, 'What we do in Vietnam will come back to haunt us.' It was a one world thesis. Well, I go to Vietnam and see the bullshit going down. Then I come back to the United States and see the same thing going on here. I'm at the 116th MI Group in Washington, DC, and as you leave the room, they have nine slots for pictures, eight of them filled: Rennie Davis, Abbie Hoffman, Ben Spock, Jerry Rubin.[16] And I'm being sent out to spot and identify these people.

"This is Phoenix," Murphy said, then added for emphasis, "*This is Phoenix!*"

"In 'Nam I had composite descriptions of a person's physical characteristics, but then I wasn't in a place where we had technology. It doesn't make any difference. The point is that it was used in Vietnam, it was used in the US, and it still is used in the United States."

In 1969, Murphy was one of precious few Americans acquainted with Phoenix, and he was determined to make it a political issue. He came to that decision in October 1969 while participating in the March Against Death outside the Pentagon. "I was being surveilled," Murphy said. "I know, because the people doing it told me so. 'I've been reading about you,' one of the officers (Sid Towle) said."

Having fought for his country in defense of its civil liberties, Murphy was enraged to learn that the 116th MIG was being used against American citizens exercising their constitutional rights to protest the war. To him, this represented "the Phoenix mentality in the United States."

"To me," he explained, "Phoenix was a lever to use to stop the war. You use what you got. I got Phoenix. I'm a former intelligence agent, fluent in Vietnamese, involved in Phoenix in the Central Highlands. That means I'm credible. I'm using it."

Intent on making Phoenix a political issue to stop the war, Murphy joined forces with two other Vietnam veterans. At news conferences held simultaneously in New York, San Francisco and Rome on 14 April 1970, the three veterans issued a joint press release laying out the horrifying facts about Phoenix. By then the program was nearly three years old.

Sid Towle's Story

A graduate of Yale University, Lieutenant Sid Towle was assigned to the 116th MIG in Washington, DC in June 1969. As chief of a counterintelligence team, he reviewed cases, including the investigation into Ed Murphy's antiwar activities.

Towle also conducted "offensive counterintelligence operations" that consisted of disrupting antiwar demonstrations by building bonfires and inciting people to riot, so the Capital Police could be called in to bash heads and arrest demonstrators. During the period he was involved in military operations against American civilians, Towle was rated by his commander as "one of the most dedicated, professionally competent and outstanding junior officers I have had the privilege to serve with anywhere."

But Towle didn't want to go to Vietnam, and in January 1971 he requested release from active duty, citing his "complete abhorrence for the Vietnam War and the continued US presence there." Towle filed for release under Army Regulation 635-100; but his request was denied and his "triple six" credentials withdrawn.[17] He was sent to Vietnam in March 1971 as the Phoenix "Phung Hoang" coordinator in Vung Liem District in Vinh Long Province.[18]

During his stint as a Phoenix coordinator, Towle spent most of his time "sifting through the District Intelligence and Operations and Coordination Center's target folders looking for aliases.[19] A sergeant assigned to the DIOCC managed funds obtained from the CIA for informers and the PRU team. The sergeant also acted as liaison with the Vinh Long PIC. Towle lived in a villa with six other people in the MACV Civil Operations and Rural Development Support (CORDS) district team.[20] Behind the villa were the PRU quarters. "We turned up the radio when we heard the screams of the people being interrogated," he said.

"I didn't know what the PRU were doing ninety percent of the time," Towle explained. "They were directed by the CIA's Province Officer in Charge."

To clear operations against the VCI, Towle had to get permission from Tom Ahern, the CIA's Province Officer in Charge.[21] Regarding operations, Towle said, "I went after an average of eight to ten VCI per week. The Special Branch people would come up with the names, which I would check. Then the PRU went out. They went out every night and always killed one or two people. But verifying whether or not they were VCI was impossible. They'd tell you who they had killed, and it was always a name on the list, but how could I know? We had charts on the wall, and we'd cross off the name, and that was it."

Towle kept score, until the day the district chief took him for a ride in a helicopter. As they were flying over a village, they saw an old man and a girl walking hand in hand down the main street. The district chief said to the door gunner, "Kill them."

The gunner asked Towle, "Should I?"

Towle said no.

"That was the beginning of the end," Towle said. "Ahern called me on the carpet. He told me the province chief was angry because I had caused the district chief to lose face."

There was another reason why Towle didn't enjoy working in Phoenix. Ahern started a bounty program in which cash prizes were offered as an incentive to inform on VCI. Ahern even arranged a contest between the Phoenix district advisors to see who could rack up the biggest body count. Disgusted, the advisors got together and decided not to participate.

A few days later John Vann, who ran all CORDS operations in IV Corps, arrived in his private helicopter.[22] "He flew right into the DIOCC," Towle recalled. "He was very critical. He asked where all the bodies and weapons were, then sent me into a funeral in progress. He had me open the casket to identify the body.

"I hated Vann," Towle said. "He was really into body counts."

On another occasion, while Towle was eating dinner in the CORDS villa, the district chief stormed into the room with the PRU team and dumped a dirty bag on the table. Eleven bloody ears spilled out. The district chief told Towle to give the ears to Ahern as proof of six VCI neutralized.

"It made me sick," Towle said. "I couldn't go on with the meal.

"After the ear thing," Towle continued, "I joined up with the air rescue team on one of its missions. I was promoted to captain while I was there, and received a message from the district senior advisor saying, 'Don't come back.' So I went to see a friend in the Judge Advocate General's office in Can Tho, and he reported the ear incident to General Cushman. The general came down in a chopper and handed the province senior advisor a letter of reprimand. After that, I knew I could never go back, so I had one of my friends in Vung Liem bring my bags up to Can Tho."

Towle was removed as the Vung Liem Phoenix coordinator on 20 July 1971. Ten days later he received orders reassigning him to Kien Phong Province. "It was the proverbial One-Way Ticket to Cambodia," he sighed. "The last two guys sent out there as Phoenix coordinators were killed by their own PRU. So I went back to see the major running Phoenix administration in Can Tho, Major James Damron, but he refused to reassign me. So from there I went back to the JAG office, where my friend and I drafted a letter to the Phoenix Directorate in Saigon."

In his letter to Phoenix Director John Tilton, Towle said

that "War crimes as designated by the Geneva Conventions were not uncommon" in the Phoenix program. He requested "immediate release" from the program under MACV 525-36.

The next day Major Damron reassigned Towle to the Tuyen Binh DIOCC – the same DIOCC where the two previous "triple sixers" had been killed. To avoid certain death, Towle hid at a friend's house in Can Tho until 10 August, when the new CORDS chief of staff, General Frank Smith, approved his release.

Referring to "the case that appalled us all," a senior CORDS official suggested that a records check be made in Saigon "before an officer or enlisted man is assigned to a Phung Hoang position in Vietnam" as a way to "reduce chances of assignment of unsuitable personnel."

At the same time "unsuitable" Sid Towle was quitting Phoenix, CORDS Director William Colby was assuring Congress that no Phoenix advisor had resigned on moral grounds through MACV 525-36.

Colby also told Congress that incentive programs (like the one Ahern organized in Vinh Long Province) were not policy. At the exact same time, however, Phoenix Director Tilton was organizing a High Value Rewards Program. In explaining the program to his wife, Tilton's deputy Colonel Chester McCoid wrote, "A very substantial reward is placed on highly placed VC political leaders, as much as $8,000 at the rate on the black market or twice that amount on the official rate of exchange. Our idea is to induce the lower-grade VCI to turn their bosses in for the bounty money."

Said McCoid with dismay, "our original proposal was watered down by the bleeding hearts, who think placing a price on your enemy's head is excessively cruel! This despite Colby's support."

Ultimately, the Phoenix concept is the sum of all the programs it coordinated, including the public information aspects – like the lies Colby told to Congress – that concealed its true goals and operational realities. All other definitions and expressions are, as Ed Murphy said, "intellectual jargon."

"The point," Murphy reminded us, "is that it was used in Vietnam, it was used in the United States, and it still is used in the United States."

WHAT WE REALLY LEARNED FROM VIETNAM: A WAR CRIMES MODEL FOR AFGHANISTAN AND ELSEWHERE

Evan Thomas and John Barry began their 6 November 2009 *Newsweek* article, "The Surprising Lessons of Vietnam", by recounting a curt telephone conversation between the commander of the International Security Assistance Force in Afghanistan, General Stanley McChrystal, and author Stanley Karnow, whose book *Vietnam* the pundits described as "the standard popular account of the Vietnam War."

McChrystal asked Karnow if there were any lessons from the Vietnam War that could be applied to Afghanistan. The 84-year-old Karnow said the lesson was simple: "We never should have been there in the first place."

Alas, the Thomas-Barry article – subtitled "Unraveling the mysteries of Vietnam may prevent us from repeating its mistakes" – was not about the costs in blood and treasure of imperial aggression. It was about improving US propaganda so that political and military leaders can build public support for the War on Terror not only in Afghanistan, but anywhere profits are waiting to be made.

Indeed, Thomas and Barry dismissed Karnow's advice as "not all that useful to General McChrystal [because] like it or not, he is already in Afghanistan."

Understanding Thomas and Barry as individuals helps to understand their militant bias. For example, in his book *The Very Best Men: The Daring Early Years of the CIA,* Thomas turned four racist, ruthless spies into daring, glamorous men who singlehandedly stopped Soviet aggression. Thomas's big wet kiss to Frank Wisner, Richard Bissell, Tracy Barnes, and Desmond FitzGerald earned him an inside track into the CIA's secret archives and access to its inner circle of supplicants. Nothing more than a paean to the CIA, his book became an instant best seller.

Barry is also graced with the love of the National Security Establishment. A British citizen hired in 1985 by media empress Katherine Graham, Barry was immediately granted an audience with CIA Director William Casey. As a sign of its commitment to Barry, *Newsweek* bought his house in England so he could afford to buy a new one in DC. He repaid his benefactors over and over again with CIA-friendly propaganda, including the 2 March 2003 article, in which he cited a high-ranking defector as insisting that Iraq had not abandoned its Weapons of Mass Destruction ambitions.[1]

Thomas and Barry exemplify that select group of national security correspondents – the old boy network – who have been so thoroughly compromised by their personal connections to the CIA that they cannot be trusted by the public. True to form, the rest of their article expanded on the fantasy of a winnable war in Afghanistan. It also engaged in shameless revisionism, contending, for example, that Karnow's sage advice reflected the wrongheaded liberal consensus that the Vietnam War was unwinnable.

Citing Hawkish Authors as Experts

Thomas and Barry insisted that the American military could have won if 1) President Lyndon Johnson had been more militant in 1965; 2) President Richard Nixon had put more effort into pacification in 1970; and 3) Democrats in Congress hadn't stabbed the military in the back in 1974.

To support their false assertions, Thomas and Barry relied on retired Army Lt. Col. Lewis Sorley and Professor Mark Moyar at the Marine Corps University at Quantico, Virginia.

The *Newsweek* correspondents cited Moyar as the source of the revisionist theory that Johnson could have won the war by leveling North

Vietnam with a 1960s version of shock and awe. "In 1964–65, the top military leadership understood that to defeat the North, it was necessary to go all-out," Thomas and Barry wrote, citing Moyar's "groundbreaking work" with its idiotic title, *Triumph Forsaken*.

Moyar claimed that "a massive bombing campaign, mining Hanoi's port, and sending troops into Laos and Cambodia to cut off the North's all-important sanctuaries and resupply route, the Ho Chi Minh Trail" would have won the war in 1965. But, Moyar contended, girly politicians and groveling military commanders prevented the hawks from going "all out"; in other words, committing genocide and annihilating the North.

"LBJ's advisors were reluctant — fearful, in part, of dragging China and the Soviet Union into a larger war," Thomas and Barry said. "The military pressed — but not very hard," making "the classic mistake of telling their political masters what they wanted to hear."

Perpetrating myths like Moyar's requires quite a bit of dissembling, and nowhere in their article do Thomas and Barry mention that the history departments at the University of Iowa and Duke rejected Moyar's job applications, based on his habit of spewing right-wing propaganda instead of facts. Moyar is to Vietnam War history what creationists are to science.[2] But that didn't dissuade Barry and Thomas.

According to their other biased source, Lewis Sorley, the Democrats stabbed the military in the back by not financing a promising counterinsurgency effort late in the war. "Sorley argues [in his 1999 book, *A Better War*] that, contrary to the conventional wisdom, the United States could have won in Vietnam – if only the U.S. Congress hadn't cut off military aid to South Vietnam," Thomas and Barry wrote.

For good measure, the *Newsweek* correspondents demeaned the books that President Barack Obama's advisors were relying upon, including Gordon Goldstein's *Lessons in Disaster*. They said that Goldstein's book "captures the conventional wisdom (at least at the center and left of the political spectrum) that Vietnam was a hopeless, unwinnable war."

"But was it [unwinnable]?" they asked with eyebrows arched, before answering their own question: "The lessons of Vietnam are not necessarily the ones we glibly assume – chief among them that Afghanistan, like Vietnam, is a quagmire, and that achieving some sort of victory is out of reach."

The Right Course

Based on the flawed theories of Moyar and Sorley, Thomas and Barry advanced the theory that the right course of action in Afghanistan was to give McChrystal all the troops and resources he wanted for a full-scale counterinsurgency campaign. In this view, de-escalating in Afghanistan or even ordering only a small troop increase was not an option, unless Obama wanted to invite questions about his resolve (a criticism adopted by Hillary Clinton in her hawkish presidential campaigns) and renewed accusations about political back-stabbing of the military.

According to Thomas and Barry, Ambassador Karl Eikenberry, a retired general who once commanded US forces in Afghanistan, fell into the camp of timid Obama advisors when, in July 2009, he questioned the wisdom of sending more troops to prop up the corrupt Afghan government of Hamid Karzai.

The bottom line of the *Newsweek* article was that the US could easily have won in Afghanistan if Obama had had the "heart" to prevail, and if Washington had learned the correct lessons from Vietnam. In advancing this theory, Thomas and Barry ignored the unprecedented violence Johnson did unleash against the North via his Rolling Thunder bombing campaign from March 1965 to November 1968, in which more than 300,000 bombing missions dropped 864,000 tons of bombs.

It's hard to determine exactly how many bombs America and NATO have dropped on Afghanistan in the 15 years since 2001; but Thomas and Barry offered no sympathy for the people they fell upon.

They also glossed over the disproven rationales for the Vietnam War, from the discredited "domino theory" to the idea of a unified Sino-Soviet strategy for world conquest. They also relied on sanitized military jargon to obscure the inhuman brutality that pervaded "death squad" operations like the Phoenix program.

The Thomas-Barry article was published on 6 November 2009. Three months later, as reported by *The New York Times*, a raid by US Special Operations forces "left three women – two of them pregnant – and a local police chief and prosecutor dead. It was one of the latest examples of Special Operations forces killing civilians during raids, deaths that have infuriated Afghan officials and generated support for the Taliban despite efforts by American and NATO commanders to reduce civilian casualties."[3]

Initially, the commando team claimed it had been fired upon by insurgents and that the women had already been murdered when they arrived. When that lie was exposed, their commander confessed they'd made "a terrible mistake." But he made no attempt to explain why, in an effort to cover-up their crime, the American commandos – practicing the Manson Family values they'd been taught by their CIA masters – carved their bullets out of the pregnant women's bodies.

Is carving bullets out of dead pregnant women really a mistake? Were the American soldiers trained to do such things, or did they think it up on the scene? None of those questions were even asked.

Murdering innocent civilians indeed has been infuriating Afghanis since early 2002 when they put down their weapons and submitted to American rule. But, as Anand Gopal explains in his book *No Good Men Among the Living*, CIA assets within its Northern Alliance started the insurgency by falsely accusing pro-American Afghanis in Maiwand of being al Qaeda sympathizers. The CIA-sponsored murders of top leaders of the Noorzai and Ishaqzai tribes forced the tribes' remaining leaders into Pakistan, where their Pashtun relatives and associates gave them shelter while they plotted their revenge on the Americans and their occupation army of collaborators.[4]

The idea that the Americans running the War on Terror are trying to reduce civilian deaths is pure propaganda, a repetition of stated policy with as much basis in fact as Colby's blatant lies about Phoenix to Congress 40 years earlier. If military commanders were trying to reduce civilian deaths, they would have arrested and tried the commandos who murdered those five people in Afghanistan. But we will never even know their names. They are free to murder to their hearts' content, because murdering civilians is unstated policy.

In the absence of punishment for war crimes and cover-ups, how can there be "efforts" to prevent civilian casualties? Indeed, you won't hear it said by the likes of Thomas and Barry, but the license to kill that is granted to American forces, along with the intentional corruption of collaborating officials, is what most closely links the barbaric War on Terror with the Vietnam War.

The Wrong Parallels

Another problem with the Thomas-Barry analysis, is that many of the tactics the *Newsweek* writers suggested should have been expanded in Vietnam have no relevance to Afghanistan. For instance, there is no North Afghanistan to bomb back to the Stone Age; there is no Soviet Union that can transform the war into a nuclear confrontation; and there is no formal Taliban army, which, like the North Vietnamese Army, could come to the rescue of civilian insurgents caught up in the conflict.

The support insurgents receive from Pashtun relatives in Pakistan – civilians the CIA has targeted for death and mutilation through a record-setting but secret number of drones strikes – is itself the product of British colonialists having invented the nation of Pakistan as a way of more efficiently looting the region. Omitting historical facts like that from their narratives is yet another trick used by propagandists like Thomas and Barry.

The parallels between the two conflicts are mostly over the narrow issue of counterinsurgency tactics, which is why the *Newsweek* article skirted any serious discussion of the Phoenix program, instead using Pentagon-friendly language about "a true counterinsurgency, focusing on protecting the population by a strategy of 'clear and hold.'"

Lifting language first employed in the Phoenix program, Thomas and Barry praised the Special Operations forces McChrystal directed in Iraq as focused "on *protecting* [my italics] civilians while ruthlessly targeting jihadist leaders." They did so without irony or reference to an earlier article authored by Barry in 2005. That article famously revealed that the Bush administration was taking to Iraq the "death-squad" strategies that had been applied in El Salvador in the 1980s, what *Newsweek* called "the Salvador option."[5]

And where, indeed, did the Salvador Option originate? With the Phoenix program in Vietnam!

The strategy was named after the Reagan regime's "still-secret strategy" of supporting El Salvador's right-wing security forces, which used clandestine "death squads" to eliminate both leftist guerrillas and their civilian sympathizers. As Barry reported at the time, "many U.S. conservatives consider the policy to have been a success – despite the deaths of innocent civilians."

Judging that those war crimes worked in Iraq, Thomas and Barry encouraged McChrystal to expand the "death squad" approach in Afghanistan. They wrote: "U.S. Special Operations Forces use the intelligence gleaned from friendly civilians to find and kill Taliban leaders. That is precisely what the Phoenix Program was designed to do 40 years ago in Vietnam: target and assassinate Viet Cong leaders."

This "true counterinsurgency," Thomas and Barry asserted, began to work in Vietnam when the top US commanders began to "smarten up."

Their article confidently asserted that in late 2009, "McChrystal is implementing a strategy that draws on the lessons of Iraq and looks an awful lot like the 'pacification' program adopted by General Abrams in Vietnam in 1968. By ratcheting back the heavy use (and overuse) of firepower, McChrystal has reduced civilian casualties, which alienate the locals and breed more jihadists."

The steady increase in civilian deaths in Afghanistan since 2010, and the emergence of ISIS in Iraq and Syria, refutes their argument[6] which relies totally on disinformation and "prejudicial" terms like "jihadist" to justify the cold-blooded murder of innocent people falsely designated as militant religious fanatics. It is the same disinformation that was used to justify Phoenix. But just as in Vietnam, where the word communist was applied to anyone who resisted the US occupation, American kidnapping and assassination programs in Iraq and Afghanistan make no distinction between "jihadists" and nationalists defending their homes and resisting foreign occupation.

The Wrong Facts

Thomas and Barry ignored some basic facts about "pacification" in Vietnam, including that:

- CIA and military Special Forces created South Vietnam's "self-defense forces" for the purpose of waging a "clear and hold" style counterinsurgency well before Abrams arrived in 1968.

- The CIA created a "general staff for pacification" in 1967 that managed the Phoenix program.

- Westmoreland's "main force" battles with the NVA bought the US military time to implement this counterinsurgency strategy, and compelled the North to initiate the Tet uprisings of 1968, which decimated the South's guerrilla forces before Abrams took command in June of that year.

The one accurate comparison Thomas and Barry cited between the situation in Vietnam and the conduct of the terror wars in Afghanistan and Iraq was already being implemented: the counterinsurgency tactic of targeting and assassinating enemy leaders. But the comparison they made was actually incomplete and misleading, since that tactic was but the exposed tip of the iceberg, riding upon a massive programmatic development below it.

The CIA's counterinsurgency effort in Vietnam was based on its Provincial Interrogation Center, Counter-Terror, Armed Political Action, Hamlet Informant, Census Grievance and Chieu Hoi "defector" programs; all made possible under extra-legal administrative detention laws and emergency decrees established by Americans to allow American participation. These cornerstones of the counterinsurgency were already in place and incorporated within the Phoenix program in 1967.

The purpose of these counterinsurgency programs was to chart the clandestine "front" organizations that drove the national liberation movement. In mapping out this "secret government" with its secret agents, the CIA came to understand how the Viet Cong Infrastructure helped average citizens cope with the massive violence that the US military and its puppet regime in Saigon were using to destroy their lives and livelihoods.

Meanwhile, the CIA established its own secret government. Through its parallel "secret government" of secret collaborators, the CIA, after 1967, directed the dictatorial regime of President Nguyen Van Thieu, and through his clique, exercised control of South Vietnam's military, intelligence, security and civil organizations.

The CIA constructs similar secret governments in many nations throughout the world, including and in particular, Afghanistan and Iraq.

The Death Lists

In Vietnam via the Phoenix program, and now in Iraq and Afghanistan through the new and improved version, the CIA sends its hit teams after a long list of targeted individuals. Targets included tax assessors and collectors; people operating business fronts for purchasing, storing or distributing food and supplies to the resistance; public health officials who distribute medicine; security and judicial officials who target American collaborators and agents; anyone proselytizing to the general population; officials involved in transportation, communication and postal services; political indoctrination cadres; military recruiters; guerrilla leaders and their forces; and anyone who funds and staffs front organizations.

As in Vietnam, all these categories of people – and their sympathizers and supporters – find their names on computerized, Phoenix-style death lists in Afghanistan and Iraq. As counterinsurgency guru David Galula noted, most of these people have honorable intentions and "do not participate directly, as a rule, in direct terrorism or guerrilla action and, technically, have no blood on their hands."[7]

In other words, non-combatants were already being targeted by McChrystal's "true counterinsurgency", which Thomas and Barry nevertheless insisted had the goal of "protecting civilians."

They knew this, of course. As reported by Brown University's Watson Institute of International and Public Affairs, "In 2009, the Afghan Ministry of Public Health reported that fully two-thirds of Afghans suffer from mental health problems."[8]

Two-thirds by 2009! How many more have been driven insane after seven years of the Thomas/Barry-endorsed steady escalation of the violence? How many have been poisoned by depleted uranium and radicalized by economic insecurity, the toxic by-products of military occupation that fuel injustice and drive people into the psychological traps set by the occupation's security forces, in the name of freedom and democracy?

The Politics of Corruption

While Thomas and Barry laid out incorrect parallels between Vietnam and Afghanistan in terms of the general dynamic of the conflicts, they ignored, in their search for lessons from Vietnam that might apply to Afghanistan, the parallels in the US strategy/tactics in these conflicts which actually were taking place.

Indeed, they turned a blind eye to the single most important strategic parallel, the pervasive corruption *by design* – including sponsorship of drug trafficking by warlords on the CIA payroll – that was endemic to the US-backed regime in South Vietnam. This systematic corruption was already operational in Afghanistan when they wrote their article, but they intentionally failed to address it.

As outlined in Chapter 2, Air Force General Nguyen Cao Ky, while serving as head of South Vietnam's national security directorate, won control of a lucrative narcotic smuggling franchise in 1965. Through his strongman, General Loan, Ky and his clique financed both their political apparatus and their security forces through opium profits. Likewise, upon occupying Afghanistan in 2002, the CIA allowed its chosen president, Hamid Karzai, and his clique to traffic in opium without fear of arrest and prosecution. Karzai even rejected a proposal that he exile his brother, Ahmed Wali, the political boss in southern Kandahar Province, after Ahmed was irrefutably linked to drug trafficking. Only Ahmed's timely assassination in 2011 spared his CIA sponsors any further embarrassment.

Another overlooked parallel is the self-delusional hubris embodied in steadfast US confidence that its forces possess accurate intelligence. But McChrystal, like every military commander before and after him, gained his intelligence about the Afghan resistance through what he referred to as "friendly civilians" like the opium trafficking warlord, Gul Agha Sherzai.

The American public is largely unaware that the Taliban laid down its arms after the American invasion in 2001, and that the Afghan people took up arms only after the CIA installed Sherzai in Kabul. In league with the Karzai brothers, Sherzai supplied the CIA with a network of informants that targeted their business rivals, not the Taliban. As Anand Gopal revealed in *No Good Men Among The Living*, as a result of Sherzai's friendly tips, the CIA methodically tortured and killed Afghanistan's most revered leaders in a series of Phoenix-style raids that radicalized the Afghan people.

If Thomas and Barry were to have addressed that fact, they certainly would have dismissed it as "a mistake".

But it wasn't a mistake. The CIA felt it was necessary to enlist Sherzai in order to consolidate the power of its drug smuggling, money-laundering, land-stealing clique of warlords. In my opinion, the National Security Establishment was always after control of the drugs and money.

As Karzai's successor, President Ashraf Ghani admitted in May 2016, "The most significant driver of corruption is the narcotic cartel." As an afterthought, Ghani noted, "the corrupt engage in the most intense propaganda when they are prosecuted and accused."[9]

But all that is ignored, as are other uncomfortable facts. For example, that America's militant leaders used 9/11 to recruit and motivate a new generation of special operations forces, whose mission is to invade private homes at midnight on snatch and snuff missions. Nowhere, in any Establishment media outlet, is it ever mentioned that our political and military leaders did this because they wanted to seize Afghanistan and use it to establish a colony in a strategic location near Russia and China.

As Dinh Tuong An stressed in his "Truth about Phoenix"

series cited in Chapter 3, friendly intelligence and false accusations are synonymous when an occupation force wages a counterinsurgency. And that's exactly what has been happening in Afghanistan and Iraq today.

Revising History

CIA and military intelligence units now operate out of a global network of bases, as well as secret jails and detention sites operated by complicit secret police interrogators. Their strategic intelligence networks in any nation are protected by corrupt warlords and politicians, the "friendly civilians" who supply the "death squads" that are in fact their private militias, funded largely by drug smuggling and other criminal activities. CIA and military intelligence officials understand that much of the intelligence they rely upon is dubious at best, but they act on it anyway, as did Sid Towle's bosses Tom Ahern and John Vann in Vietnam, because big "body counts" impress their superiors.

As a result, anyone can be an insurgent on a death list.

Phoenix program veteran Major Stan Fulcher, whom I interviewed at length in *The Phoenix Program*, succinctly explained this reality: "The Vietnamese lied to us; we lied to the Phoenix Directorate; and the Directorate made it into documented fact. It was a war that became distorted through our ability to create fiction."

The big lesson from Vietnam that applies to Afghanistan and the War on Terror is the value of gray and black propaganda in maintaining public support through emotional appeals, twisted logic, and the promulgation of revisionist history. In this game for the hearts and minds of the *US* public, US hawks have learned to play the role of victim; in the spirit of the reactionary times, they claim reverse discrimination by the so-called liberal media. Their message is carried by Fox News and intermediaries like Thomas and Barry, whose complicity assures their career advancement and wealth.

Like the German military after the First World War, McChrystal and his replacements in Afghanistan and Iraq have wholeheartedly seized upon the "stabbed-in-the-back" argument. Revising the history of the Vietnam War to insist that victory was within grasp, if only we had more "heart", is central to that deception.

That historical revisionism is what the *Newsweek* article promoted. The US and its South Vietnamese allies "finally" adopted a winning counterinsurgency strategy in the early 1970s, Thomas and Barry wrote. But "it was too late," they added, citing Sorley's *A Better War*. American public opinion had turned. President Richard Nixon signed a peace treaty with North Vietnam in 1973, but promised continued support to the GVN. The stab in the back came in 1974, Thomas and Barry said, when "Congress cut off all aid to South Vietnam. Without logistical support or air cover, the South Vietnamese Army collapsed in 1975 and the communists swept into Saigon."

Citing Sorley, the *Newsweek* correspondents claimed that key war participants – such as General Creighton Abrams and US Ambassador Ellsworth Bunker – were sure that the US would have prevailed if defeatism hadn't taken hold.

"We eventually defeated ourselves," Bunker is quoted as saying.

Having focused on this fatal betrayal, Thomas and Barry concluded that the key lessons to be drawn from Vietnam are the importance of decisive leadership and a presidential commitment to do what's necessary, including genocide, to achieve victory. They doubted that Obama was made of such stern stuff.

"Obama may decide that Afghanistan is too hard," Thomas and Barry opined, adding that if he did waver and begin "an orderly withdrawal," he must "explain to America and the world why it's necessary."

The tragedy is that Thomas and Barry's disinformation and historical revisionism worked. After their article appeared in print, Obama found the "heart" to escalate a war that has no logical end point and, in the absence of terrorist attacks on American soil, scant popular support. Now more than ever, there are growing concerns that the underlying motivation is more about economics than national security.

In a speech on 22 October 2009, former British Ambassador to Uzbekistan Craig Murray said he had concluded that the motive for the long war in Afghanistan was the desire of Western energy interests to use its territory for a natural gas pipeline to connect the Caspian Basin to the Arabian Sea. "Almost everything you see about Afghanistan is a cover for the fact that the actual motive is the pipeline they wish to build over Afghanistan to bring out Uzbek and Turkmen natural gas which together is valued at up to $10 trillion," Murray said.[10]

There is a heavy price to pay for contradicting the official narrative, and Murray, notably, "was forced out of the British public service after he exposed the use of torture by Britain's Uzbek allies." As a result of his political actions, and his advocacy of diplomacy over militancy, the US government denied him an entry visa and prevented him from presenting the Sam Adams Award for Integrity in Intelligence to CIA torture whistleblower John Kiriakou in September 2016.[11]

Then there's the question of access to Afghanistan's mineral wealth. In 2010, China signed a multi-billion-dollar deal for a copper mine contract, angering US officials and their Afghan collaborators. Other natural resources lay waiting for American businessmen with bulging pocketbooks.

It's Phoenix all over again, according to Major Stan Fulcher, the Binh Dinh Province Phoenix coordinator in 1972. "Phoenix," Fulcher said, "was a creation of the old boy network, a group of guys at highest level – Colby and that crowd – who thought they were Lawrence of Arabia."

The son of an Air Force officer, Stan Fulcher was brought up in military posts around the world, but he branded as "hypocritical" the closed society into which he was born. "The military sees itself as the conqueror of the world, but the military is socialism in its purest form. People in the military lead a life of privilege in which the state meets each and every one of their needs."

Having served in the special security unit at Can Tho Air Base in 1968, where he led a unit of 40 riflemen against the VC, Fulcher understood the realities of Vietnam better than Thomas and Barry. He told of the MSS killing a Jesuit priest who advocated land reform, of GVN officials trading with the National Liberation Front while trying to destroy religious sects, and of the tremendous US cartels – RMK-BRJ, Sealand, Holiday Inns, Pan Am, Bechtel and Vinnell – that prospered from the war.

"The military has the political power and the means of production," Fulcher explained, "so it enjoys all the benefits of society. It was the same thing in Vietnam, where the US military and a small number of politicians supported the Catholic establishment against the masses. Greedy Americans," Fulcher said, "were the cause of the war. The supply side economists were the emergent group during Vietnam."

According to Fulcher, the Phoenix program was set up by Americans on American assumptions, in support of American policies. Alas, America's allies in South Vietnam depended on American patronage and implemented a policy they knew could not be applied to their culture. In the process the definition of an insurgent was deliberately made ambiguous, and Phoenix was broadened from a rifle shot attack against the VC "organizational hierarchy" into a shotgun method of population control.

"It happened," Fulcher said ruefully, because "any policy can find supporting intelligence," meaning "the Phoenix Directorate used computers to skew the statistical evaluation of the VCI. Dead Vietnamese became VCI, and they lucked out the other five percent of the time, getting real VCI in ambushes."

What Fulcher said earlier is worth repeating: "It was a war that became distorted through our ability to create fiction. But really, there were only economic reasons for our supporting the fascists in Vietnam, just like we did in [the Shah's] Iran."

Professor Nguyen Ngoc Huy, a Vietnamese historian and former professor at Harvard, was someone Barry and Thomas might have quoted in their article, had they wanted the truth, or had they risen above their own racial prejudices and considered for a moment that a Vietnamese person's opinion might be valuable in analyzing the lessons of the war.

For what it's worth, Professor Huy believed that America "betrayed the ideals of freedom and democracy in Vietnam."

Huy added that, "American politicians have not changed their policy. What happened later in Iran was a repetition of what happened in South Vietnam. Almost the same people applied the same policy with the same principles and the same spirit. It is amazing that some people are still wondering why the same result occurred."[12]

And, one might add, the cycle is ongoing in Afghanistan, Iraq, Libya, Syria and many other places, thanks largely to the Big Lies told by propagandists like Evan Thomas and John Barry.

Chapter 6

THE AFGHAN 'DIRTY WAR' ESCALATES

NPR was badly embarrassed in 2000 when it was revealed that PSYOP (psychological operations) personnel from Ft. Bragg were working in its Washington, DC newsroom, apparently as interns.[1] Top managers were said to be unaware of the arrangement, which was blamed on people in its personnel department. However, based on NPR's cozy relationship with the military and its penchant to spew pro-military propaganda (some say the P in NPR stands for Pentagon) media watchdogs, myself included, believed the PSYOP soldiers were penetration agents meant to influence news coverage.

In any event, on 30 December 2009, I listened in dismay, but not surprise, as an NPR "terrorism" expert condemned the suicide bombing that had killed seven CIA employees in Afghanistan a few days earlier.[2] That particular act of terrorism, the expert said, was especially hideous because the murdered CIA officers were spreading economic development, democracy and love as members of a Provincial Reconstruction Team (PRT).

No less disingenuous were the comments of CIA Director Leon Panetta, who said the deceased did "the hard work that must be done to protect our country from terrorism."

Or fuel terrorism, as the case may be.

President Obama added his two cents, saying the fallen CIA officers were "part of a long line of patriots who have made great sacrifices for their fellow citizens, and for our way of life."

"Our way of life" in the twenty-first century means Full Spectrum Dominance and a burgeoning precariat.

On New Year's Day 2010 – the story of the martyred CIA officers having expired – *Washington Post* staff writers Joby Warrick and Pamela Constable ventured beyond the initial spin. Rather than cast the CIA officers as heroes, they hinted at the murderous activities they were involved in. Warrick and Constable said the CIA officers were secretly "at the heart of a covert program overseeing strikes by the agency's remote-controlled aircraft along the Afghanistan-Pakistan border."[3]

So much for spreading love and development. In 2009, CIA drone strikes killed more than 300 people (perhaps as many as 700) all of whom were invariably described as suspected terrorists, jihadists, or militants (a word never applied to the Americans), or people said to be killed by accident.

Neither the US government nor the media ever make any distinction between nationalists defending their country from foreign invaders and real terrorists who have inflicted intentional violence against civilians to achieve a political objective (the classic definition of terrorism). There is never any hint that people could have honorable reasons for resisting the American military occupation of their country, or that they are doing so because they've been driven crazy with revenge and desperation by years of relentless US air and ground attacks.

There were other reasons to doubt the hype surrounding the original story, for despite the media's description of the attack on the CIA officers as "terrorism," the act didn't fit the definition. The targets were engaged in military operations and thus were legitimate targets under the international laws of war. CIA officers managing killer drones are as guilty of terrorism as the Taliban commanders they target from the safety of their enclaves.

A few press accounts did suggest that the suicide attack was in retaliation for drone strikes on Taliban forces. In which case, ironically, from the perspective of the indigenous resistance, the offing of the CIA officers was actually "counterterrorism".

There was also speculation that the suicide attack was payback for the killing of ten people in Ghazi Khan, a village in the eastern Afghan province of Kunar. The ten Afghanis were shot to death during a raid on their home by unidentified American militants. Often Green Berets or Navy SEALs detailed to the CIA's Special Activities Division operate outside the laws of warfare. Such death squad actions also fit the classic definition of terrorism.

The rationale is that "we" must fight fire with fire; terror with terror. But do people understand, when they make such an argument, that they are calling on US personnel to murder innocent civilians with a view to terrorizing the local population in general, in order to get them to accept the US-backed client Afghan government?

As always, NATO spokespeople initially labeled the ten victims in Ghazi Khan as "insurgents" and "relatives" of an individual suspected of belonging to a "terrorist" cell that manufactured improvised explosive devices used to kill American heroes, as well as innocent Afghan civilians. However, Afghan government investigators and neighbors soon identified the dead as civilians, including eight students, aged 11 to 17, enrolled in local schools. All but one of the dead came from the same family.

Allegations of Handcuffed Victims

According to a 31 December 2009 article in *The Times* of London, the US commandos faced accusations "of dragging innocent children from their beds and shooting them. Locals said that some victims were handcuffed before being killed."[4]

An official statement posted on Afghan President Karzai's website (no less) said the raiding party "took ten people from three homes, eight of them school students in grades six, nine and ten, one of them a guest, the rest from the same family, and shot them dead."

Investigator Assadullah Wafa told the UK *Times* that the American unit flew by helicopter from a military base in Kabul and landed about two kilometers from the village. "The troops walked from the helicopters to the houses and, according to my investigation, they gathered all the students from two rooms, into one room, and opened fire." Wafa, a former governor of Helmand Province, added, "It's impossible they were al-Qaeda. They were children, they were civilians, they were innocent."

The Times quoted the school's headmaster as saying the victims were asleep in three rooms when the death squad arrived. "Seven students were in one room," said Rahman Jan Ehsas. "A student and one guest were in another room, a guest room, and a farmer was asleep with his wife in a third building.

"First the foreign troops entered the guest room and shot two of them. Then they entered another room and handcuffed the seven students. Then they killed them. Abdul Khaliq [the farmer] heard shooting and came outside. When they saw him, they shot him as well. He was outside. That's why his wife wasn't killed."

The guest was a shepherd boy, age twelve, the headmaster said, adding that six of the students were in high school and two in primary school. All the students were his nephews.

A local elder, Jan Mohammed, said that three boys were killed in one room and five were handcuffed before they were shot. "I saw their school books covered in blood," he said, according to *The Times*.

Backed into a corner, the Afghan National Security Directorate, on behalf of its owners in the CIA, tried to cover-up the war crime by saying "forces from an unknown address came to the area and without facing any armed resistance, put ten youth in two rooms and killed them."

Protests over the killings erupted throughout Kunar Province, where the killings occurred, as well as in Kabul. Hundreds of protesters demanded that American occupation forces leave the country, and that the unidentified killers from an unknown address be brought to justice.

Fat chance.

Incredibly, a NATO spokesperson claimed there was "no direct evidence to substantiate" the claim of premeditated murder. The unknown killers from an "unknown address" had come under fire from several buildings in the village. So picture these big strong American soldiers encountering sleeping children, and make an argument how they had no recourse but to tie them up then kill them.

The record of American forces engaging in indiscriminate and intentional killings of unarmed people in Afghanistan is now a long one, with testimony about premeditated executions even emerging in military disciplinary hearings, where the perps are always exonerated, like cops who routinely kill blacks in America.[5]

Engaging in war crimes, it seems, is as American as apple pie and compulsory Nuremburg-style celebrations of militant nationalism at football games. Even the United Nations must periodically warn American military forces about the dangers of conducting nighttime raids of private homes. But as the War on Terror turns into a boondoggle for US security firms and arms manufacturers, it is clear they will only increase in frequency. Obama's "surge" in 2010 added 30,000 additional troops into Afghanistan, bringing the total to about 100,000. Although that number has since been reduced and amounts to around 10,000 in 2016, the violence is escalating again thanks to an off-the-books mercenary army and ongoing military occupation that simply incites more and more revenge killings.

In 2010, Afghani patriots vowed to avenge the killings of their school children in Ghazi Khan, and the CIA in turn vowed to avenge the killing of its officers, including the base chief, a mother of three. Trapped in this cycle of violence, the surviving CIA personnel at FOB Base Chapman barricaded themselves inside and began the systematic grilling of all Afghan employees who were on duty at the time of the attack. Afghans who worked with the CIA on the outside were locked out.

Such is the downside of waging an endless but otherwise profitable war.

Provincial Reconstruction Teams

The Ghazi Khan massacre serves as an entrée into how covert CIA psyops and terror operations are conducted and then whitewashed by the American news media.

Few Americans, for example, were aware that FOB Chapman (named after Nathan Chapman, a Green Beret member of a CIA unit who was the first American killed in Afghanistan) was a CIA outpost. The local Afghanis knew, of course, that Chapman was a base for launching commando raids, like the one at Ghazi Khan. They knew the CIA used its Provincial Reconstruction Teams (PRTs) to obtain intelligence for its lethal raids, and that "reconstruction" was merely a cover. There would be nothing to reconstruct if not for the fact that the Americans have destroyed so much.

Since they were perfected in Vietnam, PRTs have been a primary means of gathering intelligence from informants and secret agents in enemy territory. Today, the PRTs are a foundation stone of the CIA's parallel government in Afghanistan, and have been a unilateral CIA operation since 2002 when the program started under the reign of US Ambassador Zalmay Khalilzad.

As evidenced by the suicide attack at FOB Chapman, the resistance has infiltrated every entity the CIA has created in Afghanistan, including the PRTs. This infiltration is made possible, ironically, by the fact that CIA officers jealously guard their elevated status and class prerogatives. It's impossible to get them to run death squads and mutilate innocent people in drone strikes unless they are very well rewarded and shielded from responsibility for their acts of terror. CIA officers, as a result, do not perform menial tasks, enabling Afghan "double-agents" to infiltrate the bases as chauffeurs, cleaning staff and security guards. Other double agents prop up inflated CIA egos by pretending to be informants or loyal members of the police and military.

In the case of the 30 December suicide bombing, the "friendly civilian" informant who carried out the deadly act was identified as Humam Khalil Abu-Mulal al-Balawi, a Jordanian national who had been captured – and supposedly turned into a double agent – by Jordanian intelligence and the CIA. Before detonating the bomb strapped to his chest, Humam lured his CIA bosses to the meeting at FOB Chapman with promises of target information relating to al Qaeda's second-in-command, Ayman Zawahiri.

The case of the Jordanian double agent raised questions about the quality of the intelligence that the CIA collects to mount its drone and death squad operations. If some informants were willing to die in order to kill CIA personnel, it was a reasonable assumption that other informants were, and still are, passing along bogus tips to discredit the CIA and sabotage its operations from within, as frequently happened in Vietnam.[6]

The likelihood that its operations had been penetrated presented CIA bigwigs in Washington with a dilemma, given that the PRTs provide CIA "Principal Agents" with a clever cover to gather intelligence from their sub-agents in the field, people in villages like Ghazi Khan who spy on their neighbors.

Unfortunately, CIA officers managing the PRTs must rely on Afghani interpreters and policemen to determine if the intelligence about "suspects" in a particular village is reliable. If any one of the CIA's hired helpers is a double agent, then the PRT death squad components can easily be misdirected and subverted.

Each PRT has an intelligence unit whose purpose is to identify members of the Taliban and al Qaeda "infrastructure." Typically, a sub-agent in a village tells the PRT intelligence unit where a suspect lives, how many people are in his house, where they sleep, and when they enter and leave. The sub-agent also provides a clandestinely obtained photograph of the target, so the commandoes know who to snatch or snuff.

But the high-toned CIA is not a social welfare outfit; its job is gathering intelligence and using it to capture, kill or defect the enemy, and it needs dependable agents to do the job. Thus, since the military occupation began, it has relied on the same brutal and corrupt warlords – mercenaries serving their own self-interest, and thus dependent on the CIA – it organized to fight the Soviets in the 1980s.

The most effective PRTs are composed of members of a warlord's militia; people who have as little empathy for the Afghan people in a particular area as do the American commandos. They are soldiers whose job is to protect the PRT while CIA-trained cadres are organizing "community defense forces" and spreading pro-American propaganda.

Afghani leaders see big bucks to be made through this arrangement. Malik Osman, leader of a Pashtun tribe in Jalalabad, offered one fighter from each Shinwari family to fight the Taliban in return for no-bid construction project contracts. Six years later his son and 12 other guests were killed in a suicide bombing, apparently engineered by an ISIS faction fighting the Taliban as well as the government and its CIA collaborators.[7]

Nation Building and the Origins of PRTs in Vietnam

Vietnam was a laboratory for military weapon and psychological warfare experimentation. Helicopter gunships made their debut, along with futuristic "psywar" strategies for pacifying civilian populations.

In the early 1960s, the CIA first developed the programs that would be combined in 1965 within its 59-man Revolutionary Development (RD) teams as part of the similarly named Revolutionary Development Cadres (RDC) program established at Vung Tau by the CIA's chief of Covert Action, Tom Donohue.[8]

The original model, known as a Political Action Team (PAT), was developed by US Information Service officer Frank Scotton and an Australian military officer, Ian Teague, on contract to the CIA. The original PAT consisted of 40 men: as Scotton told me, "That's three teams of twelve men each, strictly armed. The control element was four men: a commander and his deputy, a morale officer and a radioman.

"These are commando teams," Scotton stressed. "Displacement teams. The idea was to go into contested areas and spend a few nights. But it was a local responsibility so they had to do it on their own."

Scotton named his special PAT unit the *Trung-doi biet kich Nham dou* for people's commando teams. "Two functions split out of this," he said. First was pacification. Second was counterterror. As Scotton noted, "The PRU thing directly evolves from this."

PRU (for Provincial Reconnaissance Unit) was the name

given in 1966 to the CIA's counterterror teams, which had generated a lot of negative publicity in 1965 when Senator Stephen Young charged that the CT teams disguised themselves as Vietcong and discredited the Communists by committing atrocities.

"It was alleged to me that several of them executed two village leaders and raped some women," the *Herald Tribune* reported Young as saying.[9]

CIA officer Tom Ahern, mentioned in the previous chapter as the CIA's Province Officer in Charge in Vinh Long Province in 1971, documented a similar incident in his book *Vietnam Declassified: The CIA and Counterinsurgency.*[10] Ahern told how in October 1965 the senior CIA officer in Da Nang briefed Senator Daniel Brewster (D-MD) on the CIA's secret operations in the area. As Ahern recalled, Brewster "conducted a detailed interrogation on the structure and activity of each program, and this led (the CIA officer-in-charge in Da Nang, Robert) Haynes, in the context of countererror, into a mention of black operations. Pressured to define the term, Haynes cited as a hypothetical example a killing by a CT-team made to look like the work of the VC."

Hard to imagine now, but the Congress of that era freaked out and Haynes (who in 1967 was assigned to the original Phoenix staff) was summoned to Washington to explain himself. Afterwards, presidential advisor Clark Clifford visited the CIA station chief in Saigon and told him not to allow his minions to give congressional briefings anymore. Behind the scenes, the CIA was forced to admit that CT teams were, as Ahern reluctantly admitted, "extra-legal". As a result, "headquarters called for a GVN approval procedure whose application at the province level would allow the agency to say *in good conscience* [my italics] that the government had approved each operation as in the best interest of the war effort."

Since that incident in 1965, the CIA, in concert with its protectors in Congress and the media, has only gotten better at hiding, dissembling, and lying about its illegal and barbarous CT teams.

Fitting the Proper Profile

Staffing unilateral CIA programs like CT teams and PRTs is the foundation stone of the "nation building" aspect of American neo-colonialism. Indeed, Scotton's patented "motivational indoctrination" program developed in Vietnam is still used today. A living legend among the swaggering warrior elite, he was attached to the 1st Special

Operations Command at Fort Bragg the second time I spoke with him in 1988; his job was advising military commanders how to implement his psywar brain child.

Scotton's motivational indoctrination program was, ironically, modeled on Communist techniques. The process began on a confessional basis. "On the first day," Scotton explained, "everyone would fill out a form and write an essay on why they had joined." Then the team's morale officer "would study their answers and explain the next day why they were involved in a 'special' unit. The instructors would lead them to stand up and talk about themselves."

The morale officer's job, Scotton said, "was to keep people honest and have them admit mistakes."

Not only did Scotton copy Communist organizational and motivational techniques, he relied on VC defectors as his cadre. "We felt ex-Vietminh had unique communication skills.[11] They could communicate doctrine, and they were people who would shoot," he explained, adding, "It wasn't necessary for everyone in the unit to be ex-Vietminh, just the leadership."

The Vietnamese officer in charge of Scotton's PAT program, Nguyen Be, had been party secretary for the Ninth Vietcong Battalion before switching sides.

In 1965, Scotton was transferred to another job while Be and his new CIA advisor, Harry "The Hat" Monk, combined CIA "mobile" Census Grievance cadre,[12] PATs, and CT Teams into the standard 59-member Revolutionary Development (RD) team employed by the CIA in South Vietnam until 1975.

The RD teams were facetiously called Purple People Eaters by American soldiers, in reference to their clothes and terror tactics. To the rural Vietnamese, they were simply "idiot birds."

The Truth About Phoenix author Dinh Tuong An felt that reconstruction projects only helped the ever-adaptable VC, who simply returned from their jungle hideouts when the RD projects were done. Most Vietnamese certainly agreed with An that "Revolutionary Development only teaches the American line."

However, "nation building" was seen as the key to winning the Vietnam War, by stealing the hearts and minds of the rural Vietnamese from the Communists. Scotton's PATs were central to the strategy, and the CIA created its nation-wide RDC program based in Vung Tau on that premise.

In July 1967, the chief of the CIA's RDC program, Lou Lapham, became a member of the national-level Phoenix Committee. RD team leaders and the local Chieu Hoi (defector) program[13] representative became members of Phoenix committees at district level, so that tips on VCI gained from RD teams and defectors could be re-routed by Phoenix coordinators to the PRU-CT teams for instant "exploitation."

In this way the Phoenix "coordination" program became the centerpiece of US pacification policy in Vietnam. The program took hold after the Tet uprising of 1968, when many VCI were captured or killed and the National Liberation Front was weakened. By 1969, as defined by William Colby (the Deputy Ambassador for Civil Operations and Revolutionary Development), the first stage in "nation building" was military security, as provided by US military forces.

The second stage was territorial security – the dubious "Self-Defense Forces" put in place by RD teams.

The third and final stage was internal "political" security provided by Phoenix.

Despite Colby's claims of success, which he backed with carefully skewed statistics, the insurgency was regrouping. In a Defense Department report titled "A Systems Analysis of the Vietnam War 1965-1972", Thomas Thayer recognized that "The Revolutionary Development program had significant problems in recruiting and retaining high quality personnel." The desertion rate was over 20 percent, "higher than for any GVN military force, perhaps because they have a 30% better chance of being killed." In response, the RD teams were redirected "to concentrate on building hamlet security and to defer, at least temporarily, the hamlet development projects which formerly constituted six of the teams' eleven RD tasks."[14]

Given the drawbacks of military and territorial security, neutralizing the VCI through Phoenix replaced "nation building" as Colby's top priority. The Phoenix program, along with the CIA's RDC program, were incorporated within the CORDS Pacification Security Coordination Division and heavy-handed military personnel gradually took over civil operations, bringing about a further decline in performance. The CIA station under Ted Shackley moved CIA personnel away from nation building operations back toward classic intelligence functions. But the CIA continued to collect RDC intelligence; and obviously, it still uses the modern manifestation of the RDC program today.

The issue of "nation building" was a hot topic in the 2016

presidential campaign. Donald Trump made getting out of the nation building business, and out of NATO, the basis of his America First platform. "I do think it's a different world today, and I don't think we should be nation building anymore," he said. "I think it's proven not to work, and we have a different country than we did then. We have $19 trillion in debt. We're sitting, probably, on a bubble. And it's a bubble that if it breaks, it's going to be very nasty. I just think we have to rebuild our country."[15]

In a 30 March 2016 article for the *Huffington Post* titled "Back to Nation Building?" George Washington University Professor Amitai Etzioni implied that Hillary Clinton would engage in nation building and cited her as calling for a more "active" foreign policy. "When talking about conflicts around the world, from Syria to Ukraine to Afghanistan, she says the US needs to 'do more.' Secretary Clinton is of course not very forthcoming on the campaign trail about what exactly a more active foreign policy entails."

As America wrestles with its role as the world's only superpower, hell bent on Full Spectrum Dominance, the details of what "nation building" actually entails become ever more vital for people to understand.

PRTs in Iraq

The CIA's Revolutionary Development team concept in Vietnam was the model for its Provincial Reconstruction Team concept in Afghanistan and Iraq. The new and improved PRT program started in Afghanistan in 2002 and migrated to Iraq in 2004.

The standard PRT consists of anywhere between 50-100 civilian and military specialists. It has units for military police, psyops, explosive ordinance/de-mining, intelligence, medics, force protection (security forces that organize community defenses), and administrative and support personnel. Like Scotton's PAT teams in South Vietnam, the PRTs engage in counterterror operations as part of their political and psychological warfare function, under cover of fostering economic development and democracy.

Long ago the American public grew skeptical of the heavily censored but universally bad news they got about Iraq, and until the advent of ISIS, most were happy to forget the devastation their government has wrought. But few Iraqis are fooled by the "war as economic development" deception, or by the standards the US government uses to measure the success of its PRT program.

In his correspondence with reporter Dahr Jamail, one Iraqi political analyst from Fallujah (a suburb outside Baghdad recently occupied by ISIS) put it succinctly when he said: "In a country that used to feed much of Arab world, starvation is the norm."[16]

According to another of Jamail's sources, Iraqis "are largely mute witnesses. Americans may argue among themselves about just how much 'success' or 'progress' there really is in post-surge Iraq, but it is almost invariably an argument in which Iraqis are but stick figures – or dead bodies."

In a publication titled "Hard Lessons: The Iraq Reconstruction Experience," the Special Inspector General for Iraq Reconstruction described the mission as the largest overseas rebuilding effort in US history. In some places in Iraq, unemployment was at 40-60 percent in 2010. Repairing the damage done by US bombing was the goal, but little connection was made between how the rebuilding would or even could bring about the heralded democratic transition that never happened.

As in Vietnam and Afghanistan, the PRTs in Iraq are a gimmick to make Americans feel good about their government's imperial misadventures. The supposed successes of the PRTs are cloaked in double-speak and the meaningless statistics Phoenix coordinator Stan Fulcher referenced in the previous chapter when he said "any policy can find supporting intelligence." Achieving statistical progress is not difficult in nations whose public service infrastructures were destroyed by "shock and awe" invasions, where entire neighborhoods like Fallujah were leveled in the name of American prestige, and where the occupying power controls all information outlets.

As Fulcher also noted, it's all about business profits. The truth about US wars is less about combating Islamic terrorism or "protecting the homeland" than it is about the dark side of the American psyche, rooted in slavery and the genocidal conquest of a continent. For American businessmen, the global War on Terror with its relentless bombing campaigns and extra-legal methods shrouded in official secrecy, translates into big profits.

For politicians, war is also a good way to get elected. As ex-Vice President Dick Cheney proved, calling a political adversary soft on terror remains a fearsome club to wield. Apparently for many people, drone strikes and spectacular commando teams killing terrorists like Osama bin Laden quell carefully nurtured fears and sate the carefully cultivated hunger for revenge that was nurtured after 9/11. The same ultra-patriotic Americans who wave flags and salute the military at professional footballs games (apart from a few black players who raise their fists in defiance) seem happy as long as the outcome can be packaged as a "win" for the USA.

Pushed out of the headlines, deep into the national subconscious, are the horrendous war crimes that have promoted the policies inflicted on the peoples of Afghanistan and Iraq.

Chapter 7

VIETNAM REPLAY
ON AFGHAN
DEFECTORS

After eight years of waging a "dirty war" against the Taliban (whom Obama had described a month earlier as a "cancer" that must be irradiated out of existence), the US government and its NATO allies tried a different tack in 2010. For the first time they acknowledged that the "insurgent" enemy was, according to Defense Secretary Robert Gates, part of the "fabric" of Afghan society.[1]

Having acknowledged the humanity of Muslims in Afghanistan, the plan was now to entice low- and mid-level Taliban to switch sides. High-level Taliban and anyone connected to al Qaeda (now manifest as ISIS), however, maintained their exalted status on Obama's hit list.

In January 2010, US and NATO officials started offering bribes drawn from a multi-million-dollar program "Peace and Reintegration Trust Fund" to get Taliban fighters to betray their leaders and become, as General Stanley McChrystal said, "part of the solution in Afghanistan."[2]

In the US, the peace plan horrified some women's rights advocates, but appealed to elements of the public who were already weary of endless war. Taliban leaders condemned the buyout strategy as a "trick" and warned that offers of reconciliation were futile unless all foreign troops left Afghanistan.[3]

As ever, there was a darker CIA side to the "reconciliation" plan.

The Method in Their Madness

Historically, defector programs are an essential ingredient of brutal US pacification efforts. The Chieu Hoi "Open Arms" program in Vietnam was touted by military strategists as having produced positive results by offering "clemency to insurgents." The statistics they offered up proved the case.

But, as with every CIA covert action, the "Open Arms" program relied on deceptive advertising and media complicity to make the "pacification" of the Vietnamese countryside appear humane. In fact, "amnesty" and "open arms" programs have nothing to do with reconciliation. Rather, they serve as another component of covert CIA intelligence and counterinsurgency operations.

Former CIA Director William Colby told me that the CIA's RD teams in Vietnam (like PRTs in Iraq and Afghanistan, discussed in the previous chapter) relied on defectors whose job was to "go around the countryside and indicate to the people that they used to be Vietcong and that the government has received them and taken them in, and that the Chieu Hoi program does exist as a way of VC currently on the other side to rally."

Defectors "contact people like the families of known VC," Colby said, "and provide them with transportation to defector and refugee centers."

Master spy Colby, who perished mysteriously in a boating accident in 1996, would have agreed that information management is the key to political warfare in general and to defector programs in particular. Defector programs are ultimately aimed not at the enemy, but at the American public which, when it hears words like "clemency" and "amnesty," starts to see the war in a kinder, gentler light.

After the information managers concoct an appealing slogan, additional public approval is garnered by composing and planting articles in foreign and domestic newspapers. The stories portray CIA operations as good deeds designed to bring about peace and prosperity, while fostering freedom and democracy.

Despite the warm and fuzzy language, defector programs are a horrific aspect of dirty war. The CIA launches a covert action like the Taliban defector program only if it has the "intelligence potential" to produce information on an enemy's political, military and economic infrastructure, which in turn leads to air strikes and midnight death squad operations. Like Dinh Tuong An said in his "Truth about Phoenix" articles, they are meant to prolong a war forever, or until total victory is achieved.

In 2009, the CIA launched its defector program as a way of recruiting low and mid-level Taliban who had the best "intelligence potential" on the senior level Taliban officials it desires most to eliminate.

Not only does defection sap the enemy's fighting strength and morale, and lead to capture, interrogation and assassination of enemy leaders, genuine defectors provide accurate and timely intelligence on enemy unit strengths and locations. As a condition for "amnesty" they are required to prove their commitment by serving as guides and trackers for other pacification programs, like Counter Terror hit teams. Many are returned to their villages with a CT team to locate hidden enemy arms or food caches. Some are sent on "One Way" missions and bombed along with the targets they locate.

After being profiled and interrogated by security officers, some defectors are turned into double agents. Defectors who return to their former positions inside opposition military or political organizations are provided with a "secure" means of contacting their CIA case officer's Principal Agent, to whom they feed information leading to the arrest or ambush of enemy cadres and secret agents. Some function for years as penetration agents and provide the greatest prize of all, "strategic" information on the enemy's plans.

Defector programs also provide CIA "talent scouts" with cover for recruiting criminals into CT and RD "political action" teams. Burglars, arsonists, forgers and smugglers have unique skills and no compunctions about committing havoc. In Vietnam, the entire 52nd Ranger Battalion of the South Vietnamese Army was recruited from Saigon prisons.

Military operations, like President Obama's "surge" in 2010, provide security for CIA officers to conduct covert operations through instruments like the PRTs, which is the real reason the Taliban defector buyout program was launched concurrently with the surge.[4]

As I predicted in my 2010 article for Consortium News, the multi-million-dollar program defector program was doomed from the start. Indeed, after all the hoopla associated with its debut, it fizzled out after six months. *The Times* attributed the failure to the fact that the Pashtuns realized it was a trick, while their ethnic rivals within the CIA's parallel government feared losing whatever gains they'd made if the Taliban were incorporated.[5]

The program was revived in 2014 by President Ashraf Ghani and aimed at "high-level" reconciliation through a High Peace Council (a moniker only Madison Avenue ad men could devise). Provincial Peace Councils were installed in 33 provinces. However, disarmament was a precondition, and disarmament meant surrender.

Statistics supplied by the United Nations Development Program showed stunning success: "10,404 former combatants have so far renounced violence and joined the peace and reintegration program. Of these, 10,286 received financial assistance to reintegrate into their communities."[6]

Other statistics are less encouraging. There were over 11,000 civilian casualties in Afghanistan in 2015, marking a steady increase since Obama's surge in 2010. As a stranger could see at a glance, mounting civilian deaths indicate anything but a desire on America's part for reconciliation in Afghanistan.

Frank Scotton: A Case Study in Psyops

In Vietnam, officers within the "political and psychological warfare" branch of the CIA's Special Operations Division managed low-level defector programs. In doing so, they worked with US Information Service (USIS) officers like Frank Scotton. The USIS was the overseas branch of the erstwhile US Information Agency, and specialized in the symbolic transformation of grim realities, like CIA-sanctioned drug trafficking, into happy myths that promoted the mythological American Way.

In their effort to convert the world into one big Chamber of Commerce, the CIA and USIS employed all manner of media from TV, radio and satellites to armed propaganda teams, wanted posters and selective terror.[7]

As noted in the previous chapter, Scotton played a pioneering role in US political and psychological operations in Vietnam. After graduating from American University's College of International Relations in 1961, he received a graduate assistantship to the East-West Center at the University of Hawaii. CIA officer Lucien Conein told me that Scotton was recruited into the CIA while there, although Scotton insisted that he wasn't.

Scotton did, however, acknowledge the CIA-sponsored East-West Center's espionage function. "It was a cover for a training program in which Southeast Asians were brought to Hawaii and trained to go back to Vietnam, Cambodia, and Laos to create agent nets," he said.

Scotton told Associate Professor of History Jeff Woods about his early days in Vietnam. Here's how Woods described what psywar expert Scotton did.

> He went into the countryside alone, with a .45, a grease gun, and a bag of money. Scotton started in the central highlands arranging meetings with local officials and learning what he could about the Vietcong's people's war. He also met the wild group of multinational other warriors trying to pacify the highlands. In an abandoned shack near Anh Khe, he found Englishmen Dick Noone, Norman Hurbold, and a group of Malayans. Noone was especially interesting. His brother Pat had been an anthropologist in Malaya and the originator of Senoi Dream Theory, which held that the tribesmen's collective dream world could be shaped to influence group solidarity. Dick Noone had worked in Malaya shaping the dreams of the once peaceful Orang Asli aborigines, organizing them into the Senoi Praaq, a police unit noted for its ruthless slaughter of captured Communist guerillas. Noone convinced Scotton that his biggest problem in persuading the rural Vietnamese and Montagnards to brave the jungle and kill the VC was that he had not done it himself. The American immediately took the advice to heart: "Whoever dared the vacuum, could control the vacuum"...[8]

Determined to earn the respect of the people he intended to recruit, the novice disappeared into the jungle, alone. He slept by day and laid ambush by night. Unsure who was VC and who was not, he let several armed, black pajama-clad Vietnamese pass by without confrontation. After a few days of this, he encountered Nai Luett, a CIA-trained special forces operative who was hunting VC in the area. Luett told Scotton in no uncertain terms that any ethnic Vietnamese he encountered on the trails in the highlands at night were VC. He then handed Scotton a World War 1 bayonet and told him that if he carried it, the local Montagnards would recognize it as the sign of a VC killer and an ally. Luett then disappeared back into the jungle. By the end of his first week in the vacuum, Scotton had killed more than a half dozen VC guerrillas.[9]

Woods is describing Jason, the grotesque character wearing a goalie's mask in the popular slasher movies. When I speak of psycho CIA officers, think of Scotton. Who gave him the legal authority to go off on his own and kill all these people? Can CIA-USIS officers do anything they want, from drug dealing to mass murder?

In any event, after proving his manhood the militant American Way, Scotton turned his attention to "energizing" the Vietnamese through the carefully scripted "political action" that advanced American policies at the expense of the aspirations of average Vietnamese.

In looking for people to mold into political cadres preaching the American line, Scotton turned to the CIA's defector program, which resided under cover of the State Department's Agency for International Development, and was named the Chieu Hoi (Open Arms) program. There Scotton found the raw material needed to prove the viability of his experimental political action program.

In Pleiku Province, he worked with Captain Nguyen Tuy (a graduate of Fort Bragg's Special Warfare Center) who commanded the Fourth Special Operations Detachment, and Tuy's case officer, US Special Forces Captain Howard Walters. As part of their pilot program designed to induce defectors, Scotton, Walters and Tuy set up an ambush in VC territory and waited until dark. When they spotted a VC unit, Scotton yelled in Vietnamese through a bullhorn, "You are being misled! You are being lied to! We promise you an education!"

Full of purpose and allegory, he shot a flare into the night sky and hollered, "Walk toward the light!"

To his surprise, two men defected, convincing him and his CIA bosses that "a determined GVN unit could contest the VC in terms of combat and propaganda."

Back in camp, Scotton told the defectors to divest themselves of untruths. "We said that certainly the US perpetrated war crimes, but so did the VC. We acknowledged that theirs was the stronger force, but that didn't mean that everything they did was honorable and good and just," Scotton said.

Scotton called his method the "motivational indoctrination" program.

Going National

In 1965, Tom Donohue, the chief of the CIA's Covert Action branch in Saigon, recognized the value of intelligence obtained through defectors, and in 1965 he authorized the establishment of Chieu Hoi programs, based on Scotton's motivational indoctrination method, in each of South Vietnam's 44 provinces. In typical CIA style, there was nothing in writing, and nothing went through the central government.

CIA officers managed the Chieu Hoi program in the provinces, where the process worked as follows: upon arriving at the Chieu Hoi center, the defector was interviewed and, if he had information on the VCI, sent to the local Province Interrogation Center; if he had tactical military information, he was sent to military interrogators.

If a defector had the potential to serve in one of the RD Cadre programs, the CIA put him on a plane and sent him to its indoctrination center in Vung Tau, where he was plied with special attention and wowed with eye-popping gadgets. The training was rigorous but the defectors were treated well; they received medical care for infections, and the food was full of protein.

Next came political indoctrination, lasting from 40-60 days, depending on the individual, in which previously conscripted defectors preached the beauty of the American Way.

"They had a formal course," said Jim Ward, the CIA officer in charge of Phoenix in the Delta (1967-1969). "They were shown movies and given lectures on democracy."

Upon graduation, each defector was given an ID card, a meal, money, and a chance to gain redemption by killing former comrades.

The Chieu Hoi program was thought to be so promising that in June 1967, Nelson Brickham incorporated it within the Phoenix program. Brickham appreciated Chieu Hoi as "one of the few areas where police and paramilitary advisors cooperated." He also viewed the defector program as a means for the CIA to develop "unilateral penetrations unknown to the [South Vietnamese] police."

By 1969 the defector program was a centerpiece of "pacification" and was managed by military psyops teams (like the one that penetrated NPR), replete with posters, banners, loudspeakers mounted on trucks, and leaflets falling from the skies.

For example, on 22 January 1970, 38,000 leaflets were dropped over three villages in Go Vap District. Addressed to specific VCI cadres identified by RD teams, they read: "Since you have joined the NLF, what have you done for your family or your village and hamlet? Or have you just broken up the happiness of many families and destroyed houses and land? Some people among you have been awakened; they have deserted the Communist ranks and were received by the GVN and the people with open arms and family affection.

"You should be ready for the end if you remain in the Communist ranks. You will be dealing with difficulties bigger from day to day and will suffer serious failure when the ARVN expand strongly. You had better return to your family where you will be guaranteed safety and helped to establish a new life."

Defects in the Program

The military, CIA and USIS were so convinced by their own propaganda that they funded TV and radio shows, and produced movies with real actors to spread the word. And from the language of scripted Phoenix reports, one would think that the Chieu Hoi program was a rollicking success. All "rallied" VC (real and imagined) were included in Phoenix neutralization statistics and by 1970 more than 100,000 were said to have been processed through 51 Chieu Hoi centers.

Many so-called defectors, however, simply regurgitated the American line in order to win amnesty. They considered defector programs as a chance for R&R. They made a quick visit to their families, enjoyed a home-cooked meal, and then returned to the war for independence.

According to AID Public Safety advisor Douglas McCollum, who monitored the Chieu Hoi program in three provinces in Vietnam, "It was the biggest hole in the net. They'd come in; we'd hold them, feed them, clothe them, get them a mat. Then we'd release them and they'd wander around the city for a while, and then disappear."

As American war managers knew full well, genuine defectors were pariahs in Vietnam's village-based culture. They could never go home.

The same lesson applies in Afghanistan's tribal culture. In the 15 years of occupation, American and NATO forces are solely responsible for the deaths of thousands of innocent civilians. As a result, they have no popular support or connection to the people they wish to dominate; they can only reach the "people" through "media" like translated leaflets and bounty programs that offer rewards to traitors.

Nothing could be a clearer indication of just how detached America's war managers are from the reality of life in Afghanistan's villages. And while the CIA relies on leaflets and "motivational indoctrination" programs to sell itself, the Taliban go from person to person, speaking a common tongue, proving that technology is no substitute for human contact.

The tragedy is that America has no alternative to systematic brainwashing. And while brimming with the comic enthusiasm of an Amway convention or a Bible Belt religious revival, defector programs remain a serious business. Today, they are conducted secretly at high-security CIA bases in Afghanistan and Iraq and occasionally produce spectacular results.

For example, when the Bush regime was preparing the American public for the invasion of Iraq, the CIA recruited high-level defectors from the Iraqi army. Offers of Swiss bank accounts and positions of power in the liberated Iraq of the future were balanced with CIA-prepared scripts the defectors read to the US media. Two such defectors were channeled to *New York Times* reporter Chris Hedges, who dutifully wrote an article titled "Defectors Cite Iraqi Training for Terrorism" on 8 November 2001. The horrifying though patently untrue idea that Iraq was training terrorists to attack America had the intended effect, and public support for the pending war grew.[10]

In hopes of acquiring similar sources for domestic propaganda coups, all defector debriefing reports are sent to CIA stations for analysis and possible use against the American public, which alone can be fooled. It's a risky business, as evidenced by the Jordanian defector who turned out to be a triple agent and blew up a handful of CIA officers at FOB Chapman. But it's the only game in town.

The United States was defeated in Vietnam for just this reason. And though packaged as a new initiative, the latest Taliban defector buyout program simply heralds a replay of the Vietnam experience in Afghanistan – nothing new in the grim world of counterinsurgency.

DISRUPTING THE ACCOMMODATION: CIA KILLINGS SPELL VICTORY IN AFGHANISTAN AND DEFEAT IN AMERICA

Why, everyone wondered, did a suicide bomber target the CIA, knowing that the most violent gang on earth was going to start dropping bombs and slitting throats until its lust for revenge was satisfied?

Over the course of its seventy-year reign of terror, the CIA has overthrown countless governments, started innumerable wars, costing millions of innocent lives, and otherwise subverted and sabotaged friends and foes alike. Despite all this murder and mayhem, it has only lost around 100 officers.

No one is supposed to kill CIA officers. No matter how many innocent women and children they destroy, CIA officers are the Protected Few. Why would the terrorists in Afghanistan suddenly deviate from the norm and throw the whole game into chaos?

Consider the Afghan war veteran, Micah Johnson, the black American, who killed five Dallas cops in July 2016.[1] Johnson was enraged because it doesn't matter how many black men cops kill, they are never punished. It doesn't matter that the cops have an accommodation with the criminal underworld, or that their bosses allow their gangster informants to move drugs into black communities. Cops are members of the Universal Brotherhood of Officers. They exist above the law. The end.

Granted, the Universal Brotherhood of Officers is hard for civilians to find, let alone comprehend. It exists in the twilight zone between imagination and in reality, in Bob Kerrey's "fog of war", in the realm of the insulated ruling class. It is why officers of opposing formal armies have more in common with one another than they have with their own enlisted men.

Officers are trained to think of enlisted men as cannon fodder. They know when they send a bunch of foot soldiers up a hill, some of them will die. That's why they do not fraternize.

That's why it's illegal for a working class individual like me to speak the name of an active duty CIA officer. It's also why civilians can't know the names of CIA commandos who shoot pregnant women and dig the bullets out of their corpses. The laws only apply to the little people and the defenseless.

Only Grand Pooh-Bahs like Deputy Secretary of State Richard Armitage, who leaked the name of CIA officer Valerie Plame to syndicated columnist Robert Novak back in 2003, can get away it.[2] Not only was it a felony, it was a political crime of the highest order, given that Armitage leaked Plame's name in retaliation for her husband, Joe Wilson, a career diplomat, having disproved the Bush's regime's Big Lie that Saddam Hussein had obtained enough "yellow cake" to build a nuclear bomb.

This class distinction is the basis of the sacred accommodation.

It's why the Bush Family, despite its repeated denials, had the FBI round up the Saudi "royals" and fly them out the US the day after 9/11. If anyone was a case officer to the bombers, or knew about their plans, he was among those Protected Few.

CIA officers are at the pinnacle of the Brotherhood. Blessed with fake identities and bodyguards, they fly around in private planes, live in villas, and kill with state-of-the-art technology. They tell army generals what to do. They direct Congressional committees. They assassinate heads of state and innocent children equally, with impunity, with indifference.

In Afghanistan, CIA officers manage the drug trade from their hammocks in the shade. Opium production has soared since they purchased the government in 2001.[3] They watch in amusement as addiction rates soar among young people whose parents have been killed and whose minds have been damaged by 15 years of US aggression. They don't care that the drugs reach America's inner cities.

CIA officers have an accommodation with the protected Afghan warlords who convert opium into heroin and sell it to the Russian mob. It's no different than cops working with the Mafia in America; it's an accommodation with an enemy that ensures the political security of the ruling class.

The CIA is authorized to negotiate with the enemy, but only if the channels are secure and deniable. It happened during the Iran Contra scandal, when President Reagan won the love of the American people by promising never to negotiate with terrorists, while his two-faced administration sent CIA officers to Tehran to sell missiles to the Iranians and use the money to buy guns for the drug dealing Contras.

In Afghanistan the accommodation within the drug underworld provides the CIA with a secure channel to the Taliban leadership to negotiate on simple matters like prisoner exchanges.

The exchange of British journalist Peter Moore for an Iraqi "insurgent" in CIA custody was an example of how the accommodation worked in Iraq. Moore was held by a Shia group allegedly allied to Iran, and his freedom depended entirely on the CIA reaching an accommodation with leaders of the Iraqi resistance. The details of such prisoner exchanges are never revealed, but always lead to secret negotiations over larger issues of strategic importance to both sides.

The criminal/espionage underworld in Afghanistan provides the intellectual space for any eventual reconciliation. There are always preliminary negotiations for a ceasefire, and in every modern American conflict that's the CIA's job. For the CIA has the best intelligence on family relationships in any nation where the US is operating.

CIA officer John Mason directed the Phoenix program from 1969-1971. In a 19 August 1969 *New York Times* article, Terrence Smith quoted Mason as saying, "Sometimes family relationships are involved. We know very well that if one of our units picks up the district chief's brother-in-law, he's going to be released."

Ed Brady, an army officer detailed to the CIA and assigned to the Phoenix Directorate in Saigon, explained how the accommodation worked in Vietnam.

Brady told me how he and his Vietnamese counterpart, Colonel Tan, were lunching at a restaurant in Dalat. Casually, Tan nodded at a woman eating noodle soup and drinking coffee at the table near theirs.

Colonel Tan whispered that the woman was the Viet Cong province chief's wife. Brady, of course, wanted to grab her and use her for bait.

Colonel Tan said to Brady: "You don't understand. You don't live the way we live. You don't have any family here. You're going to go home when this operation is over. You don't think like you're going to live here forever. But I have a home and a family and kids that go to school. I have a wife that has to go to market, and you want me to kidnap his wife? You want me to set a trap for him and kill him when he comes in to see his wife? If we do that, what are they going to do to our wives?"

"The VC didn't run targeted operations against [top GVN officials] either," Brady explained. "There were set rules that you played by. If you conducted a military operation and chased them down fair and square in the jungle, that was okay. If they ambushed you on the way back from a military operation, that was fair. But to conduct these clandestine police operations and really get at the heart of things, that was kind of immoral to them. That was not cricket. And the Vietnamese were very, very leery of upsetting that."

Obama's dirty war in Afghanistan relies largely on immoral operations in which wives and children are used as bait to trap husbands – or are killed as a way of punishing men in the resistance. That is why CIA officers reign supreme; like Brady in Vietnam, they have no personal, religious, or social connection with the indigenous population. They are not bound by moral rules, and are free to slaughter with impunity.

The CIA plays the same role in Afghanistan that the Gestapo and SS Einsatzgruppen performed in France in World War Two – terrorizing the urban resistance and partisan bands in the countryside by targeting their friends and families. The CIA's objective is to rip apart poor and working class families and, in the process, unravel the fabric of Afghan society, until the Afghan people accept American domination. They don't care how long it takes, either. Afghanistan is a means to get at Russia, similar to how Nixon played the China Card in Vietnam.

And that is why CIA officers were killed in Afghanistan. The Taliban have no reason to negotiate a settlement. They know history, and that the racist elites in America will never accommodate them.

As I said in 2010, the CIA is utterly predictable. I said it would invoke the symbolic "100-1 Rule" made famous by the Gestapo, and go on a killing spree, killing 100 Afghanis for every CIA officer killed, until its lust for vengeance was satisfied.

2010 was indeed the deadliest year for civilians in Afghanistan since 2001. In 2013, the rate was still rising and included an "alarming increase in women and children casualties" which reflected "the changing dynamics of the conflict over the year…which was increasingly being waged in civilian communities and populated areas," the United Nations said.[4]

The statistics are skewed to blame civilian deaths on the Taliban, but even the US military acknowledges the steady increase. As of June 2016, "Afghans feel less secure than at any recent time, a new Pentagon report says, as Afghan battlefield deaths continue to escalate and civilian casualties hit a record high."[5]

"Perceptions of security remain near all-time lows," the report said, adding that "Only 20 percent of Afghans surveyed in March called security good. That is a drop from 39 percent a year earlier. In the latest polling, 42 percent of Afghans said security is worse now than during the time of the Taliban, which ruled the country from 1996 to late 2001 when U.S. troops invaded to eliminate an al-Qaida sanctuary. The report called the 42 percent figure a historic high."

The Afghan people hate the Americans more and more, year after year. And that makes the CIA happy, in so far as it spells protracted war and increased profits for its sponsors in the arms industry.

Afghan anger means more resistance. And more resistance provides a neat pretext for the eternal military occupation of a disposable nation strategically located near Russia and China.

The Taliban will never surrender and, for the CIA, that means victory in Afghanistan.

But it also means spiritual defeat for America, as it descends ever further into the black hole of self-deception, militarism, and covert operations.

Chapter 9

THE CIA
IN
UKRAINE

RYAN DAWSON: This is Ryan Dawson of the ANC Report. With me today is Doug Valentine. I'm going to be asking him tonight about the CIA's role in Ukraine and in infiltrating the media. Mr. Valentine, it's a pleasure to have you back on the show.

VALENTINE: It's my pleasure, thank you.

DAWSON: I want to ask you about this organization working with NGOs in the Ukraine. It's called United Action Centre. I want to read something short from their page and get your thoughts. It says: "The NGO Centre UA has a strong professional human potential. The team has experience running projects in the sphere of European and Euro-Atlantic integration. At the same time, the Centre UA consists of experts and activists who have experience in journalism, public service, PR, public activities, et cetera. Also, the Centre UA has an extensive database of contacts with international experts, politicians, and journalists. At the moment, The Centre UA is the coordinator of the New Citizen's Public Campaign which brings together around 40 NGOs."

We know from the Carl Bernstein report on the media how much the CIA has infiltrated the media. Could you give your thoughts about Centre UA and what they're doing there with 40 NGOs, supposedly to promote democracy and have activists and experienced journalists working together?

VALENTINE: The Centre UA is the organization that Pierre Omidyar co-funded two years ago. Center UA is an umbrella organization that is linked to various activist projects and NGOs,[1] one of which is the New Citizen campaign which, according to the *Financial Times*, "played a big role in getting the protest up and running".[2] In fact, according to the *Kyivpost,* the ''Center UA received more than $500,000 in 2012, … 54 percent of which came from Pact Inc., a project funded by the U.S. Agency for International Development. Nearly 36 percent came from Omidyar Network, a foundation established by eBay founder Pierre Omidyar and his wife. Other donors include the International Renaissance Foundation, whose key funder is billionaire George Soros, and the National Endowment for Democracy, funded largely by the U.S. Congress."[3] Why did Omidyar prove willing to come on board with such known regime-change sponsors as USAID and NED – to say nothing of Soros? Where else is he [co]operating? It should never be forgotten that this is the kind of company he keeps. Why?

While Omidyar was born in Paris and his parents moved to Maryland from France when he was young, he appears to be of Iranian descent. His mother was a Farsi linguist and as of 2016, is president of the Roshan Cultural Heritage Institute. As bizarre as it may seem, little information is publicly available about his father, including his name. He apparently was a urologist or surgeon at John Hopkins, and if that was the case, his name should be available. The secrecy suggests some sort of intelligence connection, perhaps to the type of upper class émigré circles the CIA cultivates in America. It is a fact that the CIA station in Iran served as one of the Agency's main bases for agent operations against the Soviets. The CIA and MOSSAD created SAVAK, the Shah's notorious internal political security service, and the Shah in turn gave the CIA a free hand to run operations against the Soviets.

Maybe Pierre Omidyar is accessible to US foreign policy agencies due to some prior family connections. Maybe that accounts for why he spent a few hundred thousand dollars (a paltry sum for a billionaire) to help put the Centre UA in place in the Ukraine: so the CIA could run operations against the Russians, like it did out of Iran. I've never heard any explanation from inquisitive Glenn Greenwald. When it comes to his sugar daddy's monkey business, Greenwald's policy is pure "see no, hear no, speak no evil." Why? Is that the quid pro quo for the handout?

What I do know is that billionaires like Omidyar and George

Soros and the Rockefellers – to say nothing of USAID and NED – aren't funding political action out of the goodness of their hearts. They're doing it to advance their interests. That's why an organization like Centre UA is created: to advance the interests of its financial backers. To me it looks like a CIA-facilitated mechanism to create a crisis in Ukraine and exploit it. The 40 NGOs it coordinates are perfectly placed to provide cover for covert CIA political action.

The Centre UA does, in fact, coordinate politicians and journalists with experts on international affairs and public relations. It says so on its website. All these people are involved in managing information; maybe they're linked on a private server like Hillary Clinton used while secretary of state. It will have occurred to the political and psywar experts in the CIA's digital Dark Army that they could easily garner public support for their color revolutions by creating websites that unite and direct people; that they could manipulate potential rebels using the same, albeit updated motivational indoctrination methods people like Frank Scotton pioneered in Vietnam.

The Centre UA's public relations experts certainly guide pro-American candidates in Kiev the same way American PR people manipulated Boris Yeltsin in Moscow. As is well known, Yeltsin gave away the store after he became President of the Russian Federation. In the same way the CIA promoted Yeltsin, Centre UA journalists certainly make sure that pro-American politicians get favorable press. They spin the facts in such a way that Omidyar, who has made their operation possible, will be happy.

The Centre UA's stated purpose was to pull Ukraine out of the Russian orbit and deliver it to Western corporations. And that's what happened, along with the obligatory political payoffs. Indeed, a few short years after Centre UA was established, Vice President Joe Biden's son joined the board of directors of the largest Ukraine gas producer Burisma Holdings. Hunter Biden heads Burisma's legal department and liaises with international organizations.

The book *Flashpoint in Ukraine*[4] provides ample evidence that the Obama regime and its privateering corporate partners overthrew the pro-Russian Ukraine government and installed a government packed with neo-Nazis and American elites. They did this for their own enrichment, and yet the US media never made it an issue. It's business as usual. The average Ukrainian citizen doesn't benefit; just the "super-predator" American elite who organized the coup. It's amazing to behold.

Biden's smash and grab operation occurred in 2014. In 2016, another super-predator, Natalie Jaresko, took control of Datagroup, the company that controls Ukraine's telecom market. Jaresko at one time held a top job at the State Department coordinating the trade and commerce agencies that dealt with the former Soviet Union, including the Overseas Private Investment Corporation. Check her out on Wikipedia. She's a part of the global elite: the IMF/World Bank /European Bank for Reconstruction and Development network. In the Clinton Administration she served as Chief of the Economics Section of the US Embassy in Ukraine, and helped paved the way for the coup d'état that occurred there 20 years later. These coups take years to organize. Many more are planned.

Jaresko acquired Ukrainian citizenship on the same day as her appointment as Minister of Finance of Ukraine in 2014. Next she squeezed her competitor, the owner of Datagroup, out of business using the kind of foreign currency loan debt scam favored by Mafia hoods and economic hitmen. That's how freewheeling capitalists work: they overload targeted nations and business people with debt and then clean them out. Again, not a word of protest from the mainstream media: it's "free trade" in action.

The CIA plays a central role in these schemes, doing the illegal but plausibly deniable things that require high tech espionage and underworld assets – reaching into police files or using private investigators to get dirt on people, then setting them up and blackmailing them. These kinds of subversion operations can't be done publicly by the likes of Biden or Jaresko or their PR people. Foreign shakedowns have to be done secretly through the criminal underworld, and that's where the CIA comes into play.

Other times the media plays the central role. In the US, for example, people win elections through negative campaigning. The Democratic Party hires investigators to get dirt on Republican candidates. Republicans do the same thing. The truth doesn't matter because events are happening instantaneously. Hyperbole becomes fact before anyone can respond. Senator Elizabeth Warren reportedly claimed to be part Native American in her application to Harvard, and once she started campaigning for Hillary Clinton, Donald Trump called her "Pocahontas" every chance he got. There are all sorts of ways, within the eternal present of spectacular domination, of influencing events through manufactured scandals and misrepresentations without it being illegal or secret. It just requires celebrity status, a Twitter account, and the attention of the networks of information control.

As Guy Debord said long before the internet in his book *Comments on The Society of the Spectacle*, "One aspect of the disappearance of all objective historical knowledge can be seen in the way that individual reputations have become malleable and alterable at will by those who control all information: information which is gathered and also – an entirely different matter – information which is broadcast. Their ability to falsify is thus unlimited."

Anyone can be smeared, and apart from the unknown Protected Few in the CIA and National Security Establishment, there's no defense. Overseas, the CIA is perpetually collecting information on adversaries like Vladimir Putin and passing it along to the Western media, which rejoices in spinning it a million different ways.

What is less well known is the CIA is engaged in tipping the balance in the domestic as well as international contests. That's why it's secret, and why all the privateers protect it. They share the same business ideology. CIA officers, PR people, journalists, politicians, and academics who get paid to give "expert" testimony on Fox or MSNBC, are knowingly manipulating social and political movements here in the US, just like they do for the Ukrainian opposition or the Venezuelan opposition.

The CIA sets up Twitter accounts and Facebook pages and social websites to move people into mass organizations to achieve its secret ends. In May 2016 Twitter "cut off U.S. intelligence agencies from a service that sifts through the entire output of Twitter's social media postings."[5] The guilty party was the CIA's Open Source Enterprise, which contracted with a private contractor, Dataminr, through the CIA's ubiquitous venture capital fund In-Q-Tel, to spy on American citizens. Such super-secret "intelligence" operations are frequently used as cover for highly illegal "offensive counterintelligence" operations.

DAWSON: We saw the National Endowment for Democracy, which is totally CIA, at the forefront in the Ukraine. But why does the CIA need so many NGOs as middlemen? What is their purpose for having 40 different non-governmental organizations?

VALENTINE: I'll give you an example. When the CIA moved into Vietnam, which had a culture the US hadn't dealt with before, the first thing it did was buy a lot of property. This was during the First Indochina War and they did this clandestinely, through cut-outs, so they'd have safe houses to set up organizations later on. It's always best for them to buy real estate during times of crisis when prices are down. Like Trump always says, "Buy low." And when are prices lowest? As Baron Rothschild famously said, "When there's blood in the streets."

The CIA bought huge tracts of property in Saigon in between 1952 and 1955, during the First Indochina War, when there was blood on the streets. The CIA bought prime property at ten percent of its value. That's the first step – get your nose in the tent. These buildings served as places where CIA officers could meet their agents and plot dirty deeds. They passed some to NGOs and civil organizations to operate.

William Colby introduced me to one of his cohorts, Clyde Bauer, the CIA officer who ran Air America in Vietnam in the early days. Bauer told me he set up South Vietnam's Foreign Relations Council, Chamber of Commerce and Lions Club, "to create a strong civil base." That's what the CIA is doing in Ukraine through the Centre UA. It's creating a pro-American civil base, from which political candidates emerge.

The CIA influences politics in foreign nations in many ways. CIA officers are constantly funneling money to all political parties, right and left, and establishing long-range agents to monitor and manipulate political developments. That's standard operating procedure.

The next thing the CIA does is seize control of a nation's secret services. That's what they did in Vietnam, and in Ukraine. As I've explained elsewhere, they offer training and high tech gadgetry to people in the secret services; they corrupt them and use them for their own purposes, like they used SAVAK in Iran. It's highly illegal to suborn officials in foreign nations. We don't like it when it's done to us, and it's not something even an influential billionaire like Omidyar is trained to do (although his private security force is probably staffed by former CIA officers who do know how to do it).

The CIA infiltrates all the political parties and as soon as a politician they own is in place, right or left, they can elevate him or her to Defense Minister or Interior Minister. These ministers are on the CIA payroll and appoint military, security and police officials who do the CIA's bidding. The CIA tries to place its people throughout the captive nation's government and civil society. In South America they recruit junior military officers via the School of the Americas (now innocuously renamed) and when the time is right, have them stage a coup with the support of all the other people they're been cultivating for years, sometimes decades.[6]

US corporations need the CIA to put these parallel governments in place. The CIA penetrates the military and security services, and simultaneously creates a civil base through deniable organizations like Centre for UA. This is how societies are ruled when there's no overwhelming popular support: through the ownership of property and by having the proper people in government and civic institutions.

The CIA recruits people in place like Lech Walesa in Poland. Often the people running the unions are on the CIA payroll; people running the education system too. The CIA can recruit these people because it has so much money. The Russians can't compete, when billionaires like George Soros are sprinkling a million here and five million there – money that goes into building civic institutions that are ideologically attuned. Whether people do it for love or money, or belief of a brighter future, the CIA is manipulating the social and political processes. Its officers and their agents are recruiting people and putting them in place, having them sign contracts that effectively say, "In exchange for working for us in advancing our interests here in Kiev you will get $100,000 in a Swiss bank account and your life will be rosy."

It's illegal. It's treasonous. You can't take money from a foreign intelligence agency and work against your own country, but that is what the CIA is doing in the Ukraine right now and around the world on a massive scale.

DAWSON: I wanted to ask you about that Human Intelligence. What is the Intelligence Community Directive 304?

VALENTINE: That came out in 2009. If anybody wants to read it, it's only four or five pages long.[7] It spells out in broad, simplistic terms what the FBI, the CIA, and the Department of Defense do for the National Director of Intelligence, in terms of HUMINT.

The position of Director of National Intelligence didn't exist until Bush became president in 2001. Until then, the person who supervised all intelligence operations was the director of the CIA, who doubled as director of all intelligence agencies. After 9/11 the CIA director was no longer officially overseeing all other intelligence agencies. That role passed to the new Director of National Intelligence, which, since 2010, is a position held by James Clapper. The DNI job was created by Bush to enable more political control over domestic intelligence operations.

In 2009, the Director of National Intelligence issued Directive 304 to define the jobs of the military, CIA, and FBI. The most recent online copy has redactions. They cut out parts about what the CIA does. It's standard to classify the names of CIA officers in the Ukraine, what their cover positions are, who they've bribed and suborned. If the president of the Rotary Club or the police chief in Kiev is a CIA agent, those things are classified, because they are illegal. But now, thanks to Directive 304, you can't even know what is unclassified about CIA operations. That is how bad it has gotten.

Again, it's all about the control of information. They don't want you to know anything. That's how they exert power over you. Your rulers are obsessed with controlling information and not letting you know what goes on, the same way Greenwald hides his treasure trove of NSA documents obtained from Snowden and dribbles out only what he wants you to see. Because a person's or an institution's power is directly equivalent to its ability to control the information upon which its power depends.

DAWSON: And to profit from it!

VALENTINE: That's the whole point. Democracy is corrupted when your government prevents you from knowing what the CIA is doing. That kind of secrecy is the antithesis of democracy. If the public doesn't know what's going on, then it has no control over its fate. Americans have given up so much control, so much freedom.

DAWSON: Every time they declassify something, we find out it had nothing to do with sensitive secrets; it's just hiding illegal activity, that's it!

VALENTINE: The CIA isn't conducting secret, illegal actions around the world to bring class, gender and racial harmony to America, or encourage Palestinians and Jews to hold hands and sing Pepsi commercials together. The CIA is doing this on behalf of the Clintons and Bushes. They do it for Omidyar and Bill Gates and George Soros and the people who rule us.

DAWSON: They are the secretive military wing of the plutocrats.

VALENTINE: Yep. Phil Agee called the CIA "Capitalism's Invisible Army". The CIA isn't doing illegal things so the minimum wage will go up, or so that bankers will be more careful about selling mortgages to people who can't afford them. They're working with the bankers. They want Ukrainians putting their money in a Morgan Stanley brokerage firm in Kiev. They want to suck the life out of Ukrainians. That is what the CIA is there for, and they are very careful and cautious about whom they recruit to achieve that goal.

DAWSON: They want things that have intrinsic value: property, farming.

VALENTINE: Yea, the first thing they want is property, and the best way to drive prices down is to start a war. People are fleeing war zones in Iraq, Libya and Syria. As soon as that happens, prices go down and corporate privateers like Omidyar, Biden and Jaresko go swooping in.

DAWSON: The IMF engages in predatory lending to push people into debt, so they have to start selling assets to pay the piper. When Ukraine started making deals with the Russians, suddenly there's a coup d'état! It just makes me laugh that the NGOs that are coordinated by the Centre UA are talking about spreading democracy, when the current government in Western Ukraine was appointed!

VALENTINE: Sure. The history of the US intelligence operations in Ukraine is educational. OSS officers in World War Two released Stepan Bandera from prison in 1944. Bandera was a Nazi collaborator whose militia slaughtered Poles, Jews and communist workers on the eastern front. The US recruited Bandera so he could fight the advancing Soviet Union. Nothing has changed. Just over ten years ago the CIA initiated its "Orange Revolution" for the same purpose – to thwart the Russians. It was one of the first color revolutions and it involved the same people the CIA employed in its coup in 2014.

DAWSON: The dioxin poison scandal.

VALENTINE: The wife of the acting president of the Ukraine (in 2014) is an American, and she's part of a Ukrainian exile faction. The CIA has a stable full of exiles from everywhere. Ngo Dinh Diem was living in exile in America when Ed Lansdale and the CIA installed him as president in South Vietnam. He was sweeping floors at Maryknoll seminary in Lakewood, New Jersey. They keep their exiles in storage and activate them and their agent networks when required. A current example is Fethullah Gülen, the America-based, Turkish exile and business magnate who tried to overthrow Prime Minister Erdoğan in July 2016.[8] As Joshua Cook reported in 2014, Gülen, "came to the United States in 1999 due to cited health problems and has stayed in the United States after gaining his visa with help from former CIA officials. The FBI previously resisted granting permanent residency status to Gülen. According to leaked cables, parts of the US government believe that Gülen "is a 'radical Islamist' whose moderate message cloaks a more sinister and radical agenda."

Cook reported that "Gülen-inspired schools are the largest charter network in the US and receive approximately $150 million a year in taxpayer money. There are about 130 of these charter schools in 26 states where the majority of the teachers are from Turkey (and) many of the contracts for construction and operation have gone to Turkish businesses. Those actions have raised red flags for the US government."

People like Diem and Gülen come out from under their rocks and fill the governmental and civic institutions the CIA creates in nations it subverts. This is another thing it does all around the world.

DAWSON: We saw in Cuba, for example, the CIA actually hired out Meyer Lansky and the Mafia to do its dirty work. Then we see the Ukrainian government hiring out a bunch of neo-Nazis.

VALENTINE: As usual, I was taking the long road to get to my point, but yes, the CIA has been operating with Ukrainian exiles since the end of World War Two, when they hired Reinhard Gehlen. Gehlen had been the chief anti-Soviet spy for the German Army. US army intelligence hired Gehlen in 1945, but as soon as the CIA was formed it grabbed him and put him in charge of Eastern Europe. The CIA used this former Nazi to re-activate the spy networks he had in Ukraine, Poland, Latvia, all the Eastern European countries, and these old Nazi spies and saboteurs went to work for the CIA.

DAWSON: They did the same thing in Japan. They got Yakuza and former

Japanese spies to spy on the Chinese. They needed that intelligence, and they didn't have enough Chinese speakers or people who could infiltrate. So they kept the same imperial Japanese who had been there during World War Two.

VALENTINE: All of this is illegal, but this is what the CIA does all around the world. It's been doing it in the Ukraine for generations. It has the grandchildren of Nazis on its payroll, an incredible infrastructure of neo-Nazi secret agents who've been battling against Russia for seventy years.

The Russians know their names, where they live, where the CIA has its safe houses. But the American public has no clue. They think the crisis began today because of the way the news is presented. The journalists, their editors, the industry owners, the publishers – which now include Omidyar – don't want you to know about all the illegal activities the CIA is involved in on their behalf. So the owners of *The New York Times* and the *Washington Post* hire editors who will direct reporters in such a way that they never report on what the CIA is doing.

DAWSON: Some of them are CIA.

VALENTINE: Journalism in the US is a traditional cover for CIA officers. And when the owners of the media aren't covering for the CIA, they're selling commercial time slots to the multi-national corporations that in turn are selling you commodities made in sweatshops in foreign nation that have been subverted by the CIA. You could almost say there's no such thing as factual reporting. It's as valuable as most of the over-priced commodities people buy to elevate their status. Everything is twisted and delivered in nine second sound bites, so you'll buy something, not know something, or forget about something.

DAWSON: If anyone is confused, just look at the reporting on Ukraine, or the reporting during the build-up to the Iraq War. Look how uniform all these three-letter networks were. The reporting got debunked online. Yet on television you had a completely one-sided story. It's pro-war, pro-coup d'état.

VALENTINE: The problem, in my opinion, is not that the CIA infiltrated journalism, but rather that the CIA is promoting the business of journalism – which is actually the advertising branch of capitalism. They're working together. The "reliable" journalists who report on the CIA – guys like Seymour Hersh – never say the things I'm saying here. The CIA and the media are part of the same criminal conspiracy. You're never going to learn anything substantive by reading what mainstream reporters dish out about the CIA. You can't take a journalism course in CIA Criminal Conspiracies 101.

DAWSON: That's why I made a documentary film called "Decades of Deception" that went over a bunch of covert operations – that have been busted wide open – that the CIA was involved with or completely in control of.[9] But, getting that out there is a drop in the bucket compared to what the mass media disseminates, and how much bull we're fed in school and from television.

VALENTINE: American society since its creation 240 years ago has had as its goal the enrichment and empowerment of a small group of property owners and their succeeding generations who, after they conquered the continent, took over the world. The civic and government institutions in the USA have been organized for over 240 years to advance that purpose. The fact that the CIA came along 70 years ago and pushed the process forward by doing illegal things on an industrial basis hasn't changed the thrust of the American empire and its front men.

The people who control the Centre UA and manage its operations in Ukraine are doing the same thing here. It's the same rulers. It's the same PR people and journalists, the same politicians, and they are doing the same things. Just trace the provenance of so many of them.

DAWSON: And they can distort massive events. I mean trying to get one newspaper or one talking head to mention that Palestine is under occupation. It will never happen. Never.

VALENTINE: And yet people really think that they have freedom here. I guess it is all relative, but if you start to know a little bit, you realize you don't know much "truth" at all.

DAWSON: The internet is making a small dent in it, but not enough. Not yet, but I have hope in it anyway.

VALENTINE: I'm sixty-six; when I started writing back in the early 1980s, it could take a month to get in touch with someone to learn a particular fact. Things are faster now. But CIA is faster now too. It created a new Digital Directorate so it can more perfectly control internet information. The control of scientific and technological information is as important as the control of words – the intellectual information that is written down or broadcast. Control of scientific information is a means of controlling our ideas and assumptions about things. Just as the CIA is at the forefront of propaganda on the Internet, its science and technology division is at the forefront of shaping the industries than run the world.

The CIA is at the forefront of drone and weapons technology – any kind of technological advancements that only serve and enrich the ruling class. The CIA is at the forefront of that research and development, and that goes for the Internet, too.

Back in the mid-1990s I took a class in the hypertext language. And to my surprise, we were taught that all information was routed through super processors in Langley. Putin recently said that the Internet was a CIA special project and he was right. I remember when the Defense Advanced Research Project Agency came out with ARPANET, which started helping us to access information in college libraries back in the early 1990s. It was all done under the Department of Defense, which was fronting for the CIA.

So our Internet capabilities are a new freedom, but at the same time we enjoy this freedom by the leave of the CIA. If they wanted to, they could shut it down in a minute. They control it and they monitor every aspect of it. If we actually were doing something that threatened them, they would know about it in a nanosecond and our activities would be stopped. But we're just mosquitos.

DAWSON: The FCC has already moved to destroy net neutrality in the US. I see that Internet freedom as kind of a black swan. You have all these commercial purposes, definitely: people like Omidyar making money selling things online, but I am not sure if they worried that there would be people who would become self-made journalists and start reporting on all the horrible things they do.

VALENTINE: People are addicted to the Internet now and if Bill Gates or Omidyar wanted to, they could start charging you a dollar a day. It's like a drug. The first shot is for free. Now it's the time for them to start charging. Nothing happening on the Internet right now is indicative of what's going to be going on in five years. This whole Internet fantasy could turn nightmarish very soon.

DAWSON: Well, that's pretty dark, but you may be right. At least they are charging people on the service end to provide it, and they are not happy about it. But you can completely control information if you can decide who is fast and who is slow; that is all it takes.

VALENTINE: If you were an Internet entrepreneur, how many different ways do you think you could come up with making millions off it? People are addicted to iPhones and texting. The entrepreneurs are hanging around the school yard and they are giving you free Skype. The CIA too. If the Brits could get away with pushing opium on China in 1848, what makes you think the CIA won't do it here, now?

DAWSON: Do opium? Ha!

VALENTINE: We'll have to come back in five years and see if I'm right.

DAWSON: I'm not arguing against you. I just don't *want* to believe it. You know, because it's dark.

VALENTINE: Enjoy the good times, because these little bits of freedom that we have now may be the last. "You don't need a weatherman to know which way the wind blows." It's like Directive 304, which you could once find online, but is now classified. Civil liberties are diminishing, not increasing. The Supreme Court just said that nobody can challenge Obama's right to detain.

DAWSON: He kills without trial, too.

VALENTINE: They can do anything and it's not going to get better, as resources diminish, as the income inequality gap widens, these trends are just going to get worse.

DAWSON: Yeah, they had the largest corporate bailout in history, and no one went to jail. There were some protests, but then it faded away. And that was after a sixteen-trillion-dollar bailout of these financial institutions, plus the Federal Reserve jumping in after that with even more money.

VALENTINE: That is the perfect example of why we do not live in a democracy. At the time they did some polls, and ninety percent of the American public did not want the government to bail out the banks. These were decisions made by our secret rulers. All the big decisions in our democracy are made by them.

DAWSON: And mass media agreed with it: "Too big to fail!"

VALENTINE: Yea, that's a catchy slogan. And there are fewer rulers all the time and more of us schleppers on the outside who are paying their bills.

DAWSON: Well, get out your pitchforks, people!

Chapter 10

WAR CRIMES
AS
POLICY*

In February 2013, the *Guardian* and *BBC Arabic* unveiled a documentary film exploring the role of retired Colonel James Steele in the recruitment, training and initial deployments of the CIA-advised and -funded Special Police Commandos in Iraq.

The documentary was a departure from mainstream reporting, in that it told how the Commandos tortured and murdered tens of thousands of Iraqi men and boys. But the Commandos are only one of America's many weapons of human destruction in Iraq. Along with US military forces that murder indiscriminately, CIA-funded death squads that murdered selectively, and the CIA's palace guard – the Iraqi Special Operations Forces – the Commandos are part of a genocidal campaign that had killed about 10% of the Sunni Arabs of Iraq by 2008, and driven half of all Sunnis from their homes.

Including economic sanctions and a 50-year history of sabotage and subversion, America and its Iraqi collaborators have visited far more death and destruction on Iraq than Saddam Hussein and his Ba'athist regime. Driven into fanaticism by the brutal invasion and occupation, many thousands of Sunnis then formed the Islamic State of Iraq (ISI). After being decimated by US forces, ISI was reinforced by former Ba'athist military and intelligence officers, as well as foreign mercenaries

---

* Co-authored with Nicholas J.S. Davies

from places like Chechnya. Now known as ISIS, the militant Sunni resistance seized vast stretches of land in Iraq and Syria. Only as recently as June 2016, was it finally driven out of Fallujah.

In the weeks after the documentary, American pundits began cataloguing the horrors that had piled up by 2013. They told how the Bush and Obama regimes killed more than a million Iraqis, displaced around five million, and imprisoned and tortured hundreds of thousands without trial. The photos that were released of brutality at Abu Ghraib Prison give but an inkling of the terror to which the Iraqis were subjected.

The draconian administrative detention laws, systematic torture and executions that characterize the occupation are still in place in 2016. The prime minister's office, a position now held by Haider Jawad Kadhim Al-Abad, is where the CIA-managed Counter Terrorism Service is still ensconced. In May 2016, the CTS gained fame for leading the US offensive to take back Fallujah from ISIS forces that had occupied the city since 2014. Iraqi soldiers and the national police forces assisted.

The systematic oppression the Americans imposed upon Iraq meets the definition of genocide in the Genocide Convention, and violates multiple articles of the Geneva Conventions guaranteeing protection to civilians in time of war. But the guilty Americans have gone unpunished for their war crimes, not least of which was falsifying intelligence about Iraq's non-existent weapons of mass destruction. British legal advisors repeatedly warned their government in 2003 that invading Iraq would be a crime of aggression, which they called "one of the most serious offenses under international law."

For anyone familiar with the CIA, the systematic oppression was predictable. But the US Government, as usual, destroyed and conceals most of the hard evidence of its war crimes, making it harder to prove. And the media is content to revise history and focus public attention on front men like Steele, rather than the institutions – in particular the CIA – for whom they work.

History, however, provides contextual evidence that what happened in Iraq amounts to an official but unstated policy of carefully planned war crimes. Indeed, the CIA modeled the Iraqi Special Police Commandos on the Special Police forces it organized and funded in Vietnam. In November 2000, Counterpunch published an article describing how former Congressman Rob Simmons, while serving as a CIA officer in Vietnam, created the Special Intelligence Force Unit

(SIFU) on which the Iraqi Special Police Commandos are very likely modeled.[1]

There are other examples. As we were reminded by the *Guardian*, Steele headed the US Military Advisory Group in El Salvador (1984-1986), where US-advised Salvadoran units were responsible for thousands of cases of torture and extra-judicial killing. Operating in both rural and urban areas, they were directed against anyone opposing US policy – always leftists advocating the things most hated by the CIA – land reform and redistribution of wealth from oligarchs to workers.

The CIA's death squads in El Salvador were periodically moved from one administrative cover to another to confuse investigators. The CIA played this shell game with its Special Police Commandos in Iraq as well, rebranding them as the "National Police" following the exposure of one of their secret torture centers in November 2005. In its finest Madison Avenue marketing traditions, the CIA renamed the Commandos' predatory Wolf Brigade "the Freedom Brigade", bringing to mind Reagan's description of the Contras as "freedom fighters".

In Vietnam, the CIA built an archipelago of secret torture centers to process the hundreds of thousands of suspects that were kidnapped by its mercenary army of "counterterrorists". All around the world, CIA officers and their military sidekicks teach modern torture techniques and design the torture centers concealed within the National Security Establishment's network of military posts. Along with the CIA's stations, those posts are the secret government's infrastructure for Full Spectrum Dominance.

Major Joe Blair, the Director of Instruction at the School of the Americas (1986-89), described the training the US gave to Latin American officers as follows: "The doctrine that was taught was that if you want information you use physical abuse … false imprisonment … threats to family members … and killing. If you can't get the information you want, if you can't get that person to shut up or to stop what they're doing, you simply assassinate them, and you assassinate them with one of your death squads."[2]

In 2000, the School of the Americas was renamed the Western Hemisphere Institute for Security Cooperation, but, as Blair testified at a trial of SOA Watch protesters in 2002, "There are no substantive changes besides the name. They teach the identical courses that I taught, and changed the course names and use the same manuals."

General Paul Gorman, who commanded U.S. forces in Central

America in the mid-1980s, defined this type of warfare based on systematic war crimes as "a form of warfare repugnant to Americans, a conflict which involves innocents, in which non-combatant casualties may be an explicit object."[3]

Another problem with the official narrative, apart from historical amnesia, is that each new war crime is viewed as an isolated incident; and when the dots are connected, the media's focus is always on some shadowy character like Steele. To its credit, the *Guardian* made a feeble attempt to connect Steele to the former Director of the Central Intelligence Agency, David Petraeus, and former Defense Secretary Donald Rumsfeld. But it ignored the overarching reality that the entire National Security Establishment is staffed by the same right-wing ideologues who power the US Government's unstated policy of waging systematic war crimes for profit.

We know perfectly well who these militants are. The problem is that they regularly have lunch with the reporters whom the American public, in its naiveté, trusts to expose them and their criminal conspiracy.

For example, on 17 March 2013, CNN talking head Fareed Zakaria had Donald Gregg on his show to discuss North Korea. Zakaria introduced Gregg as President George H.W. Bush's national security advisor in the 1980s. But he did not mention that Gregg, while the senior CIA officer in III Corps in Vietnam, helped to develop the "repugnant" form of warfare described by General Gorman. Nor did Zakaria explain how Gregg oversaw its application in El Salvador through the CIA's back-channel "counterterror" network.[4]

Gregg's plan, adopted by Steele in El Salvador and then Iraq, requires CIA advisors to coordinate the occupied nation's civilian security services, like the Iraqi Special Police, with military intelligence and civil affairs units, in order to provide reaction forces units with timely information on the location of guerrillas, whose hideouts are bombed by US warplanes and then ravaged in My Lai-style cordon and search operations in which counterterror death squads hunt enemy cadres in their homes.

In Vietnam, Gregg and his CIA companions – many of whom migrated to El Salvador – put together a chart of VC political cadres from "battered" detainees. The abused detainees were forced to point out on a map where their comrades were hiding. Next, the CIA officers piled the detainees into a helicopter and had them point out the hiding places on the ground. A CT team would then snatch the targeted VC cadres and bring them to the CIA's secret torture center, run by a CIA-paid and owned Special Police officer, the kind of guy Steele advised in Iraq.

"We brought guys in from the national prison to flesh out the reports," Gregg said about one particular operation. "We had guys analyzing reports, marking photographs, putting the pictures together on the wall, and then photographing that. That led to 96 people in the organization. Using military intelligence, we took photos of the houses where they lived. Then we took the photos back to the helicopter where we had the 23 people, who were hooded, and they circled the faces of the cadres."

There's more historical evidence of CIA tactics, but the "Pink Plan" developed by CIA officers Gregg, Rudy Enders and Felix Rodrigues in Vietnam is the same basic plan the CIA exported to El Salvador, and that Steele applied in Iraq.

After finishing with Gregg, Zakaria took a commercial break and returned with Paul Wolfowitz, President George W. Bush's Deputy Secretary of Defense and a member of the Bush's Office of Special Plans, which planned and promoted the terror war on Iraq.

> ZAKARIA: "How do you think about, as an American policy maker, the issue of – was it worth the price in American lives and treasure, by some estimates $1 trillion?"
> WOLFOWITZ: "I would like as much as anyone to be able to say, let's forget about the Persian Gulf. Let's forget about the larger Middle East. But that part of the world isn't leaving us alone. Al Qaeda isn't leaving us alone. Pakistan isn't leaving us alone. I think our interests and our values would be advanced if we stick with it."

Zakaria did not ask Wolfowitz what he meant by "leaving us alone."

War Criminals Wave Press Passes

Given the history of America's genocidal wars in Vietnam and Central America, it is unfortunate that the *Guardian* limited itself to establishing that Steele and his administrative bosses, General David Petraeus and Donald Rumsfeld, underwrote systematic torture and extrajudicial killing.

What needs to be stressed is that thousands of Americans, including unelected political cadres like Wolfowitz, and scores of journalists with access to them like Zakaria, know that the CIA-owned Ministry of Interior operates more than a dozen secret prisons. They know what goes on in them, too. As one Iraqi general told the film-makers, "drilling, murder, torture – the ugliest sorts of torture I've ever seen."

Likewise, the composition and operations of Special Police death squads, an American interviewee said, "were discussed openly, wherever it was, at staff meetings," and were "common knowledge across Baghdad."

Common knowledge never shared with the public.

It is a testament to the power of US "information warfare" that this policy of systematic war crimes comes as a surprise to the general public. Such is the power of National Security State insiders like David Corn and Michael Isikoff, who happily turned a policy of calculated war crimes into the "hubris" of a few sexy mad patriots whom the Establishment is glad to scandalize, but never prosecute.[5]

Certainly people have to be reminded, and the young have to learn, that America's policy of war crimes for profit cannot exist without the complicity of the mainstream media, which shamelessly exploits our inclination to believe that our leaders behave morally. As George Orwell wrote in 1945, "The nationalist not only does not disapprove of atrocities committed by his own side, but he has a remarkable capacity for not even hearing about them."

Belligerent nationalism is understood in America as the essence of patriotism, and this veneration for militants is taught to all budding reporters at journalism schools, along with the sacred Code of Silence. Which is why, when insider Seymour Hersh reported that the CIA and Israel were training Special Forces assassination squads for deployment in Iraq based on the Phoenix program model, he described it in a bloodless manner that made it seem necessary and, at worst, a mistake.

But war crimes are not a mistake; they are a "repugnant" and thoroughly intentional form of modern American warfare.

Hersh quoted a former CIA station chief as saying, "We have to resuscitate Iraqi intelligence, holding our nose, and have Delta and agency shooters break down doors and take them" – the insurgents – "out."

Hold your nose, Seymour, and cheer the war crimes. When insider Amy Goodman at Democracy Now interviewed Hersh about the Phoenix-style murder program, she didn't ask if it amounted to a policy of war crimes. When insider Zakaria had Wolfowitz on the hot seat, he failed to question him about the war crimes he plotted and committed.

All this media psywar is waged in the name of maintaining morale – to make us feel good about our leaders – Wolfowitz, Perle, Frum and Feith – and the war crimes they commit in our name.

After the CIA death squads eliminated the senior leadership of the Iraqi government in 2003, they targeted "mid-level" Ba'ath Party members – a large portion of Iraq's middle class. Cover for this needless rampage was provided by *Newsweek's* top national security propagandist, John Barry, who quoted an army officer as saying, "The Sunni population is paying no price for the support it is giving to the terrorists. From their point of view, it is cost-free. We have to change that equation."[6]

How did they change the equation? In one case, US forces held a general's three sons as hostages to persuade him to defect. But instead of releasing his sons as promised, they staged an elaborate mock execution of his youngest son, before torturing the general himself to death.

All of it covered up. Not one victim featured on TV. All you'll ever see is ISIS beheading people.

If you were to believe *The New York Times* – America's newspaper of record – it doesn't know the names of the CIA officers in Iraq behind these barbaric practices. Publishers may claim that the Intelligence Identity Protection Act prevents them from naming names, but they could describe the jobs and tell us what's being done. But they don't even do that, and that self-censorship is what the policy of war crimes depends upon. *The Times* conceals the criminal conspiracy waged by militant elites that undermines our "democracy." We will never learn the truth about how the CIA nurtured the exile leadership it installed in Iraq, or how it organized the Ministry of Interior as its private domain, replete with a computerized list of every Iraqi citizen and every detail of their lives.

The Times could at least describe the CIA as "Keeper of the Hit Lists: Blackmail Central." But it won't, because it's a family affair. As we know, the Iraqi National Congress was headed by Ahmed Chalabi, the CIA-sponsored source on the myth of weapons of mass destruction, hand-delivered to *Times* reporter Judy Miller, now a member of the

Council on Foreign Relations and a Fox News analyst. Chalabi's lies, and Miller's dutiful reporting of them, were a major pretext for the war on Iraq.

What is never mentioned is that the Iraqi National Congress was founded and funded by the CIA, and that one of its leaders was the exiled General Hassan al-Naqib. The CIA handpicked al-Naqib's son, Falah al-Naqib, as Interim Interior Minister in Iraq and, in return for the favor, Falah appointed his uncle General Thavit to lead the Special Police Commandos.

Times reporters undoubtedly lunch with Thavit and his CIA case officer, which may be why they never explain the CIA's systematic methods of dominance: for example, that any American working for the Interior Ministry or Prime Minister's office is reporting to a publicly acknowledged administrative boss in the military or State Department, while secretly reporting to a CIA case officer, his operational boss.

The Times never explains that every unit in the Special Commandos has a CIA advisor handing out hit lists to its counterpart American "Special Police Transition Team". Up to 45 US Special Forces soldiers work with each Iraqi unit. These teams are in round-the-clock communication with their CIA bosses via the Special Police Command Center. There is no record of the Special Police or Special Commandos ever conducting operations without US supervision, even as they massacred tens of thousands of people.

Every militia and Iraqi Special Forces unit has a CIA case officer in a similar management position. Every top Iraqi politician and ministry official has a CIA case officer too. And *New York Times* reporters drink with these advisors inside the Green Zone. It's the family secret that enables atrocity.

American journalists do not report the truth. Consider their deference to the Interior Ministry's CIA advisor Steven Casteel after his Special Police Commandos launched their reign of terror in Baghdad. All reports of a Phoenix-style terror campaign were conveniently forgotten and instead, Knight Ridder reporters regurgitated Casteel's black propaganda – that all atrocities were either rumor or innuendo or perpetrated by "insurgents in stolen police uniforms."[7]

Forget about "mistakes." Casteel's explanation is as ludicrous as General Petraeus claiming that the Iraqis formed the Special Police Commandos on "their own initiative."

In its profile, Knight Ridder did not mention that Casteel had managed DEA operations in Latin America. It did not say that he'd been the DEA's Chief of Intelligence before being sent to Iraq or that the CIA has controlled the DEA's overseas targeting for 40 years. It wasn't noted that Casteel served as a CIA asset in Latin America, attacking left wing drug traffickers and letting right wing traffickers flourish, supporting the CIA-sponsored Los Pepes-AUC death squads who were responsible for about 75% of civilian deaths in the Colombian civil war over the next ten years.

Knight Ridder did investigate Commando atrocities and might have uncovered the whole story but its Iraqi reporter, Yasser Salihee, was shot and killed by an American sniper in June 2005. Heeding what was an unmistakable warning, Knight Ridder instead blamed the abuses on infiltration of the Commandos by "Shiite militias".

After the exposure of the al-Jadiriyah torture center, journalists reported that heads would roll. But CIA asset Adnan al-Asadi, the Deputy Interior Minister, maintained command of the National Police and prevented reforms promised by the Interior Minister at the time, Jawad al-Bulani.

Throughout his CIA-sponsored tenure, Asadi's police forces were implicated in human rights abuses. During demonstrations in Tahrir Square in Baghdad in March 2011, demonstrators spotted Asadi on a rooftop directing snipers as they shot peaceful protesters in the square below. But no war crime goes unrewarded, and Asadi was eventually elected to Parliament, where the big money is to be made. Such are the advantages of working for the CIA.

Today, Iraq's prisons are still rife with rape, torture, executions and disappearances. The *Guardian* and the BBC made a good start, but US journalists need to launch an investigation into the full extent of US command and control of the Special Police Commandos, and all the death squads and torture centers the US imposed on Iraq. Such an investigation must honestly examine the roles of the CIA and of US Special Forces, including the secret "Nightstalkers" who worked with the Wolf Brigade in 2005. The investigation must lead to accountability for every war crime committed, all the way to the top.

American journalists were glad to demonize Saddam Hussein for his war crimes – real and imagined. Now they need to identify and humanize the dead bodies that piled up every month in Baghdad. They need to follow up with Iraqi human rights groups like the Organization for Follow-Up and Monitoring, which matched 92% of the bodies of execution victims with names and descriptions of people detained by US-led Interior Ministry forces.[8]

America's ruling National Security Establishment has expanded covert paramilitary operations from 60 nations in 2008, to 120 in 2013. If we are ever to have a whiff of democracy, we need our journalists to reveal the extent to which the CIA commands and controls these operations in Iraq, Afghanistan, Libya and Syria. We need them to explain on a daily basis how the National Security Establishment corrupts foreign nations, intelligence, and "news" for the same racist, imperial purposes that have defined US foreign policy since its inception 240 years ago.

Chapter 11

NEW GAMES, SAME AIMS: CIA ORGANIZATIONAL CHANGES

GUILLERMO JIMENEZ: Welcome to De-Manufacturing Consent. I am your host, Guillermo Jimenez. Our guest today is Douglas Valentine. How are you today?

VALENTINE: I'm well. Thanks for having me on the show.

JIMENEZ: *The Phoenix Program* has recently been republished by Open Road Media as part of their Forbidden Bookshelves series. Would you mind sharing with us how your book was chosen for the series? What do you make of this new-found interest in Phoenix; what the CIA was up to in Vietnam; and what the CIA is up to generally?

VALENTINE: When the book came out in 1990, it got a terrible review in *The New York Times.* Morley Safer, who'd been a reporter in Vietnam, wrote the review. Safer and the *Times* killed the book because in it I said Phoenix never would have succeeded if the reporters in Vietnam hadn't covered for the CIA.

   Several senior CIA officers said the same thing, that "So and so was always in my office. He'd bring a bottle of scotch and I'd tell him what was going on." The celebrity reporters knew what was going on, but they didn't report about it in exchange for having access. I said that in the book specifically about *The New York Times.* So I not only got the CIA angry at me, I also got the Vietnam press corps angry at me too.

Between those two things, the book did not get off to an auspicious start.

The Times gave Safer half a page to write his review, which was bizarre. The usual response is just to ignore a book like *The Phoenix Program*. But *The New York Times Book Review* serves a larger function; it teaches the media elite and "intelligentsia" what to think and how to say it. So Safer said my book was incoherent, because it unraveled the bureaucratic networks that conceal the contradictions between policy and operational reality. It exposed Colby as a liar. Safer was upset that I didn't portray his friend and patron, Bill Colby, as a symbol of the elite, as a modern day Odysseus.

Luckily, with the Internet revolution, people aren't bound by *The Times* and network news anymore. They can listen to *Russia Today* and get another side of the story. So Mark Crispin Miller and Philip Rappaport at Open Road chose *The Phoenix Program* to be the first book they published. And it's been reborn. Thanks to the advent of the e-book, we've reached an audience of concerned and knowledgeable people in a way that wasn't possible 25 years ago.

It's also because of these Internet developments that John Brennan, the director of CIA, thought of reorganizing the CIA. All these things are connected. It's a vastly different world than it was in 1947 when the CIA was created. The nature of the American empire has changed, and what the empire needs from the CIA has changed. The CIA is allocated about $30 billion a year, so the organizational changes are massive undertakings.

If you want to understand the CIA, you have to understand how it's organized.

JIMENEZ: Exactly, and that's what I want to talk to you about next. But first I'd like to touch upon the CIA's infiltration of the US media. I find it curious, because the way that you describe it, it's not so much a deliberate attempt to censor the media. There's a lot of self-censorship as a result of that already existing relationship. Is that how you see this?

VALENTINE: Yes. The media organizes itself the way the CIA does. The CIA has case officers running around the world, engaged in murder and mayhem, and the media has reporters covering them. The reporter and the case officer both have bosses, and the higher you get in each organization, the closer the bosses become. The ideological guidelines get more restrictive the higher up you go. To join the CIA, you have to pass a psychological assessment test. They're not going to hire anybody who is sympathetic towards poor people. These are ruthless people who serve capitalist bosses. They're very rightwing, and the media's job is to protect them. Editors only hire reporters who are ideologically pure, just like you can't get into the CIA if you're a Communist or think the CIA should obey the law.

It's the same thing in the media. You can't get a job at CNN if you sympathize with the Palestinians or report how Israel has been stealing their land for 67 years. The minute you say something that is an anathema or upsets the Israelis, you're out. The people who enforce these ideological restraints are the editors and the publishers. For example, while covering the merciless Israeli bombardment of civilians in Gaza in 2014, Diana Magnay was harassed and threatened by a group of bloodthirsty Israelis who were cheering the slaughter. Disgusted, Magnay later referred to them as "scum" in a tweet. She was forced to apologize, transferred to Moscow, and banished forever from Israel.[1]

In a similar case, NBC correspondent Ayman Mohyeldin was playing soccer with four young boys in Gaza when Israel shelled the playing field. Mohyeldin witnessed their murders, which he reported in a series of tweets. Without ever providing a reason, NBC pulled Mohyeldin from Gaza and prevented him from ever returning. NBC replaced Mohyeldin with Israeli sympathizer Richard Engel.

Any dictator would be happy with the way American media is organized. The minute you step out of the box, they fire you or send you off to Siberia. It's a homogenous system. Not just the media and CIA, but politicians too. As the 2016 primaries proved, you can't be a candidate for either party unless you pass the ideological test. You must be a freewheeling capitalist. You must support Israel with billions of tax payer dollars. You must give the military whatever weapons it wants. That's the nature of the American state. These things naturally work together because that is the way it has been structured for 240 years.

JIMENEZ: We've seen pseudo alternatives emerge in the Internet posing as adversarial or anti-establishment when they're anything but. We've seen this growing trend, and it's something to be mindful of as we look for these sources on the Internet.

VALENTINE: The Internet is a free for all, so you have to approach it the way any enlightened person approaches every part of America, which is buyer beware. Capitalism is not designed to protect poor people or make sure people lead healthy, fulfilling lives. It's designed to make sure the super-rich can steal from the poor. There's only so much wealth and the rich want it.

The rich want to monopolize information too. Is a particular piece of information on the Internet coming from a reliable source? Who knows? Just because some of it is true doesn't mean that all of it is true. To be able to discern whether the information is accurate or complete, you must be grounded in the reality that the capitalist system and all its facets are organized to oppress you, keep you in the dark and off balance as much as possible. It's a game of wits and you've got to be smart about it. Buyer beware.

JIMENEZ: Exactly. Now I'd like to talk about the recent organizational changes in the CIA. It stems from an article in The *Washington Post* by Greg Miller. The headline is "CIA Director John Brennan Considering Sweeping Organizational Changes." What the article is saying is that Brennan wants to restructure the CIA using the model of their Counterterrorism Center; merging different units and divisions, combining analysts with operatives into hybrid teams that will focus on specific regions of the world. This sounds to me like the organizational changes that were born out of Phoenix and that were exported to other parts of the world over the years. The CIA appears to be applying the same structure to all of its operations. Is that how you read this?

VALENTINE: Yes, and it's something that, from my perspective, was predictable, which is why *The Phoenix Program* was re-released now, because what I predicted 25 years ago has happened. And you can only predict if you know the history.

The CIA initially, and for decades, had four directorates under an executive management staff: Administration, Intelligence, Operations, and Science and Technology. Executive management had staff for congressional liaison, legal issues, security, public relations, inspections, etc. Administration is just that: staff for finance, personnel, and support services like interrogators, translators and construction companies. Science and Technology is self-explanatory too, but with a typical CIA twist – science for the CIA means better ways to kill and control people, like the MKULTRA program. And now there's a fifth directorate, Digital, that keystrokes and hacks foreign governments and corporations.

The Operations people overthrew foreign governments the old fashioned way, through sabotage and subversion. The Operations Directorate is now the National Clandestine Service. The Intelligence Directorate, which is now called Analysis, studied political, economic and social trends around the world so that executive management could mount better operations to control them.

The Operations Directorate was divided into several branches. The Counterintelligence (CI) branch detected foreign spies. Foreign Intelligence (FI) staff "liaison" officers worked with secret policemen and other officials in foreign nations. They collected "positive intelligence" by eavesdropping or by recruiting agents. The Covert Action branch engaged in deniable political action. The Special Operations Division (now the Special Activities Division) supplied paramilitary officers. There was also a Political and Psychological branch that specialized in all forms of propaganda.

These branches and directorates were career paths for operations officers (operators) assigned to geographical divisions. An FI staff officer might spend his or her entire career in the Far East Asia Division. The managers could move people around, but those things, generally speaking, were in place when the CIA began.

The events that led to the formation of the current Counterterrorism Center began in 1967, when US security services began to suspect that the Cubans and the Soviets were infiltrating the anti-war movement. Lyndon Johnson wanted to know the details, so his attorney general, Ramsay Clark, formed the Interdepartmental Intelligence Unit (IDIU) within the Department of Justice. The IDIU's job was to coordinate the elements of the CIA, FBI and military that were investigating dissenters. The White House wanted to control and provide political direction to these investigations.

The Phoenix program was created simultaneously in 1967 and did the same thing in Vietnam; it brought together 25 agencies and aimed them at civilians in the insurgency. It's political warfare. It's secret. It's against the rules of war. It violated the Geneva Conventions. It's what Homeland Security does in the US: bringing agencies together and focusing them on civilians who look like terrorists.

The goal of this kind of bureaucratic centralization is to improve intelligence collection and analysis so reaction forces can leap into the breach more quickly and effectively. In 1967, the CIA already had computer experts who were traveling around by jet. The world was getting smaller and the CIA, which had all the cutting edge technology, was way out in front. It hired Ivy Leaguers like Nelson Brickham to make the machine run smoothly.

Brickham, as I've explained elsewhere, was the Foreign Intelligence staff officer who organized the Phoenix program based on principles Rensis Likert articulated in his book *New Patterns of Management*. Brickham believed he could use reporting formats as a tool to shape the behavior of CIA officers in the field. In particular, he hoped to correct "the grave problem of distortion and cover-up which a reporting system must address."

Likert organized industries to be adaptable, and the CIA organized itself the same way. It was always reorganizing itself to adapt to new threats. And in 1967, while Brickham was forming Phoenix to neutralize the leaders of the insurgency in South Vietnam, James Angleton and the CIA's Counteriintelligence staff were creating the MHCHAOS program in Langley, Virginia, to spy on members of the anti-war movement, and turn as many of them as possible into double agents.

Chaos was the codename for the Special Operations Group within Angleton's Counterintelligence staff. The CIA's current Counterterrorism Center, which was established in 1986, is a direct descendent of Chaos.

Starting in 1967, White House political cadres, through the IDIU in the Justice Department, coordinated the CIA's Chaos program, the FBI's COINTELPRO Program, and the military's domestic spying programs. When Nixon took office in January 1969, he immediately grasped the partisan political potential of the IDIU and these various domestic spying programs. The Nixon White House expanded Chaos and assigned its chief, Richard Ober, a deputy and a case officer. The Chaos staff occupied a vault in the basement at CIA headquarters in Virginia. It had a room where files were kept and where slides of suspects and potential recruits were viewed. A group of female secretaries managed the super-secret files.

Chaos was super-secret because it was illegal for the CIA to engage in domestic operations. Assignment to it was considered a "command performance." There was a communications system exclusively for Chaos cables and couriers to CIA stations overseas. The Chaos "back-channel" could by-pass the division chiefs and station chiefs and work directly with its unilateral assets in a country. Chaos "traffic" had the highest security classification, was restricted to only those officers involved in the operation, and was inaccessible to everyone but the CIA's top administrators.

In October 1969, based on names provided by the FBI, the Chaos case officer began recruiting double agents from the Black Power and anti-war movements. I never learned his name, but the case officer only approached people with "radical" credentials. Radicals who passed polygraph and psychological assessment tests were recruited, trained in the clandestine arts, supplied with gadgetry and cash, given a cover, and sent overseas. The case officer called his 40-50 double agents "dangles" because their job was to act like normal radicals and hope that a gullible KGB agent would make an approach.

Chaos dangles also spied and reported on their American colleagues. That's the illegal domestic part. A folder was created for each dissident. The folder contained the dissident's 201 "personality" file from the FBI, and included everything from arrest records to report cards to surreptitious photos taken of the person with other radicals. Some 7,000 -10,000 hard files were eventually assembled.

In 1970 the Chaos squad started entering its information on radicals onto IBM cards and compiling it in a data base codenamed HYDRA that ultimately contained the names of some 300,000 people. HYDRA was developed domestically at the same time as the Phoenix information system (PHMIS) in Vietnam, by the same people. Chaos included a mail intercept program codenamed HTLINGUAL.

I'm sure the anthrax scare after 9/11 was a CIA provocation designed to justify a mail intercept program similar to HTLINGUAL. All of these things I'm talking about are happening today on a much grander scale within the Muslim American community.

In 1971, the IDIU's Intelligence Evaluation Committee was managed by Robert Mardian, the Nixon Administration's assistant attorney general in charge of Internal Security. The Chaos squad was helping the Pentagon track army deserters, as well as foreign nationals who were trying to coax soldiers to desert from US military bases in Germany. Chaos dangles were sent to North Vietnam and Cuba, and one agent, possibly Timothy Leary, was launched against Eldridge Cleaver in Algeria. Another Chaos agent played a critical though undisclosed role at the May 1971 anti-war demonstrations in Washington. Even Nixon's National Security Advisor, Henry Kissinger, monitored Chaos operations in regard to his secret peace negotiations with the North Vietnamese.

By 1972, the Chaos squad was working with Nixon's infamous Plumbers. One Chaos agent may have been involved in the botched Watergate burglary that brought Nixon down. The mastermind of the burglary, Gordon Liddy, sat on Mardian's Intelligence Evaluation Committee and leveled requirements on CIA officer Richard Ober at Chaos. Liddy and his partner in crime, CIA officer E. Howard Hunt, are known to have directed Ober to spy on members of other government agencies. They also targeted Nixon's political enemies, including people like Daniel Ellsberg who could in no way be considered terrorists. Which gives you an idea of the prominence of political cadres in these operations, and how they used their power to conduct all manner of dirty tricks.

Incredible power was concentrated in the Chaos office. Ober worked with the National Commission on Civil Disorders, the protean Law Enforcement Assistance Administration, and the Special Services units (Red Squads) of America's major metropolitan police departments. The CIA has always recruited cops as contractors to organize and advise foreign police forces, and local police forces certainly helped the CIA amass its Chaos files. As head of the Counterintelligence staff, James Angleton was the CIA's official contact with all federal law enforcement agencies, including the Bureau of Narcotics.

Chaos exemplifies how the White House, through the CIA's network of law enforcement contacts, could use the Homeland Security apparatus as a cover to conduct all manner of illegal domestic operations. It shows how the CIA could use participating Homeland Security agencies for its own insidious institutional purposes, and that individuals like Hunt and Liddy could exploit it for partisan political purposes.

Hunt and Liddy's many misadventures resulted in the Watergate scandal, which cast a bright light on CIA's shenanigans and eventually led to the exposure of the Chaos squad. William Colby was the CIA's Executive Director at the time. Colby had returned to the United States in 1971 to testify to Congress about Phoenix, and had stayed on to take charge of the CIA's organizational affairs. After the arrest of the Watergate burglars, Colby worked with the Justice Department to have the IDIU abolished, and he made sure the Chaos "case officer" was reassigned but not disciplined.

After he became Director of Central Intelligence in September 1973, Colby personally minimized the damage by leaking some of the gory Chaos details to Seymour Hersh. Colby also sacrificed his bitter rival James Angleton, who as chief of Counterintelligence was held responsible for Chaos and the mail intercept program. Colby's "limited hangout" and scapegoating of Angleton were part of a shell game, however, and the Chaos squad continued to track radicals and respond to FBI and military requirements. Everything was the same as before, including the ultra-secure communications system and restricted filing system, except that now, and from then on, it was done under the aegis of counterterrorism.

Colby started the ball rolling in July 1972 when he made Ober chief of the CIA's International Terrorism Group (ITG). Ober's new job was to set up and manage a "central program" on international terrorism and airplane hijackings. Building on the Chaos files, the ITG started penetrating terrorist training camps in Algeria and Libya. It kept track of black militants with international connections, and its reports, like Chaos reports, were sent to Kissinger at the National Security Council.

Ober's appointment as chief of ITG coincided with the establishment of Nixon's Cabinet Committee to Combat Terrorism, the first US Government entity of its kind.

After the official termination of Chaos in March 1974, the ITG continued to occupy the same space in the CIA's basement. A new ITG chief was assigned and was assisted by the same female secretaries who kept updating the Chaos files and computer tapes. As of 1975, no Chaos files had been destroyed, because the CIA could not adequately define a "dissident."

In 1977, veteran CIA officer Howard Bane became the third ITG chief. The notion of state-sponsored terrorism had emerged and was attributed to Libya and Iraq, both of which were said to have Soviet backing. As a result, Jimmy Carter's DCI, Stansfield Turner, directed Bane to organize the CIA against this new threat.

According to Bane, counterterrorism was a "hot potato" but a "low priority" because of ongoing Congressional investigations into CIA abuses. Bane said Turner was "hung up" on the legal definition of terror. Turner insisted that CIA officers refer to counterinsurgency as "low intensity warfare," and in his effort to polish the CIA's image, Turner renamed the ITG the Office of Terrorism.

Again, it was a shell game. Bane moved into the Chaos/ITG space in Langley's basement. He described it as a windowless room as large as the ground floor of a house, divided into cubicles. "There were ten or twelve little old ladies running around in tennis shoes," he said.

Operations were compartmentalized and there was a "vault mentality." Little was happening. The acting chief was the former ITG operations officer and his job was following US citizens overseas.

An avid proponent of covert action, Bane had served as chief of the CIA's North Africa Division and in other top operational posts. He was nearing retirement and approached his new assignment with the fervor of a man seeking to enshrine his legacy. He summoned everyone to a staff meeting and said, "Let's advertise ourselves to divisions." He set up a reference system to service each of the CIA's divisions, and each "little old lady" became an expert on a specific geographical area.

Bane started meeting with his counterparts at State, Treasury, the FBI, the Pentagon, the White House and the NSA. As the Office of Terrorism began to serve a visible function, he moved the office to a fourth floor suite with windows. He was given an operations officer and recruited young men to replace the older women as his liaison officers to the divisions. He began working with Jim Glerum, the chief of the CIA's Special Operations Division,[2] to beef up the paramilitary operational forces at his command.

Meanwhile, the US Army had created Delta Force to respond to the well-publicized terrorist incidents that occurred in the 1970s. Delta and later the Navy's SEAL Team Six served as the CIA's vanguard in the nascent War on Terror. Within the context of "low intensity warfare", the Office of Terrorism and its paramilitary units adopted a new lexicon in which "anti-terrorism" was the term for broad policy, and "counterterrorism" applied to specific, immediate actions.

Bane got a bigger budget and high tech gadgets like silenced weapons and bugging equipment for use in hostage rescue operations. He acquired a fleet of black choppers and formed a Crisis Management Training Program team, composed of a psychiatrist and a few case officers, which advised US and foreign law enforcement officers on how to negotiate with terrorists.

Bane set up a two-man intelligence unit at Delta headquarters at Fort Bragg, at which point Delta became a "customer" of CIA intelligence. Bane's Office of Terrorism sent daily reports profiling known terrorists and their activities to the Defense Intelligence Agency and the FBI. Very quietly his unit began to coordinate actual counter-terror operations. "Say someone in Frankfurt had access to the Red Army," Bane explained. "Then Delta would send a team."

Bane's Office of Terrorism handled each incident on a case-by-case basis, depending on whether it was defined as "international terrorism" (meaning the terrorists crossed borders or had foreign support) or "domestic terrorism" if terrorists were operating within their own country. If the incident related to domestic terrorism, the Office of Terrorism could not get involved, unless authorized through a presidential executive order called a "finding."

The need for a finding was a stumbling block. Bane cited the time Colombia's M19 terror group took 20 foreign diplomats, including the US ambassador, hostage at a party at the Dominican Embassy. Thinking the transnational nature of the incident qualified it as "international terror," Bane, with the approval of the State Department's terrorism unit, launched a Delta operation in conjunction with the CIA's new SOD chief, Rudy Enders. Bane provided intelligence on the terrorists, while Enders provided Delta with the equipment it needed to stage a rescue operation. Meanwhile the Crisis Management Team assembled in Florida and prepared to jump into Colombia.

But the operation came to a screeching halt when the CIA's Assistant Deputy Director of Operations, John Stein, revealed the operation to Turner's Deputy Director of Operations, John McMahon. As Bane recalled, McMahon asked him, "Are you trying to send us all to jail?" McMahon put the operation on hold and Bane was forced to call his officers back to Langley where they waited while "the lawyers" met with Carter's National Security Council staff. Only after the lawyers gave their approval did Carter issue the required "finding."

In another instance, Bane was not allowed to mount an operation to rescue Italy's Prime Minister Aldo Moro. According to Bane, his superiors determined that Moro's captors were Italian nationals and thus were deemed to be operating domestically.

Let me stress that all this was happening within the context of the Cold War. The Office of Terrorism was a feature of the broader "low intensity warfare" strategy designed to thwart Soviet "aggression" in Third World countries like El Salvador. Not until 4 November 1979, and the takeover of the American Embassy in Tehran, did the context start to change. This seminal event marked the emergence of Islamic "fundamentalists" as America's new bête noire. (And it allowed Ronald Reagan to crush Jimmy Carter in the 1980 presidential election.)

In the wake of the Embassy takeover, Carter ordered Bane and the CIA's Office of Terrorism to work with Delta Force to rescue the 53 hostages. Bane told me the plan was based on a covert action plan to obtain "current intelligence" on the status of the hostages, including Tom Ahern, the CIA's station chief in Tehran.[3] Bane needed this information to know where to direct what he called "the black and gray propaganda necessary to disguise the CIA's actual intentions." There was also a need to quickly train Delta Force to operate in the Iranian desert.

The needed intelligence was obtained, but the government's first major counterterror operation, the Desert One rescue mission, failed to get off the ground. Several aircraft malfunctioned and one crashed on 25 April 1980, killing eight soldiers. As with the Benghazi tragedy, Republican politicians jumped for joy at the chance to criticize Democrats; the hostage crisis dragged on for six months and enabled Reagan to characterize Jimmy Carter as weak, which means instant death for any American politician.

There was other collateral damage as well. Reagan's flamboyant Director of Central Intelligence, William Casey, fired Bane and replaced him with William Buckley, a veteran CIA officer who had served several tours in Vietnam. From 1969-1971, under his patron Ted Shackley, Buckley had directed the CIA's national counterterror program in Vietnam.

In April 1981, Casey and Buckley traveled together to Saudi Arabia to pave the way for the construction of an underground network of secret military bases that would be available to US forces. If the remarks attributed to Osama bin Laden are true, the presence of those bases under Saudi soil was one of the reasons he staged the 1998 Embassy bombings and the 9/11 terror attacks.

The War onTerror took its next Great Leap Forward in October 1981 with the assassination of Egyptian President Sadat by his personal bodyguards, whom Buckley had trained. The assassination nullified the Camp David Accords and freed Israel to target PLO bases in Lebanon. In May 1982, Israeli assets in the fascist Christian Phalange militia organized one of the greatest acts of terror of all time – the massacre of hundreds of Palestinians in the Sabra and Shatila refugee camps.

In August 1982 Buckley returned to CIA headquarters to coordinate anti-terrorism policy through the Domestic Terrorism Group. Meanwhile, Casey appointed veteran CIA officer David Whipple as the CIA's National Intelligence Officer (NIO) for counterterrorism. A veteran operations officer with extensive service in the Far East, Whipple had been serving as CIA station chief in Switzerland.

Whipple told me that Casey's executive staff consisted of

16 NIOs; eight handled geographical divisions, while the other eight handled issues like narcotics, nuclear weapons, and in Whipple's case, terrorism. Under Casey's direction, every government agency established a counterterror office as part of a secret apparatus. Whipple as NIO coordinated the CT offices and assisted the CIA's division chiefs, making sure their station chiefs were properly handling counterterror issues in their area of operations.

Whipple ran the Office of Domestic Terrorism (ODT) from 1982 until 1986. His staff included an operations chief, intelligence analysts, photo interpreters, and case officers.[4] Because it had the authority to access any division's files and co-opt its penetration agents, the ODT was resisted by the divisions – especially the Near East Division, which was on the front lines of the War on Terror.

As you can see, the evolution of "offices" and later "centers" that transcended and coordinated the CIA's divisions was well underway by 1982. Throughout this early stage of its evolution, the CIA's terrorism office retained the legal authority to conduct unilateral domestic operations for a specific period of time before being required to notify and involve the FBI. (The guidelines are more honored in the breach than the observance, I'm sure.) The ODT also maintained the super-secret communications system instituted during Chaos that by-passed the CIA's normal chains of command.

As part of this back-channel "counterterror network", Casey recruited Oliver North, a doe-eyed Marine lieutenant colonel assigned to the National Security Council (NSC). Whipple served as North's case officer in the monumental political misadventures North embarked upon.

Cut from the same fascist cloth as his ideological forefathers Hunt and Liddy, North formed a crisis management center along with REX 84, "a plan to suspend the Constitution in the event of a national crisis such as nuclear war, violent and widespread internal dissent, or national opposition to a U.S. military invasion abroad."[5] North's plan called for "the round-up and internment of large numbers of both domestic dissidents (some 26,000) and aliens (3,000 – 4,000), in camps such as the one in Oakdale, Louisiana."[6]

Certain trusted members of Congress were witting (despite that august body's periodic protestations that the CIA operates as a "rogue elephant") and Senator Daniel Inouye cut off all debate about North's plan to suspend the Constitution when the subject was raised during the televised Iran-Contra Hearings in 1987.

In April 1984, North created the Terrorist Incident Working Group (TIWG) specifically to rescue several American hostages held in Lebanon, including the aforementioned William Buckley, who had been kidnapped the month before. North became TIWG's chairman and in October 1985 managed its first successful operation – the capture of the hijackers of the Achille Lauro.

A few months earlier, after the June 1985 hijacking of TWA Flight 847 while it was flying from Athens to Beirut, George H. W. Bush had created the Vice President's Task Force on Combating Terrorism. As the NSC's liaison to the Task Force, "North drafted a secret annex for its report which institutionalized and expanded his counterterrorist powers, making himself the NSC coordinator of all counterterrorist actions."[7]

North continued to acquire greater and greater powers, and on 20 January 1986, National Security Decision Directive 207 made him "chief coordinator" of Casey's secret counterterror network through the Office to Combat Terrorism (OCT). Working through the NSC's Operations Sub-Group, North coordinated the back-channel CT network with Major General Richard Secord's "off-the-shelf" Enterprise in a series of illegal operations. Among them were Israel's facilitation of arms sales to Iran; American civilians supplying arms to the Contras; and Contra drug smuggling into America.

North also planned for the repression of domestic dissent and criticism. As P. D. Scott has noted, "the Office to Combat Terrorism became the means whereby North could coordinate the propaganda activities of Carl "Spitz" Channel and Richard Miller (and) the closing of potential embarrassing investigations by other government agencies."[8]

The evolution climaxed in 1986 with the creation of the Counter-Terror Center under Duane Clarridge. Yet another right wing ideologue, Clarridge had been chief of the CIA's station in Turkey in the late 1960s and early 1970s, when the fascist Grey Wolves went on a terror rampage, bombing and killing thousands of public officials, journalists, students, lawyers, labor organizers, social democrats, left-wing activists and Kurds. Since then, Turkey's military has been one of America's strongest allies, despite the recent coup attempt staged by the America-based, CIA-connected exile, Fethullah Gülen.

A body-builder and scion of the old boy clique that runs the CIA, Clarridge was chief of Latin America Division from 1981 until 1984, when Nicaraguan harbors were mined and the CIA's "murder manual" was distributed to the Contras. Clarridge helped Secord's off-the-shelf

Enterprise move PLO weapons captured by Israeli forces during their bloody invasion of Lebanon, through Manuel Noriega in Panama, to the Contras. That's the kind of stuff the CT Center still does today; moving weapons from chaotic places like Benghazi in Libya, to deniable terrorist surrogates in Syria.

As chief of the Europe Division, Clarridge had also provided the back channel in Lisbon that Secord's Enterprise used to sell HAWK and TOW missiles to the Iranians, in exchange for the release of American hostages. According to Scott, "The intrigues of North, Secord, Clarridge and (Robert) Oakley (at the State Department) at this point showed a concern for politics rather than security."[9]

When I interviewed him, Clarridge described the CT Center, which has coordinated CIA back-channel activities since 1986, as a central unit with members from the directorates operating under a committee at the National Security Council. With input from the division chiefs, the CT Center "divines" (as he put it) anti-terrorism policy and then "constructs entities" that conduct operations. It is not a function of US Special Forces, as often portrayed in the media, but of CIA "action teams" trained to capture suspected terrorists and bring them to the United States to stand trial.

During his tenure as CT Center chief from 1986 to 1988, Clarridge worked directly with George H. W. Bush. He was lucky in that regard; Clarridge was indicted on seven counts of lying to Congress, but his case never went to trial, thanks to a last minute pardon Bush issued on 24 December 1992.

When called to task about his crimes, North blamed the peaceniks who lost the Vietnam War. If liberal politicians hadn't investigated the CIA, he argued, then fascists like him wouldn't have had to resort to dirty tricks. North's hatred of the peace movement was palpable. North believed that "the most pressing problem is not in the Third World, but here at home in the struggle for the minds of the people."[10]

North was out of control; when Jack Terrell told the Justice Department that North was involved in Contra drug smuggling, North labeled Terrell a terrorist and sicced the FBI on him. But neither North nor any of the other Iran-Contra criminals were ever punished, because, as Michael McClintock noted at the time, "the very notion of counter-terror as terrorism was forbidden, while circumlocution was the norm."[11]

That's how the CIA's CT Center evolved from the Chaos domestic spying mechanism into the nerve center of the CIA's clandestine staff. Same thing happened with the CIA's Counter-Narcotics Center at the same time. Both are modeled on Phoenix, and both are wonderful tools for White House cadres to exercise political control over the bureaucracies they coordinate. These "centers" are the perfect means for policing and expanding the empire; they make it easier than ever for the CIA to track people and events in every corner of the world. The need for the old-fashioned directorates is fading away. You don't need an entire directorate to understand the political, social and economic movements around the world anymore, because the United States is controlling them all.

The US has color revolutions going everywhere. It's got the World Bank and the IMF strangling countries with debt, like the banks are strangling college students and home owners here. The War on Terror is the best thing that ever happened to US capitalists and their secret police force, the CIA. Terrorism is the pretext that allows the CIA to coordinate and transcend every government agency and civic institution, including the media, to the extent that we don't even see its wars anymore. Its control is so pervasive, so ubiquitous; the CIA has actually become the Phoenix.

JIMENEZ: Right.

VALENTINE: It's the eye of god in the sky; it's able to determine what's going to happen next because it's controlling all of these political, social and economic movements. It pits the Sunnis against the Shiites. It doesn't need slow and outdated directorates. These Phoenix centers enable it to determine events instantaneously anywhere. There are now Counterterror Intelligence Centers all over the world. In Phoenix they were called Intelligence Operations Coordinating Centers. So it's basically exactly the same thing.

It's been evolving that way and everybody on the inside was gearing themselves for this glorious moment for 30 years. They even have a new staff position called Targeting Officers. You can Google this.

JIMENEZ: Right, right, exactly.

VALENTINE: The centers represent the unification of military, intelligence and media operations under political control. White House political appointees oversee them, but the determinant force is the CIA careerists who slither into private industry when their careers are over. They form the consulting firms that direct the corporations that drive the empire. Through their informal "old boy" network, the CIA guys and gals keep America at war so they can make a million dollars when their civil service career is over.

JIMENEZ: The *Washington Post* and subsequent articles frame it as if these changes are drastic. But to hear you, it's a natural progression. So what does this announcement mean? Is the CIA putting out their own press release through the *Washington Post* just to give everyone the heads up?

VALENTINE: Well, everybody in the CIA was worried that if the directorates were reorganized, it would negatively affect their careers. But executive management usually does what its political bosses tell them to do, and Brennan reorganized in 2015. He created a fifth directorate, the Directorate for Digital Innovation (DDI) ostensibly as the CIA's "mantelpiece". But, as the *Washington Times* reported, "it is the formation of the new 'mission' centers – including ones for counterintelligence, weapons and counter-proliferation, and counterterrorism – that is most likely to shake up the agency's personnel around the world."[12]

The CIA's "ten new Mission Centers" are designed to "serve as locations to integrate capabilities and bring the full range of CIA's operational, analytic, support, technical and digital skillsets to bear against the nation's most pressing national security problems."[13]

This modernization means the CIA is better able to control people politically, starting with its own officers, then everyone else. That's the ultimate goal. Politicians, speaking in a unified voice, create the illusion of a crime-fighting CIA and an America with a responsibility to protect benighted foreigners from themselves. But they can't tell you what the CIA does, because it's all illegal.

Well, it's all a lie. In order for the politicians to hold office, they have to cover for the CIA. Their concern is how to explain the reorganization and exploit it. They squabble among themselves and cut the best deals possible.

JIMENEZ: That makes complete sense. Talking about all the illegal activity the CIA is involved in, I couldn't help but think of the drug running. I'd like to point out to our listeners the article you wrote, which offers everything they ought to know as far as the history of the CIA in drugs. It's entitled, "The CIA and Drugs: A Covert History" (Counterpunch, 7 November 2014).

Meanwhile, I'd like to hear your opinion on the influence of counterterrorism and counterinsurgency tactics in local law enforcement. Local police departments are adopting many of the same tactics. We're seeing the US government use counterterrorism and counterinsurgency tactics against its own people. Perhaps one of the most vivid examples is what happened in Ferguson, Missouri. Is that too a natural progression of Phoenix?

VALENTINE: Absolutely. The very last paragraph in my book *The Phoenix Program* says you'll know the Phoenix has arrived when you start seeing police forces advancing on protestors in paramilitary formations, and driving around in armored vehicles.

That's what the CIA does in foreign nations; it militarizes police forces so it can control that country's political, economic and social movements. The CIA's influence is pervasive here, too; it advises all the major police departments in the US. The Phoenix model of coordinating agencies happens under the "cognizance" of the CIA, because the premier threat is a terrorist infiltrating the US with nukes. It goes back to Chaos thinking: maybe ISIS is recruiting black radicals in Ferguson. If so, we need paramilitary police forces and administrative detention laws to neutralize them. The Missouri governor can say a protester in Ferguson is violating national security laws and hold him indefinitely.

The media loves it. FOX News said the Black Lives protesters were holding "us" (meaning white people) hostage. If it's a hostage situation, they're terrorists. Tucker Carlson said (I paraphrase), "You can talk about race all you want. It's a hostage situation and race doesn't matter."

So the racists in government and law enforcement are elated. Now they can send in provocateurs (maybe an Afghanistan veteran like Dallas shooter Micah Johnson, who got wiped out by a robot carrying a Claymore mine) and start riots and crush the protestors because they're terrorists. And that's how, over the last 40 years, dissent has come to equal terrorism. It's how the one percent wants us to see non-violent protest. They want the public to believe that anybody who resists law enforcement is a terrorist. All the pieces have been put in place, through the corporate media, to make the lies seem true. These Counterterror

Intelligence Centers are already operating in the United States through the Department of Homeland Security's fusion centers, which do the same thing.

JIMENEZ: Exactly.

VALENTINE: The American empire consists of hundreds of military bases and a CIA station in every country. It's Pepsi being sold in Vietnam. "We are the world." It's not just 50 states and a few protectorates. It's crazy for average Americans to think their fate is not directly connected to the fate of every other person in the world, or that the one percent considers them higher-class peasants than the other worker bees elsewhere around the world.

There are diminishing resources and other strategic problems that the CIA is forecasting 20 years into the future. It's planning stratospheric aerosol injections to cure climate change. The reorganization of the CIA is another incremental step in anticipation of America reaching that tipping point. Gated communities are the future; the centers replicate them.

JIMENEZ: Indeed. Something you said just now really struck me. And that's the way that Americans separate themselves from the Other. It reminds me of these arguments we hear in the media regarding the use of militarized police. It's okay in Afghanistan, but not in Ferguson. The use of Predator drones to kill somebody in Yemen is okay, but not in Montana. It's murder either way, but most of the American public doesn't see it that way. We can discuss this, but unless the American people do something to change this, then we run the risk of these things just becoming normal and accepted. For example, the CIA's drug running now we see in feature films, in Hollywood productions.

VALENTINE: They think, "Well, that's what the CIA does, everybody knows it." If you watch a pro football game, you know the US military owns the NFL. There's F-14s flying over the stadiums. Every spectator has to stand and salute and plant a big wet kiss on the military's fat bloated butt.

In my opinion, what it will take is for the men and women in the military to realize they're part of a self-defeating enterprise. Before you can change the CIA, you have to change some other things. You have to shrink the military establishment and end the war on drugs, which can be done. When given the chance in state referendums, people are voting for medical marijuana and adult recreational use.

When given a chance to vote, people express common sense. Marijuana is not going to make you go out and massacre school kids or abortion providers. That happens because we live in a country that glorifies the god of violence and his sacred warriors.

Demilitarizing American society is a start, like decriminalizing marijuana is a first step in ending the war on drugs. It's easier than challenging an arcane thing like the CIA that's covered with grey and black propaganda. It's hard for people to understand how huge bureaucratic systems work together. They get frustrated and vote to leave the European Union, or they cling to Trump or Clinton, thinking things will change.

Maybe next year all the students will default on their loans and bring the system down. Maybe they'll say to hell with the bankers for mortgaging my future. We're taking it back. If something like that can happen, if that kind of consciousness can spread among young people being held in economic bondage and groomed to administer the empire, then there's hope. If they see they have nothing to lose, they'll come together and start making a fuss.

JIMENEZ: That would be something to behold.

VALENTINE: You have to use your imagination.

PART II

HOW THE CIA CO-OPTED AND MANAGES THE WAR ON DRUGS

"The whole history of spectacular society called for the secret services to play the pivotal role; because it is in them that the characteristics and means of execution of such a society are concentrated to the highest degree."

Guy Debord, Comments on The Society of the Spectacle

Chapter 12

CREATING A CRIME: HOW THE CIA COMMANDEERED THE DRUG ENFORCEMENT ADMINISTRATION

The outlawing of narcotic drugs at the start of the 20th century coincided with Secretary of State John Hay's "Open Door" policy toward China. This is one of the ironies of American history, given that the Open Door policy originated with Great Britain's First Opium War (1839–1842) against China.

At the time, the British insisted that "free trade" civilized the world by making it wealthier. Free trade, they said, gave them the divine right to push Indian opium on China in exchange for tea. They shared this principle with Confederate Americans who fought for their "right" to own slaves.

America's "Open Door" policy placed it in competition with the world's other imperial powers. From that point on, the federal government was committed to maintain, through military might, open markets in every nation in the world on behalf of American businesses.

Not coincidentally, the outlawing of narcotic drugs turned the issue of addiction from a matter of "public health" into a pretext for expanding police forces and reorganizing the criminal justice and social welfare systems. The new health care industry was placed in the hands of businessmen seeking profits at the expense of despised minorities, the poor and working classes.

Private businesses established civic institutions to sanctify this policy. Public educators developed curriculums that doubled as political indoctrination promoting the Business Party line. Bureaucracies were established to promote the expansion of corporate interests abroad, while suppressing resistance to the oligarchy that benefited from it.

It takes a library full of books to explain the economic foundations of the war on drugs, and the reasons for America's laissez faire regulation of its medical, pharmaceutical and drug manufacturing industries. Suffice it to say that investors used the government to unleash and transform their economic power into political and military might; and by World War Two, the "free trade world" was relying on the United States for its opium derivatives, under the guardianship of Harry Anslinger, the Commissioner of the Federal Bureau of Narcotics (FBN).

Narcotic drugs are a strategic resource, and when Anslinger learned that Peru had built a cocaine factory, he unilaterally confiscated its stash before it could be sold to Germany or Japan. In another instance, Anslinger and his counterpart at the State Department prevented a drug manufacturer in Argentina from selling drugs to Germany.

At the same time, according to Douglas Clark Kinder, Anslinger permitted "an American company to ship drugs to Southeast Asia despite receiving intelligence reports that French authorities were permitting opiate smuggling into China and collaborating with Japanese drug traffickers."[1]

Federal drug law enforcement's relationship with the espionage establishment matured with the creation of the Office of Strategic Services (OSS). Prior to World War Two, the FBN was the government agency most adept at conducting covert operations at home and abroad. As a result, OSS chief William Donovan asked his friend Harry Anslinger to provide senior FBN agents to help organize the OSS. FBN agents trained OSS agents to manage agent networks, engage in sabotage and subversion, and work undercover to avoid security forces in hostile nations.

The relationship grew during the war when FBN executives and agents assisted OSS scientists in "truth drug" experiments involving marijuana. The "extra-legal" nature of the relationship continued after the war: when the CIA decided to test LSD on unsuspecting American citizens, FBN agents were chosen to operate the CIA safe houses where the experiments were conducted.[2]

The relationship was formalized overseas in 1951, when Agent

Charlie Siragusa opened an office in Rome and began to develop the FBN's foreign operations. In the 1950s, FBN agents posted overseas spent half their time doing "favors" for the CIA, such as investigating diversions of strategic materials and Marshall Plan largesse behind the Iron Curtain. A handful of FBN agents were actually recruited into the CIA while maintaining their FBN credentials as cover.

Officially, FBN agents set limits. Siragusa, for example, claimed to object when the CIA asked him to mount a "controlled delivery" into the US as a way of identifying the American members of a smuggling ring with Communist affiliations. In his autobiography, Siragusa said, "The FBN could never knowingly allow two pounds of heroin to be delivered into the United States and be pushed to Mafia customers in the New York City area, even if in the long run we could seize a bigger haul."[3]

In 1960 the CIA asked Siragusa to recruit assassins from his stable of underworld contacts. Siragusa again claimed to have refused. But Mafia drug traffickers, including most prominently Santo Trafficante Jr, were soon participating in CIA attempts to assassinate Fidel Castro.

Siragusa did open a CIA safe house in 1960. FBN agents in New York maintained the MKULTRA "pad" and used it to make cases and debrief informants. When the CIA wanted to use the pad, it would call the district supervisor in New York City and tell him to keep the agents away for a few days.

FBN Agent Arthur Fluhr served as New York District Supervisor George Belk's administrative assistant from 1963-1968. As Fluhr recalled, "Belk was given a CIA contract. George said that he never actually met anyone from the CIA, but that Siragusa told him to cooperate if and when he was contacted. Later the CIA did call. They told Belk: You'll have this checking account, but don't write any checks other than for rent and the maintenance of the 13th Street apartment."

The CIA used Belk's account – which at times held a million dollars and at other times was empty – as a slush fund for foreign officials on its payroll. "Sometimes we were told to baby sit people for the CIA while they were in town," Fluhr said. "One time it was a group of Burmese generals. They came for a few days and when they weren't at the UN, they used the money in Belk's account to go on a shopping spree. They went down to the electronics shops on Canal Street and filled suitcases full of stuff."

The CIA chaperoned the visiting Burmese generals through

Customs without their bags being checked. One can imagine what they brought into New York City in those same suitcases.

The CIA used the safe houses to conduct all manner of illegal domestic operations behind the FBI's back. Indeed, in the course of investigating illegal FBI wiretaps in January 1967, Senator Edward Long learned that the FBN was managing the CIA's safe houses. No one in Congress knew about it. Treasury officials held meetings with the CIA's Assistant Deputy Director of Plans, Desmond FitzGerald, and MKULTRA boss Sid Gottlieb. After a few days of dissembling, Gottlieb admitted that the CIA had used the pads to obtain information "which was of obvious interest to us in connection with our own investigative work."[4]

That particular pad was shut down. "We gave the furniture to the Salvation Army," Fluhr recalled, "and took the drapes off the windows and put them up in our office."

And FBN Agent Andrew Tartaglino opened a more luxurious CIA safe house on Sutton Place.

As the dominant partner in the relationship, the CIA exploited its affinity with the FBN. "Like the CIA," FBN Agent Robert DeFauw explained, "narcotics agents mount covert operations. We pose as members of the narcotics trade. The big difference is that we're in foreign countries legally and through our police and intelligence sources, we can check out just about anyone or anything. Not only that, we're operational. So the CIA jumped in our stirrups."

Jumping into the FBN's stirrups afforded the CIA deniability. To further ensure that the CIA's criminal activities are not revealed to the public, narcotics agents are organized militarily within the sacred chain of command. Highly indoctrinated, they blindly obey on a "need to know" basis. This institutionalized ignorance sustains the illusion of American righteousness, in the name of national security, upon which their motivation to commit all manner of crimes depends.

But, as FBN Agent Martin Pera explained, "If you're successful because you can lie, cheat, and steal, those things become tools you use in the bureaucracy."

Institutionalized corruption originated at headquarters in Washington, where FBN executives provided cover for CIA assets engaged in drug trafficking. In 1966, Agent John Evans was assigned as an assistant to FBN Enforcement Chief John Enright. "And that's when I got to see what the CIA was doing," Evans told me. "I saw a report on the Kuomintang saying they were the biggest drug dealers in the world and that the CIA was underwriting them. Air America was transporting tons of Kuomintang opium." Evans bristled. "I took the report to Enright. He said, 'Leave it here. Forget about it.'

"Other things came to my attention," Evans added, "that proved that the CIA contributed to drug use in America. We were in constant conflict with the CIA because it was hiding its budget in ours, and because CIA people were smuggling drugs into the US. We weren't allowed to tell and that fostered corruption in the Bureau."

Heroin smuggled by "CIA people" into the US was channeled by Mafia distributors primarily to African American communities. Local narcotics agents then targeted disenfranchised blacks as an easy way of subduing or criminalizing them, reducing their community organizing and voting power, and thereby preserving the white ruling class's privileges.

"We didn't need a search warrant," explained former New Orleans narcotics chief Clarence Giarusso. "It allowed us to meet our quota, and it was ongoing. If I find dope on a black man, I can put him in jail for a few days. He's got no money for a lawyer and the courts are ready to convict. There's no expectation on the jury's part that we have to make a case. So rather than go cold turkey, the addict becomes an informant, which means I can make more cases in the neighborhood, which is all we're interested in. We don't care about Carlos Marcello or the Mafia. City cops have no interest in who brings dope in. That's the job of the federal agents."

The Establishment's race and class privileges have always been equated with national security, and FBN executives preserved the social order. Not until 1968 were black FBN agents allowed to become group supervisors and manage white agents.

The war on drugs is a projection of two conditions peculiar to America. First is the institutionalized white supremacy that has defined it since slave owner Thomas Jefferson declared "All men are created equal." Second is the policy of allowing anti-Communist allies to traffic in narcotics. These deniable but official policies reinforce the belief among CIA and drug law enforcement officials that the Bill of Rights is an obstacle to national security.

Blanket immunity from prosecution for bureaucrats who translate these policies into practice fosters corruption in other forms. The FBN's premier "case-making" agents, for example, routinely "created a crime" by breaking and entering, planting evidence, using illegal wiretaps and falsifying reports. They tampered with heroin, transferred it to informants for sale, and even murdered "straight" agents who threatened to expose them.

All of this was known at the highest level of government and in 1965 the Treasury Department launched a corruption investigation of the FBN. Headed by Andrew Tartaglino, the investigation ended in 1968 with the resignation of 32 agents and the indictment of five. That same year the FBN was reconstructed in the Department of Justice as the Bureau of Narcotics and Dangerous Drugs (BNDD).

But, as Tartaglino said to me, dejectedly, "The job was only half done."

The First Infestation

Richard Nixon was elected president based on a vow to restore "law and order" to America. To prove, symbolically, that it intended to keep that promise, the White House launched Operation Intercept along the Mexican border in early 1969. There were, however, unintended consequences; the massive "stop and search" operation so badly damaged relations with Mexico that National Security Advisor Henry Kissinger formed the Ad Hoc Committee on Narcotics (aka the Heroin Committee) to coordinate drug policy and prevent further diplomatic disasters.

The Heroin Committee was composed of cabinet members represented by their deputies. James Ludlum represented CIA Director Richard Helms. A member of the CIA's Counterintelligence staff, reporting directly to James Angleton, Ludlum had been the CIA's liaison officer to the FBN since 1962.

"When Kissinger set up the Heroin Committee," Ludlum recalled, "the CIA certainly didn't take it seriously, because drug control wasn't part of their mission."

As John Evans noted above, and as select members of Congress were aware, the CIA for years had sanctioned the heroin traffic from the Golden Triangle region of Burma, Thailand and Laos into South Vietnam as a way of rewarding top officials for advancing US policies. This reality presented the White House with a dilemma; either curtail the CIA and risk losing the war, or allow tons of heroin to be smuggled into the US for use by rebellious middle-class white kids dabbling in cultural revolution.

Nixon's compromise solution was to make drug law enforcement part of the CIA's mission. This decision forced the CIA to target its clients in South Vietnam. Although reluctant to do so, CIA Director Richard Helms told Ludlum: "We're going to break their rice bowls."

This betrayal occurred incrementally. Fred Dick, the BNDD agent assigned to Saigon, passed the names of complicit South Vietnamese military officers and politicians to the Heroin Committee. But, as Agent Dick recalled, "Ambassador [Ellsworth] Bunker called a meeting in Saigon at which CIA Station Chief Ted Shackley appeared and explained that there was 'a delicate balance.' What he said, in effect, was that no one was willing to do anything."

Meanwhile, to protect its global network of drug trafficking assets, the CIA began infiltrating the BNDD and commandeering its executive management, internal security, intelligence and foreign operations branches. This act of bureaucratic piracy required the placement of CIA officers in influential positions in every federal agency concerned with drug law enforcement.

CIA Officer Paul Van Marx, for example, was assigned as an assistant on narcotics control to the US Ambassador in France. Van Marx thereafter ensured that BNDD conspiracy cases against European traffickers did not compromise CIA operations and assets. He also vetted potential BNDD assets to make sure they were not enemy spies.

The FBN had never had more than 16 agents stationed overseas, but Nixon dramatically increased funding for the BNDD with the result that hundreds of agents were soon posted abroad. The success of these overseas agents depended entirely on CIA intelligence and cooperation, as BNDD Director John Ingersoll understood.

BNDD agents soon felt the sting of CIA involvement in drug law enforcement operations within the United States. Operation Eagle was the flashpoint. Launched in 1970, Eagle targeted anti-Castro Cubans smuggling cocaine from Latin America to the Trafficante crime family in Florida. Of the dozens of Cuban traffickers arrested in June, many were found to be members of Operation 40, a CIA terror organization active in the US, the Caribbean, Mexico, and Central and South America.

Operation 40 was one of several narco-terrorist groups created, funded and directed by the CIA.

The revelation that CIA narco-terrorists were operating within the US led to the assignment of CIA officers as "advisors" to mid-level BNDD enforcement officials, including Latin American Division chief Jerry Strickler. CIA officers tasked to work with the enforcement division served as political cadre; their job was not to make cases, but to protect CIA drug trafficking assets from exposure and prosecution, while facilitating the recruitment of these assets as informants for the BNDD.

Many of the anti-Castro Cuban exiles arrested in Operation Eagle were indeed hired by the BNDD and sent throughout Latin America to expand its operations. They got "fantastic information," Strickler noted. But many were playing a double game.

The Second Infestation

By 1969, Ingersoll's inspections staff had gathered enough evidence to warrant the investigation of several corrupt FBN agents who had risen to management positions in the BNDD. But Ingersoll could not investigate his top managers without subverting the organization's drug investigations. So he asked CIA Director Helms for help building a "counterintelligence" capacity within the BNDD.

The result was Operation Twofold, in which 19 CIA officers were infiltrated into the BNDD to spy on corrupt BNDD officials. According to Chief Inspector Patrick Fuller, "A corporation engaged in law enforcement hired three CIA officers posing as private businessmen to do the contact and interview work."

CIA Officer Jerry Soul, a former Operation 40 case officer, was the primary recruiter. In selecting CIA officers for Twofold, Soul chose junior officers whose careers had stalled due to the reduction of forces in Southeast Asia. Those hired were put through the BNDD's training course and assigned to spy on the BNDD's 16 regional directors. No records were kept and some participants have never been identified.

Chuck Gutensohn was one of several Twofold "torpedoes" I interviewed. Prior to his recruitment into the BNDD, Gutensohn had spent two years at the CIA's base in Pakse, a major heroin transit point between Laos and South Vietnam. "Fuller said that when we communicated, I was to be known as Leo Adams for Los Angeles," Gutensohn said. "He was to be Walter DeCarlo, for Washington, DC."

Gutensohn's cover, however, was blown before he got to Los Angeles. "Someone at headquarters was talking and everyone knew," he recalled. "About a month after I arrived, one of the agents said to me, 'I hear that Pat Fuller signed your credentials'."

Twofold existed at least until 1974 and was deemed by the Rockefeller Commission to have "violated the 1947 Act which prohibits the CIA's participation in law enforcement activities." It also, as shall be discussed later, served as a cover for clandestine CIA operations.[5]

The Third Infestation

The Nixon White House blamed the BNDD's failure to stop international drug trafficking on its feeble intelligence capabilities, a condition that opened the door to further CIA infiltration. In late 1970, CIA Director Helms arranged for his recently retired Chief of Continuing Intelligence, E. Drexel Godfrey, to review BNDD intelligence procedures. Among other things, Godfrey recommended that the BNDD create Regional Intelligence Units (RIUs) and a Strategic Intelligence Office (SIO).

The RIUs were up and running by 1971, with recycled CIA officers assigned as analysts, prompting regular BNDD agents to view the RIUs with suspicion, as repositories for Twofold torpedoes.

The SIO was harder to implement, given its arcane function as a tool to help senior BNDD managers formulate plans and strategies "in the political sphere." As SIO Director John Warner explained, "We needed to understand the political climate in Thailand in order to address the problem. We needed to know what kind of protection the Thai police were affording traffickers. We were looking for an intelligence office that could deal with those sorts of issues, on the ground, overseas."

Organizing the SIO fell to CIA officers Adrian Swain and Tom Tripodi, both of whom were infiltrated into the BNDD. In April 1971, Swain and Tripodi accompanied Ingersoll to Saigon, where they were briefed by Station Chief Ted Shackley. Swain had worked in Laos and Vietnam, and through former CIA contacts, he surreptitiously obtained maps of CIA-protected drug smuggling routes in Southeast Asia.

Upon their return to the US, Swain and Tripodi expressed frustration that the CIA had access to people capable of providing the BNDD with additional intelligence, but these people "were involved in narcotics trafficking and the CIA did not want to identify them."[6]

Seeking a way to finesse the situation, Swain and Tripodi recommended the creation of a "special operations or strategic operations staff" that would function as the BNDD's own CIA "using a backdoor approach to gather intelligence in support of operations." Those operations would rely on "longer range, deep penetration, clandestine assets, who remain undercover, do not appear during the course of any trial and are recruited and directed by the Special Operations agents on a covert basis."[7]

The White House approved the plan in May 1971, along with a $120 million proposal for drug control, of which $50 million was earmarked for BNDD special operations. Three weeks later Nixon declared a "war on drugs," at which point Congress responded with funding for the SIO and authorization for the extra-legal operations Swain and Tripodi envisioned.

Director John Warner was given a seat on the US Intelligence Board so the SIO could obtain raw intelligence from the CIA. But, in return, the SIO was compelled to adopt CIA security procedures; a CIA security officer was assigned to establish the SIO's file room and computer system; safes and steel doors were installed; and witting agents had to obtain CIA clearances.

Three active-duty CIA officers were assigned to the SIO as desk officers for Europe and the Middle East, the Far East, and Latin America. Tripodi was assigned as the SIO's chief of operations. Tripodi, notably, had spent the previous six years in Florida with the CIA's Security Research Services, where his duties included the penetration of peace groups, as well as setting up "notional" private investigation firms to conduct black bag jobs. It is of historical importance that White House "Plumber" E. Howard Hunt inherited Tripodi's Special Operations unit, which included several of the Watergate burglars.

SIO ops chief Tripodi liaised with the CIA on matters of mutual interest, including the covert collection of intelligence outside of routine BNDD channels. As part of his operational plan, code-named Medusa, Tripodi proposed that SIO agents hire foreign nationals to blow up contrabandista planes while they were refueling at clandestine air strips. Another proposal called for ambushing traffickers in America, and taking their drugs and money – which, as I've reported elsewhere and in my books on the subject, case-making agents had been doing for decades, albeit unofficially.[8]

Enter Lucien Conein

The creation of the SIO coincided with the assignment of CIA officer Lucien Conein to the BNDD. As a member of the OSS, Conein had parachuted into France to form resistance cells that included Corsican smugglers. As a CIA officer, Conein in 1954 was assigned to Vietnam to organize anti-Communist forces in the North, and in 1963 he achieved infamy as the intermediary between the Kennedy White House and the cabal of generals that murdered President Diem and his brother Nhu.

In *The Politics of Heroin in Southeast Asia,* historian Alfred McCoy alleged that in 1965, Conein arranged a truce between the CIA and drug trafficking Corsicans in Saigon. Conein apparently knew some of these gangsters from his work with the French resistance. The truce, according to McCoy, allowed the Corsicans to traffic in narcotics as long as they served as contact men for the CIA. The truce also endowed the Corsicans with "free passage" at a time when Marseilles' heroin labs were turning from Turkish to Southeast Asian morphine base.[9]

In a letter to McCoy's publisher, Conein denied McCoy's allegation and insisted that his meeting with the Corsicans was solely to resolve a problem caused by Daniel Ellsberg's "peccadilloes with the mistress of a Corsican."[10]

It is impossible to know who is telling the truth. Ellsberg denies that his CIA friends were involved in drug trafficking; McCoy and all the evidence indicate they were. What is definitely known is that in July 1971, on Howard Hunt's recommendation, the White House hired Conein as an expert on Corsican traffickers in Southeast Asia. Conein was assigned as a consultant to the SIO's Far East Asia desk, then under CIA officer Walter Mackem, a veteran of Vietnam. Conein's activities will be discussed in greater detail.

The Parallel Mechanism

In September 1971, the Heroin Committee was reorganized as the Cabinet Committee for International Narcotics Control (CCINC) under Secretary of State William Rogers. The CCINC's Congressional mandate was to "set policies which relate international considerations to domestic considerations." By 1975, its budget amounted to $875 million and the war on drugs had become a boondoggle for bureaucrats.

Concurrently, the CIA formed a unilateral drug unit in its operations division under Seymour Bolten. Known as the Special Assistant to the Director for the Coordination of Narcotics, Bolten directed CIA division and station chiefs in unilateral drug control operations. In doing this, Bolten worked with Ted Shackley, who in 1972 was appointed head of the CIA's Western Hemisphere Division. Bolten and Shackley had worked together in post-war Germany, as well as in anti-Castro operations, including Operation 40, in the early 1960s. Their collaboration would grease federal drug law enforcement's skid into moral and legal oblivion.

"Bolten screwed us," BNDD's Latin American Division Chief Jerry Strickler said bitterly. "And so did Shackley."

Bolten also screwed the judicial system by setting up a "parallel mechanism" using a computerized register of international drug traffickers and a CIA-staffed communications crew that intercepted calls from drug traffickers in the US to their accomplices around the world. The International Narcotics Information Network (INIS) was modeled on the Phoenix information system (PHMIS) the CIA had used to terrorize the underground resistance in South Vietnam.

Bolten's staff also "re-tooled" dozens of CIA officers and slipped them into the BNDD. Several went to Lou Conein at the SIO for clandestine, highly illegal operations.

Factions within the BNDD, CIA and military were opposed to Bolten's parallel mechanism, but CIA Executive Director William Colby supported Bolten's plan to preempt the BNDD and use its agents and informants for unilateral CIA purposes. The White House also supported the plan for political purposes related to Nixon's reelection. As part of the CIA's secret government, BNDD officials who resisted were expunged; those who cooperated were rewarded.

The Bureau of Narcotics Covert Intelligence Network: BUNCIN

In September 1972, DCI Helms (then immersed in Watergate intrigues), told BNDD Director Ingersoll that the CIA had prepared files on specific drug traffickers in Miami, the Florida Keys and the Caribbean. Helms said the CIA would provide Ingersoll with assets to pursue the traffickers and develop information on tangential targets of opportunity. The CIA would also provide operational, technical, and financial support.

The result was the Bureau of Narcotics Covert Intelligence Network (BUNCIN) whose methodology reflected Tripodi's Medusa Plan and included unconventional warfare tactics like "provocations, inducement to desertion, creating confusion and apprehension."[11]

Some BUNCIN intelligence activities were directed against "senior foreign government officials" and were "blamed on other government agencies or even on the intelligence services of other nations."[12] Other BUNCIN activities were directed against American civic and political groups.

BNDD officials managed BUNCIN's legal activities, while Conein at the SIO managed its extra-legal jobs. According to Conein's administrative deputy, Rich Kobakoff, "BUNCIN was an experiment in how to finesse the law. The end product was intelligence, not seizures or arrests."

CIA officers Robert Medell and William Logay were chosen to manage BUNCIN operations in the field.[13]

A Bay of Pigs veteran born in Cuba, Medell was initially assigned to the Twofold "counterintelligence" program. Medell was BUNCIN's "covert" agent and recruited its agents from the anti-Castro Cuban drug smuggling underworld. All of his assets had previously worked for the CIA, and all understood that they were working for it again.

Medell started running agents in March 1973 with the stated goal of penetrating the Santo Trafficante organization in Florida. To this end the BNDD's Enforcement Chief, Andy Tartaglino, introduced Medell to Sal Caneba, a retired Mafioso who'd been in business with Trafficante in the 1950s.

Caneba in one day identified the head of the Cuban side of the Trafficante family, as well as its organizational structure. But the CIA refused to allow the BNDD to pursue the investigation, because it had employed Trafficante in its assassination attempts against Fidel Castro, and because Trafficante's Operation 40 associates were performing similar functions for the CIA around the world.

Medell's Principal Agent was Bay of Pigs veteran Guillermo Tabraue, whom the CIA paid a whopping $1,400 a week. While receiving this princely sum, Tabraue participated in the "Alvarez-Cruz" drug smuggling ring.

Medell also recruited agents from Manuel Artime's anti-Castro organization. Howard Hunt, notably, had been Artime's case officer, and many members of Artime's narco-terror organization had worked for Bolten and Shackley while Shackley was the CIA's station chief in Miami in the early 1960s.

Bill Logay was the "overt" agent assigned to the BUNCIN office in Miami. A member of the CIA's "jeweler" program for junior officers, Logay had been Shackley's bodyguard in Saigon in 1969. From 1970-1971, Logay served under Tully Acampora as the CIA's special police liaison and drug coordinator in Saigon's Precinct 5. Logay was asked to join Twofold, but claimed to have refused.

Medell and Logay's reports were hand delivered to BNDD headquarters via the Defense Department's classified courier service. The military was in charge of emergency planning and provided BUNCIN agents with special communications equipment. The CIA supplied BUNCIN's assets with forged IDs that enabled them to work for foreign governments, including Panama, Venezuela and Costa Rica.

Like the Twofold canard, BUNCIN had two agendas. The first, according to Chief Inspector Fuller, "was told" and had a narcotics mission. The second provided cover for the Plumbers and their dirty tricks. Orders for the domestic subversive political facet emanated from the White House and passed through Conein to Gordon Liddy and his "Operation Gemstone" squad of anti-Castro Cuban narco-terrorists from the Artime organization.

BNDD enforcement chief Tartaglino was unhappy with the arrangement and gave Agent Ralph Frias the job of screening the anti-Castro Cubans the White House sent to the BNDD. Frias was assigned to the BNDD's international affairs staff. When Nixon's chief of staff Bob Haldeman sent three Cubans to the BNDD, Frias discovered they were "plants" who, once in possession of BNDD credentials, were to act on behalf of their political patrons at the White House. Those three were not hired, but, Frias told me, many others were successfully infiltrated inside the BNDD and other federal agencies.

Under BUNCIN cover, CIA assets reportedly kidnapped and assassinated people in Colombia and Mexico. The Nixon White House sponsors also used BUNCIN assets to gather dirt on Democratic politicians in Key West.

Thanks to the CIA, through BUNCIN, federal drug law enforcement sank to new lows of political repression and corruption.

Novo Yardley

The Nixon White House exploited the "operations by committee" management method to ensure political control over its illegal drug operations. As the various agencies involved in drug law enforcement "pooled" resources, the BNDD's narcotics mission was further diluted and diminished.

As the preeminent agency in the federal government, the CIA

used Bolten's "parallel mechanism" to commandeer the BNDD's global network of agents. The process advanced in South America when, at their introductory meeting in Mexico City in 1972, Western Hemisphere Division chief Shackley ordered the BNDD's Latin American Division chief Jerry Strickler to hand over all BNDD files, informant lists, and cable traffic.

"Bad things" happened as a result, according to Strickler. The worst abuse was that the CIA allowed drug shipments into the US without telling the BNDD.

"Individual stations allowed this," SIO Director John Warner confirmed.

In so far as evidence acquired by CIA electronic surveillance is inadmissible in court, the CIA was able to protect its controlled deliveries simply by monitoring them. The significance of this strategy cannot be overstated. The courts have terminated numerous investigations as a result of the CIA spying on traffickers. Likewise, dozens of narcotics prosecutions have been dismissed on national security grounds due to the participation of CIA assets operating in trafficking organizations around the world.

Strickler knew by name which CIA people were guilty of sabotaging cases in Latin America and wanted to indict them. He brought his list to BNDD headquarters, but at Bolten's insistence, Strickler was immediately kicked out of the enforcement division. Meanwhile, CIA assets from Bolten's unilateral drug unit were kidnapping and assassinating traffickers as part of Operation Twofold.

Ingersoll confirmed the existence of this covert facet of Twofold. Its purpose, he told me, was to put agents under deep cover to develop intelligence on drug trafficking from South America. The regional directors weren't aware of the program. Ingersoll said he got approval from Attorney General John Mitchell and passed the operation on to his successor, John Bartels, the first administrator of the Drug Enforcement Administration (DEA). Ingersoll said the unit was not supposed to operate inside the US, which is why he thought it was legal.

Ingersoll said he was surprised that no one from the Rockefeller Commission asked him about it.

I was fortunate to interview Joseph DiGennaro, a member of this covert operation.

Joey DiGennaro's entry into the covert facet of Twofold began when a family friend, who knew Jim Ludlum, suggested that he apply for a job with the BNDD. Then working as a stockbroker in New York, DiGennaro met Chief Inspector Fuller in 1971 in Washington. Fuller gave DiGennaro the code name Novo Yardley, based on his posting in New York and as a play on the name of the famous codebreaker.

After DiGennaro obtained the required clearances, he and several other recruits were "spun-off" from Twofold into the CIA's "operational" unit. The background check took 14 months, during which time he received intensive combat and tradecraft training.

In October 1972 DiGennaro was assigned to a New York City enforcement group as a cover for his CIA activities. His paychecks came from BNDD funds, but the program was reimbursed by the CIA through the Bureau of Mines. The program was authorized by the "appropriate" Congressional committee.

DiGennaro's unit was a component of the Special Operations Division, which at the time was managed by former Phoenix program director Evan Parker. The US military provided assets within foreign military services to keep exfiltration routes (air corridors and roads) open. The military cleared air space when captured drug trafficking suspects were brought into the US. DiGennaro spent most of his time in South America, but the unit operated worldwide, including in Lebanon, France, and the Far East. The unit numbered about 40 men, including experts in printing, forgery, maritime operations and telecommunications.

DiGennaro would check with Fuller and take sick time or annual leave to go on missions. There were lots of missions. As his BNDD group supervisor in New York, Joseph Quarequio, said, "Joey was never in the office."

The job involved tracking, kidnapping and, if they resisted, killing traffickers. Kidnapped persons were incapacitated by drugs and dumped in the US. As DEA Agent Gerry Carey recalled, "We'd get a call that there was 'a present' waiting for us on the corner of 116th Street and Sixth Avenue. We'd go there and find some guy, who'd been indicted in the Eastern District of New York, handcuffed to a telephone pole. We'd take him to a safe house for questioning and, if possible, turn him into an informer. Sometimes we'd have him in custody for months. But what did he know?"

If you're a Corsican drug dealer in Argentina, and men with police credentials arrest you, how do you know it's a CIA operation?

DiGennaro's last operation in 1977 involved the recovery of a satellite that had fallen into a drug dealer's hands. Such was the extent of the CIA's "parallel mechanism."

The Dirty Dozen

With the formation of the DEA in July 1973, BUNCIN was renamed the DEA Clandestine Operations Network (DEACON). A number of DEACONs were developed and funded as Special Field Intelligence Programs. As an extension of BUNCIN, DEACON 1 developed intelligence on traffickers in Costa Rica, Ohio and New Jersey; politicians in Florida; terrorists and gun runners; the sale of boats and helicopters to Cuba; and the venerable Trafficante organization.

Under DEA boss John Bartels, administrative control of the DEACONs fell under DEA intelligence chief George Belk and his assistant for special projects, Phil Smith. Through Belk and Smith, the Office of Special Projects became a major facet of Bolten's "parallel mechanism". It housed the DEA's air wing (staffed largely by CIA officers), conducted "research programs" with the CIA, provided state-of-the-art technical aids and false documentation to agents, and handled fugitive searches.

As part of DEACON 1, Smith sent covert agent Bob Medell "to Caracas and Bogota to develop a network of agents." As Smith noted in a memorandum, reimbursement for Medell "is being made in backchannel fashion to CIA under payments to other agencies and is not counted as a position against us."[14]

Thoroughly suborned by the CIA, DEA Administrator Bartels established a priority on foreign clandestine narcotics collection. Thus, when Belk proposed a "special operations group" in the office of intelligence, Bartels immediately approved it. In March 1974, Belk assigned the special operations group to Lou "Black Luigi" Conein.

As chief of the Intelligence Group/Operations (IGO), Conein administered the DEA's Special Operations Group (DEASOG) and its National Intelligence Officers (NIO) program. The chain of command, however, was "unclear" and while Medell reported administratively to Smith at Special Projects, Conein directed him through a separate chain of command reaching to William Colby, who had risen to the rank of CIA Director in the summer of 1973, concurrent with the formation of the DEA.

Conein had worked for Colby in Vietnam, and through Colby's personnel assistant, Jack A. Mathews, he hired a "dirty dozen" CIA officers to staff DEASOG. As NIOs (not regular DEA agents), the DEASOG crew did not buy narcotics or appear in court, but instead used standard CIA operating procedures to recruit assets and set up agent networks for the long-range collection of intelligence on trafficking groups. They had no visible connection to the DEA and were housed in a safe house outside headquarters in downtown Washington. The space was provided by Conein's drinking buddy from Vietnam, John "Picadoon" Muldoon, who had formed a private investigative firm as cover for CIA domestic ops. Muldoon's PI firm was located in the same building.

The first DEASOG recruits were CIA officers Elias P. Chavez and Nicholas Zapata. Both had paramilitary and drug control experience in Laos. Jack Mathews had been Chavez's case officer at the Long Thien base, where General Vang Pao ran his secret drug-smuggling army under Laos station chief Ted Shackley's auspices from 1966-1968.

A group of eight CIA officers followed: Wesley Dyckman, a Chinese linguist with service in Vietnam, was assigned to San Francisco; Louis J. Davis, a veteran of Vietnam and Laos, was assigned to the Chicago RIU; Chris Thompson from the CIA's Phoenix program went to San Antonio; Hugh E. Murray, veteran of Pakse and Bolivia (where he participated in the capture of Che Guevara) was sent to Tucson; Thomas D. McPhaul had worked with Conein in Vietnam and was sent to Dallas; Thomas L. Briggs, a veteran of Laos and a friend of Shackley's, went to Mexico; Vernon J. Goertz, a Shackley friend who had participated in the Allende coup, went to Venezuela; and David A. Scherman, a Conein friend and former manager of the CIA's interrogation center in Da Nang, went to sunny San Diego.

Gary Mattocks, who ran the CIA counterterror teams in Vietnam's Delta, and interrogator Robert Simon were the eleventh and twelfth members. Terry Baldwin, Barry Carew and Joseph Lagattuta joined later.

According to Lou Davis, Conein created DEASOG specifically to do Phoenix program-style jobs overseas: the type where a commando breaks into a trafficker's home, steals his drugs and slits his throat. The NIOs were to operate overseas and target traffickers the local cops couldn't touch for political reasons – the prime minister's son or the police chief in Acapulco if he was the local drug boss. If the NIOs couldn't assassinate the target, Conein and the CIA would arrange to bomb his labs or use psychological warfare to make him look like he was a DEA informant, so his own people would kill him.

The DEASOG people "would be breaking the law," Davis observed, "but they didn't have arrest powers overseas anyway."

Conein envisioned 50 NIOs operating worldwide by 1977. But a slew of Watergate-related scandals forced the DEA to curtail the program and reorganize its covert operations staff in ways that have since corrupted federal drug law enforcement beyond repair.

Assassination Scandals[15]

The first scandal focused on DEACON 3, which targeted the Aviles-Perez organization in Mexico. Eli Chavez, Nick Zapata and Barry Carew were the NIOs assigned.

A veteran CIA officer who spoke Spanish, Carew had served under Tully Acampora as a special police advisor in Saigon before joining the BNDD. Carew was assigned as Conein's Latin American desk officer and managed Chavez and Zapata (aka "the Mexican Assassin") in Mexico. According to Chavez, a White House Task Force under Howard Hunt started the DEACON 3 case. The Task Force provided photographs of the Aviles-Perez compound in Sinaloa, from whence truckloads of marijuana were shipped to the US.

Funds were allotted in February 1974, at which point Chavez and Zapata traveled to Mexico as representatives of the North American Alarm and Fire Systems Company. In Mazatlán, they met with Carew, who, according to Chavez, stayed at a fancy hotel and played tennis every day, while Chavez and Zapata, whom Conein referred to as "pepper-bellies," fumed in a flea-bag motel.

Eventually a female informant arranged for Chavez, posing as a buyer, to meet Perez. A deal was struck, but DEA chief John Bartels made the mistake of instructing Chavez to brief the DEA's regional director in Mexico City before making "the buy."

At this meeting, the DEACON 3 agents presented their operational plan. However, when the subject of "neutralizing" Perez came up, analyst Joan Bannister took this to mean assassination. Bannister reported her suspicions to DEA headquarters, where the anti-CIA faction gleefully leaked her report to *Washington Post* columnist Jack Anderson.

Anderson's sensational allegation that the DEA was providing cover for a CIA assassination unit was supported by revelations that the Senate had investigated Conein for shopping around for assassination devices, including exploding ashtrays and telephones. Conein kept his job, but the investigation exposed Muldoon and led to Conein's comrade from the OSS, Mitch Werbell.

A deniable asset Conein used for parallel operations, Werbell had sold silenced machine pistols to DEACON 1 target Robert Vesco. Then living in Costa Rica, Vesco was surrounded by drug trafficking Cuban exiles from the Trafficante organization. Trafficante was also, at the time, living in Costa Rica as a guest of President Figueres. Figueres' son had purchased weapons from Werbell and used them to arm a death squad he had formed with DEACON 1 asset Carlos Rumbault, a notorious anti-Castro Cuban narco-terrorist and fugitive drug smuggler.

Meanwhile, in February 1974, DEA Agent Anthony Triponi, a former captain in the army Special Forces and a Phoenix program veteran, was admitted to a hospital in New York "suffering from hypertension." DEA inspectors found Triponi in the psychiatric ward, distraught because he had broken his "cover" and now his "special code" would have to be changed.

Thinking he was insane, the DEA inspectors called former chief inspector Patrick Fuller in California, just to be sure. As it turned out, Triponi was an active member of Operation Twofold and everything he said was true! The incredulous DEA inspectors called the CIA and were stunned when they were told: "If you release the story, we will destroy you."[16]

By 1975, Congress and the Justice Department were investigating the DEA's nefarious relations with the CIA. In the process they stumbled upon Tripodi's Medusa Program, as well as DEA plots to assassinate Moises Torrijos (brother of Panamanian President Omar Torrijos) and Panama's chief of military intelligence, Manuel Noriega.

In a draft report, DEA Inspector Richard Salmi described Medusa as follows: "Topics considered as options included psychological terror tactics, substitution of placebos to discredit traffickers, use of incendiaries to destroy conversion laboratories, and disinformation to cause internal warfare between drug trafficking organizations; other methods under consideration involved blackmail, use of psychopharmacological techniques, bribery and even terminal sanctions."

The Cover-Up

Despite the flurry of investigations, Nixon's successor, Gerald Ford, reconfirmed the CIA's arrangement with DEA. The CIA continued to have its way. Much of its success is attributed to Seymour Bolten, whose staff, perhaps not coincidentally, handled all requests for files from the US Senate Select Committee to Study Governmental Operations with Respect to Intelligence Activities. The Church Committee, as it was known, was investigating the CIA's many and varied illegal activities. But rather than bring about the total destruction of the Agency, the Church Committee concluded that allegations of drug smuggling by CIA assets and proprietaries "lacked substance."

The Rockefeller Commission likewise gave the CIA a clean bill of health, falsely stating that Operation Twofold was terminated in 1973. As Ingersoll noted, the Commission completely ignored the existence of the CIA's operational unit hidden within the inspections program.

However, as a result of the DEASOG assassination scandals, Ford did task the Justice Department to investigate "allegations of fraud, irregularity, and misconduct" in the DEA. Under US Attorney Michael DeFeo, the ensuing investigation examined allegations that DEA officials had discussed killing Omar Torrijos and Manuel Noriega. In March 1976, Deputy Attorney General Richard Thornburgh announced there were no findings to warrant criminal prosecutions.

In 1976, Congresswoman Bella Abzug submitted questions to Ford's CIA director, George H.W. Bush, about the CIA's role in international drug trafficking. Bush's response was to cite a 1954 agreement with the Justice Department that gave the CIA the right to block prosecution and keep its crimes secret in the name of national security. In its final report, the Abzug Committee wryly noted: "It was ironic that the CIA should be given responsibility of narcotic intelligence, particularly since they are supporting the prime movers."[17]

Acknowledging the operational realities, Congress in 1976 through the Mansfield Amendment sought to curtail extra-legal activities by prohibiting DEA agents from kidnapping suspects without the consent of the host government. The CIA, of course, was exempt and continued to sabotage DEA cases against its "prime movers" while further tightening its stranglehold on DEA executive management.

In 1977, having reached the end of his rope, the DEA's enforcement chief, Daniel Casey, sent a memo co-signed by the enforcement division chiefs to DEA Administrator Peter Bensinger. The memo stated, "All were unanimous in their belief that present CIA programs were likely to cause serious future problems for DEA, both foreign and domestic."[18]

Casey and his division chiefs specifically cited CIA "controlled deliveries" into the United States, and the fact that the CIA "will not respond positively to any discovery motion," as the biggest impediments.

"Many of the subjects who appear in these CIA-promoted or controlled surveillances," the DEA officials complained, "regularly travel to the United States in furtherance of their trafficking activities." The "de facto immunity" from prosecution the traffickers enjoyed, due to the CIA's "electronic surveillance" of the controlled deliveries, enabled the CIA assets to "operate much more openly and effectively."

But Bensinger suffered the CIA at the expense of America's public health and the DEA's integrity. Under Bensinger, the DEA created its CENTAC program to target trafficking organization worldwide. But the CIA subverted CENTAC too: as CENTAC chief Dennis Dayle famously said, "The major targets of my investigations almost invariably turned out to be working for the CIA."[19]

Murder and Mayhem

DEACON 1 inherited BUNCIN's anti-Castro Cuban assets from Brigade 2506, which the CIA had organized to invade Cuba in 1960. Controlled by Nixon's secret political police, these CIA assets, operating under DEA cover, had parallel assignments involving "extremist groups and terrorism, and information of a political nature."[20]

DEACON 1's downfall, however, had more mundane origins and began when overt agent Bill Logay charged that covert agent Bob Medell's anti-Castro Cuban assets had penetrated the DEA on behalf of the Trafficante organization. In other words, the CIA was using its narco-terrorists to spy on the DEA, so it could better protect its anti-Castro Cuban narco-terrorist networks.

DEACON 1 secretary Cecelia Plicet fanned the flames by claiming that Conein and Medell were using Principal Agent Tabraue to circumvent the DEA, and thus more easily bring drugs into the country. In what amounted to an endless succession of controlled deliveries, all monitored by the CIA, Tabraue financed loads of cocaine and used DEACON 1 assets to smuggle them into the US. Plicet told me that Medell and Conein worked for "the other side" and wanted the DEA to fail. These accusations prompted yet another cover-up, in which Logay was reassigned to the DEA's Inspections staff and Medell was replaced by Gary Mattocks, an NIO member of the Dirty Dozen.

According to Mattocks, Western Hemisphere Division Chief Ted Shackley (whom Mattocks had worked for in Vietnam) helped Colby set up DEASOG and brought in "his" people, including Tom Clines, whom Shackley placed in charge of the CIA's Caribbean Operations Group. Clines, like Shackley and Bolten, knew all the exile Cuban narco-terrorists on the DEASOG payroll. CIA officer Vernon Goertz, notably, worked for Clines in Caracas as part of the CIA's parallel mechanism under DEASOG cover.

As cover for his DEACON 1 activities, Mattocks set up a front company designed to improve relations between Cuban and American businessmen. Meanwhile, he hired members of the Artime organization, including Watergate burglars Rolando Martinez and Bernard Barker, and Che Guevara's killer, Felix Rodriguez. These anti-Castro narco-terrorists were allegedly part of a hit team that Shackley and Clines employed for private as well as professional purposes – a distinction no longer relevant in the 21st century.

In late 1974, DEACON 1 finally expired when Robert Simon's daughter was murdered in a drive-by shooting by Mattocks' crazed anti-Castro Cubans. Simon at the time was managing the CIA's drug data base and had linked the exile Cuban narco-traffickers with "a foreign terrorist organization." As Mattocks explained, "It got bad after the Brigaders found out Simon was after them."

It was bad, yes, but it was business as usual, and none of the CIA's narco-terrorists were arrested for murdering Simon's daughter. Instead, Conein issued a directive prohibiting DEACON 1 assets from reporting on domestic political affairs or terrorist activities. The murder was swept under the carpet for reasons of national security.

DEACON 1 unceremoniously ended in 1975 after Fred Dick was assigned to head the DEA's Caribbean Basin Group. In that capacity Dick, who hated Seymour Bolten, visited the DEACON 1 safe house and found, in his words, "a clandestine CIA unit using miscreants from Bay of Pigs, guys who were blowing up planes." Dick hit the ceiling and in August 1975 DEACON I was terminated.

No new DEACONs were initiated and the rest quietly ran their course. Undeterred, the CIA redeployed its anti-Castro Cuban miscreants to the terror organization CORU in 1977. Others would go to work for Ollie North in the Reagan regime's Iran-Contra narco-terror network.

Conein's IGO was disbanded in 1976 after a grand jury sought DEACON I intelligence regarding several drug busts. But, as noted earlier, CIA-acquired intelligence cannot be used in prosecutions, and the CIA refused to identify its assets in court, with the result that 27 prosecutions were dismissed on national security grounds.

Gary Mattocks was thereafter unwelcome at the DEA. But his patron Ted Shackley had become DCI George H. W. Bush's assistant deputy director for operations, at which point Shackley rehired Mattocks into the CIA and assigned him to the CIA's narcotics unit in Peru.

At the time, drug kingpin Santiago Ocampo was purchasing cocaine in Peru and his partner Matta Ballesteros was flying it to the usual Cuban miscreants in Miami. One of the receivers, Francisco Chanes, an erstwhile DEACON asset, owned two seafood companies that allegedly served as fronts in North's Contra supply network, receiving and distributing tons of Contra cocaine.

Mattocks soon joined the Contra support operation as Nicaraguan guerrilla leader Eden Pastora's case officer. In that capacity Mattocks was present in 1984 when a CIA case officer handed pilot Barry Seal a camera and told him to take photographs of Sandinista official Federico Vaughn loading bags of cocaine onto Seal's plane. A dual CIA/DEA "special employee," Seal was running drugs for Jorge Ochoa Vasquez and using Nicaragua as a transit point for his deliveries.

North asked DEA officials to instruct Seal to steal $1.5 million in cash from Ochoa and deliver the money to the Contras instead. When the DEA officials objected, North leaked a blurry photo to the right-wing *Washington Times*. Purportedly taken by Seal, the photo showed Vaughn loading cocaine onto the plane.

For partisan political purposes, North blew the DEA's biggest case at the time. And the DEA did nothing about it, even though DEA Chief Jack Lawn said in 1988, in testimony before the Subcommittee on Crime of the Committee on the Judiciary, that leaking the photo "severely jeopardized the lives" of agents.[21]

The criminal conspiracy climaxed in 1989 when the CIA instructed Gary Mattocks to testify as a defense witness at the trial of DEACON 1's Principal Agent Gabriel Tabraue. Although Tabraue had earned $75 million from drug trafficking while working as a CIA/DEA asset, the judge declared a mistrial based on Mattocks' testimony. Tabraue was released without a scratch. Some people inferred that President George H.W. Bush had personally ordered Mattocks to torpedo the case.

Other examples of the CIA's use of narco-terrorists abound. In 1981, for example, DEA Agent Dick Salmi recruited Roberto Cabrillo, a drug smuggling member of CORU, another organization of crazed

Cuban exiles formed by Frank Castro and Luis Posada while George Bush was Director of Central Intelligence.

The DEA had arrested Frank Castro in 1981, but the CIA engineered his release and hired him to establish a Contra training camp in the Florida Everglades. Castro's colleague, Luis Posada, reportedly managed drug shipments for the Contras in cahoots with Felix Rodriguez. Charged in Venezuela with blowing up a Cuban airliner and killing 73 people in 1976, Posada was shielded from extradition by President George W. Bush in the mid-2000s.

Having been castrated by the CIA, DEA officials could only ask their CORU assets to please stop blowing up people like Orlando Letelier in the US. They could maim and kill people anywhere else, just not here in the Happy Homeland. By then, Salmi noted, the Justice Department had a special "gray-mail section" to fix cases involving CIA terrorists and drug dealers.

The Joke Is On You

Director of Central Intelligence William Webster formed the CIA's Counter-Narcotics Center (CNC) in 1988. Staffed by over 100 agents, it ostensibly became the springboard for the covert penetration of, and paramilitary operations against, top traffickers protected by high-tech security firms, lawyers and well-armed private armies.

Under CIA political control, the CNC brought together every federal agency involved in the illusory war on drugs. Former CIA officer and erstwhile Operation Twofold member, Terry Burke, then serving as the DEA's Deputy for Operations, was allowed to send one liaison officer to the CNC.

The CNC quickly showed its true colors. In late 1990, Customs agents in Miami seized a ton of cocaine from Venezuela. To their surprise, a Venezuelan undercover agent said the CIA had approved the delivery. DEA Administrator Robert Bonner ordered an investigation and discovered that the CIA had, in fact, shipped the load from its bulging warehouse in Venezuela.[22]

The "controlled deliveries" were managed by CIA officer Mark McFarlin, a veteran of Reagan's terror campaign in El Salvador. Bonner wanted to indict McFarlin, but was prevented from doing so because Venezuela was in the process of fighting off a rebellion led by leftist Hugo Chavez. This same scenario has been playing out in Afghanistan for the last 15 years, largely through the DEA's Special Operations Division

(SOD), whose sole purpose is to provide cover for CIA operations worldwide.

The ultimate form of imperial corruption, the SOD's job is not simply to "create a crime" as freewheeling FBN agents did in the good old days, but to "recreate a crime" so it is prosecutable, despite whatever extra-legal methods the CIA employs to obtain the evidence. That way, law enforcement agencies can make arrests without probable cause.

As Reuters reported in 2013, "The unit of the DEA that distributes the information is called the Special Operations Division, or SOD. Two dozen partner agencies comprise the unit, including the FBI, CIA, NSA, Internal Revenue Service and the Department of Homeland Security. It was created in 1994 to combat Latin American drug cartels and has grown from several dozen employees to several hundred."[23]

The utilization of information from the SOD, which like DEASOG operates out of a secret location in Virginia, "cannot be revealed or discussed in any investigative function" according to a DEA document cited by Reuters, which added that officials are specifically directed "to omit the SOD's involvement from investigative reports, affidavits, discussions with prosecutors and courtroom testimony."

Agents are told to use *"parallel* construction" (my italics) to build their cases without reference to SOD's tips, which may come from sensitive CIA "intelligence intercepts, wiretaps, informants and a massive database of telephone records," Reuters reported.

Citing a former federal agent, Reuters reported that SOD operators would, like Joey DiGennaro's CIA unit, tell law enforcement officials in the US to be at a certain place at a certain time and to look for a certain vehicle which would then be stopped and searched on some pretext. "After an arrest was made, agents then pretended that their investigation began with the traffic stop, not with the SOD tip, the former agent said."

An anonymous DEA official told Reuters that this "parallel construction" approach is "decades old, a bedrock concept" for law enforcement seeking to avoid probable cause requirements.

The SOD's approach does indeed replicate techniques from the early 1970s used in Operation Twofold and Bolten's parallel mechanism. But it is a "bedrock concept" only in so far as revising reports in order to convict defendants, which was always conducted as unstated policy, is now official policy: no longer considered corruption, it is how your government manages the judicial system on behalf of the rich political elite.

As FBN Agent Bowman Taylor caustically observed, "I used to think we were fighting the drug business, but after they formed the BNDD, I realized we were feeding it."

The corruption was first "collateral" – a function of national security performed by the CIA in secret – but has now become "integral," the essence of an empire run amok. I'll elaborate on that, below.

BEYOND DIRTY WARS: THE CIA/DEA CONNECTION AND MODERN DAY TERROR IN LATIN AMERICA

GUILLERMO JIMENEZ: On today's show I am joined by Mr. Douglas Valentine, an expert on the CIA and the DEA and their adventures in terror and narcotics trafficking. Doug, thank you for being on the show.

VALENTINE: You're very welcome.

JIMENEZ: I'm trying to piece together how modern-day narco-terrorists, the notorious cartels that we hear and read so much about, may connect with the Phoenix program, and how by studying and understanding this history we can better understand what is happening today. Perhaps we could begin with a summary on what we need to know about Phoenix before we can explore the program's expansion, and how it's been implemented in other parts of the world.

VALENTINE: The Vietnam War was a unique experience for the American military and the CIA. They were fighting the North Vietnam Army (NVA) in what they called "a main force war." The US was quite prepared to fight that main force war because it had the biggest military in the world. What America wasn't prepared to fight was a guerrilla war, a political war. Ho Chi Minh had said he'd rather have two political cadres in every village than a battalion in the field. And that's what happened. The Communists organized the people of South Vietnam to fight the oligarchy that was working for the CIA and following American policies.

The guerrilla war in the villages baffled the Americans, so the CIA started experimenting with a lot of political and psychological ways of fighting the insurgency in the villages. They called it "the other war." Pacification. The job fell to the CIA because it meant killing civilians not soldiers. The military isn't supposed to go into a village and kill everybody. They did it anyway, plenty of times, but it turned the people against the US and its puppets in the South Vietnamese government.

So the job of killing civilians was given to the CIA, which isn't hampered by any rules of engagement related to the laws of any country. There is nothing to stop the CIA's hired killers from going into the villages and snuffing and snatching Uncle Ho's cadres. The cadres are teachers, laborers, mailmen, farmers; but they're not soldiers. They provide support for the NVA and the guerrillas. They're the backbone of the insurgency.

The CIA realizes it has to "eliminate" these people to win the war. It works through its assets in a country's judicial system to create administrative detention laws that allow Americans and their subsidiary counterterrorism teams to snatch the cadres from their homes at midnight, without charging these targeted cadres with having committed criminal offenses. It builds secret interrogation centers where the cadres and their friends and family members can be tortured and turned into double agents. It creates a system that terrorizes everyone, in order to create millions of informers. Once it finds out who the cadres are, the CIA sends out its death squads. The CIA calls them counterterrorism teams like the ones it uses today in Afghanistan and Iraq and other countries around the world. They creep into the cadres' homes in the middle of the night, drag them away to the interrogation centers, or slit their throats and kill their friends and their families for psychological reasons, and run away before anybody knows what happened.

In 1967 the CIA brings together all these methods of fighting the guerilla war in the Phoenix program. Phoenix combines all these things plus a lot I haven't mentioned. It pulls together people from the army, navy, air force and Special Forces. It includes the Vietnamese secret services. It coordinates everybody that's involved in the war and brings every resource to bear on the political people in the villages, in an effort to wipe them off the face of the earth. That's what the Phoenix program is. The total number of people killed was between 25,000 and 40,000.

JIMENEZ: Wow. Hearing you speak about this tactic of going into someone's home at night, which is happening in places like Iraq and Yemen, and taking out an entire family, associates and friends, and doing so in a public and violent way as a form of psychological warfare. I see a lot of parallels between what you just described and what is happening now in Northern Mexico with these drug cartels. They employ the same or similar tactics and it's not a coincidence as we look at the history of the Phoenix program and how it transitioned into Central America. Many of the founding members of the more violent and notorious drug cartels in Mexico today, namely Los Zetas, are directly linked to the death squads that were trained during this transition of the Phoenix program to Central America.

Why did Phoenix become the go-to strategy in El Salvador, Guatemala, and later Iraq?

VALENTINE: Phoenix was a program in Vietnam, a methodology, but it is also a concept based in a speculative philosophy of history in which self-made America is exceptional, and its will to power is determinant. Phoenix the program goes through organizational changes. Over the eight years it existed, pieces were put into it and taken out. The pieces were called different things; different labels were put on the jar up on the shelf. But it is also a method of thinking about and controlling perceptions of, and events in, the ever present spectacular moment, and as such is transferable and adaptable to any situation.

The United States never met a war it didn't like, especially now that it has the biggest military and the best intelligence service the world has ever known. They're the biggest and best because they're always fighting to expand the empire. They're always finding a reason to start a war, so they can send the next generation of young men into battle, to learn how to kill people in the most brutal fashion. The US has an imperative to be as super-aggressive as it can be, so it doesn't lose its edge. If its predatory impulse to dominate was stilted in Vietnam, that doesn't mean the soldiers and spies aren't going to pop up some place else. They're always going to pop up someplace else. They always do.

As Vietnam was winding down, the CIA was beset by

Congressional investigations that revealed some of the criminal activities it was involved in, like MKULTRA. The military took a big hit with the release of the Pentagon Papers in 1971. The military had lied to the American public about why it was fighting the Vietnam War. During the Watergate period the CIA had a reduction of forces in Southeast Asia. But the impulse to dominate was still there and Phoenix was the perfect template to apply elsewhere, so the CIA and military could release their repressed aggressive forces. Phoenix is both the methodological and programmatic way these repressed impulses to dominate gradually emerge.

By 1973 the people who had been running Phoenix were overthrowing the elected socialist government in Chile. One of them was Ted Shackley, who'd been station chief in Saigon. By 1973, Shackley was head of the CIA's Western Hemisphere Division and helped engineer the coup in Chile. From there the CIA and military fanned out through Latin America. If you review the history, you'll see that there's an infusion of American covert forces into Latin America as the war in Vietnam winds down.

Nowhere was this more evident than in El Salvador, where Lieutenant Colonel Stan Fulcher served from 1974 until 1977 as an intelligence advisor with the US Military Advisory Group. Fulcher had run Phoenix operations in Binh Dinh Province in South Vietnam in 1972. Two years later in El Salvador, as he told me when I interviewed him, he saw the same "old boys" who'd run the war in South Vietnam. The big difference in El Salvador was that the CIA effected US policies through proxies from allied countries as a result of the reduction in the CIA's paramilitary forces.

Fulcher watched while Israeli advisors taught El Salvador's major landowners how to organize criminals into vigilante death squads. The death squads used intelligence from El Salvador's military and security forces to target and murder labor leaders and other opponents of the oligarchy. But they were deniable.

Fulcher watched while Taiwanese military officers taught Kuomintang political warfare techniques at El Salvador's Command and General Staff College: Phoenix-related subjects like population control through psychological warfare, the development and control of agent provocateurs, the development of political cadres within the officer corps, and the placement of military officers in the civilian security forces. He saw political prisoners put in insane asylums he described as being "like Hogarth's paintings."

Fulcher saw Americans smuggle weapons and money to the death squads. He was outraged by what he saw and organized at his own home a study group of young military officers who supported land reform, nationalization of the banks, and civilian control of the military. In 1979 these reformist officers staged a successful but short-lived coup. As a result of that coup the Salvadoran National Security Agency (ANSESAL), which the CIA had formed in 1962, was disbanded and reorganized as the National Intelligence Agency (ANI).

This reorganization didn't put an end to the death squads. Instead, the landowners and the fascist military officers moved to Miami and Guatemala, where they formed a political front called Arena, to which the CIA channeled funds for the purpose of eliminating the reformers. Major Roberto d'Aubuisson was chosen to head Arena. D'Aubuisson was a former member of ANSESAL, and he transferred its files to general staff headquarters where they were used to compile blacklists. Operating out of Guatemala, under CIA supervision, D'Aubuisson's death squads murdered Archbishop Oscar Romero and El Salvador's attorney general in early 1980. In December of that year, six members of El Salvador's executive council were kidnapped, tortured, and killed by a death squad. The death squads went on a rampage which included the murders in January 1981 of the head of the land distribution program, along with his American advisors, Michael Hammer and Mark Pearlman.

At this time, according to Salvadoran Army officer Ricardo Castro, death squad supervision passed to Department 5, the civil affairs branch of the Salvadoran general staff. "Department 5 suddenly started coordinating everything," said Castro, a West Point graduate with a master's degree in engineering.[1]

Formed in the mid-1970s by the CIA, Department 5 became "the political intelligence apparatus within the general staff." Although it was designed as an investigative, not an operating, agency, Department 5 had "a large paramilitary force of people dressed in civilian clothes," and because it targeted civilians, "They can knock someone off all by themselves, or capture them," Castro said.

When military as opposed to political targets were involved, Department 2, the intelligence branch of the general staff, would send information from its informant nets to Department 3 (operations), which then dispatched its own death squad. Whether the people to be killed were guerrillas or civilians, Castro explained, "The rich people – the leading citizens of the community – traditionally have a great deal of input. Whatever bothers them, if they've got someone who just came into their ranch or their farm and they consider them a bad influence, they just send a messenger to the commander."

So Latin America was, for economic reasons, the place the US aimed its aggression after Vietnam. The Phoenix people brought their techniques and ideas into South and Central America, the Caribbean and Mexico and began applying and perfecting the Phoenix model in various ways in these countries. All this erupts in 1980 when the Reagan regime comes to power.

JIMENEZ: The Salvador Option, is that synonymous with the Phoenix program? Is it essentially the same thing under a different name?

VALENTINE: Yes. in fact, the people who created and imposed the Salvador Option were Phoenix veterans. The "Pink Plan" approved by Vice President Bush for use in El Salvador in 1981 was developed by CIA officers Donald Gregg, Rudy Enders and Felix Rodrigues in Vietnam, and exported to El Salvador and Iraq.

I did interviews with Gregg and Enders in 1988. Gregg was Bush's national security advisor at the time, and he called me from the White House one afternoon when, as he put it, he had nothing to do. He described the whole process in detail. The interview is in my book, *The Phoenix Program*.[2]

Like I said, you can change the label on the jar on the shelf. It's still poison.

JIMENEZ: The same poison, the same concept you mentioned earlier. To me this sounds like standard operating procedure in every theater of war that America is involved in today. It's amazing.

VALENTINE: I was just reading a book about Daniel Siqueiros, the muralist. There's a passage where a peasant woman says that the foreman who's beating the peasants does what the hacienda owner says, and the hacienda owner does what the North Americans say. Every working class person in South America understands that. That Americans don't understand it is just a testament to the media here.

There's a lot of anti-Americanism in South America and Mexico. The poor people understand that the hand of the Americans – the CIA, FBI, State Department – has always been corrupting high officials in their countries. They do it a number of ways. One way is through drug trafficking.

People think this is something that started in Central America during Iran-Contra, but it started in China when the US backed Chiang Kai-shek in the 1920s. The only way that Chiang Kai-shek could finance his government was through the opium trade. There were laws restricting the opium trade, but the US turned a blind eye to Chiang's opium business because they didn't want the Communists taking over China. The United States has been engaged in an unstated policy since the 1920s of supporting its political allies by allowing the leadership to make fortunes dealing drugs.

The CIA allowed General Vang Pao, the leader of the CIA's "secret army" of Hmong tribesmen in Laos, to make a fortune through the opium trade in the 1960s and 1970s. FBN Agent Bowman Taylor told me about it. Taylor had been an agent in Dallas since 1951, and in 1963 he was assigned to run the Bureau's newly created office in Bangkok. "There was no preparation," Taylor noted. "I just packed bags and went."

Finding friends in Thailand wasn't easy for Taylor, who had no diplomatic training or skills. The war on drugs wasn't a sexy thing yet, and no one at the US Embassy wanted to jeopardize his career by helping an FBN agent whose job was to make drug cases on the most important people in the Kingdom of Opium. Shunned by his American colleagues, Taylor forged relations with a colonel in the Thai army. Three months after his arrival, he received additional help when FBN Agent Charles Casey arrived. Casey teamed up with a Chinese-American FBN undercover agent from San Francisco to make a case against Kuomintang drug smugglers in the Shan states of Burma. For CIA-related reasons of so-called national security, which everyone is acquainted with by now, the case collapsed after several months.

At Taylor's direction, Casey next made a case against two Thai lieutenants serving with the CIA-advised Border Police. But they were the CIA's "best" lieutenants, according to Taylor, so after their arrest the CIA simply sent them to manage a drug network in Laos. In another instance, a CIA pilot left a suitcase full of opium at the Air America ticket counter in Bangkok. Taylor and a Thai police officer tailed the pilot to an American airbase outside Tokyo; but the pilot was whisked away to the Philippines and put under protective custody by CIA security officers.

Joining Taylor and Casey in 1965 was agent Al Habib. "I went on a ninety day TDY," Habib recalled in our interview, "and after the initial shock, I wound up staying two years."[3]

The initial shock was the CIA. "Taylor had gotten in trouble in Laos," Habib recalled, "and he sent me there to patch things up. I reported to the Embassy in Vientiane where I was met by a CIA officer. He asked me what I wanted, and I told him I was there to make narcotics cases. That made him nervous so he called the Marine guard. He said, 'Stay here until we come to get you.' And I sat there under guard until they took me to see Ambassador William Sullivan."

Habib laughed. "I'm sitting in Sullivan's office surrounded by a gang of menacing CIA officers. Sullivan introduces himself and asks if I would please explain what I'm doing in Laos. I say I'm there to work undercover with the police, to locate morphine labs. To which he replies, 'Are you serious?'

"At that point a CIA officer says to me, 'You! Don't do nothing!' Meanwhile Sullivan goes to his office and composes a yard-long telegram to Secretary (of State Dean) Rusk saying, in effect, 'Don't they know that Laos is off limits?'

"They tell me how Taylor set up an undercover buy from a guy. He got a flash roll together and went to the meet covered by the Vientiane police. When the guy steps out of the car and opens the trunk, the police see it's the King of the Meos.[4] The police run away and Taylor busts General Vang Pao, alone."

"It's true," Taylor laughed when I asked him about it. "I made a case on Vang Pao and was thrown out of the country as a result. What you weren't told was that the Laotian Prime Minister gave Vang Pao back his Mercedes Benz and morphine base, and the CIA sent him to Miami for six months to cool his heels. I wrote a report to (FBN Commissioner Henry) Giordano, but when he confronted the CIA, they said the incident never happened.

"The station chiefs ran things in Southeast Asia," Taylor stressed, adding that the First Secretary at the Vietnamese Embassy in Bangkok had a non-stop drug smuggling airline to Saigon. "I tried to catch him, but there was no assistance. In fact the CIA actively supported the Border Police, who were involved in trafficking." He shrugged. "The CIA would do anything to achieve its goals."

According to several FBN agents I interviewed, the CIA actually flew opium to its warlords in South Vietnam. In one documented case that supports this assertion, Major Stanley C. Hobbs, a member of

MACV Advisory Team 95, was caught on 30 August 1964 smuggling 57 pounds of opium from Bangkok to a clique of South Vietnamese military officers. Hobbs flew into Saigon on the CIA's proprietary airline, Air America. His court martial was conducted in secret at Ryukyu Island for "security" reasons. The witnesses were all US Army and South Vietnamese counterintelligence officers. The records of the trial have been lost and though convicted Hobbs was fined a mere $3,000 and suspended from promotion for five years. As a protected drug courier, he served no time.

FBN Commissioner Giordano wrote a letter to the Assistant Secretary of Defense complaining about the light sentence Hobbs received. After his request for a record of the trial was denied, Giordano wrote to Senator Thomas J. Dodd asking for help obtaining information. But Dodd was similarly stonewalled; which only goes to show that in the 1960s, the CIA was powerful enough to subvert federal drug law enforcement even at the legislative level. It still is today.

"A kid in the slums who steals a loaf of bread will draw stiffer punishment than that," columnist Carl Rowan quoted Missouri Senator Stuart Symington as saying about the Hobbs case.[5]

With the support and blessings of the CIA, several top generals in South Vietnam had franchises in the drug trade. According to Al McCoy, the three men at the head of the syndicate were Air Force General Nguyen Cao Ky, President Thieu, and Prime Minister Tran Thien Khiem, who worked hand in hand with William Colby running the Phoenix program.[6]

According to Nguyen Ngoc Huy, a Vietnamese historian and former professor at Harvard, General Dan Vang Quang, Admiral Chung Tan Cang, Prime Minister Khiem, Air Force chief Ky, and Thieu's military chief of staff, Cao Van Vien, ran the rackets in Vietnam through their wives.[7]

None of this officially sanctioned corruption was made public until the US decided to get out of Vietnam. Then, when it served US interests (as with Manuel Noriega in Panama in 1990), it was "Oh, my god! We've got drug traffickers on our hands. We can't deal with these people anymore."

But the fact is that the CIA organized the drug trade out in the Far East and used it to reward the generals and politicians who pushed American policy even though it was against the interests of their people. The CIA buys American politicians in the same way.

Corrupting the leadership of a country in order to keep it in your pocket is integral to maintaining an empire. It is a well-established colonial policy. The two main facets of Phoenix – controlling the "upper tier" people in a foreign government by corrupting them, and terrorizing the lower tier into submission – come together in the mid-70s in Central America and explode with Iran-Contra in the 1980s.

In *The Great Heroin Coup*, author Henrik Kruger advanced the theory that, with the loss of Vietnam and its networks in Southeast Asia, the CIA shifted its drug headquarters to Mexico through drug trafficker Alberto Sicilia-Falcon, a Cuban exile who popped up in Mexico in 1973. Kruger theorized that the CIA put Sicilia-Falcon in business using the old French Connection network of corrupt officials in Mexico. The Mafia and its connections in the French Corsican underworld had operated there for decades with top Mexican politicians, generals and security forces, just like in Vietnam. I write extensively about that in my books. Anyway, Sicilia-Falcon claimed that he was working for the CIA and with the same corrupt officials, and that his real job was to provide weapons to anti-Communist forces in Central America.

In 1977, Senator Sam Nunn held a hearing to investigate arms smuggling from the US to drug lords like Sicilia-Falcon and other criminal organizations in Mexico.[8] It was quite a scandal; President Echeverria said in 1975, "External forces are trying to destabilize our country."[9]

At the Nunn Hearings, the director of the Bureau of Alcohol Tobacco and Firearms (ATF) said that there was a tremendous mark-up for American manufactured weapons and that hundreds of people were smuggling automatic rifles into Mexico. The same thing happened again with the Fast and Furious scandal 40 years later. That case also ended up in front of Congress. In that case the ATF allowed guns to be smuggled into Mexico, ostensibly to locate big crime bosses, none of whom were ever arrested. The guns just ended up in the hands of criminals, like the gun that was used to kill a US Border Patrol agent. The true intent of the operation was never revealed.

So the corruption, the drugs for arms trafficking, and the death squads aren't divorced from each other. They are systematically related and, historically, dependent on one another. That's Phoenix.

JIMENEZ: To what extent is this being done strictly for political reasons – aligning themselves with a given cartel, for example, because they have the same goal of keeping the same group of people in a given country in or out of power. How much is based on profiting financially from the narcotics trade? Your thoughts on how this plays out in today's illicit black markets.

VALENTINE: The illicit drug trade produces some $300 billion a year in cash that exists off the books until it's deposited in a bank. Everyone wants to have the US $100 bill, so the majority of the narco-dollars end up in banks that hold US dollars. A lot of that money buys arms that are used for political purposes, to overthrow governments, like in Syria. We're often told that drug money helps support ISIS and other so-called terrorist groups.

But it's impossible for $300 billion, no matter what currency it's in, to float around the world economy undetected.

The great white fathers who control world finances know where it comes from and where it goes. The CIA has a new Digital Division that keeps track of all this. We're talking about people who can arrange economic sanctions on Iran. It's amazing to see what they can do, but it is impossible for me to explain how they do it. But that $300 billion has a lot to do with buying people's loyalty. Controlling that $300 billion is a very high priority of the CIA.

JIMENEZ: It's clear that this is being managed by the powers that be. So how much of what we are seeing today in places like northern Mexico can be traced to the training of the death squads like the Kaibiles in Guatemala? A couple of the founding members of Los Zetas were Kaibiles, and others were trained in the School of the Americas. Officially they defected from the Mexican Special Forces and went into the narcotics trade for themselves. Is this a matter of blowback, of people trained in Phoenix tactics going bad? Or is it by design? Bill Conroy of Narco News has done a lot of investigative work into the drug cartels in Mexico, and he doesn't even consider them cartels. He considers them factions of the Mexican government itself vying for control.

VALENTINE: The US has had an unstated policy of smuggling guns to militant factions in Mexico's Northern states that are continuously fighting against the central government. It's one of ways of keeping the central government weak, so that Mexico can never develop into a strong economic or political adversary. The US effects the same secret policy in every nation south of Mexico, too. Hillary Clinton staged a coup in Honduras in 2009.

Corruption is the best way of destabilizing a country. If a nation's top officials are corrupt and don't represent the people, then it's not the people's government. America has made sure this happens in Mexico. After World War Two, the CIA started to effect this policy. Several presidents of Mexico have been agents of the CIA, working not to advance policies that help average people, but to effect American policy.

The CIA uses Phoenix techniques because these techniques are deniable, affordable and effective. Neither country can afford to have the US military bombing Mexican villages, so the oligarchs unite and do the job in this dirty underhanded way. Political factions in Mexico compete for power and money, and in pursuit of short-term profits, they become pawns in the CIA's double game to destabilize Mexico by keeping it in a constant state of violence against itself. CIA officers in Mexico contribute to this by guiding and manipulating the arms for drugs trade. As you noted, the CIA has trained some of the Mexican Special Forces people in one of the cartels in the modern techniques of guerrilla warfare. Opposing cartels, whether wittingly or unwittingly, have likely been assisted by the CIA too, just to keep them at each other's throats. It's an underworld and there's a lot going on that never gets publicly revealed.

No one talks about it, but the CIA has an operations officer engaged in covert actions in every province and state in Mexico, including along the border. These CIA officers work with the local DEA agents, reporting to the fusion center, and the Counterterrorism and Counter Narcotics centers, in Mexico City. As in Fast and Furious, they monitor the guns for drugs networks so they can 1) blackmail and turn the political bosses into assets, and 2) keep the various cartels armed and fighting each other. They're not interested in disarming Mexico. If Trump was elected and built a wall, the CIA would put trap doors in it.

At the other end of the pipeline, as Gary Webb revealed, they monitor the delivery of drugs to disenfranchised minorities in America, whom the police pit against each other and use as commodities to pack the prisons, where they are then exploited as slave labor. Here the social engineering is based on institutional racism. Again, you're not allowed to talk about it, but people see it. Very sophisticated methods of social engineering are behind this, and the Black Lives Matter people have a hard time articulating it. And even if they find the language, the media shuts them down, because you're not allowed to talk about systematic repression. We're a free country and that isn't supposed to be possible.

JIMENEZ: I agree completely with everything you just said. The idea is to corrupt foreign leaders and keep them in your pocket. There's no better example than Mexico, and as you just alluded to, this is happening right here within our own borders.

I want to read a short excerpt from your book to illustrate the point. You quote a Salvadoran army officer, Ricardo Castro. He was running a death squad in El Salvador and he described what they would do as a sort of daily routine. He said: "Normally you eliminate everyone. We usually go in with an informant who is part of the patrol and who has turned these people in. When you turn somebody in, part of your obligation is to show us where they are and identify them. We would go in and knock on people's houses. They'd come out of their house and we'd always tell them we were the left and we're here because you don't want to cooperate with us or whatever. And then we'd eliminate them all, always with machetes."[10]

This is exactly what we're seeing today in Mexico; the cartels going into someone's home, always with machetes. Again, not a coincidence. I was always a fan of rap and hip hop, groups like NWA and Public Enemy in the early to mid-90s, and back then I was hearing through this music that the CIA was bringing in drugs to South Central Los Angeles to neutralize the black population. This became the stuff of urban legend. Then Gary Webb introduced us and the world to Freeway Ricky Ross, and that confirmed that indeed the CIA was facilitating the trafficking of crack cocaine to LA. This is done for political and financial reasons, but also as a means of social engineering through the drug trade. They can manufacture a crisis like the crack epidemic.

VALENTINE: These things were planned 70 years ago. After World War Two, the big brains in industry and government prepared to rule the world. So this is not something that a magician pulled out of a hat. If you read the news, Americans are surprised every day by institutionalized racism and its attendant cycle of violence: the cops kill a black man, and then a black man kills some cops. We've been seeing it every day of our lives, but it's always "news" that's characterized as an aberration. But all these things, and the way they're happening, were plotted decades ago. It was known back then that social engineering would be a more potent weapon then the atomic bomb.

The CIA and the military hire the smartest anthropologists, sociologists and psychologists to figure out how to do this stuff. They have it down to a science called Human Factors. The way they have perfected things like Phoenix is beyond my knowledge. I don't get to drive the latest Lamborghini. I have a Toyota. I was able to figure out some of these things 30 years ago, but the methods of preventing people from finding out have also improved and it's harder than ever to know exactly what's going on.

That's why you need a broad historical view. If you focus just on what's happening now, you're shocked every day by what you see. We need to develop a collective historical consciousness to understand the predicament and to be able to do something about it, to stop being manipulated by the press on a daily basis. The media have us trained like sex-texting teenagers to focus on things that have nothing to do with how our perceptions of events are being controlled. It is important for people to take a broader view and to try to put these things in perspective, not only to understand what is happening now, but to see where things are going in the future and to plot a way to deal with it.

JIMENEZ: I couldn't agree more with what you just said, Doug. I follow these stories as they're breaking – like the news of the IRS targeting certain political groups and AP reporters, or the Edward Snowden NSA scandal – and I find myself falling into this trap. I have to check myself and say "Slow down here, let's process this stuff again" with a broader more historical view, because these are not mistakes, the interventionism overseas, the bungles in Iraq and Afghanistan. This is by design and if you understand the historical context you can better understand what is happening.

VALENTINE: The media needs its *crise du jour.* The news can't last more than 24 hours without being refreshed; you need a new headline to get people's attention so you can sell them something. Of course partisan political politics is poison and does nothing to help. The endless bickering creates the political gridlock within the government we see; meanwhile the bureaucracies grow more powerful.

When I first started studying the DEA, I looked at its predecessor organization, the Bureau of Narcotics, which was created in 1930. It had a \$3 million budget and 300 agents up until 1968. Now there are 600 agents in New York City alone, and the industry is so profitable that Congress gives the DEA around \$20 billion annually. It has something called the Special Operations Division which was featured by Reuters a couple of days ago.[11]

The DEA's Special Operations Division was created in 1994 to go after Pablo Escobar. It was a unit of about 12 people from the CIA, FBI and NSA organized on the Phoenix model. It used the latest surveillance technology to find Escobar. Over the last 20 years, the SOD has become a giant Phoenix-type center in the DEA with hundreds of agents. Through the NSA, they listen in on everyone's conversations on the pretext that someone might have something to do with drug trafficking. This information is used for political and economic purposes by the bureaucrats who have run these operations for ten years. After they get out of the NSA or DEA or CIA, the bosses go to work for corporations that benefit from the knowledge they've acquired through these secret surveillance operations, because, despite what they say publicly, they are not throwing away the extraneous information. They're using it for their personal benefit. It really pays nowadays to get involved in the domestic spy business as a DEA or CIA agent, because you're set for life. It's another way the CIA has corrupted our society.

JIMENEZ: Absolutely. Regarding the correlation between the DEA, CIA and NSA, a story broke this week that the NSA is indeed feeding the DEA information that they're collecting through these wiretapping programs to go after a small drug smuggler. That sort of information to someone like you, Doug, who has been following the history of this probably comes as no surprise at all.

VALENTINE: In my book I tell how the NSA and DEA were doing that in 1970. It's nothing new. What's so dangerous is that the intelligence that the DEA gets from the CIA and the NSA is inadmissible in court. The CIA can promote a drug trafficker and use him as an agent simply by wiretapping him. If the CIA wiretaps a drug trafficker, the DEA can't take him into court and the guy has a license to deal.

At first the DEA was upset. But after ten years, the executives saw the writing on the wall and joined in the fun and games. The CIA corrupted the DEA the same way it corrupts foreign governments. The CIA is corrupting the NSA and the military in the same fashion. It corrupts our bureaucracies the same way it corrupts foreign governments. They say it's for national security, but really it's for the money.

It's gotten to the point where the Justice Department allows the DEA to lie. They can't say they acquired the evidence from a CIA wiretap, which they did, so they say they acquired it from a confidential informant whose name, they say, they can't reveal. They present that fiction as evidence in court. The judges, who've also been corrupted, won't ask where it came from and the defendant goes to jail for 20 years.

The moral to the story is that you don't have to commit a crime anymore to go to prison. The law enforcement agencies can frame you and send you to prison for thinking bad thoughts. The powers that be coordinate all the bureaucracies on the Phoenix model, and they've all been corrupted because it's the most effective way to ensure political control. If the bureaucrats subvert the Bill of Rights, they can own two houses and afford a trophy wife, send their kids to the best colleges. All our democratic institutions are so corrupt, are involved in so many illegal activities, that their main focus now is how to keep it quiet.

JIMENEZ: Earlier you called the CIA a criminal conspiracy and I think that's true. As you just mentioned, this is how the social order is kept through engineered instability, even within our own country. So much of what was once criminal has become standard operating procedure.

Just to emphasize your points about information gathering and intelligence: Russell Tice, an NSA whistleblower, did an interview with Peter B. Collins and Sibel Edmonds of Boiling Frogs Post a few weeks back in which he said all content in all our conversations – telephone, electronic or otherwise – is indeed being collected and stored.[12] Not only that, but they're targeting everyone in the country including politicians, Congressmen, even Barack Obama himself from the time he was a Senator.

So to emphasize your point again, this is about corrupting and/ or compromising the leaders of a country to keep them under control. We can look at the FBI program COINTELPRO and how it targeted political groups like the Black Panthers. When they were thoroughly destabilized and discredited and splintered, members of the Black Panthers went on to form the Bloods, the Crips in South Central and elsewhere around the country. All of this is connected and explains how we ended up in the mess we're in. Earlier I laughed when we were talking about this, but that's just a defense mechanism to keep from screaming at this insanity.

VALENTINE: Another defense mechanism is to read the right books, like Sam Greenlee's book *The Spook Who Sat by the Door*. Forty years ago, black people were aware of everything that is happening now. Nothing has changed for them, except the bureaucracies that repress them are more powerful. As I've mentioned elsewhere, from the time the Bureau of Narcotics was created in 1930 until 1968, black agents were not allowed to become managers and supervise whites. Drug law enforcement has always been run by supremacists for the purpose of incarcerating blacks and Mexicans and anyone considered inferior. Nothing has changed. The presence of a black president hasn't changed these bureaucracies. They still exist with that purpose in mind and despite appearances, that's still the policy.

JIMENEZ: I understand. In closing I'd like to read from the final chapter of *The Phoenix Program*. It's the perfect way to end this conversation. I'd like folks to listen and consider what is happening not just in other parts of the world today, but within our own borders as well.

You finish the book with this paragraph: "Where can Phoenix be found today? Wherever governments of the left or the right use military and security forces to enforce their ideologies under the aegis of anti-terrorism. Look for Phoenix wherever police checkpoints ring major cities, wherever paramilitary police units patrol in armored cars," – this sounds like Boston just a few months ago – "and wherever military forces are conducting counterinsurgency operations. Look for Phoenix wherever emergency decrees are used to suspend due process; wherever dissidents are interned indefinitely; and wherever dissidents are rounded up and deported. Look for Phoenix wherever security forces use informants to identify dissidents; wherever security forces keep files and computerized black lists on dissidents; wherever security forces conduct secret investigations and surveillance on dissidents; and wherever security forces (or thugs in their hire) harass and murder dissidents, and wherever such activities go unreported by the press."

So again, just take that in and consider what is happening not just around the world but within this country, in this supposed land of the free and home of the brave.

So, Doug, your final thoughts on this before we wrap this up.

VALENTINE: I'd say it's all about consciousness. It sounds like a fake term from the '60s. But if you become aware of the problem, you'll see the way out.

| Chapter 14 |

PROJECT GUNRUNNER

KEN MCCARTHY: Welcome to Brasscheck TV. Our guest today is Doug Valentine. The story we're going to talk about is Project Gunrunner and Operation Fast and Furious. Gunrunner started under the Bush administration and continued under Obama, and here's the story.

The Bureau of Alcohol, Tobacco and Firearms allowed and encouraged people with criminal backgrounds and known connections to Mexican cartels to buy guns from shops in Arizona and send them to Mexico. More than 1,000 military grade weapons were involved. Not only did the ATF allow it, the gun store owners in Arizona were concerned. They'd tell the ATF, "This guy keeps coming by and buying 20 or 30 AK-47s. Can you look into him? He seems to have a criminal background." And the ATF would get back and say, "Let him buy them."

Some of the guns ended up in Mexico. Some were involved in crimes. In one case a US border agent was killed by one of these guns. That's the official story. Now it's come out that about a dozen drug cartels in Mexico were operating independently of one another for years. They were prosperous and stayed out of each other's hair. Everybody was happy. Then in 2006 a war broke out and they started killing each other and a lot of Mexican civilians as well. About 50,000 people have been killed, often in a very gruesome manner. One of the cartels, Los Zetas, has an interesting pedigree. It is made up of people who were trained by the US Special Forces. They were trained to kill drug cartel leaders and then decided they'd rather run their own cartel.

A member of the Sinaloa cartel, Vicente Zambada-Niebla, is currently in prison in the US "on charges of trafficking more than a billion dollars in cocaine and heroin."[1] Zambada's attorney is saying that since the late 1990s, the Sinaloa cartel has provided various US law enforcement agencies with information about the other cartels. They help the US eliminate their rivals and in exchange they're allowed to import limitless quantities of drugs into the US. Chicago is one of their main drop-off points.

So, Doug, has there ever been a case when the US government through its various law enforcement agencies gave a pass to drug dealers in exchange for something else? How often does it happen and how far back does this go?

VALENTINE: An old FBN agent, Lenny Schrier, once told me: "The only way you can make cases is if your informant sells dope." So, yes; not only has it happened, and not only does it still happen, but giving dealers a free pass to deal drugs is the foundation stone upon which federal drug law enforcement is based. Once you realize that, you have to look beyond, at the political and economic context that makes such an extra-legal practice possible. Allow me to explain.

In the 1920s, the US threw its weight behind Chiang Kai-shek, whose Kuomintang Party was fighting the Communists and several other warlords for control of China. The US was competing with the other colonial nations for control of China, which had a cheap labor force and represented billions in profits for US corporations and investors. The problem was that the Kuomintang supported itself through the opium trade. It's well documented in the diplomatic cables between the US government and its representatives in China. Historians Kinder and Walker said the Commissioner of the Bureau of Narcotics, Harry Anslinger, "clearly knew about the ties between Chiang and opium dealers."[2]

Anslinger knew that Shanghai was "the prime producer and exporter to the illicit world drug markets," through a syndicate controlled by Du Yue-sheng, a crime lord who facilitated Chiang's bloody ascent to power in 1927. As early as 1932, Anslinger knew that Chiang's finance minister was Du's protector. He'd had evidence since 1929 that American t'ongs were receiving Kuomintang narcotics and distributing it to the Mafia. Middlemen worked with opium merchants, gangsters like Du, Japanese occupation forces in Manchuria, and Dr. Lansing Ling, "who supplied narcotics to Chinese officials traveling abroad." In 1938 Chiang Kai-shek appointed Dr. Ling head of his Narcotic Control Department.[3]

In October 1934, the Treasury attaché in Shanghai "submitted reports implicating Chiang Kai-shek in the heroin trade to North

America." In 1935 the attaché reported that the Superintendent of Maritime Customs in Shanghai was "acting as agent for Chiang Kai-shek in arranging for the preparation and shipment of the stuff to the United States."[4]

These reports reached Anslinger's desk, so he knew which KMT officials and trade missions were delivering dope to American t'ongs and which American Mafia drug rings were buying it. He knew the t'ongs were kicking back a percentage of the profits to finance Chiang's regime.

After Japanese forces seized Shanghai in August 1937, Anslinger was even less willing to deal honestly with the situation. By then Du was sitting on Shanghai's Municipal Board with William J. Keswick, a director of the Jardine Matheson Shipping Company.[5] Through Keswick, Du found sanctuary in Hong Kong, where he was welcomed by a cabal of free-trading British colonialists whose shipping and banking companies earned huge revenues by allowing Du to push his drugs on the hapless Chinese. The revenues were truly immense: according to Colonel Joseph Stilwell, the US military attaché in China, in 1935 there were "eight million Chinese heroin and morphine addicts and another 72 million Chinese opium addicts."[6]

Anslinger tried to minimize the problem by lying and saying that Americans were not affected. But the final decisions were made by his bosses in Washington, and from their national security perspective, the profits enabled the Kuomintang to purchase $31 million worth of fighter planes from arms dealer William Pawley to fight the Communists, and that trumped any moral dilemmas about trading with the Japanese or getting Americans addicted.

It's all documented. Check the sources I cite in my books. Plus, US Congressmen and Senators in the China Lobby were profiting from the guns for drugs business too. They got kickbacks in the form of campaign funds and in exchange, they looked away as long as Anslinger told them the dope stayed overseas. After 1949, the China Lobby manipulated public hearings and Anslinger cooked the books to make sure that the Peoples Republic was blamed for all narcotics coming out of the Far East. Everyone made money and after 1947 the operation was run out of Taiwan, with CIA assistance.

The US government's involvement in the illicit drug business was institutionalized during World War Two. While serving on General Joseph Stilwell's staff in 1944, Foreign Service officer John Service reported from Kunming, the city where the Flying Tigers and OSS were headquartered, that the Nationalists were totally dependent on opium and "incapable of solving China's problems."

Service's reports contributed to the Truman Administration's decision not to come to Chiang Kai-shek's rescue at the end of the war. In retaliation, Chiang's intelligence chief, General Tai Li, had his agents in America accuse Service of leaking the Kuomintang's battle plans to a leftist newsletter. Service was arrested. After Service was cleared of any wrongdoing, the China Lobby persisted in attacking his character for the next six years. He was subjected to eight loyalty hearings, and dismissed from the State Department in 1951.

Service's persecution was fair warning that anyone linking the Nationalist Chinese to drug smuggling would, at a minimum, be branded a Communist sympathizer and his reputation ruined. That is how the US drug operation is still protected today, although security for the operation has improved, and whistleblowers are smeared in other ways.

After World War Two the business of managing the government's involvement in the illicit narcotics trade was given to the CIA, because it could covertly conduct support operations for, among others, the Nationalist Chinese in Taiwan. The CIA also relocated and supplied one of Chiang's armies in Burma. This KMT army supported itself through the opium trade and the CIA flew the opium to places where it was converted to heroin and sold to the Mafia. The other bureaucracies – the military and the Departments of State, Justice and Treasury – provided protection along with the China Lobby congressmen and senators who controlled the little information that was made public.

Mexico fits into this equation. The history of US relations with Mexico is the determinant factor in why the drugs-for-guns business is booming in Mexico right now. It has a lot to do with the United States treating Mexico not as the kind of ally Nationalist China was against the Communists, but as an ongoing threat that needs to be perpetually destabilized. The US has been destabilizing Mexico since Mexico made slavery illegal. American slaves were escaping into Mexico and the Southern states saw this as an act of war. Militias from the Southern states would launch raids into Mexico to get their slaves back, and Mexico would give the slaves sanctuary.

There is a big dose of traditional US racism involved. Mexicans are considered inferior. They're said to be uneducated and all immigrants are criminals and poor. So that's a big element too.

The animosity grew in World War One when Mexico entered into relations with Germany. Check out the famous Zimmermann telegram.[7] Since then the US has been wary that Mexico, with its impoverished population, harbors Communist sympathies. It does everything it can to prop up the elite and help it brutalize the lower classes and keep them down so they can't organize themselves politically and economically. With help from the government, US corporations bribe the elite who run the civic and political institutions, so that Mexico can never support progressive nations in Latin America.

The 1968 Tlatelolco massacre in Mexico City is an example of the CIA's efforts to stifle political reform in Mexico. CIA heretic Phil Agee witnessed the event and wrote about it. It was Mexico's version of Tiananmen Square, but the 300 demonstrators who were gunned down were said to be Communists, so the bloodbath was, in the American press, said to be justifiable. As Ronald Reagan was fond of saying, Mexico is "our backyard." People were made to fear that Mexican labor leaders, farmers and sociologists were about to invade and conquer us, so we had to slaughter them in self-defense. That's the context you have to see these things in. It's Communism versus Capitalism. White versus black. Donald Trump plays on the same fears today.

MCCARTHY: So Fast and Furious was not just a gun sting operation that went awry. Supposedly the US goal, according to Vicente Zambada-Niebla's attorney, was to create a mega cartel. Does that make sense in some way based on your experience of watching how these things unfold?

VALENTINE: I think the CIA is the mega cartel. It might serve the CIA's purposes to have one central cartel in Mexico. But, certainly, no other organization in the world knows as much about drug trafficking. The CIA has computer systems that contain every bit of information about every trafficker and trafficking group; it knows where they bank and where they invest; it can predict their moves, whether in Afghanistan or Mexico. It uses all this information to manipulate events.

Since 1973 the CIA has been in control of US narcotics intelligence worldwide. The function was taken away from the DEA and given to the CIA, which is the unseen hand in this Fast and Furious melodrama. The ATF and DEA are straw men in this drama; as law enforcement agencies, they're shoved out in front of the CIA. But it's the CIA and State Department that arrange what's happening in Mexico, because, quite simply, US law enforcement agencies have no authority in Mexico.

The State Department's concerns about political relationships in the region trump any law enforcement concerns. Any time a law enforcement operation is conducted in a foreign nation it has to be approved by the State Department and the CIA. The CIA has the final say on anybody being recruited by any US law enforcement agency in Mexico. If I'm in the DEA or ATF and I want to recruit the Sinaloa cartel, or anyone in a cartel, I have to check with the CIA. The CIA runs a background check to find out whether the guy is working for the Russians or the North Koreans. The CIA is always worried that Mexicans are working for our enemies. You always hear about Hezbollah in Mexico. So the CIA has control over all informants recruited by the DEA and the ATF in Mexico, and the media knows this. Every reporter who works the Mexican beat knows this, but if they were to tell you, they'd be accused, like John Service or Chelsea Manning, of aiding the enemy. If they tell, they're revealing national security secrets.

So the media is prevented from mentioning that the CIA plans the little melodramas you see. The script is written by politicians in the White House and Congress. The CIA carries out their illegal operations and if one goes bust, it's pinned on some hapless law enforcement agency. So the view the public has of these operations is totally skewed.

The CIA's purpose in having an informant in some Mexican cartel, or running a mega-cartel, has nothing to do with law enforcement. The CIA is not a law enforcement agency. It's our Mafia operating in foreign nations. I don't know which politicians and business people the CIA is backing in Mexico through these guns-for-drugs activities. But that's what it's about. It's about promoting politicians and business people who will enact policies helpful to America while suppressing the Mexican people. Those are the motivations behind who the CIA selects as an informant in a particular cartel.

MCCARTHY: So the ATF, the FBI, these are the fall guys.

VALENTINE: The others, yes, but the FBI is never a fall guy. The FBI also has an "internal security" mandate. Sometimes there's conflict, but the CIA will work with the FBI to pin it on someone else. The CIA's object is making foreign nations abide by American policy. The FBI is protecting the US from any leftist threats. Its counterintelligence operations spill into Mexico, but they're classified and you'll never hear about them in the news. They don't talk about the FBI in this kind of context in the news either.

The FBI is the premier law enforcement branch of the US government but it has no authority over the CIA. It resisted the creation of the CIA for that reason. Under J. Edgar Hoover, the FBI also denied the existence of organized crime and the Mafia until 1963. It took decades to get to that point, because the crooks were anti-Communist and enforced racial repression.

In 1951 Senator Estes Kefauver formed a committee to investigate organized crime in an attempt to delineate lines of authority. It tracked back to drug smuggling in Mexico. That's in my books.

According to a 14 July 1947 State Department report, Chinese Nationalist forces were, at that moment, "selling opium in a desperate attempt to pay troops still fighting the Communists." The Commissioner of the Bureau of Narcotics, Harry Anslinger, knew that Kuomintang narcotics were reaching Mexico. In a November 1946 report to Anslinger, the FBN's supervisor in New Orleans reported that, "Many Chinese of authority and substance gain their means from this illicit trade" and that, "In a recent Kuomintang Convention in Mexico City a wide solicitation of funds for the future operation of the opium trade was noted." The agent listed the major Chinese traffickers by name.

In February 1947, Treasury attaché Dolor DeLagrave, a former OSS officer, reported from Mexico City that three major drug rings existed, but he made no mention of Virginia Hill's connections, Albert Spitzer and Alfred C. Blumenthal. Bugsy Siegel was killed in Virginia Hill's house on 15 June 1947.

In 1939, Meyer Lansky had sent Hill to Mexico where she seduced a number of "top politicians, army officers, diplomats and police officials."[8] Hill soon came to own a nightclub in Nuevo Laredo and started making frequent trips to Mexico City with Dr. Margaret Chung. "Mom" Chung was an honorary member of the Hip Sing T'ong and had served as the attending physician to the Flying Tigers, the private airline formed under China Lobby luminary General Claire Chennault to fly supplies to the Nationalists in Kunming, a city infused with OSS agents and opium.

As investigative journalist Ed Reid reported in *The Mistress and the Mafia*, the FBN knew that Dr. Chung was "in the narcotic traffic in San Francisco."[9]

Chung took large cash payments from Siegel and Hill, and delivered Kuomintang narcotics to Hill in New Orleans, Las Vegas, New York and Chicago. And yet, despite the fact that the FBN agents "kept her under constant surveillance for years," they "were never able to make a case against her."[10]

Why not? Because she was protected by her many influential friends in Washington, including Admiral Chester A. Nimitz.

Agent Joe Bell, the FBN's district supervisor in Chicago, theorized that Siegel's murder, "paved the way to complete control of illegal narcotics distribution in California by the Mafia."[11]

Bell was referring to a related drug smuggling operation Lansky initiated in Mexico in 1944 under Harold "Happy" Meltzer. Described as "the man who most feared Bugsy's grab at Mexico," Meltzer based his operation in Laredo, as fate would have it, directly across the border from Hill's nightclub. He worked with the Mexican consul in Washington, who located suppliers and bribed border guards, and moved drugs to the Mafia in California. Bankrolled by Lansky, Meltzer traveled between Mexico City, Cuba, Hong Kong and Japan.

Meltzer was an occasional CIA asset and in December 1960, the CIA asked him to join an assassination team. His proximity to Virginia Hill in Laredo suggests that he was a recipient of Dr. Chung's Kuomintang narcotics. If that was the case, Siegel may not have been murdered by the Mafia, but by agents of the US government, because Bugsy's grab for control of the CIA's Mexican connection threatened to expose Dr. Chung's protected Kuomintang operation. Even the way Siegel was murdered – by two rifle shots to the head – was characterized as very "ungangsterlike."[12]

Anslinger knew that Spitzer and Blumenthal were Lansky's associates and that large opium shipments were coming out of Mexico "under police escort," but the FBN did nothing. In 1948 the FBN declared that Mexico was the source of half the illicit drugs in America – but did nothing about it because the drug trade enabled the CIA, which had been created in 1947, to destabilize the Mexican government. The CIA apparently connected Captain Rafael Chavarri, founder of Mexico's version of the CIA, the Federal Security Directorate (DFS), with Mexico's top drug smuggler, Jorge Moreno Chauvet.

According to Peter Dale Scott, at this point the CIA "became enmeshed in the drug intrigues and protection of the DFS, its sister agency."[13]

By 1950, Chauvet was receiving narcotics from the new Lansky-

Luciano French connection, and the mob-connected former mayor of New York, William O'Dwyer, was now the US Ambassador to Mexico.

All of this was known to Senator Kefauver. He and other top government officials were also aware that the government's Faustian pact with the Mafia during World War Two had allowed the hoods to insinuate themselves into mainstream America. In return for services rendered during the war, Mafia bosses were protected from prosecution for dozens of unsolved murders, including the 11 January 1943 assassination of *Il Martello* publisher Carlo Tresca in New York.

The Mafia was a huge problem in 1951, equivalent to terrorism today. But it was also a protected branch of the CIA, which was co-opting criminal organizations around the world and using them in its secret war against the Soviets and Red Chinese. The Mafia had collaborated with Uncle Sam and had emerged from World War Two energized and empowered. They controlled cities across the country. Congress looked into this mess through the Kefauver Committee.

Estes Kefauver was a Democratic senator from Tennessee whose goal was to run for President in 1952. His plan was to achieve favorable national attention by exposing the Mafia's role in political corruption and labor racketeering. In order to embark on such a perilous mission, the ambitious senator needed only the approval of President Truman and Judiciary Committee Chairman Pat McCarran, a rabid segregationist, anti-Communist, and lynchpin in the China Lobby.

A conservative with no love for Big City Democrats, McCarran recognized the self-promotional merit in Kefauver's idea. But Nevada was dominated by organized crime figures, to the extent that McCarran was facetiously referred to as "the Gambler's Senator." So he decided to run the investigation himself. Then Senator Joe McCarthy claimed to have a list of 205 people in the State Department who were "known members" of the American Communist Party. McCarran at that point became preoccupied with setting up the Internal Security Subcommittee and joining the politically more promising Communist witch-hunt. Unable to manage both projects simultaneously, he came to terms with Kefauver.

Kefauver formed the Special Committee to Investigate Organized Crime in Interstate Commerce in 1951 and immediately hit a roadblock. By investigating the so-called "gambling syndicate", he was destined to expose the Mafia's ties to J. Edgar Hoover's Establishment patrons, so Hoover refused to let FBI agents serve as investigators for the Committee.

Hoover claimed he was too busy saving the country from Communists, and that it would be counterproductive to devote FBI resources toward investigating what he deemed to be consensual crimes – gambling and drugs.

So Kefauver turned to Commissioner Anslinger for help, and Anslinger assigned his top agents as expert witnesses and investigators. Kefauver and his team of FBN agents visited the major cities and conducted their investigation, and at the end determined that "the vice squad" pattern "gave control of vice payments to a few officials and demoralized law enforcement in general."[14]

The Committee concluded that local law enforcement managed local crime and that federal agencies were powerless to stop it. Street cops were taking payoffs from pimps, gamblers and drug dealers and kicking a percentage up to their bosses, who kicked another percentage back to the politicians who appointed them. The industrialists who put the politicians in power were happy, as long as the cops made sure the Mafia sold dope to blacks and Puerto Ricans.

Nothing has changed. The CIA, FBI, ATF and DEA are performing the same function for their political bosses. They manage crime to maintain social divisions, and so capitalism can thrive. The Kefauver Committee said there's nothing we can do about it.

As Guy Debord famously said, "The Mafia is not an outsider in this world; it is perfectly at home. Indeed, in the integrated spectacle it stands as the model of all advanced commercial enterprises."

People have been aware of it for 65 years but can't do anything about it because the national security state is an impregnable fortress and average citizens can't get inside. Even if you understand what's going on, five seconds later you're chasing it out of your mind because there's not a thing you can do about it. We can't vote to end the secrecy that enables these rackets to exist. Clinton and Trump are rubbing it in our faces. They're saying, "You can't do a damn thing about it." Cops killing blacks is unfortunate but cops are hardly ever punished. The CIA controls the world's rackets the same way, and the federal government and its media allies keep it secret, and there's nothing you can do about it except get riled up personally.

MCCARTHY: It's amazing how skillful they are at keeping the focus on a tiny part of the story and not even getting into the real story. It is interesting how they muddy issues.

VALENTINE: Right now America has 5% of the world's population and 25% of its prisoners. Most of them are in prison for drug-related offences. Talk about human rights abuses. After they joined forces with the Mafia, the capitalists got their Congressmen to keep increasing sentencing for drug offenses. They created a vast, privatized, profitable prison industry which in turn props up a huge law enforcement industry. Taken together, this is not freedom and democracy.

Instead, the government/media propaganda machine has succeeded in demonizing the people who pack the prisons, just as it demonizes Muslims, in order to keep the homeland security industry growing. The disenfranchised minorities who are arrested for drug offenses get court-appointed lawyers who never seriously contest their cases; they cop pleas and go to prison. Human beings are the grist for this crime-mill that churns out money for investors; it's systemic corruption, just like NAFTA, which has led to increased poverty and suffering in Mexico. And this provides the pretext for a surveillance state that's equipped by companies staffed by former FBI, DEA, ATF and CIA agents. It's creating terrorism to subvert the justice system and assure them political control of Americans. That's the domestic end of this drugs-for-guns boondoggle.

MCCARTHY: So overseas we use it as a tool of policy supporting the people we like and eliminating the people we don't like. At home we use it to keep people under political control.

VALENTINE: Yep. All the evidence is there. If you look at what the CIA has done – the coups d'état of leftist governments and alliances with crooks and fascists – and what they're doing now and what they say behind the scenes, it becomes evident that what I'm saying is fact. But the media bosses are partners in this enterprise, and they won't allow their networks to report on anything of substance. If rogues among them do, they're expelled.

MCCARTHY: And there's the horrible example of Gary Webb. I mean if that's not a warning to journalists what can happen to them...

VALENTINE: Lots of journalists have been harassed for even having hinted at the truth. Lots of other people have suffered the same way, starting with the Foreign Service officer I mentioned earlier, John Service.

MCCARTHY: If drugs were to be decriminalized, then that whole thing goes up in smoke. You can't have all these cops on the payroll doing nothing except taking bribes. You can't have the CIA running drug cartels. They always say it would be a humanitarian disaster if we let drugs be legal; there'd be people dying in the streets from overdoses, and that's why we're keeping all this going for you.

VALENTINE: If you look at every other country where they don't have these, to use the cliché, "draconian drug laws", people are not dead in the streets with needles sticking out of their arms and coke pipes shoved up their nose. People want to live healthy lives, but political and economic factors keep them down. Discrimination and lack of economic opportunity turns segments of society to the underground drug business, both as sellers and users. Among the protected rich and famous it's a kick and something they can get away with because they have lawyers and access to the Betty Ford Clinic.

The government is creating conditions across the board that are conducive to taking drugs. The pharmaceutical industry is part of the problem, along with its co-conspirators in the advertising industry; every time you turn on the TV there's a commercial telling you to take a pill. The next commercial says don't take that pill, take this pill. This is the free market at work, sucking the life out of people.

It would help if the air waves were publicly and not privately owned, and if we could get rid of all this advertising. It would help if we could nationalize the pharmaceutical industry and take the profit out of healthcare and law enforcement. Then maybe we could experience something like democracy. But as long as the vulture capitalists control the national security state and the media, that isn't going to happen.

MCCARTHY: We started out with a limited discussion about Mexico, but once you start unraveling one thread, it really does lead to this discussion we're having – because it's not about the gun- and drug-running into Mexico. It's not even about the history of the US supporting drug operations all over the world. It's about domination and control. It's about a few people conspiring, literally, to keep the majority of people in a controlled and controllable state.

VALENTINE: Yep. While you're looking at this one particular shell game, 40 other shell games are going on. If they can keep you focused on the sensational operations, like Gunrunner, you're not going to be looking at what's important: the big picture.

MCCARTHY: It's all about misdirection, the greatest magician's trick. Even in warfare, the ultimate skill is to misdirect the attention of your enemy. So, Doug, thank you so much. You're the guy doing all the digging. You're the one looking at this every day and I can understand the cynicism. But since you brought that up, if one more person understands what's going on it's a victory; not a massive victory, but it's a victory. Big victories have to start with small victories.

PART III

THE PHOENIX FOUNDATION OF HOMELAND SECURITY

"Such a perfect democracy constructs its own inconceivable foe, terrorism. Its wish is to be judged by its enemies rather than by its results. The story of terrorism is written by the state and it is therefore highly instructive. The spectators must certainly never know everything about terrorism, but they must always know enough to convince them that, compared with terrorism, everything else must be acceptable, or in any case more rational and democratic."

Guy Debord, Comments on the Society of the Spectacle

Chapter 15

THE SPOOK
WHO BECAME A
CONGRESSMAN:
WHY CIA OFFICERS
CANNOT BE ALLOWED TO
HOLD PUBLIC OFFICE

While running for Congress as a Republican candidate in 2000, Robert R. "Rob" Simmons posted on his website and in TV ads a picture of himself standing in front of an American flag in an army uniform. The symbolic meaning was obvious: Simmons was glorifying himself as a soldier/patriot above all else.

But in the final week of the campaign, his identification with militancy took an unexpected turn when he was scandalized by allegations that he had committed war crimes while serving not as a soldier, but as a CIA officer in Vietnam. Simmons called the accusation a "smear tactic."

"Any veteran, anybody who served his country in war, should be offended," Simmons said, appealing directly to the patriotism of undecided voters in a last ditch effort to win the election, while inadvertently castigating the CIA.

Adding to his indignation was the undisputed fact that the charges had emanated from the staff of his opponent, Congressman Sam Gejdenson, who had represented Connecticut's 2nd District since 1981.

Rocked by the outpouring of sympathy for Simmons, Gejdenson fired a campaign worker for inciting two (yes, two) college students to plan (yes, plan) a rally against Simmons. The students were intimidated – politically suppressed, in CIA terms – into cancelling their protest.

The local newspaper, the *New London Day*, headlined the Gejdenson aspect of the story, calling it a "dirty trick," but refusing to delve into the substance of the charges. So I wrote to the editor and said that I'd interviewed Simmons twelve years earlier. I offered to write an article about him; but the newspaper decided to wait until after the election.

It seemed like the newspaper was trying to help Simmons win the election. And win he did; though trailing in the week before the election, he won by less than 3,000 votes. It was the allegation that he was a torturer that propelled him to victory.

God bless America

When the *Day* finally featured a story on Simmons' sordid CIA past, it admitted that the war crimes charge wasn't a "dirty trick" but stemmed from a profile of Simmons the *Day* itself had published in 1994. In a rare moment of candor, Simmons in 1994 had confessed that while managing the Phú Yên Province Interrogation Center (PIC), he would threaten to withhold medicine from injured prisoners in order to obtain information. But, he added piously, he never made good on the threat.

According to Simmons, a coercive tactic like threatening to withhold medical treatment did not reach the threshold of a war crime. On the contrary, "If I hadn't involved myself, many people would have lost their limbs or their lives," Simmons said with a straight face.

Simmons' denial was enough for the *Day*. It didn't ask if he'd withheld medicine for hours or days, or if his victims included children and the elderly. It wasn't concerned with the guilt or innocence of the people Simmons abused, or if they were forced to sign false confessions to stop the bleeding. Steeped in the same racist stereotypes that military propagandists spewed during the war, the newspaper assumed that every Vietnamese in the PIC was a terrorist deserving of whatever atrocities were committed against him or her. They were all trying to kill heroic Americans like Rob Simmons, weren't they?

I wasn't surprised by the newspaper's shenanigans. From the time *The Phoenix Program* was published in 1990, I'd witnessed a gradual escalation of belligerent nationalistic rhetoric, accompanied by an outpouring of revisionist Vietnam War history. The reactionary Reagan, Bush and Clinton regimes had waged a series of increasingly militant and covert action initiatives, from El Salvador to Iraq to Serbia, in a calculated and well-publicized attempt to purge the Vietnam Syndrome from the fragile American psyche.

The floodgates opened in the wake of 9/11. Suddenly, the practice of withholding medicine became CIA standard operating procedure as part of the Bush-Cheney-Rumsfeld repertoire of torturous "enhanced" interrogation techniques. Torture became so popular that in 2003 the US Supreme Court approved the practice of withholding medical treatment for *domestic* law enforcement purposes. In a 6-3 decision, the Court exonerated several California cops who'd withheld medical treatment from a Hispanic suspect they'd shot five times. The cops, like Simmons, claimed they were merely trying to get him to talk.[1]

Withholding medical treatment, however, was not always applauded by American militarists as a cool way of coercing bad guys. When John McCain ran for president in 2008, withholding medical treatment was characterized as the dastardly sort of thing only subhuman Commies would do.

McCain, who spent five and a half years in captivity in North Vietnam, was shot down while dropping bombs on civilians in the heart of Hanoi. Taken prisoner with fractures in his right leg and both arms, he received minimal care and was kept in wretched conditions. As he tearfully recalled, "They kept saying, 'You will not receive any medical treatment until you talk'."[2]

McCain suffered. "I thought that if I just held out, that they'd take me to the hospital. I was fed small amounts of food by the guard and also allowed to drink some water. I was able to hold the water down, but I kept vomiting the food.

"I looked at my knee. It was about the size, shape and color of a football. I remembered that when I was a flying instructor a fellow had ejected from his plane and broken his thigh. He had gone into shock, the blood had pooled in his leg, and he died, which came as quite a surprise to us – a man dying of a broken leg. Then I realized that a very similar thing was happening to me."

McCain cracked. Thereafter known as "Songbird", McCain told the guards, "I'll give you military information if you will take me to the hospital."

I've repeated McCain's sorrowful story to show how easy

it was for the *Day* to manipulate information to minimize the charge against Simmons. We didn't hear the screams of pain and fear in the background like we did in McCain's account. Simmons' victims were given no voice at all.

This magical ability to portray the same thing as good in one case and bad in another is the essence of the political and psychological warfare campaign being waged against Americans by rehabilitated war criminals like Simmons and McCain and their supporting cast in the old boy network that has manipulated public opinion for 70 years. But the differences between McCain and the Vietnamese Simmons tortured, are that McCain was wounded while terror bombing innocent civilians in a major city in a foreign country while Simmons remained unscathed, and the people he terrorized were snatched from their homes at midnight or in Phoenix round ups.

As his well-rehearsed story illustrates, Simmons is an expert at dissembling, which, as I explained to the *Day*, is why he shouldn't have been allowed to hold public office. He can't be trusted to tell the truth about anything. But the sad fact is that many Americans are soothed by the double standard, which absolves them of complicity in the crimes their country commits.

What's worse is that he has legions of allies in the media to censor his critics, fellow CIA officers to back his alibi, and corrupted historians to lend an air of authenticity to his propaganda.

Stated Policy vs Operational Reality

Early in my research into the Phoenix program, I filed an FOIA with the CIA asking it to release all its records about the PICs. That request was denied.

Forty years after they were abandoned, the PICs are still as big a secret as what happened inside the gulag archipelago of black sites the CIA built after 9/11 in eight countries, including Thailand (where al Qaeda commander Abu Zubaydah was waterboarded), Afghanistan, and "several democracies in Eastern Europe".[3]

The CIA will never release to the public its secret files about the PICs, which certainly served as models for its black sites. And even if it did release them, they should not be believed. CIA officers are trained never to incriminate themselves in written reports or spoken words. Not to do so, after all, is key to achieving plausible deniability.

The way to understand the operational realities of running a PIC, as opposed to the stated policies Simmons and his co-conspirators cite chapter and verse, is by studying the political, psychological and bureaucratic contexts in which they occur. By doing so, one realizes that war crimes like those committed in the PICs are unstated, but carefully crafted US policy.

The mindset of CIA officers and their media co-conspirators is the unifying factor in this conspiracy. McCain, the tortured, and Simmons – by the same standards – the torturer, truly believe the heroic myth they have created about themselves. Indeed, the "Myth of the Hero" has informed Western literature and philosophy since the Greek elite paid Homer to pen the *Iliad* and *Odyssey,* forever endowing the warrior class with the highest social virtues, while justifying the tragic consequences of their imperial marauding as "fate."

Since then the theme of the warrior hero has determined Western social development. The Old Testament would be a short story without it. How many times have Hollywood's leading men quoted the rousing speech Shakespeare had Henry V deliver to his soldiers on Saint Crispin's Eve:

> For he today that sheds his blood with me
> Shall be my brother; be he ne'er so vile
> This day shall gentle his condition…

Being initiated into a secret society – a "band of warrior brothers" that exists apart from and is superior to civil society – can be intoxicating. Even Confederate soldiers are venerated as heroes; for however vile they were as individuals, they obeyed their officers and killed and died on command. Much of America's rhetorical identity as "exceptional" is based on this Marlboro macho man myth.

What distinguishes CIA officers is their transcendent ability, through their bureaucratic association with the National Security Establishment and its Homeric scribes in Hollywood, to promulgate their myths as fact, while guaranteeing that the truth is concealed.

McCain's exalted status as a US Senator enabled him to enact legislation that sealed thousands of documents pertaining to Vietnam War POW briefings. He claimed he did it to protect the privacy of POWs, but his real motive, according to Sydney H. Schanberg, was to keep the lid on the details of his collaboration with his captors.[4]

Simmons pulled a similar stunt. While serving as a legislative aide in the US Congress, he helped author and enact the Intelligence Identities Protection Act, which makes it a crime to name CIA agents. It was already a crime to report CIA "sources and methods," but this Act added another layer of legal chain mail to the protective shield already separating CIA officers from the consequences of their crimes. Once they are safely ensconced in this legally-gated community, they have only to sculpt their Boy Scout persona.

Every crime boss knows how to act in front of the press. In 1958, reporter Dom Frasca managed to get an interview with Vito Genovese, just before he went to prison for drug trafficking. Don Vito liked golf, wore yellow tinted glasses, and lived alone in a five-bedroom cottage. He did his own cooking, mostly traditional Italian dishes. Eight grandkids often visited. When Frasca asked him about the rackets, Vito blamed all his troubles on his ex-wife going through menopause. Most significantly, Vito's wry humor kept Frasca at an impeccable distance without offending.

It's easy to put on an act. The best politicians, criminals and CIA officers do it naturally. The problem for the rest of us is that, over time, the actors come to believe it. The myths they internalize are the fatal "lie in the soul" Plato warned about. "Fate" isn't what makes someone murder and torture for profit; it is deceiving oneself into believing one has no choice.

Not everyone is a victim of this mass delusion. Warren Milberg, a CIA officer I interviewed for *The Phoenix Program,* told me how, in 1967, the Pentagon invited him and two other Air Force officers to join a secret CIA counterinsurgency program in Vietnam. Volunteers were given extensive training and sent to Vietnam to serve at the discretion of senior CIA officers in Saigon and the regions. Most were assigned to the provinces as paramilitary officers. Several became Phoenix coordinators.

Milberg, who identified himself as one of the "Protected Few," joined the program. But the other two officers withdrew, one "as a matter of conscience." Jacques Klein withdrew because "he felt the means and methods that he thought were going to be used in [Phoenix] were similar to the means and methods used by the Nazis in World War Two."

Klein took individual responsibility. Simmons sacrificed his and is forever corrupted. It's that simple.

"What Did You Do in the War, Daddy?"

Simmons enlisted in the army in July 1965. He went to the army's intelligence school that fall and, upon graduating, was commissioned as a first lieutenant. He arrived in Vietnam in April 1967 and served a year with the 219th Military Intelligence Detachment in Bien Hoa, a major city in III Corps near Saigon.

Simmons liked the war and volunteered for another tour, serving until December 1968 with MACV Team 96 in Can Tho City, where the CIA was headquartered in IV Corps.[5] His job was to work with South Vietnamese military and police forces to interdict the Viet Cong's secret supply system. Secret agents and smugglers were moving weapons, drugs and other contraband through market places along the Cambodian border. Simmons was successful and, as a reward, was sent to brief Ambassador Ellsworth Bunker on his findings, which led to the initiation of the Cambodian Border Watch Program.

While in Can Tho, Simmons worked with CIA officers. "I liked the Agency guys," he said to me. "They listened, and they asked the smartest questions."

The CIA guys liked Simmons too and arranged a job interview for him at CIA headquarters. He was hired and entered the junior officer trainee program, which involved paramilitary training – handling weapons and making bombs – and intelligence training – surveillance, spy craft, running agent nets, setting up proprietary companies, etc. This was the same program Milberg joined and Klein quit. Similar programs have proliferated since 9/11.

Simmons returned to Vietnam in November 1970 as a CIA officer posing as a civilian employee of the Defense Department within MACV's Pacification Security Coordination Group.[6] He was slated to return to Can Tho, but a CIA officer in Phu Yen Province had "flipped out" and locked himself in a room with a gun. That sorry soul was sent home, as was his predecessor. According to Simmons, the officer he replaced was fired for hitting a priest, "a Don Luce-type" who, ironically, was at that very time investigating abuses at the Phu Yen PIC.[7]

Other ironies awaited Simmons.

Located in II Corps, Phu Yen was a "heavy VC province." CIA officers were confined to the compound, wore flak jackets, carried machine guns, periodically came under mortar attack, and had a personal force of "Nung" Chinese bodyguards.

Simmons was assigned to the CIA compound in Tuy Hoa, the province's capital city. He did not name his boss, the Province Officer in Charge (POIC), but described his counterpart, Special Police Chief Nguyen Tam, as a former French Foreign Legionnaire and paratrooper in the South Vietnamese Army. Tam was a tough veteran who didn't trust Simmons and could not control his freewheeling subordinates. Simmons initially reported on police corruption, but, he said, "Morales never passed the reports to Saigon."[8]

In 1970, CIA Station Chief Ted Shackley distanced the CIA from the pacification programs it had initiated earlier in the war, including Phoenix. Negotiations for a ceasefire were underway by 1971 and the CIA receded into the shadows. Simmons was not allowed to meet the CORDS Province Senior Advisor. Relations with military intelligence and with the Special Police were strained as well.

Shackley told me that the CIA still oversaw Phoenix in 1972, but only "to iron out problems." Was there a province chief not willing to cooperate with the PIC? Maybe there was overcrowding in a PIC that the province or region couldn't resolve. What to do? Well, the Phoenix director would go to the secretary-general (of the National Police) and cite specific cases. There might be a knowledgeable source in a PIC who needed to be brought to Saigon.[9] Were the line managers looking at the dossiers?

"Phoenix," Shackley insisted, "had nothing to do with intelligence operations. It was completely separate from Special Branch trying to penetrate the Vietcong. Any guy who could be used as a penetration agent was spun out of Phoenix."

Under Shackley, Phoenix evolved into a massive screening operation under military control, while the Special Branch had the mission of "keying on important VCI political leaders and activists so as not to clog up the system with volumes of low-level VCI cadre or front members."[10]

A typical Special Branch operation began when an agent submitted a report on a VCI suspect. The Special Branch would assign people to watch him or her. Special Police officers worked in two-man teams around the clock. They'd find where the suspect lived and worked and where his "contact points" were. Other agents were set up in business, perhaps a soup shop close to the suspect's house, or a bicycle repair shop near his favorite cafe. Places the suspect visited were kept under surveillance. The Special Police wanted to know, for example, if the suspect and his comrades were printing leaflets in a safe-house for the Women's Revolutionary Association. If the suspect was involved in revolutionary activity, he was secretly arrested and interrogated and, ideally, made to inform on his bosses. More arrests would follow and the best candidate among them would be coerced into working for the Special Police as a penetration agent, secretly channeling information to his case officer, which would lead to more arrests.

For security purposes, photos of the penetration agent were taken in the company of Special Police personnel. He/she would also be forced to sign a sworn statement indicating that he/she was working for the GVN. The photos and documents would find their way to the VCI if the agent did not cooperate in the future.

Such was nature of the spy business Simmons was in. When he arrived in Tuy Hoa, his boss had three other CIA officers on his staff. One advised Korean army forces in the province. Another oversaw "unilateral" operations and was isolated from every South Vietnamese agency, all of which were penetrated by the VCI. The POIC spent most of his time with the unilateral operations officer, a veteran who had over 20 years of spy experience. Simmons was low man on the totem pole and his boss gave him little supervision; he was, after all, working with counterparts who were not trusted.

"We met and we talked," Simmons explained, "but [the POIC] focused on the unilateral operations guy, on political reporting on dissident groups, who is running in elections, who is going to win."

The third officer advised the PIC Chief and vacated Vietnam soon after Simmons arrived. He was not replaced, due to the Reduction in Forces policy in place, and Simmons inherited the thankless job.

But all was not doom and gloom. "In late 1970," Simmons said, "there was a feeling that we were winning the war. Not conquering Hanoi. Not pacifying the countryside. But reducing the VCI threat and driving the NVA main forces back."

Simmons' job involved intelligence and paramilitary operations. In regard to intelligence, he directed Special Police Chief Tam in operations designed to identify members of the VCI, with the goal of controlling the political environment by penetrating the VCI. This was not an easy thing to do; those in GVN-controlled areas had cover jobs – doctor, teacher, farmer – while filling positions within the insurgency, such as messenger to VCI in the hamlets and villages. Those in the countryside were armed and hiding in secret lairs.

Knowing how the CIA worked with the Special Police in Vietnam is helpful in understanding how the CIA operates in Afghanistan, Iraq, and elsewhere. As recently as May, 2016, the Pentagon announced that dozens of American "advisors" had been deployed to Yemen over the past two weeks. "They are working with Saudi and Arab coalition troops seeking to assert control over southern portions of the country, including the areas controlled by al Qaeda in the Arabian Peninsula (AQAP)."[11]

As noted, CIA advisors like Simmons often work under military cover. Today, in Yemen and elsewhere, they are doing exactly what he did. More to the point, the CIA funds, equips, and manages the special police forces it has created worldwide, but you won't hear about it on the news.

In Vietnam, the CIA organized the Special Police into sections. At the top was the chief and under him were (among others) an Interrogation Section, a "Studies and Plans" Section, and the all-important Secret Services Section (SSS).

The SSS was split in two sub-sections. The first would watch, track, arrest and recruit low level VCI sympathizers. The more important Special Operations Sub-Section ran infiltration and penetration operations. Because special operations involved strategic intelligence, the Special Police chief jointly supervised SSS cases with his CIA advisor, who met directly with and helped the SSS case-officers running agents in the field.

Agent recruitment was compartmentalized. When the Special Police spotted an insider who could be recruited to infiltrate the VCI or an outsider in a position to approach members of the VCI, the first step was to determine if he/she could be turned into an agent. What did he do? Did she live in the area where the VCI were operating? Did the person have contact with someone inside the VCI?

Such a person was known as a PIRL – a potential intelligence recruitment lead. If he or she was found to be suitable, they were recruited.

Next the Special Police drafted a Preliminary Plan to train the recruit in "tradecraft": how to collect information, what matters to focus on, how to maintain a cover story, and how to make contact with and secretly report to a case officer. All of this was discussed with the CIA advisor. If a CIA advisor like Simmons approved the plan, he dipped into his black bag and supplied the cash to pay the agent. He also provided the necessary equipment: cameras, tape-recorders, safe-houses and items like antibiotics to purchase the target's cooperation.

The Special Police Chief, SSS Chief and SSS case-officer would periodically meet with the CIA advisor to evaluate the agent's Information Report. When things were running smoothly, an Operational Plan was made. If the agent succeeded in transforming himself into a VC activist, the plan was upgraded to an Infiltration Plan. If the agent succeeded in turning a VCI cadre into a defector – a spy inside the VCI – the plan reached its highest level and became a Penetration Plan. At that point – and this is the crucial part – the running of the operation was turned over to the CIA, and the Special Police were ordered to protect, maintain, and not interfere in the plan.

In every case, the Special Police had to follow the CIA advisor's directions and satisfy his every need. This involved a significant degree of humiliation, for CIA advisors like Simmons rarely spoke Vietnamese. And even with a translator, they could not comprehend the subtleties of Vietnamese culture, let alone the intricacies of a penetration operation, which is why neither party trusted the other.

Within this perverse environment, a CIA officer like Simmons was constantly asserting his dominance, and misunderstandings and resentments proliferated. Inevitably, CIA officers like Simmons internalized yet another integral part of the hero myth - the Lord Jim "warlord" mentality.

Megalomaniacal warlords intriguing against one another to control the political environment is the dynamic that defines America's hidden corridors of power.

Phoenix in Phu Yen

The Special Police sent a representative to the Phu Yen Province Phoenix/Phụng Hoàng Committee, along with information and documents from its Studies and Plans Section. But they did not direct the Committee or its field operations. Consequently, Simmons considered Phoenix a duplication of Special Police operations. The Special Police "might send reports" to the Phoenix center, he observed, "which was out on Point, not downtown," and consisted of "a bunch of people keeping files."

Just as the CIA knew that the VCI had penetrated the Special Police, so too the Special Police knew that Phoenix had been penetrated.

Phoenix was more exposed and an easier target of enemy collection efforts. In Phu Yen Province, the Phoenix DIOCCs were often attacked and files stolen.

"We would go to Phoenix and they'd show us a file," Simmons said, "and we'd use the file to help build a case. Every report we generated, we sent to the PIOCC. But Special Branch had its own files. And if at the PIC we got someone who cooperated, we would withhold his file if he was going to be doubled, because we knew the PIOCC was penetrated."

Simmons and the PRU

By 1971 the CIA was distancing itself from its PRU counter-terror teams as well as from Phoenix and the Special Branch. Simmons was never responsible for the PRU. He knew the South Vietnamese PRU chief, whom he described as "a smart, upstanding, responsible guy," and he allowed the PRU to use his radio, but that was the extent of his involvement.

According to Simmons, the Phoenix coordinator in Phu Yen Province worked more closely with the PRU than he did. The PRU, when developing information on VCI cadre in a village or hamlet, would acquire targeting information from the DIOCCs. The PRU would ask, "Who do you have in that village," and then the PRU chief would check out the DIOCC's files on likely candidates.

The region's PRU advisor, Jack Harrell, had attended the same CIA training class as Simmons. Harrell paid the PRU once a month out of the CIA's bottomless black bag. Thirty years later, Simmons would call upon Harrell to support the story he told to the *New London Day*, that no one was ever tortured at the Phu Yen PIC. Harrell went along with the fiction.

Simmons and the PIC

Under Simmons' supervision, the Special Police placed suspected members of the VCI, including children, on a blacklist. If they appeared to act suspiciously, or were accused by an informer, they were snatched and placed in the PIC. Simmons was involved at every stage of every operation.

The PIC was a one-storey building with a tin roof in downtown Tuy Hoa. Simmons' office was "around the corner" in a Quonset hut on the grounds of the National Police station. His translator had good relations with the PIC Chief, an Interrogation Section officer who reported to the Special Police Chief and to Tran Quang Nam, the ranking National Police Chief in the province. Simmons described the PIC chief as "smart, educated, from Saigon, a progressive."

The PIC Chief's staff provided reports for Simmons to peruse. After reading the translated reports, Simmons would interrogate prisoners who, in his estimation, could become penetration agents. He conducted the interrogations himself but, he emphasized, he "never" let himself get in "untenable situations."

The PIC Chief did not manage penetration operations; he helped the SSS case officer interrogate and single out leads for the Special Police chief to exploit. But Simmons was a control freak and considered the PIC "the key place for recruiting double agents."

The PICs, like almost every CIA operation, were kept secret from the American public, but were a grim reality, like US military bases, to the people living around them. The PICs were notorious and South Vietnamese citizens were constantly complaining about them. Theoretically, a PIC advisor played a mediating role with the local population; while staying in the shadows, he helped improve conditions in response to citizen complaints for more light, more windows, more water, more space, more food and medicine. This public relations consideration was the reason why Simmons had access to Vietnamese medics and, in rare instances, American doctors.

PICs were also a way station. Prisoners were supposed to be rotated out within a few days and their cases sent to Province Security Committees (PSC) for disposal. If enough evidence was presented to convict someone as a "national security offender," he/she was placed in "administrative detention" without access to a lawyer or due process. There were detention centers in every province, apart from the PICs and prisons. This same system exists in every nation America currently occupies. Private US companies make out like bandits building the facilities.

High level VCI were sent to the National Interrogation Center in Saigon. People convicted of national security offenses were sent to various prisons or the infamous facility at Con Son Island where they were stuck and often shackled in Tiger Cages – rows of submerged concrete cells shaped like coffins, built by French colonialists, with iron gates for roofs so that guards could look down on the prisoners from above – whose existence was revealed to the public by Don Luce in 1970.

The Special Intelligence Force Unit

The PRU teams were controversial and known for war crimes. Called "The CIA's Hired Killers" by journalist Georgie Anne Geyer in a 1970 article for *True* magazine, the PRU were recruited by CIA talent scouts from Vietnam's minority ethnic and social groups. PRU teams were composed of Chinese Nungs, Montagnards, Muslim Chams, Cambodians, convicts and former VC. The one thing they had in common was the ability to kill without remorse.

By 1971 the CIA was distancing itself from the PRU, and Simmons was instructed to develop his own paramilitary unit for capturing and killing individual VCI. As a trained paramilitary officer, he was fully prepared and willing to mount operations designed to kill "targeted" members of the VCI.

During our interview in 1988, Simmons produced reports of his paramilitary operations in Phu Yen Province. One report told how a Special Police team killed three VCI in November 1970. Based on a tip provided by an informer, the VCI were ambushed at night while digging a spider hole outside Vinh Phu hamlet. One of the people killed, Nguyen Van Toan, was described in the report as the Secretary of the Communist Party Chapter Committee and chairman of the Village People's Revolutionary Committee. Toan was 20 years old and a native of Vinh Phu hamlet. He was killed in his neighborhood.

As a result of this successful operation, Simmons was ordered to develop the province's paramilitary capability. To that end he created one of several prototypes for "special action" teams in Military Region II. Called the Special Intelligence Force Unit (SIFU), it was formed in late 1971. Recruits came from nearby districts. All were volunteers from the Special Police and the National Police Field Forces. Eventually there were six teams, each consisting of four men from the Special Police and four from the Field Forces. The Phu Yen Province SIFU had its own facility and was commanded by Special Police officer Nguyen Van Quy. It was advised and funded by Rob Simmons.

Simmons did not say if he accompanied the SIFU team on its missions, but in order to command respect, CIA paramilitary officers routinely went on missions.

In a report dated December 1971, the National Police Commander in Phu Yen Province discussed several SIFU operations. Simmons objected to the word "assassinate," so Colonel Nam used the word "exterminate" to describe a mission in which two VCI were killed in an ambush.[12]

As an example of SIFU effectiveness, Simmons produced a copy of a 29 January 1972 letter he sent to his CIA superiors. The letter was a request for medals for SIFU members who had participated in "the recent Lien Tri operation."

The Lien Tri operation began when an informer reported that elements of the Tuy Hoa City Party Committee Action Team were planning to enter Lien Tri hamlet to build hiding places in preparation for an attack against Tuy Hoa and its northern suburbs. The North Vietnamese were, at the time, laying the groundwork for the spring offensive of 1972. The SIFU moved into the area the following day to intercept the VC Action Team. At 9:00 pm, four confirmed VC, along with three women and seven youths, were seen digging a hole and were "taken under fire." Killed were Trinh Tan Luc, a Tuy Hoa Party Committee member, and Nguyen Dung of the Tuy Hoa Current Affairs Committee.

Under laws written by Americans, it was legal for Simmons to target for death South Vietnamese civilians such as the three women and seven youths digging the hole. Given that two of the VCI had organized a recent attack on Tuy Hoa, Simmons was pleased to "exterminate" them. The operation was over by 11:00 pm.

"This operation epitomizes the type of operation we encourage the police to run against the VC/VCI in Phu Yen province," Simmons boasted to his boss. "The special police prepared detailed information on the individual VC, tasked their local sources for information on the individuals targeted, which was of immediate value, and then were able to mount a strike force which was sufficiently well-equipped to effectively react to the information in a timely manner. The results speak for themselves."

Prior to leaving Vietnam in June 1972, Simmons conducted one last operation. That spring the NVA and VCI had attacked the Phu Yen PIC and CIA compound. Binh Dinh Province, bordering Phu Yen on the north, was overrun by enemy forces, which were advancing on Tuy Hoa, when Simmons leaped into action.

Everyone was in a panic. For several harrowing days they were cut off from the rest of Region II. Simmons spent a night alone in the compound monitoring the radio, and the next day, after crawling out from under his desk, he helped move reinforcements and supplies across the beachhead. It was touch and go, and after the main attack was repulsed, Simmons and his homeboys were confronted with a dicey situation. Thousands of refugees were fleeing Binh Dinh and the VCI were using them as cover to sneak in their own assassins. CIA officers had been targeted for "assassination" (a word Simmons uses when people target Americans) in Binh Dinh, and reports indicated that the CIA officers in Phu Yen were next on the list.

The fear and apprehension were palpable, but Simmons saved the day. Documents captured in March revealed that the VCI were planning to infiltrate Tuy Hoa in mini-vans called Lambros. "So," Simmons explained, "we rolled [the Lambro drivers] up and we put them all in the PIC. That's fifteen to twenty people. We interrogated the Lambro drivers and learned they had all been conscripted. They were bringing VC cadres posing as farmers into Tuy Hoa. The Lambros were driven by VCI, including a few women. They had weapons hidden under seats to attack government offices."

As Simmons is fond of saying, the results speak for themselves. But is there another side of the story of his CIA activities in Vietnam? What did the South Vietnamese and their government, which the US was ostensibly there to support, think of his operations?

Mythological Transformations

"'I'm a poor farm girl,'" Simmons said in a shrill, falsetto voice, mocking a woman he'd snatched and confined without due process in the PIC. "So we released her and watched her for three months, then we put her name in the paper. Arresting and watching her suppressed her and the organization too."

What Simmons described is the application of terror to suppress people. He traveled 12,000 miles to terrorize and kill Vietnamese citizens like 20-year old Nguyen Van Toan in their backyards, because they believed in agrarian reform and resisted foreign domination. As an "exceptional" American he did so unflinchingly, under the pretext of bringing self-determination to the Vietnamese. Meanwhile, some of the Communist sympathizers he terrorized were, despite his best efforts, being freely elected into public office as part of the ceasefire agreements.

Although Simmons would insist that PICs and PRUs were synonymous with democratic institutions, many South Vietnamese disagreed. As early as June 1969, South Vietnam's National Assembly had questioned the Ministers of Defense, Justice and Interior about abuses by Phoenix officials, including illegal arrest, torture and corruption. Eighty-six deputies signed a petition asking for an explanation. Justice Minister Le Van Thu noted that the extra-legal facet of the system, the Province Security Committees, had the power to sentence VCI cadre for up to two years in detention without convicting them of any crime. Thu said the practical difficulties of amassing solid evidence made it necessary to arrest everyone suspected of complicity. That explanation was not well received.[13]

One legislator charged the Vinh Binh Province police chief with "knowingly" arresting innocent people for the purpose of extortion. Another said VCI suspects were detained for six to eight months before their cases were heard, and that suspects were frequently tortured to extract confessions. She said the people "hated" the GVN for starting Phoenix.

Other deputies were incensed that American troops forcefully and illegally detained suspects during military operations, a charge Colby would deny at Congressional hearings in 1971.

Congressman Reid asked Colby, "Do [Phoenix advisors] perform any actual arrests or killings, or do they merely select the individuals who are to be placed on the list who are subject to killing or capturing and subsequent sentencing?"[14]

Colby replied, "They certainly do not arrest, because they have no right to arrest." But, he added speciously, "Occasionally a police advisor may go out with a police unit to capture somebody [but] he would not be the man who reached out and grabbed the fellow."

At the same hearings, Army intelligence officer Michael Uhl testified that all civilian detainees were listed as VCI and that, despite Colby's denials, Americans exercised power of arrest over Vietnamese civilians. "In Duc Pho," Ulh said, "where the 11th Brigade base camp was located, we could arrest and detain at will any Vietnamese civilian we desired, without so much as a whisper of coordination with ARVN or GVN authorities."

As for the accuracy of information from "paid sources who could easily have been either provocateurs or opportunists with a score to settle," Uhl said, "The unverified and in fact unverifiable information, nevertheless was used regularly as input to artillery strikes, harassment and interdiction fire, B-52s and other air strikes, often on populated areas."

No Vietnamese citizen was fooled by Colby's double talk. Grass roots opposition to American occupation and systematic repression existed and was not confined to Communists. At senate hearings held in 1970, Foreign Relations Committee Chairman William Fulbright asked Colby "Where is Mr. (Truong Dinh) Dzu, the man who ran second in the last election?"[15]

"Mr. Dzu is in Chi Hoa jail in Saigon," Colby said, adding that Dzu was not arrested under Phoenix, but under Article 4, which made it a crime to propose the formation of a coalition government with the Communists.[16]

Apart from Colby and his co-conspirators, no one made a distinction between Vietnamese officials the Americans corrupted, or the Americans advising Phoenix, or the ubiquitous American-created and jerry-rigged judicial system that enabled all the atrocities that occurred.

For its part, the CIA lumped together peaceniks, neutralists and political opponents as VCI, but again, the Vietnamese people weren't fooled. They knew the CIA didn't want to end the war if it meant sharing power with Communists. As it is in Afghanistan today, the CIA's goal in Vietnam was to prevent rapprochement, which it tried to do by making advocating peace with the Communists punishable by death or imprisonment without trial under the An Tri Laws.

Despite the Vietnamese peoples' efforts at political accommodation, the CIA in 1972 still considered neutralists and anyone advocating peace as legitimate targets for extermination. And Congressman Rob Simmons was an agent of this genocidal endeavor to suppress the will of the Vietnamese people to live in peace.

The same can be said of the American militants who lead America into war after war in Islamic states, pushing young Muslim men into fundamentalism, and provoking within them the lust for revenge that our leaders then insidiously use as a pretext to restrict civil liberties and institute a police state in the US.

Being in Simmons' presence was disturbing, the way being around CIA officers always is. One senses that the abuse they have heaped on their victims has forever warped their souls. They no longer need to psych themselves up to dehumanize their imaginary enemies; it's second nature to them.

My argument to the *New London Day* was that it is necessary to ask how Simmons' prolonged abuse of people affected him and those like him, and how their sick sensibilities might determine their actions if they moved from clandestine operations into public office.

The newspaper dismissed my argument as irrelevant, but the detrimental effects of engaging in torture are known. In December 2014, the *Washington Post* cited from the Senate Report on CIA torture. The Report said that "numerous" CIA agents engaged in torture in Iraq and around the world had "serious documented personal and professional problems" that "should have called into question" their employment by the CIA and access to classified information. The author of the article asked, "What can we expect for the future of those who carried out the rectal feedings, waterboardings, and other harsh treatment of detainees that the report described?"[17]

I was muzzled in 2000 when Simmons was running for Congress. But time has justified my fears that the public embrace of Simmons and those like him represented a dangerous drift toward fascism in America. Indeed, he and his CIA co-conspirators have applied the same tactics they used in South Vietnam against their "liberal" enemies in America, as I shall demonstrate later in this book.

When I asked Simmons about the morality of interrogation centers and hit teams, he said, "Most of what we did was benign." He assumed no responsibility. He admitted only to negligent cruelties and thanks to CIA secrecy, there is no official evidence to contradict him. But there is circumstantial evidence.

Residual Responsibility

When the *Day* ran its feature article on Simmons, it avoided the overarching issue of American responsibility for systematic repression in Vietnam, and focused solely on Simmons' good intentions. In support of Simmons' claim, it cited Gary Mattocks, who managed the CIA's PRU teams in IV Corps in 1971. Mattocks (whose CIA escapades are chronicled in a prior chapter) said he visited Simmons and never observed any torture at the PIC. He qualified that statement, however, by adding, "Our orders were to vacate the premises if anybody was being mistreated. But we couldn't tell them what to do. They ran the show."

Mattock's statement, "They ran the show," is patently untrue. And while the *Day* let it stand, there is plenty of evidence to prove it is false.

The Special Police were well aware of who "ran the show." One of the top Special Police officers told me that his organization – along with the entire South Vietnam government – "was like a needy person, and any gift given to her or him was precious and heartily welcomed. Every year the gifts were newer and better than before, and so the government willingly followed whatever directions and instructions accompanied the gifts."

The Special Police officer quoted a proverb used in South Vietnamese financial circles, a proverb that applied when CIA promises were accompanied by action (meaning money): "Who pays, governs."

Simmons admitted as much. When I interviewed him in 1988, I asked about his relationship with his counterparts. He replied that the PIC Chief reported administratively "up through the police structure, but he also knows that the building was built [by the CIA] and then turned over. Okay. But he also knows that, 'Hey! You know this building came from the guy in the Quonset hut.'"

I asked if the CIA paid Special Branch salaries. "That's right," he replied. "And also the agents. If you've got a hot agent that you want to recruit, the money comes from [the CIA].

"I was very interested in some of the quality of interrogation that was going on," Simmons added, "and I had access to resources so that I could manage [phone rings], so that I could get what I wanted."

Simmons could get anything he wanted. And as we know, "He who pays, governs."

In a letter to the editor, I suggested that if the *Day* really wanted to confirm, as the editor had said, that Simmons was a good public figure with clean hands, it should send a reporter to Vietnam to interview any surviving civilians who had been held in the Phu Yen PIC while it was under Simmons' supervision. Get the other side of the story, I suggested; let the victims be the judges. But the newspaper preferred the Homeric myths about Simmons, whom it endorsed. It never sent anyone to Vietnam. It didn't even try to contact knowledgeable Vietnamese officials and historians.

There are, however, contemporaneous reports regarding conditions in the PICs. One of them is a 9 September 1973 letter from David and Jane Barton to Congressman Robert N. C. Nix at the Asian and Pacific Affairs Sub-Committee. From May 1971 until May 1973, the Bartons were field directors with the American Friends Service Committee's Rehabilitation Center in Quang Ngai Province. Quang Ngai is close to Phu Yen and what the Bartons said about the Quang Ngai PIC mirrored events in the PIC supervised by Simmons. I'll cite portions of their letter to give a sense of what went on.

The Bartons addressed the withholding of medicine as a torture technique. They noted that medical care for prisoners was "almost nonexistent." During their two years in Quang Ngai, they said, "no Vietnamese doctor nor medical person visited any of the prisoners and there were few medicines stronger than aspirin." Prisoners were seriously ill with, among other things, pneumonia, unset broken bones, infected wounds and malnutrition. Some were chained to their beds and prison officials rarely isolated prisoners with communicable diseases, such as tuberculosis.

"A second problem," they said, was that "many prisoners [in the hospital] were returned [to the PIC] for further interrogation even though they were diagnosed as seriously ill and under treatment. One such example is that of a nineteen-year-old woman whom our doctor discovered had a cardiovascular problem of potentially serious consequences. In addition, the patient had a three-month-old fractured femur due to a bullet wound and was unable to walk. The AFSO doctor asked both the American and Vietnamese officials to allow him to remove the bullet and evaluate this prisoner's heart condition. The American and Vietnamese officials were fully aware of the danger to this prisoner's life if she did not receive medical treatment, and yet [she] was returned to the Interrogation Center and denied medical care."

On the subject of torture in PICs, they wrote:

The majority of the prisoners to whom we gave medical treatment had been tortured. We were able to gather evidence of torturing through the physical examination … through interviews and personal accounts … and from X-rays and photographs. During interrogation at the Province Interrogation Center prisoners explained that they are forced to drink large amounts of water mixed with [lime], soap, or salty fish sauce. After their stomachs are bloated, the Interrogator jumps on their stomachs. One APSO doctor examined several patients who had "petit mal" seizures and memory lapses. He felt that this was due to brain damage caused by drinking such toxins. Prisoners also told an AFSO doctor that they were forced to lie on a table and if they didn't respond to questioning properly, the interrogator would reach underneath their ribcage and crack or break the prisoner's rib. The same doctor examined and had X-ray evidence of several prisoners with cracked or broken ribs. Frequently prisoners suffered from internal bleeding and internal injuries. These prisoners described how they were placed upright in water-filled oil drums which were then beaten on the sides giving the prisoners internal injuries without leaving external marks of torture on their bodies. Many prisoners showed very visible signs of being beaten and in several cases skull fractures, brain hemorrhages, and various forms of paralysis resulted. Prisoners were also tortured with electricity. Electrical wires were attached to their toes, fingers, or [genitals]. When the electrical shocks were administered ... they would become unconscious. Upon regaining consciousness, the prisoners would again be interrogated and if their interrogators were not satisfied with their answers, the electrical shocks would be repeated. The electrical torturing seemed to cause strange physiological phenomenon, fits and seizures, especially among the female prisoners. We knew as many as 25 women who routinely had 8 to 10 such seizures a day. During our routine medical visits with prisoners, we were able to witness and document the permanent mental and physical damage which prisoners sustained as a result of the tortures mentioned above.[18]

Ultimately, the Bartons were trying to convince Congress to stop funding the systematic political repression it imposed on the Vietnamese. To that end they said:

We were distressed to hear stories of torture going on in the American-built Interrogation Center and to see men and women rice farmers from the Quang Ngai countryside continually being arrested and transported [there] in American-purchased vehicles. Similarly, it was upsetting to speak with a Vietnamese National Police Commander who had been trained at the US

International Police Academy and discover that this official expected a large bribe from us for the release of the brother of one of our Vietnamese staff. Incidents such as these were just a few of the constant superficial reminders of how American money and supplies were being used to mistreat and imprison Vietnamese civilians.

Based on reports of torture in PICs, Congressman Paul McCloskey visited Vietnam in early 1971. While there, he asked CIA officer John Mason, the director of the Phoenix program, to arrange a visit to a PIC. It wasn't easy getting in. McCloskey was met at the gate by a red-headed CIA officer with a revolver on each hip, cowboy style. A combat veteran of Korea, McCloskey brushed him aside and pushed his way in.

To its credit, the *Day* cited McCloskey as saying, "There were instruments of torture in the interrogation room – whips and manacles, things of that nature."

The *Day* did not add that, upon returning to the US, McCloskey and several colleagues stated their belief that "torture is a regularly accepted part of interrogation" and that "US civilian and military personnel have participated for over three years in the deliberate denial of due process of law to thousands of people held in secret interrogation centers built with U.S. dollars."

Despite the censorship, taken together, the statements of the Bartons, McCloskey, and the anonymous Special Police chief I cited earlier are irrefutable: the CIA and its individual officers were responsible for any crimes the Special Police engaged in, including torture in PICs.

As Jacques Klein observed, the CIA was an occupation force that functioned systematically like the Gestapo and SS Einsatzgruppen in France.

Residual Responsibility and Systematic War Crimes

Phoenix, the PRU, the PICs and the Special Police were part of a system of repression the CIA designed and implemented in Vietnam for the political control of people. But was everything – from assassination to extortion, massacre, Tiger Cages, terror, and torture – legitimate and justifiable? By 1971 the system's legality was questioned not just by antiwar activists, but by the House Subcommittee on Foreign Operations and Government Information.[19]

As usual, a whistle-blower provided Congress with its ammunition. In late 1970, army intelligence officer Barton Osborn gave an aide on the Subcommittee's staff a copy of the training manual he had been issued at Fort Holabird. According to the aide, William Phillips, "it showed that Phoenix policy was not something manufactured out in the field, but was sanctioned by the US government. This was the issue: that it is policy. So we requested, through the Army's congressional liaison officer, a copy of the Holabird training manual, and they sent us a sanitized copy. They had renumbered the pages."

This stab at disguising policy and avoiding responsibility is what had prompted McCloskey to visit the Phoenix Directorate in April 1971, in preparation for hearings to be held that summer. Phoenix training officer Colonel James Hunt was there with CORDS Director Jake Jacobson and Phoenix Director Mason. "And just as I was getting up to go to the platform to give my briefing," Hunt said, "Mason whispered into my ear, 'We gotta talk to them, but the less we say, the better.' Well, the first question McCloskey asked was if anyone in the program worked for the CIA. And Mason denied it. He denied any CIA involvement. Jake, too."

It bothered Hunt that Mason and Jacobson "blatantly lied." It also bothered McCloskey, who returned to Washington and charged that Phoenix "violated several treaties and laws." The legal basis for his charge was Article 3 of the Geneva Conventions, which prohibits "the passing of sentences and the carrying out of executions without previous judgment pronounced by a regularly constituted court, affording all the judicial guarantees which are recognized as indispensable by civilized peoples."

Article 3 also prohibits mutilation, cruel treatment (withholding medicine, for example) and torture.

Having agreed to the Conventions, Congress was aware of Article 3 but chose to ignore it. But a problem arose when the American ambassador to the International Committee of the Red Cross (ICRC) wrote a letter to Congress. In his 7 December 1970 letter, Imer Rimestead said, "With respect to South Vietnamese civilians captured by US forces and transferred by them to the authorities of the RVN (Republic of South Vietnam), the US Government recognizes that it has a residual responsibility to work with the Government of Vietnam (GVN) to see that all such civilians are treated in accordance with the requirements of Article 3 of the Conventions."

To the consternation of America's war managers, Rimestead's letter meant they could no longer dismiss the thousands of civilian detainees corralled in the Phoenix dragnet as an internal matter of the GVN. Rimestead reasoned that by funding Phoenix, the Special Police, and the Directorate of Corrections, America automatically assumed "residual responsibility" for detainees – for as we know, without US aid there never would have been an RVN – or puppet governments in Iraq and Afghanistan.

Rimestead's letter implied that American war managers were war criminals, prompting CIA, State Department and Pentagon lawyers to review Phoenix procedures and contest their illegality at the House Subcommittee on Foreign Operations and Government Information hearings in the summer of 1971. Luckily for them, on June 13, *The New York Times* began printing excerpts from *The Pentagon Papers* which, by name, deflected attention away from the CIA. Consequently, the public paid little attention when, in July, Congressman Reid asked Colby, "Are you certain that we know a member of the VCI from a loyal member of the South Vietnamese citizenry?"

Colby said "No." But that didn't stop Rob Simmons from throwing people in the PIC. On the contrary, the CIA, as part of the inter-agency Vietnam Task Force, insisted the Conventions afforded no protection to civilian detainees because "nationals of a co-belligerent state are not protected persons while the state of which they are nationals has diplomatic representation in the state in whose hands they are."

The CIA said that Article 3 "applies only to sentencing for crimes and does not prohibit a state from interning civilians or subjecting them to emergency detention when such measures are necessary for the security or safety of the state." Skirting the issue of executions carried out "without previous judgment pronounced by a regularly constituted court," it asserted that administrative detention procedures did not violate Article 3 precisely because they involved "no criminal sentence."

After the Bush regime began detaining suspects in Afghanistan, Iraq and Guantanamo, legal scholar Jennifer Van Bergen and I examined its assertion that administrative detention was legal. Our conclusion was that where you find administrative detentions, you are likely to find torture. The connection exists even where it is clear that investigations and screenings leading to such detentions are, as Bush's White House Counsel Alberto Gonzales put it, "not haphazard, but elaborate, and careful ... reasoned and deliberate."[20]

This conclusion derives from the faulty elements of administrative detention: the absence of human rights safeguards and normal legal guarantees such as due process, habeas corpus, fair trial, confidential legal counsel, and judicial review; vague and confusing definitions, standards, and procedures; inadequate adversarial procedural oversight; excessive Executive Branch power stemming from prolonged emergencies (the War on Terror being the ultimate example); and the involvement of the CIA and other secret, thus unaccountable, Executive Branch agencies.

When butchered in such a fashion, the judicial system is a charade and human rights are jeopardized. As William F. Schultz, Executive Director of Amnesty International, said: "This year we are witnessing not just a series of brutal but fundamentally independent human rights violations committed by disparate governments around the globe. This year we are witnessing something far more fundamental and far more dangerous. This year we are witnessing the orchestrated destruction by the United States of the very basis, the fragile scaffolding, upon which international human rights have been built, painstakingly, bit by bit by bit, since the end of World War Two."[21]

The "scaffolding upon which international human rights have been built" has been destroyed forever by the Bush and Obama regimes, by a carryover of practices first applied in Vietnam. The similarities between systematic repression in Vietnam and what's happening in the War on Terror and its domestic flipside, Homeland Security, are not limited to policies and procedures, but include the psychological warfare campaigns that create the fear, and thus the public support, for the policies and procedures.

The linkage between administrative detention, torture and repressive police states is evident for all to see, but remains unrecognized due to the systematic censorship of information. The US and Israel are at the forefront of this ominous development, manufacturing crisis after crisis to maintain a perceived national emergency with its corresponding emergency decrees that target the unprotected classes and specifically US citizens such as blacks and Muslims. Intelligence laws that permit spying on suspects without probable cause of criminal activity are secretly revised and expanded; secret torture centers ensure confessions; and Star Chamber "security courts" are convened specifically to operate outside international law. And that's to say nothing of all the secrecy that surrounds Guantanamo.

When backed into a corner, the government's public relations experts insist that torture is necessary to defend freedom. Cheney stood by it. Trump promised to bring back waterboarding and worse. That was a factor in his appeal.

Behind this twisted logic are beastly impulses rooted in the dark side of the human psyche – the kind of impulses the CIA and the Mafia harness and use to achieve dominance. What differentiates the CIA and the Mafia, inter alia, is that the CIA more perfectly controls public institutions and information. The CIA, for example, owned and operated three newspapers in Saigon.

One wonders how many it owns in America.

Determined not to repeat the mistakes made in Vietnam, the Bush and Obama regimes prevented the media from publishing photos of dead US soldiers returning from Iraq and Afghanistan. Like Bush, Obama uses censorship, disinformation and propaganda to conceal the brutality of his policies and practices. We don't see the mutilated bodies after drone strikes. The purpose is to disguise criminal intent and practice.

But any public official who engages in such a criminal conspiracy, including Rob Simmons, should be held responsible for the predictable result – which is why the nation needs a war crimes tribunal. At a bare minimum, Simmons could be tried for the human rights violation of denying due process.

Due process is a human right recognized in international law to be enjoyed by all persons. But when Congressman Reid asked if civilian detainees had a right to counsel, Colby replied "No."

Flabbergasted, McCloskey asked Colby, "The administrative detention applies to those against whom there is insufficient evidence to convict, isn't that right?"

Colby agreed.

But, McCloskey blurted, "the defendant informed against, or identified, has no right to appear in his own defense, no right to counsel, no right to confront his accusers, no right to see his dossier; is that correct?'"

"That is correct," Colby said.

"That brings me to the real problem with the Phoenix program that I saw while I was there," McCloskey said. "If the evidence is insufficient to convict a man, and also insufficient to show a reasonable probability that he may be a threat to security, then he may still be sent to the PIC."

Congressman Reid added in utter exasperation: "At least as shocking as the assassinations, torture, and drumhead incarcerations of civilians under the Phoenix program is the fact that in many cases the intelligence is so bad that innocent people are made victims."

Reid produced a list (signed by the CIA's Special Branch advisor in Binh Dinh Province) of VC cadre rounded up in February 1967. Reid said, "It is of some interest that on this list, 33 of the 61 names were women and some persons were as young as eleven and twelve."

Did the people of Vietnam feel the CIA was protecting them from terrorism?

CORDS official Ted Jacqueney testified before Congress in 1971 that "arrest without warrant or reason" was a major complaint of the people of Da Nang. "I have personally witnessed poor urban people literally quaking with fear when I questioned them about the activity of the secret police in the past election campaign. One fisherman in Da Nang, animated and talkative in complaining about economic conditions, clammed up in near terror when queried about the police, responding that 'he must think about his family.' After many personal interviews in Vietnam on this subject, I came to the conclusion that no single entity, including the feared and hated Vietcong, is more feared and hated than the South Vietnamese secret police."

Jacqueney added, "In every province in Vietnam there is a Province Interrogation Center – a PIC – with a reputation for using torture to interrogate people accused of Vietcong affiliations.

"Last year the senior AID police advisor of Da Nang City Advisory Group told me he refused, after one visit, to ever set foot in a PIC again, because 'war crimes are going on in there.'. . . Another friend, himself a Phoenix advisor, was ultimately removed from his position when he refused to compile information on individuals who would, he felt, inevitably be 'targeted' however weak the evidence might be."

Army intelligence officer Bart Osborn agreed: "I had no way of establishing the basis on which my agents reported to me suspected VCI. There was no cross-check; there was no investigation; there was no second opinion." Osborn added, "I never knew of an individual to be detained as a VC suspect who ever lived through an interrogation in a year and a half, and that included quite a number of individuals."

"They all died?" Congressman Reid asked incredulously.

"They all died," Osborn replied. "There was never any reasonable establishment of the fact that any one of those individuals was, in fact, cooperating with the VC, but they all died and the majority were either tortured to death or things like thrown out of helicopters."

At the end of the hearings Representatives McCloskey, John Conyers, Ben Rosenthal and Bella Abzug stated their belief that, "The people of the United States have deliberately imposed on the Vietnamese people a system of justice which admittedly denies due process of law. In so doing, we appear to have violated the 1949 Geneva Convention for the protection of civilian peoples at the same time we are exerting every effort available to us to solicit the North Vietnamese to provide Geneva Convention protections to our own prisoners of war.

"Some of us who have visited Vietnam," they added, "share a real fear that the Phoenix program is an instrument of terror; that torture is a regularly accepted part of interrogation ... and that the top US officials responsible for the program at best have a lack of understanding of its abuses."

They concluded "that US civilian and military personnel have participated for over three years in the deliberate denial of due process of law to thousands of people held in secret interrogation centers built with US dollars," and they suggested that Congress owes a duty to act swiftly and decisively to see that the practices involved are terminated forthwith.

It is as a participant in that genocidal endeavor that Rob Simmons should be tried as a war criminal.

The Making of a Psychological Warrior

Rob Simmons was trained and is highly skilled in the art of duplicity, of tricking people, and of torturing them into telling things that they didn't want to tell. He was also involved in setting up a hit team that went out and assassinated people in their own backyards.

How did doing those things affect him? One would have to have been inside a PIC and see the squalid conditions that the prisoners endured, and hear their screams, to understand the traumatic impact being in one of them for 18 months straight would have had on a 28-year-old CIA officer like Rob Simmons.

When I met Simmons in September 1988, he not only exhibited signs of Post-Traumatic Stress Syndrome, he admitted having it. "People never resolve war experiences," he said with a lugubrious sigh. He seemed ready to explode and unleash the hatred he harbored against the anti-war left that sabotaged the patriots. He raged at "how the VC manipulated media in US, people like Walter Cronkite, who created the notion that Phoenix was an assassination program."

A super patriot in the Barry "bomb them into the Stone Age" Goldwater mold, Simmons believes the First Amendment "was never intended to be a free ride for individuals to say and do whatever they want." He reserves to himself, as one of the Protected Few, the right to determine when it is not okay for Black Lives Matter protestors to speak freely. He seamlessly structures his moral universe on a double standard in which the flag is a sacred symbol of liberty, and burning it should be outlawed.

In 2001, in one of his first votes as a Congressman, he supported an anti-flag desecration amendment, and in June 2003 he voted yes on a constitutional amendment prohibiting flag desecration.

When I wrote about him in 2000, I said his ideology, his activities at the PIC, and his actions on behalf of the CIA while staff director of the Senate Select Committee on Intelligence raised doubts about his fitness to govern in an open society, within the framework of a Constitution that guarantees due process to all Americans, including flag burners, anti-war protestors, and leftists.

Based on what he did after Vietnam, I still feel that way. In the short term, he stayed in the CIA as an Operations Officer. Between 1975 and 1978 he ran a major operation that prevented the Taiwanese from obtaining material for a nuclear weapon. Sensitive files the Taiwanese needed were stolen, and attempts to buy materials were "choked off." It was a feather in his coonskin cap.[22]

But, as Simmons told author Joseph Persico, he got mad at Jimmy Carter's CIA Director, Stansfield Turner. In what was called the Halloween Massacre of 1977, Turner fired an estimated 600 employees in the CIA's covert operations branch.

"I'd served overseas, risking myself and my family in some rough spots, and was damn poorly rewarded for it," Simmons whined, then expressed resentment at CIA critics on the left. "People outside treated us like scum, like pariahs."[23]

His rant had the ring of a prepared script delivered by a practiced actor, and his ostensible exit in 1979 did not translate into severed relations with the CIA. On the contrary, Simmons kept his TOP SECRET security clearance and went to work as a legislative assistant to neocon Senator John H. Chafee at the Select Committee on Intelligence, while simultaneously obtaining a degree in Public Administration from

Harvard. This period in his Curriculum Vitae has all the earmarks of a covert action.

It looked to me like Simmons was being "double-hatted," an arrangement through which an officer works under administrative cover for an organization while secretly taking orders from the CIA. Many junior military officers enter this relationship with the CIA while advancing to field officer grade and studying at the Command and General Staff College.

It appeared to me that Simmons had a specific CIA assignment. While serving on Chafee's staff, he helped draft and facilitate passage of the Intelligence Identities Protection Act. This legislation was ostensibly a result of the magazines *CounterSpy* and *Covert Action Quarterly* naming CIA officers. CIA dropout Philip Agee and the aforementioned Bart Osborn were associated with the magazines. The CIA hated them with a purple passion and, largely through its unofficial public relations firm, the Association of Former Intelligence Officers, publicly but falsely blamed them for the murder of CIA Officer Richard Welch in Athens in December 1975.

The Intelligence Identities Protection Act makes it a crime to name CIA agents. John Kiriakou, who blew the whistle on CIA torture in 2007, is one of only two people convicted under it.

Having proven his value as a "money-maker," Simmons in 1981 became staff director of the Republican-controlled Senate Select Committee on Intelligence. Reagan had been elected president and Democrats were pushing for an investigation of William Casey, whom Reagan had nominated as Director of the CIA. According to Persico, the committee's conservative chairman, Barry Goldwater, hired Simmons precisely to "button up" the investigation of Casey. And, lo and behold, Simmons dutifully produced a truncated, five-page report describing Casey as "not unfit" to hold the job.[24]

There was no mention of Casey's associations with underworld character Robert Vesco, his connection with an ITT bribery scandal, and various other criminal escapades in self-aggrandizement. Simmons told Persico, "[Casey] wasn't screwing widows or orphans. He was taking advantage of the law."[25]

Taking advantage is par for the course for the rich and powerful people Simmons serves – like Donald Rumsfeld; one day they're routing nerve gas to Saddam Hussein, the next day they're killing him, his family and followers, and stealing everything they own.

The Democrats' fears about Casey were realized once he was confirmed as DCI. He reversed the Turner policies that Simmons hated, and jumped in the stirrups of the counterterrorism network established by CIA careerists behind Carter's back. Casey used the network to bypass Congress and launch the Enterprise, the network of companies established by Major General Richard Secord to secretly sell arms to Iran, through Israeli agents, as a way of financing the illegal Contra war in Nicaragua. At Casey's direction, the CIA formed death squads, demolished an oil facility, and mined a harbor in Nicaragua – all violations of international law that had as their intent the terrorizing of civilians, the sort of thing former CIA dropout John Stockwell described as "destabilization."[26]

Destabilization, said Stockwell, means "hiring agents to tear apart the social and economic fabric of the country. It's a technique for putting pressure on the government, hoping they can make the government come to the U.S.'s terms, or that the government will collapse altogether and they can engineer a coup d'état, and have the thing wind up with their own choice of people in power.

"What we're talking about is going in and deliberately creating conditions where the farmer can't get his produce to market; where children can't go to school; where women are terrified inside their homes as well as outside; where government-administered programs grind to a complete halt; where the hospitals are treating wounded people instead of sick people; where international capital is scared away and the country goes bankrupt.[27]

"Of course," Stockwell added, "they're attacking a lot more."

And, of course, the CIA is doing this everywhere around the world, every day. You just don't hear about it on NPR. But Simmons knows how it works, that's why the CIA appears to have placed him on Senator Goldwater's staff.

While in the prominent position of staff director of the Select Committee on Intelligence, Simmons was chaperoning "fact-finding" delegations to secret CIA installations for discussions not about the virtue of subverting US laws and foreign nations, but on how best to go about it. Surrounded by old boys, he had his hands on the controls, but somehow failed to uncover Casey's "self-sustaining, off-the shelf" drugs-for-guns apparatus that provided $1 million a month to the Contras.

When the Iran-Contra scandal erupted, Simmons claimed that another CIA officer had deceived him, despite the fact that he'd talked to every major player and had read every secret document. But it was merely his "administrative" job to find out the truth and tell it to the American people. His prevailing "operational" job was to protect the secret old boy cabal that runs the CIA.

Simmons rationalized Casey's deception of Congress as inconsequential. "For people who served in war," author Bob Woodward said, "Simmons thought that was the primary experience, real danger. Everything else paled by comparison. They had sent people to certain death. So to hustle some bucks was nothing. It was easy. To be criticized was nothing. So some judge or senator or reporter or cartoonist was beating on you. So what? You have served in war and survived."[28]

For such militants, steeped in the Homeric myth of the warrior hero, the ultimate test is murdering another man; you can't understand what life's about unless you've done it. Fifty thousand American soldiers were sacrificed on that pagan altar in Vietnam, so the crime bosses could build an empire on their bones.

To Lie, Cheat and Steal

Simmons left Congress in 1985, after receiving awards from Casey and the Senate, to become a visiting lecturer at Yale, where he taught classes titled "Congress and the US Intelligence Community" and "The Politics of Intelligence". In 1991 he was elected to Connecticut General Assembly, where he remained for eight years.

While campaigning for the Senate in 2009, Simmons said, "I am honored to have served in the US Army and the CIA, putting my life on the line on difficult and dangerous missions abroad to protect our people and our interests."

Some things never change, including Simmons' jingoism and self-glorification. But was he really honored to have participated in the genocide of 2 million people who never threatened the US?

Apparently he was. Such is the power of self-delusion, of constructing a persona and coming to believe in it so thoroughly it replaces the actual human being, like a bite from the Walking Dead. But do we want self-deluded ideologues whose loyalty is to the CIA and the military, not to the American public or democracy, as public officials?

In 2000, in my article for Counterpunch, I asked if voters could be certain Simmons would tell them everything they needed to know in order to govern themselves. How could anyone know for sure he wasn't playing a double game or hiding secrets, consistently promoting militarism and war, no matter its necessity or cost?

As Simmons once said, "In intelligence, you have to lie, cheat, and steal to get the truth. The reason for it is for your national security."

Unfortunately, as FBN Agent Martin Pera explained, "You can't check your morality at the door – go out and lie, cheat, and steal – then come back and retrieve it. In fact, if you're successful because you can lie, cheat, and steal, those things become tools you use in the bureaucracy."

That's exactly what Simmons did while serving as a legislative aide and staff director for the Senate Intelligence Committee. I'm guessing that he was intentionally placed in that position to effectuate the secret policies of the CIA. His career illustrates how the old boy network coordinates the executive, legislative and judicial branches of government on behalf of the arms industry, to which the military and CIA are joined at the hip, while simultaneously imposing increasingly systematic repression on the American people.

It is rule by organized crime under the rubric of patriotism and national security. Just figure: the CIA runs the arms for drugs trade through its covert paramilitary army, while its logistics experts handle "off-the-shelf" shipping companies, and its financial experts create off-shore banks to recycle the cash into new operations. All of it is highly compartmented, with intelligence officers suborning foreign customs agents and special policemen, some of whom arrange, without their own government's knowledge, the construction and operation of black sites.

Simmons is naturally endowed with the persona needed for a PR position in this enterprise. He was a Lector at his Episcopalian Church in toney Stonington, Connecticut when I interviewed him. He knew I'd spoken with Colby and was glad to discuss aspects of his CIA activities that advanced the myths he was creating about himself as he prepared to re-enter the national political arena as a US Congressman – a career move that seemed preordained.

In 2000 I also asked the overwhelming question: where, in a nation sharply divided along ideological lines, would a hardline political and psychological warrior like Simmons stand if the Bush administration embarked on another genocidal campaign against another manufactured enemy, like Johnson and Nixon did in Vietnam, and Reagan and Bush did during Iran-Contra? Would he betray the will of the American people to live in peace, as a way to reward his patrons in the CIA? Where would Simmons stand if America entered an age of dissent?

His voting record "speaks for itself", as Simmons is fond of saying. Claiming that "Intelligence is the first line of defense in the war on terrorism," he voted to allow the Bush regime to authorize electronic surveillance without a court order to acquire foreign intelligence information. He voted to allow the security services to spy on Americans without a warrant and without going to the FISA court. He voted for intelligence gathering without civil oversight, which erodes our basic constitutional rights.[29]

He voted to declare that Iraq was part of the War on Terror, and to invade and occupy it forever.

He voted to steal up to $78.9 billion in public funds and give it to arms manufacturers as "emergency" funds for the terror wars on Afghanistan and Iraq: that's $62.5 billion for military operations in Iraq and the War on Terror, $4.2 billion for homeland security, $8 billion in aid to allies and for Iraqi relief and rebuilding, $3.2 billion for US airlines to cover additional security costs, and $1 billion in aid to Turkey, which in turn dutifully allows CIA agents to infiltrate Syria.

He voted to give more and more public money to the War Machine while more and more Americans slipped out of the middle class into poverty. He voted YES on making the Bush tax cuts permanent, and was warned by the AARP not to use its name in his campaign ads.

He received a Grade A from the NRA, and voted to continue military recruitment on college campuses.

He voted YES on building a fence along the Mexican border, and YES for comprehensive immigration reform without amnesty.

While Chairman of the Homeland Subcommittee on Intelligence, Information Sharing, and Terrorism Risk Assessment, he advocated improved intelligence coordination between federal, state, and local authorities on the Phoenix program model.

He voted to create a Phoenix-style National Intelligence Director and National Counterterrorism Center.

He voted YES on making the PATRIOT Act permanent; YES on protecting the Pledge of Allegiance; YES on disallowing R-rated movies and coffeepots in prison cells; YES on military border patrols to battle drugs and terrorism; on allowing school prayer during the War on Terror; YES on the Bush regime's national energy policy; and YES on keeping the Cuba travel ban until its political prisoners were released.

Finding himself a Congressperson at the most critical point in America's legislative history in the past 50 years, he was a consistent and prominent advocate for the Bush regime's extra-legal policies and practices regarding the administrative detention and torture of suspects in the War on Terror.

In 2006, the host of Talk Nation Radio in Connecticut, Dori Smith, interviewed Wells Dixon, an attorney at the Center for Constitutional Rights. Dixon worked on Guantanamo-related issues. Simmons had argued "that suspects in the War on Terror are exceptions to the Geneva Conventions and that rules that have been used in the past do not apply to them." Smith asked Dixon if Simmons was correct.[30]

Dixon replied that Simmons was wrong. He emphasized that "the Geneva Conventions and Common Article Three are part of US military law and training. They are part of the Uniform Code of Military Justice and they are also part of Army Regulation 190.8, which governs the treatment of prisoners. The Geneva Conventions, of course, have also protected our soldiers for more than 50 years and will continue to do so as long as we adhere to them fully ourselves."

Simmons had also insisted that because the War on Terror is not fought against sovereign nations or organized liberation movements, the rules of prisoner's engagement are "non-existent." He insisted that the laws were vague and soldiers posted at Guantanamo and Abu Ghraib couldn't figure out how to treat prisoners.

Simmons again was dissembling. As Dixon noted, "the Supreme Court held in the Hamdan case that there was no basis for concluding that compliance with the Uniform Code of Military Justice was impracticable in the War on Terror."

In a particularly outrageous assertion, Simmons said that conditions at Gitmo were more open than at the Osborn Correctional facility in Connecticut.

Dixon again corrected Simmons. "The conditions at Guantanamo are ... not more open than at Osborn Correctional facility. For one thing there is no question that the detainees at Guantanamo have been tortured and abused by US military personnel and (CIA) agents. The Center for Constitutional Rights has documented this in a report issued in July that provides firsthand accounts from current detainees and their lawyers of many of the abuses they have suffered while they have been detained in Guantanamo."

Dixon reminded the audience that Rumsfeld approved a list of techniques, including the "exploitation of phobias." One detainee was deprived of sleep for 49 out of 50 days, subject to an induced hypothermia, and led to believe that he was in Egypt and he would be tortured unless provided information to the Government.

Dixon said that Rumsfeld's "enhanced interrogation" methods rose to the level of torture. "The General Counsel of the Navy Alberto Mora said in 2004 in a memorandum that it was his opinion that these sorts of activities would be not only unlawful but unworthy of military service, and that in his view they would rise to the level of torture. He raised a number of rhetorical questions such as, what does deprivation of light and auditory stimuli mean? Can a detainee be locked in a completely dark cell and if so, for how long: a month, a year? Another question he asked was, can phobias be applied until madness sets in?

"If you consider the conclusions of people like Mr. Mora, I don't think that there is any credible dispute at this point that the detainees in Guantanamo have been subject to torture and abuse."

Smith noted that Simmons backed legislation that would send detainees to military courts that could withhold classified evidence from suspects – which is exactly the system the US imposed on South Vietnam, as Simmons knew from having sent suspects to the Stalinist security courts there.

Dixon again cited the Hamdan case, saying the Supreme Court ruled there is no basis to argue that the Uniform Code of Military Justice is inadequate to try terrorism suspects. He noted that after four years, suspects could not possibly have any intelligence value or pose a threat to the United States. They were pawns in a public relations game. Even the CIA had concluded in a 2002 report that most of the people at Gitmo "were there because they were captured at the wrong place at the wrong time. They had nothing to do with terrorism. This is a statement that's been echoed by many former military officials including the former Guantanamo Commander Jay Hood who said, "Look, sometimes we just didn't get the right folks.' So I think it's important to remember that."

Dixon raised another troubling issue. "A provision in the Military Commissions Act suspends Habeas Corpus for any alien detained by the United States," he said. "This would include lawful immigrants picked up on the streets of New Haven or Hartford, and it therefore deprives them of any meaningful opportunity to challenge their detention. So as a result of this provision we expect that the United States will move to dismiss a number of the pending Habeas cases and we will then challenge the law on the ground that it's an unconstitutional suspension of Habeas Corpus."

Next, Smith raised the issue of withholding medical care from wounded prisoners, as Simmons did when he was the PIC in Vietnam. "That was a violation of the Geneva Conventions wasn't it?" she asked.

"Absolutely," Dixon replied. "The denial of medical care to someone in the custody of the United States certainly would be illegal and unconscionable and it would violate the Geneva Conventions. No question about it."

Last but not least, Smith asked, "Do you think that he should have been more open about this when he argued for changes to US law and the way we interpret the Geneva Conventions?"

Dixon noted that military regulations do not apply to the CIA. He then stressed that "torture has proved to be extremely unreliable and in fact extremely dangerous." He noted that the CIA had rendered Mahar Arar to Syria, "where he was tortured and then confessed." Arar, however, was innocent and eventually cleared by the Canadian Government. "And so I think that you can see from that example that coercion and torture really is not useful for interrogation practices," Dixon said.

"The other instance that I would point to," Dixon added, "is the case of Ibn al-Sheikh al-Libi, a suspected Bin Laden associate who was captured a few months after September 11th in Afghanistan. He was rendered by the CIA to Libya where he was tortured and under torture provided information concerning the connection between Iraq and al Qaida. This information formed the basis for Colin Powell's presentation to the United Nations in February of 2003 in which he said essentially that there was a connection between Iraq and al Qaida. We now know that that's not the case; that the information [al-Libi provided] was false, and we now know what the unfortunate results are of that information [i.e. the invasion of Iraq]. So to the extent that Congressman Simmons or any other interrogator would employ coercive or other means to obtain information I would be very suspicious."

Suspicious, indeed: Simmons always finds a way to clear the CIA of any wrongdoing. He is, after all, clearing himself when he clears the CIA.

That's what happens when a nation is ruled by a "Protected Few," regulated[31] only by one another.

MAJOR GENERAL BRUCE LAWLOR: FROM CIA OFFICER IN VIETNAM TO HOMELAND SECURITY HONCHO

In August, 2002, I wrote an "Open Letter" to Major General Bruce Lawlor at the Office of Homeland Security. Lawlor had recently been named as Homeland Security's Senior Director for protection and prevention. By coincidence, he was a former CIA officer whom I had interviewed at length for *The Phoenix Program.*

Given that Lawlor had been involved in Phoenix operations in Vietnam, it seemed fitting that he would get a job at Homeland Security, which is modeled on Phoenix. But I was still surprised; when I met him in 1988, Lawlor was a small town lawyer in Vermont, feeling unappreciated and resentful of his former bosses at the CIA.

He was still mad at the left, too. He'd run for attorney general in Vermont's 1984 Democratic primary; and in the spirit of full disclosure, he had listed his CIA service in the Phoenix program on the resume his campaign staff handed out to the press. Then the unexpected happened; a small radical magazine published a scathing article about Lawlor and Phoenix. Soon thereafter the state's anti-imperialist and pacifist groups produced briefs for delegates at the Democratic convention that said, "No Assassins for Attorney General."

Lawlor lost the primary, even though William Colby, a native of Vermont, visited the state during the campaign to speak on Lawlor's behalf.

How times have changed. A decade after the Vietnam War ended, it was still possible to persuade voters that a former member of a covert torture and assassination program wasn't suitable to be a state's chief law enforcement officer. Since 9/11, it has become a badge of honor.

In any event, four years after he lost in the primary, Lawlor still held a grudge against the peaceniks who, in his opinion, had smeared him. When I wrote my "Open Letter" in 2002, I wondered exactly what he had in store for people like me, now that he was in charge of the homeland's Protection and Prevention.

Here We Go Again

Having former CIA officers in important government positions is nothing new. I refer you to the previous chapter about former Congressman Rob Simmons, who ran a torture chamber in Vietnam. Another example, Yale graduate and Bush family insider Porter Goss served in the CIA's operations division for over ten years, attacking Cuba, handling agents in Mexico, and eventually serving in London. None of what Goss actually did is known, but he had tons of campaign money and was elected to Congress in 1988. He served the neocon cause until 2006 when Bush named him Director of the Central Intelligence Agency. Goss was in Pakistan in early 2001, just prior to the 9/11 attacks, having lunch with the head of Pakistan's version of the CIA, General Mahmud Ahmed, whose agent network "had ties to Osama bin Laden and directly funded, supported, and trained the Taliban."[1]

Other slimy CIA spooks walk the halls of Congress, like William Hurd, who slithered around Afghanistan, Pakistan, and India. Like Simmons and Goss, the CIA apparently greased his slide into Congress, so it could more effectively repress American society the way it does foreign nations.

The question needs to be asked: is having people who are in actuality war criminals in positions of legislative and executive authority in America an expression of a free society? Or is the CIA antithetical to democratic institutions, given that it is a secretive organization whose modus operandi is similar to that of an organized crime outfit and corrupts everyone it comes in contact with? Should CIA officers be disqualified from holding public office? What is to prevent them from treating their domestic enemies the same way they treat their foreign enemies?

I admit, it was frightening to learn that "Bruce" was now a major general and a top-ranking official in the ominous Office of Homeland Security. Suddenly he had access to whatever political blacklists the Bush regime had assembled, as well as control over any covert action teams that might be used to neutralize dissidents. As a replica of the Phoenix "coordination" program, the Homeland Security apparatus is a perfect cover for all manner of clandestine blackmail and extortion operations.

My fear was that Lawlor was still working for the CIA – and even if not, still had that mentality – and thus posed a threat to democracy in America. One reason for that concern was that nowhere in Lawlor's online biographies was there any mention of his CIA service. That omission indicated intent to deceive.

The Executive Session on Domestic Preparedness, "a standing task force of leading practitioners and academic specialists concerned with terrorism and emergency management" (sponsored by Harvard and the Departments of Defense and Justice) posted a biography of Lawlor. It mentioned that he'd been the first commanding general of the Joint Task Force - Civil Support (JTS-CS) at Fort Monroe. The JTS-CS, it explained, had been formed to provide "command and control over Department of Defense consequence management forces in support of a civilian Lead Federal Agency following a weapon of mass destruction incident in the United States, its territories or possessions."

Could that civilian Lead Federal Agency be the CIA, I wondered?

The JTF-CS's mission sounded like a self-fulfilling prophesy, in view of the fact that it was founded a mere two years before the 9/11 terror attacks. In its 2000 policy paper "Rebuilding America's Defenses," the neocon Project for a New American Century worried that the transformation of American armed forces through "new technologies and operational concepts" was likely to take too long, "absent some catastrophic and catalyzing event – like a new Pearl Harbor."

Many people felt this too was a self-fulfilling prophesy. And, of course, Lawlor commanded the JTF-CS through 9/11 until October 2001, when it was merged with Northcom.

Nowhere in the Executive Session's biography did Lawlor's patrons at Harvard (he's a graduate of its National Security Fellows Program), say that he had once been a CIA officer.

Why not?

In another biography that at one time was posted on the internet but has since been removed (the Wikipedia link goes nowhere), Lawlor was said to have been "assigned as the Deputy Director, Operations, Readiness and Mobilization within the Office of the Deputy Chief of Staff for Operations and Plans in May 1998. As Deputy Director, he monitors Army operations worldwide and oversees National Guard and Reserve Forces Integration efforts."[2]

This is significant too, in so far as National Guard and Reserve forces are, like JTF-CS, integral parts of Northcom, the military component of the Homeland Security apparatus. Northcom was formed after 9/11 specifically to enhance the military's ability to coordinate with civilian law enforcement agencies. Since then, the military has steadily expanded its influence over domestic law enforcement, with eerily predictable results. The most drastic effect has been the militarization of police forces across the nation, and the intimidating presence of soldiers in airports and train stations. Over time, the American people have accepted their subordination to this systematic expression of state omnipotence and violence. They've been pacified.

Police departments nationwide are given "gee whiz" gadgets developed by the military, like the Stingray cell-site simulator and the IMSI catcher. Such surveillance technologies chip away at our Fourth Amendment right to privacy. They're often deployed in secret, and cops who use them are compelled to sign nondisclosure agreements with the FBI. Such gadgets are used to identify every person at a Black Lives Matter demonstration or meetings to boycott Israel.

Many cops have military experience. They return from overseas duty and still consider themselves heroes protecting the empire. Then the FBI or CIA comes along and recruits them into the secret boys club and they think they're above the law. They're perfectly willing to use the same extra-legal tactics they learned in the colonies on dissidents at home.

Their sensibilities are informed by the crimes they participated in overseas. In the colonies, they got to bust into the homes of Iraqi and Afghan civilians, guns blazing. When they return and become cops, they automatically know who to target: the poor, blacks, leftists, environmentalists, and anti-war activists who disrespect their sacrifices on behalf of the nation.

Political cadres own and control cops in America like they own and control special policemen in occupied countries. A favorite "gee whiz" gadget they dispense is PredPol software for "predictive" policing. "PredPol was designed for 'tracking insurgents and forecasting casualties in Iraq,' and was financed by the Pentagon. One of the company's advisors, Harsh Patel, used to work for In-Q-Tel, the CIA's venture capital firm. If, for instance, the software depends on historical crime data from a racially biased police force, then it's just going to send a flood of officers into the very same neighborhoods they've always over-policed. And if that happens, of course, more personnel will find more crime — and presto, you have the potential for a perfect feedback loop of prejudice, arrests, and high-tech 'success.' To understand what that means, keep in mind that, without a computer in sight, nearly four times as many blacks as whites are arrested for marijuana possession, even though usage among the two groups is about the same."[3]

I'll expand on the CIA/FBI/Pentagon infiltration of law enforcement in the next chapter. Meanwhile, let's address one more problem with Lawlor's official biography, which states that, "The General's military service began in 1967. After service in Vietnam from 1971 to 1973, he received a Direct Commission in 1974 as an Intelligence Officer."[4]

Again, the information is intentionally misleading with no mention that Lawlor was a CIA officer. In fact, the unsuspecting reader is led to believe he was in the military.

Might Lawlor have consented to this subterfuge, because he was still serving the CIA undercover as a military officer when he took the job at Homeland Security?

Bruce Lawlor in Vietnam

I first read about Lawlor in *Everything We Had* by Al Santoli. The interview was provocative, to say the least. In a section of his book titled "The Phoenix," Santoli identified Lawlor as having been a CIA case officer in I Corps from November 1971 through December 1973. He quoted Lawlor as saying that in order to win the war, "what we had to do was get in and eliminate the ability of the VC to control or influence the people. That's what pacification was all about. The buzzword was 'root out.' We tried to go in and neutralize their political structure."[5]

For anyone unfamiliar with Phoenix jargon, "neutralize" meant to assassinate, imprison, or turn someone into a defector or double agent. Political control, of course, is the name of the game.

Lawlor made some other provocative statements, including this zinger which echoes my own conclusions about the CIA: "We permitted the Vietnamese to corrupt the system and we did it because we basically were corrupt ourselves."

In an effort to find out how Lawlor came to the conclusion that the CIA was corrupt, I wrote to him and requested an interview. He agreed, and what he told me confirmed everything Santoli had attributed to him, along with some additional, startling details.

Lawlor told me that he joined the CIA (not the military) in 1967, while he was getting his BA at George Washington University. After he graduated, the CIA sent him to its training school. He took the paramilitary course in weapons and military tactics, and was trained as an intelligence officer, the kind who manages interrogation centers and secret agents. After that he was assigned to the Vietnam Desk at Langley headquarters, where he received specialized training in agent operations in Vietnam. He also took a language course in Vietnamese.

While at CIA headquarters, Lawlor formed a rapport with the Vietnam Desk officer, Al Seal, and when Seal was assigned as the base chief in Da Nang, he invited Lawlor to go along.

Lawlor arrived in Saigon in November 1971 and joined the Embassy's translation section. He transferred to Da Nang a few weeks later and was assigned to the CIA's counterintelligence office. He worked at that job through the Easter Offensive of 1972, during which time he developed a friendship with Patry Loomis, who would later achieve notoriety as an associate of Ed Wilson.[6]

In the summer of 1972, Loomis was made the Region's PRU advisor. Just as a reminder, the CIA's PRU program was staffed by blood-thirsty mercenaries. Their job was to go into VC areas, in CIA jargon, "to do unto them what they were doing to us." This is a reference to "selective terrorism", the Viet Minh guerrilla tactic of murdering low-ranking colonial officials (and collaborators) who worked closely with the people; policemen, mailmen, teachers, etc. The murders were gruesome – a bullet in the belly or a grenade lobbed into a café – and were designed to achieve maximum publicity and demonstrate to the people the power of the nationalists to strike crippling blows against their oppressors. For the CIA, this tactic meant kidnapping, killing and mutilating political, i.e. civilian cadres, along with their families and neighbors.

When Loomis was promoted to head the PRU in Region I,

Lawlor replaced him as the Quang Nam Province officer in charge and liaison to the Special Police. In that capacity, Lawlor did what Simmons had done in Phu Yen Province; with his Special Branch counterpart, Captain Lam Minh Son, he organized the most aggressive Special Branch officers into a Special Intelligence Force Unit that hunted members of the Viet Cong Infrastructure in the hamlets and villages.

"Lam recognized that his own people could not run paramilitary operations in rural villages," Lawlor explained. "So we trained a unit of Special Branch guys – taught them infantry formations." They did this in anticipation of the pending ceasefire, at which point the PRU were to be placed under the control of Special Branch and integrated within Lam's Special Police paramilitary unit.

Bored with filing reports, Lawlor started going out on PRU operations with Loomis. He dressed in tiger fatigues and went on ambushes and traditional "snuff and snatch" operations. By then the PRU had become, Lawlor recalled, "an adjunct duty of the Special Branch advisor in each province. The CIA funneled PRU salaries in I Corps through the Special Branch to the region PRU commander, Major Vinh, who then doled it out to the province PRU chiefs."

In his Congressional testimony in 1971, Colby described the PRU as "special groups which were not included in the normal government structure. Since that time, this has been more and more integrated into the normal government structure, and correspondingly conducted under the government's rules of behavior."

In her article "The CIA's Hired Killers," Georgie Anne Geyer told how, "In the absence of an American or South Vietnamese ideology, it was said in the early days, why not borrow the most workable tenets of the enemy's. After all," she quoted Dan Ellsberg's friend Frank Scotton as saying, 'they stole the atomic bomb secrets and all from us'."[7]

As a result, Geyer wrote, "Scotton and a few other Americans started a counter-guerrilla movement in northern Quang Ngai Province. Terror and assassination were included in their bag of tricks. At one point, [Scotton's parent agency, the US Information Service] printed 50,000 leaflets showing sinister black eyes. These were left on bodies after assassination or even - 'our terrorists' are playful - nailed to doors to make people think they were marked for future efforts.[8]

"But," Geyer said, "whereas Scotton's original counter-guerrillas were both assassins in the night and goodwill organizers of the people, the PRUs are exclusively assassins in the night." Furthermore, she said, "the PRUs are excellent torturers. Torture has now come to be so indiscriminately used that the VC warn their men to beware of any released prisoner if he has not been tortured."

"Sometimes we have to kill one suspect to get another to talk," Geyer quoted a CIA PRU advisor as saying. Another PRU advisor told her that "he ate supper with his PRUs on the hearts and livers of their slain enemies." Another one said, "I've been doing this for 22 years all over the world." He cited Egypt when Nasser was coming to power and the Congo "when we were trying to get rid of Tshombe." Geyer said about the PRU advisor: "His job, like that of many Americans in South Vietnam, was terror."

Geyer called American PRU advisors "really the leaders," a view that contradicted Colby's claim that Americans were limited to "advice and assistance."

Things changed dramatically for Lawlor after the ceasefire in January 1973. Prior to that, his "easy, striped pants" job as Special Branch advisor amounted to coordinating with Captain Lam and getting reports from the Hoi An PIC. He had no dealings with the US military or the province senior advisor and "rarely acted on Phoenix information – just PRU and unilateral sources. There was little Special Branch input, because no one talked to anyone."

One big problem concerned the PRU. Although the PRU were placed under the jurisdiction of the Special Branch after the ceasefire, the CIA still controlled the purse strings. But it wasn't providing as much money as before and had lost control over the PRU leadership. According to Lawlor, top ranking PRU officers turned to graft, drug dealing and shakedowns to make up the differential. Bad things started happening. Region 1 PRU Chief Vinh began putting the arm on the Quang Nam PRU chief, Phan Van Liem, who in turn began changing money for the VC.

Eventually one member of the Quang Nam PRU team went to Lawlor and said, "It's getting out of hand." Ever the idealist, Lawlor investigated. The investigation ended when he walked into the Hoi An PIC and saw that a woman, who knew about the region PRU chief's dirty dealings, had been raped and murdered. Her body was stretched over a table.

"All of a sudden," Lawlor told me, "Mr Liem wants me to go on a [one-way] mission with him, and the other PRU guys are telling me, 'Don't go!'"

After the Easter Offensive of 1972, according to Lawlor, the

North Vietnamese Army concentrated on repairing its infiltration routes in preparation for the next offensive. Then came the ceasefire, at which point each village identified itself as controlled by the GVN or by the VC. As Lawlor recalled, "all of a sudden there was a lot of business, because as soon as someone put a VC flag on their roof, they're gone. Not in the sense that they were killed, but we could pick them up and interrogate them. And we basically were flooded."

It was also after the ceasefire that "the country club set" took over. Tom Flores, a veteran of the CIA's Western Hemisphere Division, replaced Al Seal as the Region Officer in Charge. Flores brought his own deputy and chief of operations, and the entire CIA contingent moved into the Da Nang Consulate under State Department cover. Their involvement in PIC and PRU operations was now thoroughly illegal.

Lawlor described Flores as "a very senior officer on his last tour" whose objective "was to live well, not rock the boat, and take advantage of the amenities that were readily available." That attitude was prevalent. Lawlor, as an example, cited the Public Safety advisor to the Field Forces as "one of the guys who used to set up the shakedowns of merchants. He came out of that war wealthier than you or I will ever be. But you can't prove it."

When Lawlor brought the matter to the attention of his bosses, he was told, "Don't bother me," or asked, "What do you want me to do?"

As with the Homeland Security boondoggle, many Americans went along for the profitable ride. "The Special Branch liaison in Hue became the Thua Thien Province Observer," Lawlor recalled. "He had been a retired cop and he liked the good life. But he had no enthusiasm. He thought it was a joke. He wanted to stay over there when his contract was up, so he became the Province Observer. He liaised."

Contributing to the decline in morale after the ceasefire was the fact that the Special Intelligence Force Units were disbanded and the PRU were placed under the National Police Command within the Special Branch. "This caused many problems," Lawlor explained. "We started seeing more ghost soldiers, more extortion, and more protection money. We couldn't pay them at all, so we lost control."

The PRU had the same mission as before and maintained their agents in field, "but because the CIA advisor was no longer a participant, there were fewer operations and more excuses for not going."

Lawlor tried to maintain control by providing "gee whiz" gadgets like Night Hawk helicopters with mini-guns and spotlights, and by being able to get wounded PRU into the hospital in Da Nang.

"Phoenix coordination," according to Lawlor, "was dead. There was nothing left. The Vietnamese gave it lip service but there was no coordination with the Special Police. When the MSS and Special Branch got together, they tried to take away rather than share information."

As soon as the Special Branch began paying PRU teams at province level, "Major Vinh got concerned. Now he has to answer to Saigon. He has to give them a cut. That resulted in Vinh cheating somebody out of his cut, and that fractured what had been a unified unit."

So it was that the PRU program devolved into a criminal enterprise, like Frankenstein's monster, beyond the control of its criminally insane creator.

The last straw for Lawlor occurred just before the end of his tour in November 1973. Having worked in Da Nang's counterintelligence office, he knew that an NVA spy ring existed in the area, and that the Special Branch had sacrificed a number of low-level cadres instead of flushing out the most important spies. "It was a great deception operation," Lawlor said. "The high-level people continued to operate."

One of the NVA agents was the girlfriend of Tom Flores's operations chief. But when Lawlor reported this to Flores, he did nothing but accuse Lawlor of having "gone native."

Lawlor then committed the cardinal sin: he defiled the sacred chain of command by slipping a copy of his report to the CIA station's security chief in Saigon. The operations officer was sent home, but Lawlor was finished; security teams visited his office, confiscated his furniture, and presented him with a ticket back home.

"After that I became disillusioned," Lawlor confessed. He returned to Langley headquarters, where Ted Shackley – then chief of the Far East Division – accepted his resignation.

Lawlor was embittered. "The Agency betrayed us," he said. "To go after the VCI, we had to believe it was okay. But we were too young to understand what happens when idealism cracks up against reality. We risked our lives to get information on the VCI, information we were told the President was going to read. Then guys who didn't care gave it to superiors more interested in booze and broads."

Reprisal Is the Name of the Homeland Security Game

But there's something weird about Lawlor that keeps him coming back for more, despite whatever scruples he may have manifested above. After his bid to be the Democratic Party's nominee for attorney general failed in 1984, Colby intervened and got him a job interview at Langley. He was interviewed by Rudy Enders, the chief of the CIA's paramilitary Special Operations Division. However, despite his willingness to return to the fold and help do the CIA's dirty work in Central America, details of the Da Nang incident surfaced during the interview, and Lawlor was not rehired; at least, not officially.

People look for vindication in different ways. Take, for example, the reaction of the militant right wing to America's humiliating defeat at the hands of the Vietnamese. Phoenix creator Nelson Brickham compared it to the frustration and bitterness of the German nation after the First World War. As we all know, that frustration and bitterness (plus the financial support of fascist sympathizers like Henry Ford) enabled Hitler to rise from the ashes of the Weimar Republic.

The same thing happened in America after the preordained terror attacks of 9/11. Symbolically, 9/11 wiped the slate clean. All the moral prohibitions on the rabid right were lifted, and all the rage they had cultivated during the degenerate Clinton regime was unleashed, under the aegis of counterterrorism, on nations sitting on vast oil reserves, as well as suspected terrorists, domestic dissidents, and the flag-waving American public as well.

Lawlor, like Simmons, resembled a bitter man looking for revenge. They probably subscribe to the fascist theories of Michael Ledeen, who blamed the 9/11 terror attacks on Clinton, "for failing to properly organize our nation's security apparatus."[9]

Others blamed 9/11 on a conspiracy between the MOSSAD, Saudi Arabia, and those members of The Project for the New American Century who landed in the Bush regime's Office of Special Plans. But, according to Ledeen, the problem was Clinton's "sneering lack of respect for security."

"New times require new people with new standards," Ledeen asserted. "The entire political world will understand it and applaud it. And it will give [Office of Homeland Security chief] Tom Ridge a chance to succeed, and us to prevail."

A lot of people with an axe to grind were jumping on the Homeland Security bandwagon, hoping to help Ridge succeed in crushing the left, and paving the way for neocons to prevail. Knowing this, and fearing that Lawlor was of the Ledeen reprisal persuasion, I tried to get an interview with him. I called his office and spoke with his secretary. She said he would call me back, but he never did.

Knowing, from personal experience, that the macho men of the CIA never forget an insult, I was concerned for everyone who had fought to end the Vietnam War, as well as those who, in 2002, were lining up to oppose the Bush regime's police state policies at home and imperialism abroad.

So in 2002 I wrote my Open Letter in Counterpunch to Bruce Lawlor. Here it is.

> As far as I know, General Lawlor, we still live in a democracy. Although the Bush regime seems hell bent on using the uninvestigated terror attacks of 11 September as a pretext to turn America into a military dictatorship, we are not yet (as far as I know) under martial law. Public officials, like you, still have a responsibility to respond to our concerns. Speaking on behalf of people concerned by the opportunity for the abuse of human rights and civil liberties presented by the corrupt Bush regime, through its Homeland Security apparatus, here are the questions that need to be answered:

> 1) What happened in July 1995 to make you leave your law practice and go to the Army War College? Did the CIA have a role in that decision?

> 2) How did your education at the War College pave the way for your assignment as Special Assistant to the Supreme Allied Commander in Europe from June to October 1996? CIA officers often go by the term "Special Assistant." Were you serving as the CIA's liaison to the Supreme Commander?

> 3) In May 1998 you became Deputy Director of Readiness and Mobilization within the office of the Deputy Chief of Staff for Operations and Plans. Your job was managing National Guard and Army Reserve units around the world. The job had international

functions and fell under the CIA's cognizance. Did the CIA help you get this job? How were you involved with the CIA in this position?

4) You were the first commander of the Joint Task Force, Civil Support. Your job was to work with civilians. Was this a CIA assignment? Did you liaise with the CIA? Was this assignment based in any way on your experiences as a CIA officer in Vietnam, and was your main qualification the Phoenix sensibility that you brought to the job? What are your other qualifications?

5) In a 24 March 2000 statement to Congress, you seemed to be preparing for the Homeland Security job you have now. In a way you even predicted the calamitous events of 9/11. Did you, in fact, have any foreknowledge of those attacks?

6) In your statement you said that as commander of the JTF-CS, you created Civil Support Teams (CSTs) to assist in case of a weapon of mass destruction incident. The CSTs, you said, were "National Guard assets, and thus can function under state or federal authority. They are equipped with sophisticated communications systems that will enable local first responders to talk with neighboring jurisdictions or link up with federal centers of expertise. CSTs are also being equipped with state of the art detection equipment that will enable them to help local first responders quickly identify potential WMD agents."

That's what you told Congress. Would you now please tell us what role the CIA plays in CST operations? It sounds like a great CIA cover to me. Is there a Civil Support Team near me? Will you allow me to observe how it functions?

7) What is your relationship with the CIA in your role as Senior Director for Protection and Prevention at

the Office of Homeland Security? What do you do? Is it true that the Office of Homeland Security will be the strategy-making part of the apparatus, and that the forthcoming Department of Homeland Security will be the tactical and operational part? What is the function of the Homeland Security Council, and what is your relationship with it? Can we have organization charts of these entities, including ones that show where the CIA is hiding its covert assets?

8) Last but not least, please explain the conspicuous absence of any reference to your CIA background in your official biographies. This seems to suggest that you are still CIA. Are you? And tell us, please, if you and others like you intend to use your power to seek revenge against your ideological opponents?

Bruce Lawlor never responded.

But then, I hadn't expected him to. The point of the (admittedly rhetorical) Open Letter was not just to expose the CIA connection and its ramifications, but to broadcast this possibility of revenge and hopefully thereby forestall it.

Red Squads and Red Herrings

Where the CIA is involved, there are always trap doors and deadly deceptions. Recall Operation Twofold and how the CIA hid a hit squad within the DEA's internal security unit.

The CIA does nothing unless it can be assured of plausible deniability, and the Homeland Security apparatus is an infinitely large space in which the CIA can hide operations aimed at manipulating society and managing the political control of the American people.

Twofold isn't the only example of the hidden dangers of such a setup. In its 1970 End of Year Report, the Phoenix Directorate quoted from a captured VC circular titled "On the Establishment of the Enemy's Phung Hoang Intelligence Organization in Villages."

The VC circular was referring to the fact that the CIA had instructed each Special Branch case officer to organize and maintain ten People's Intelligence Organization (PIO) cells. Each cell consisted of three agents in a hamlet. Apart from fingering VCI, the PIO agents engaged in psywar, "to jeopardize the prestige of the revolutionary families, create dissension between them and the people, and destroy the people's confidence in the revolution."

PIO agents also made lists of the VCI cadres to be murdered when the ceasefire took place. "Their prescribed criteria are to kill five cadres in each village in order to change the balance between enemy and friendly forces in the village," the circular said. In doing so, the primary task of GVN village chiefs was to "assign Phoenix intelligence organization and security assistants to develop and take charge of the People's Self-Defense Force and select a number of tyrants in this force to activate 'invisible' armed teams which are composed of three to six well trained members each. These teams are to assassinate our [Viet Cong civilian infrastructure] key cadre, as in Vinh Long Province."

Throughout this book I've given examples of how the CIA uses "civic actions" as a cover for "invisible" armed teams aimed at political enemies. Ensuring deniability is the first step, and to that end Phoenix employed the motto "Protecting the People from Terrorism" to present itself as goodness and light. And yet the CIA was inserting secret hit teams inside the Self-Defense Force that were ostensibly "Protecting the People from Terrorism" in order to kill (without trial and based on all the flawed sources we have discussed) those whom they presumed might be aiding the Viet Cong in some way – people who were civilians and had rights as such.

It is exactly this type of duplicity that informs the Homeland Security apparatus. The DHS has even adopted the Phoenix motto, "Protecting the People from Terrorism," and for the same exculpatory purposes. The big question is: will these security forces conduct Phoenix-style paramilitary and psywar operations against dissident Americans in a crisis?

Consider Bruce Lawlor. He reported the rape and murder of a woman at the PIC and when nothing happened, went about his business. Rob Simmons spent 18 months inside a PIC and never saw anything inappropriate. Bob Kerrey, as will be discussed in a forthcoming chapter, led a team of Navy SEALs into a Vietnamese village and murdered its men, women and children.

They did these things, came home, uttered the magic words "God and country" and all was forgiven. What have they proven but their intense commitment to kill? And as a result, they have again been inducted into the gang of the Protected Few, and can get away with murder, like cops killing blacks.

They crossed the line and lost perspective. Lawlor was aware that CIA officers systematically corrupt entire societies and, in the process, become corrupt. He even admitted it. Yet he still desired to take his place among the Protected Few. Why? Was it the chance to get revenge? But paradoxically, on whom?

The brother of Frank Scotton's mentor, Dick Noone, manipulated the dreams of a peaceful tribe of people in Malaysia for the purpose of turning them into a police unit "noted for its ruthless slaughter of captured Communist guerillas." Scotton did the same thing to Mountain tribes in Vietnam.

Americans' dreams are being shaped too. Hollywood producers make billions extoling the violent virtues of the ruling warrior class. Video games make killing and mutilating Muslims a consummation every young American man desires. It makes them feel powerful, and provides an antidote to their social alienation.

The CIA shapes our dreams of democracy by controlling the information we receive. The Senate's 6,000 page report on CIA torture was whittled down to a 525 page summary, with redactions. The summary nonetheless told how CIA officials tortured more suspects than acknowledged and in more gruesome fashion than imagined, misled Congress and the media, and jerry-rigged the program for deniability. It said that torture served no purpose other than making CIA officers feel good.

We aren't allowed to know the details and the names of the victims. The evidence is concealed and no CIA officers were indicted. But at least we know why CIA officers commit crimes. They do it because they like it and it is how they become rich and powerful and protected.

John Kiriakou, the CIA officer who revealed waterboarding in 2007, was one of two CIA officers sent to prison for the empire's post 9/11 crime spree. His crime was telling the truth. His conviction and imprisonment was a blunt warning to other CIA officers: in the underworld of organized CIA crime, omerta is the only law that matters.

Epilogue

Why be concerned with buttonmen like Lawlor and Simmons when Mafia generals like George H. W. Bush are giving the orders?

As DCI, Bush laid the groundwork for the off-the-shelf counterterror network that facilitated the Enterprise and the illegal selling of arms to Iran to finance the illegal Contra war in Nicaragua. He laid the basis for the global Phoenix program.

As lame duck president in December 1992, Bush invaded Panama and killed hundreds of innocent people in order to kidnap former CIA asset Manuel Noriega; and he pardoned six loyal Republican officials involved in the Iran-Contra scandal, in one of the greatest criminal cover-ups in history.[10]

As David Johnston said in *The New York Times*, "Bush swept away one conviction, three guilty pleas and two pending cases, virtually decapitating what was left of [Iran-Contra prosecutor] Walsh's effort, which began in 1986." He added that there was "evidence of a conspiracy among the highest ranking Reagan Administration officials to lie to Congress and the American public."[11]

Bush's idiot son, W, honored the family tradition of mass murder by launching the illegal war on Iraq and the global War on Terror with all its horrors. Like his father, he is venerated among the Ultras who profited as a result of his militancy and disdain for international law.

Bruce Lawlor wasn't quite that powerful, but he was influential at a decisive moment. According to the *Washington Post*, his boss at Homeland Security, Tom Ridge, delegated most tasks to him.[12] The *Post* described Lawlor as having "alienated many people in the White House and in the department with a brusque and secretive manner."

Perhaps Lawlor was "secretive" because he was a CIA agent. When he left in 2003, the *Post* described the six-month-old Department of Homeland Security as "hobbled by money woes, disorganization, turf battles and unsteady support from the White House, and has made only halting progress toward its goals, according to administration officials and independent experts."

The *Post* blamed Lawlor for the problems, saying he "at times helped lead Ridge in the wrong direction," and "was involved in perhaps the most bitter dispute in the department's short history."

Lawlor had reviewed and approved an agreement that Ridge signed with Attorney General John Ashcroft that made the Justice Department – not the DHS – the lead agency investigating the financing of terrorism. The memo enraged the Secret Service, "which was required to halt hundreds of probes and forego its tradition of financial investigations. Ridge apologized (but) the rift took months to heal…"

As a result of Lawlor's actions, real power remained centered in Bush's 50-member Homeland Security Council, which is ruled by the CIA. Jerry-rigged like Phoenix, DHS lacked "a political infrastructure at the top of the department."

"The department's roles and missions are still being defined," one official said.

Lawlor won't say if he accomplished his mission, stated and unstated, or even what it was. My guess is that his job was to keep the organization off-balance so the CIA could step into the vacuum and assert control in its formative stage.

In any event, Lawlor stayed in Washington and became a Beltway bandit, capitalizing on his contacts to serve on various security-related boards and academic posts, including the Homeland Security Advisory Council. He achieved his personal ambitions, but at what price?

How the DHS advanced secret CIA missions is the subject of the next chapter.

Chapter 17

HOMELAND SECURITY: THE PHOENIX COMES HOME TO ROOST

In the articles I wrote about Homeland Security between 2001-2003, I said that America has been in an ideological state of siege since 9/11, when the Twin Towers came crashing down and all the moral and psychological prohibitions on the Ultra conservatives were lifted forever. All the anger and frustration they had nurtured during the Vietnam War and the Carter and Clinton administrations was unleashed in a torrent of war mongering. The anthrax-challenged Democrats climbed on the war wagon; on 15 September 2001, Congress, save for one glorious dissenter, gave Bush $40 billion and the authority to use "all necessary and appropriate force" against those who could be said to have been involved in what would remain largely uninvestigated terrorist attacks.

Bush embarked on his Holy Crusade against Islam, but directed at Afghanistan and Iraq, not at Saudi Arabia where his family's business partners and the majority of those officially blamed for the 9/11 attacks came from. To protect this misadventure into neo-colonialism in the Middle East, Bush on 8 October 2001 signed into law the Office of Homeland Security to detect, prevent, and recover from terrorist attacks, and/or "weapons of mass destruction" attacks on American soil. The Homeland Security juggernaut was born.

Less than three weeks later, again with overwhelming Congressional support, Bush signed the Patriot Act, vastly expanding the government's domestic intelligence gathering and law enforcement powers, while rolling back individual rights and protections from government intrusions.

The stigma of public accusations of his having stolen the 2000 election was replaced with a popular war of revenge against Afghanistan. Bush's approval ratings doubled in polls.

In the absence of political opposition, the Bush regime's rationale for neo-colonial aggression was set in stone in September 2002 with the promulgation of The National Security Strategy of the United States. Through this manifesto, the National Security Establishment effectively conferred upon itself the divine right to launch murderous, preemptive attacks on any Muslim nation with valuable natural resources. Russia and China were long range strategic targets.

A first-degree murder strategy may make many Americans *feel* safer because US terror is directed at the Islamic "Other". But there are hidden clauses in the manifesto's fine print. As an exercise in neo-colonialism disguised as "protecting the American people", the eternal War on Terror constantly recreates the urgent need for its existence;[1] and by destroying the lives and livelihoods of millions of innocent people, it automatically fuels more terrorism – though within the United States itself terror attacks are few and far between, and most of what passes for terrorism derives from FBI incitement and entrapment. Of 508 defendants prosecuted in federal terrorism-related cases in the decade after 9/11, 243 were involved with an FBI informant, while 158 were the targets of sting operations.[2] This is to say nothing of what many people regard as false flag operations.

Moreover, neo-colonialism constantly fuels political dissent within the United States. There are, after all, enlightened Americans who recoil in horror at their government's aggression. But increased dissent is what the National Security Establishment wants. You can call it a vicious cycle or a self-fulfilled prophesy, but dissent provides the ruling elite with the pretext it needs to impose the repressive measures required to maintain and expand its political dominance. It's a "win-win" for the capitalists, in so far as a police state delivers a wide range of economic benefits to those who invest in its requirements.

And make no mistake: homeland security is a euphemism for "internal security", a term that cannot be used (along with "separate but equal") because it has the nasty ring of McCarthyism and the anti-Communist witch-hunts of the 1950s.

In this overarching sense, the War on Terror and homeland security are flip sides of the same class warfare coin. It is the same voracious, capitalist ideology applied to foreign and domestic policy, especially as the upper class in "class warfare" itself becomes a smaller and proportionately more powerful ruling elite, the omnipotent one percent, forever pitting the middle classes against the lower classes.

Psychologically, the homeland security phenomena is the culmination of the right wing's obsession to overcome the Vietnam Syndrome and reassert "white" America's dominance not just abroad but at home. Since America's ignoble defeat in 1975, each successive act of US aggression abroad and repression at home has brought the architects and participants of the Vietnam War closer to redemption.

For those who participated in war crimes in Vietnam, 9/11 was a cathartic event. For their leaders it was an apotheosis. All the crimes they were despised for committing, were suddenly the magic tricks that would make them and ambiguous America, as Trump promised, "great again."

The psychological warfare campaign blossomed on 9/11; the warmongers saturated the airwaves and editorial columns with propaganda calling anti-war protesters "un-American" and equating them with terrorist sympathizers. The propaganda has never stopped. As it was during the Vietnam War, peace protestors and civil rights activists have become enemies of the state and, hence, targets of the Homeland Security infrastructure.

The Bureaucratic Method in Their Madness

High level bureaucrats like Dick Cheney and Donald Rumsfeld understand that political, economic and military power is harnessed through complex organizational structures. Their staffs are packed with people like Phoenix program creator Nelson Brickham, who know exactly how to do it.

After 9/11, the Ultras began implementing their long-range plans to consolidate power. Bush signed the Homeland Security Act on 25 November 2002, creating the Department of Homeland Security (DHS) to coordinate the anti-terror elements of dozens of federal agencies. The Act created the policy-making Homeland Security Council with four standing members: the president as chairman, along with the vice president, secretary of defense and attorney general. The Homeland

Security Council is the National Security Council applied domestically.

The Homeland Security Council can be understood as grander version of the Phoenix Committee in Vietnam, which consisted of the Deputy for CORDS (William Colby) as chairman, plus the CIA's station chief, MACV's assistant chiefs of staff for intelligence and operations, and the CIA chief of Revolutionary Development.

The homeland security apparatus further evolved in May 2003 when, as part of the White House coordinating mechanism, Bush created the Terrorist Threat Integration Center (TTIC) under future DCI John O. Brennan. Based at CIA headquarters, the TTIC was staffed by counterterrorism experts from the CIA, FBI, DOD and DHS. It reported directly to the White House political staff, beyond public and congressional scrutiny.

The apparatus congealed in late 2004, when the TTIC was renamed the National Counterterrorism Center (NCTC) and placed under the newly created position of Director of National Intelligence (DNI).[3] Operating like a global Phoenix Directorate with a computerized blacklist of suspects, the NCTC has access to all military and law enforcement databases, foreign as well as domestic, which it skims for High Value targets. High Value targets are captured and incarcerated, and if possible, recruited as penetration agents at home and abroad. Failing that, they are placed on Obama's "kill list" and "neutralized" by the all-seeing "predator" drone or some CIA/Special Forces hit team packed with psycho killers.

Instruments like the NCTC facilitate the merging of foreign and domestic counterterror operations. The NCTC collects, stores, and analyzes data on US citizens from every available surveillance data base as a "pre-crime" pacification effort. The CIA manages the NCTC Operations Center, and if a suspected threat emerges, it is able to direct every homeland component, the same way it used Phoenix to coordinate every cooperating agency in Vietnam. The network extends from the White House into America's tiniest villages, and includes everyone from Congresspersons and corporate executives, to cops shooting black teenagers or chasing homeless veterans off the streets.

Parallel Mechanisms

Within the federal bureaucracy, the Department of Justice (DOJ), CIA and military have their own separate chains of command, jealously guarded "parallel mechanisms" that exist apart from their "coordinated" homeland security functions.

With 800 military bases around the world, its own legal system, and a budget that devours the highest percentage of federal taxpayer dollars, the military is the elephant in the room. Apart from a mutiny by the lower ranks, as happened in Vietnam, the military and its arms industry sidekicks will continue to be the driving force behind US aggression abroad and mass surveillance at home. The military's Northcom component is the backbone of the homeland security apparatus, alternately intimidating, assisting, and spying on its civilian counterparts.

The National Security Agency (NSA) is the apparat's eyes and ears. Instituted by Bush after 9/11, the NSA's Terrorist Surveillance Program was ruled unconstitutional in 2006, but the lawsuit was dismissed on appeal and a similar program called PRISM now exists in its place. As revealed by whistleblower Edward Snowden, PRISM collects communications from major US internet companies.[4]

The DOJ operates its back-channel through the FBI's Joint Terrorism Task Forces (JTTF). Based in over 100 cities and at 56 FBI field offices, these Phoenix-style coordination centers focus on "upper tier" targets that cross state lines. The FBI defines the task forces on its website as "small cells of highly trained, locally based, passionately committed investigators, analysts, linguists, SWAT experts, and other specialists from dozens of U.S. law enforcement and intelligence agencies."

The FBI has had "internal security" as its mandate since its inception, and in 1996 it launched its InfraGard program in Cleveland. InfraGard is a "non-profit" organization serving as a public-private partnership between businesses and the FBI. It's a private sector Phoenix in which business people, college presidents, state and local law enforcement agencies, and other civil guardians funnel tips to the FBI to prevent hostile acts against America's "critical infrastructure". It operates in secret and has over 50,000 members. The ACLU described InfraGard as "a corporate TIPS program" and "surrogate eyes and ears for the FBI."[5]

Since 2003, the DHS – under FBI supervision – has shared responsibility for InfraGard assets.

It is important to note that the FBI has no jurisdiction over the CIA, which, like the military, exists above and beyond the laws the rest of us must obey. But while the military is an elephant trampling on everyone, the CIA is the serpent in the garden.

The CIA's back-channel is its Counterterrorism Center (CTC) network. Formed in 1986, it is a direct descendent of Operation Chaos (as outlined in Chapter 11: New Games, Same Aims). The CTC network operates globally through Phoenix-style Counterterrorist Intelligence Centers, in collaboration with the suborned military, police and intelligence services of infected nations. The unilateral CTC network has its own communications system and is used to bypass the DOJ, State Department and Pentagon, as well as the regular CIA bureaucracy. It has its own paramilitary Special Operations Unit that functions like a global PRU team.

The CTC works with the CIA's Crime and Narcotics Center (CNC) to manage strategic aspects of the international arms and drug trade out of drug producing nations like Bolivia and Afghanistan.

Supposedly there is a legal firewall between the CIA and domestic law enforcement organizations, just as Posse Comitatus laws once banned the military. The CIA, however, infiltrates officers within the FBI's Joint Terrorism Task Forces, and within the DHS. I've described elsewhere how the CIA infiltrated the DEA. CIA officers are not listed on anyone's organizational charts, in accordance with their status as the Protected Few; but they're there.

For example, four months after 9/11, DCI George Tenet personally arranged with New York City's Muslim-hating Mayor Michael Bloomberg to slip senior CIA officer David Cohen inside the NYPD as its deputy commissioner for intelligence. *The New York Times* and *Daily News* dutifully buried the story. As Matt Apuzzo noted, "Nobody questioned the wisdom of taking *someone trained to break the laws of foreign nations and putting him in a department responsible for upholding the rule of law* [my italics]. Nobody even checked out Cohen's hand-prepared résumé, which said he had a master's degree in international relations from Boston University.[6] The misstatement itself was inconsequential. That it went entirely unquestioned was indicative of the lack of media scrutiny Cohen could expect in his new job."[7]

An expert on Israeli methods of repressing Palestinians, Cohen launched a private, Bloomberg-approved jihad against Muslims in New York City. As he explained: "In the case of terrorism, to wait for an indication of crime before investigating is to wait far too long."[8]

Concepts and Programs

Phoenix is the conceptual model for the DHS. Both are based on the principle that governments can manage societies through implicit and explicit terror. The strategic goal is to widen the gap between the elites and the mass of the citizenry, while expunging anyone who cannot be ideologically assimilated.

Phoenix, like the DHS, was an organization that evolved. At the top was the Phoenix Committee. Under the Committee was a Directorate in Saigon, managed by a senior CIA officer with a staff of CIA, military, and State Department personnel. The Directorate coordinated intelligence gathering agencies and anti-terror operations in Vietnam's provinces (equivalent to states in America) and districts (counties).

The DHS executive management team operates like the Phoenix Directorate, overseeing a jerry-rigged labyrinth of overlapping offices and directorates most Congresspersons can't unravel. Put another way, central power is held by the senior bureaucrats who run federal agencies. The bureaucrats in Washington are held in check by the states, which, as part of a republic, traditionally resist federal intrusion. As a result, the bureaucrats running the DHS (and their White House and Congressional sponsors) are constantly suborning acquisitive state legislators, governors and business leaders with federal pork.

Briefly, the DHS has a deputy undersecretary for intelligence and analysis. This deputy reports to the DHS Secretary and manages the Office of Intelligence and Analysis (I&A), which consists of about 1000 analysts, many from contributing agencies. I&A coordinates intelligence with appropriate officials in state, local, tribal and territorial governments. More importantly, it runs vast agent networks like InfraGard with the private sector through what is called, without irony, the Homeland Security Enterprise.

Complementing the Office of Intelligence is an Office of Operations Coordination and Planning which oversees the DHS National Operations Center (NOC). The NOC collects and "fuses" information from the same federal, state, territorial, tribal, local, social media, and private sector agencies as I&A. The DHS intelligence and operations offices work together to issue advisories and bulletins relating to perceived or provoked threats. They also organize specific but classified protective measures you have no right to know about.

DHS has an Emergency Operations Center (EOC). The EOC is the culmination of decades of devolution, originally manifested as Civil Defense (famous for building bomb shelters and teaching grade school kids how to duck under their chairs in case the Russians nuked America) and later as the Federal Emergency Management Agency (FEMA). Absorbed within the DHS in 2003, FEMA and its predecessor outfits created "continuity of government" plans for press censorship and internment of suspected radicals in times of national crisis. The EOC's tentacles can be found in gentrified bomb shelters and corporate offices everywhere, secretly ingesting rumors about "security risks" by word of mouth and encrypted emails.

The DHS has over 250,000 employees, including detectives it deploys within its own departments, every agency it coordinates, and every branch of the military. These DHS employees have vast discretionary powers, including the authority to open mail coming to US citizens from foreign nations whenever it's deemed necessary – another internal security measure once considered illegal.

The DHS has another investigations unit that oversees international operations and intelligence functions. This unit has about 7,000 special agents operating in 200 US cities and 60 countries around the world. It works with the CIA and assigns agents to the FBI's Field Intelligence Groups, through which they jointly run vast informant networks. Several DHS investigation units maintain paramilitary Special Response Teams, which are very likely trained and managed by CIA paramilitary officers.

The DHS has its very own counterterrorism unit, and a war crimes unit that assiduously avoids the CIA. When an Italian court indicted a group of CIA officers for kidnaping an innocent man in Milan and sending him to Egypt to be tortured, DHS agents looked away. Like FBI agents, DHS agents have no authority over the CIA, which is free to terrorize anyone, anywhere.

Last but not least, the DHS has fusion centers which operate in every state and major city, just like Phoenix intelligence and operations coordinating centers were set up in Vietnam. Every law enforcement entity in a state or city sends a representative to the local fusion center, which tries to anticipate threats through analysis of shared intelligence. State and local police provide space and resources (including snitches) for the majority of the fusion centers. There is even a fusion center in Mexico City.

The ACLU compared fusion centers with the corporate TIPS program because of the involvement of private Terrorism Liaison

Officers (TLO). A TLO is a citizen trained to detect and report suspicious activities. TLOs function like the People's Intelligence Organization cadres mentioned in Chapter 16, paying close attention to what customers, passers-by and neighbors say, and then reporting "suspicious utterances" (or, when bored or nervous, inventing them) for entry into the proper database.[9]

By 2014, California had more than 14,000 TLOs. Some are cops, others are wannabe cops; paramedics, utility workers, railroad employees, etc.[10] TLOs have been used to monitor Occupy Wall Street and Black Lives Matter protests and activists.[11]

Fusion center employees occupy themselves by playing video war games and fantasizing about being armor-clad super heroes. When bored, they target political activists and despised minorities. The Missouri fusion center targeted supporters of Ron Paul, pro-life activists, and so-called conspiracy theorists. Anti-war activists and Islamic lobby groups were targeted in Texas. A DHS analyst in Wisconsin targeted anti-abortion activists; a Pennsylvania DHS contractor spied on environmental activists and a Second Amendment rally; the Maryland state police put anti-death penalty and anti-war activists in the FBI's database; and in 2009, the Virginia fusion center published a terrorism threat assessment identifying historically black colleges as potential hubs for terror related activity. It also identified hacktivism as a form of terrorism.

Along with the FBI's task forces, fusion centers serve as cover for domestic CIA operations. This is nothing new, as the CIA has always placed officers inside state police forces and the Special Services (aka "Red Squad") units of police forces in major cities. CIA Chaos-style officers specialize in the recruitment of American citizens who travel abroad, as well as foreign students, diplomats, scientists and businesspeople willing to sell out their countries for an SUV or a pat on the back.

Homeland Security as Implicit Terrorism

Ultimately, the DHS is about protecting the haves from the have-nots, just like Phoenix coordinators were protecting large land owners from VCI revolutionaries fighting for agrarian reform.

"It's the problem of supporting personalities rather than democratic institutions," Colonel Stan Fulcher explained when we spoke in 1987, "The Vietnamese were victims of our corruption. We smothered them with money. It's the same thing you see in Central America today. You can't take a Salvadoran colonel in a patron army without the corruption he brings along."

The billions of dollars pouring from your pay checks into the DHS "internal security" boondoggle are smothering America in corruption too.

Given the dearth of actual terrorist acts in America, the Homeland Security Enterprise exists primarily to protect critical infrastructure assets in the private sector from disenfranchised citizens seeking justice and accountability from government and corporations. In this capitalist sense, DHS is the key component in the state-sponsored legal criminality Johan Galtung spoke about.

"Personal violence is for the amateur in dominance," Galtung said, "structural violence is the tool of the professional. The amateur who wants to dominate uses guns; the professional uses social structure. The legal criminality of the social system and its institutions, of government, and of individuals at the interpersonal level, is tacit violence. Structural violence is a structure of exploitation and social injustice."

Indeed, the stated goal of the Homeland Security Enterprise is the protection of critical infrastructure assets in the public and private sectors. Not the protection of people. To that end, the DHS assigns Intelligence Officers and Protective Security Advisors to fusion centers. This operation is run out of the DHS National Protection and Programs Directorate and focuses on physical (concrete blocks around buildings) and cyber security.

Given that your chance of being killed by a terrorist is less than dying from a bee sting, this joint business venture has achieved nothing in terms of saving lives. Instead, fusion centers and their DHS managers function as political police enforcing the ultra-conservative, free-wheeling capitalist ideology that drives corporate America. In advancing this ideology, DHS managers seek to promote public support for, and indeed, reverence toward, cops, soldiers and the Homeland Security Enterprise. They also generate the attendant apprehension within the general public that persons with contrarian views are suspect. You can count on DHS cadres not to support the Constitutional right of anyone, like pro football player Colin Kaepernick, who refuses to stand during the National Anthem.

Like the Phoenix program it was modeled on, the DHS helps coordinate the systematic corruption and repression of grassroots

American society on behalf of the rich political elite. Consider this: the Act that created the DHS stripped 180,000 government employees of their union rights – because there "might be" an emergency. On behalf of its private sector patrons, Congress eliminated civil service and labor protections for DHS employees, who can be reassigned or dismissed without notifying their union representatives. Emboldened by Congress, DHS executive management sought the power to override any provision in a union contract, but for some reason the federal courts blocked that attempt at union busting.

The key stakeholders in the Enterprise are the owners of the private businesses that comprise the critical infrastructure of the National Security Establishment: anything related to war and law enforcement. Their intellectual partners occupy vastly overpaid management positions in elite law firms, hospitals, universities, nongovernmental organizations, and nonprofit groups looking to advance their careers while eliminating the competition.

What CIA officer Lucian Conein said to me about Phoenix applies to Homeland Security: it's a great blackmail scheme for the central government: "If you don't do what I want, you're VC."

This is what homeland security has become: a protection racket. At the strategic political level it consists of bankers and corporate lobbyists paying elected officials to create tax loop-holes for the rich, blanket domestic surveillance that compels working people to live in terror of being fired if they make suspicious utterances, and corrupt officials rewarding their arms industry contributors by laundering taxpayer dollars into the war machine.

For stakeholders in the National Security Establishment, the Enterprise is the biggest boondoggle ever: and not just for the lavish public spending devoted to their military-defense projects; it is a dream come true for their cadres, too – people like Bruce Lawlor and Rob Simmons (see Chapters 15 and 16) who sold their souls to the CIA's Cult of Death, and also understand the arcane mechanics of internal security.

Remember, the CIA believed that the US could win the Vietnam War through military force. But the Communists represented the interests of the people and for this reason, the people sided with them. In response, operators like Lawlor, Simmons and Frank Scotton recruited spies to map out the VCI's organization, and then targeted its "upper tier" leaders for neutralization. In the process of going after the enemy's political leadership, they terrorized the leadership's friends and families and supporters as well – the "lower tier" they sought to pacify through psychological warfare.

The same pattern is unfolding in America. Homeland Security cadres, through the DHS and the various parallel mechanisms, are identifying and targeting the National Security Establishment's "political and administrative" opponents in America for neutralization. For upper tier dissidents it means being the target of "compromise and discreditation" campaigns launched by Ultras, often through deniable assets like the Association of Former Intelligence Officers (AFIO) and other Swift Boat-style organizations.

Since the creation of the Homeland Security protection racket, over eight trillion taxpayer dollars has been moved from social programs into "internal security" programs that have provided the National Security Establishment with over 250,000 cadres to pacify the flag-waving American public. For the average American this means eternal debt and subservience, as their tax dollars are given to their "protectors". The psychological warfare aspect of the pacification program is handled by network news and Hollywood, which erase historical memory and with it, any moral imperative on the part of average Americans to pretend they don't live in segregated communities; all that matters is dominance over some Other, and anyone can dominate others by becoming a spy for homeland security.

The methods for doing so are as ancient as language, and the myth of Cronos overthrowing Uranus. Since the dawn of civilization, effete old men have created gods and religions to organize young men into warrior clans. They indoctrinate the youths with patriotic slogans, make them feel special, and then send them to rape and pillage their neighbors. Organizing society in this fashion protects the old men, and their wives and wealth and power, from those young men who have the urge to kill them and take everything they own.

Within America, cops are organized and indoctrinated to function like a warrior clan that uses "explicit violence" to pacify the public. They execute teenagers for wearing baggy pants or casting disrespectful looks at them while they're on safari in black communities. They shower tear gas and rubber bullets on heretical white anti-war protesters, and then happily rough them up during arrest. Everyone knows the cops will never be punished for excessive use of explicit force, and therein lies the power of "implicit terror": cops enforce the law, they do not obey it.

DHS cadres in mufti serve the same "armed propaganda" purpose. They understand that terror, whether explicit or implicit, is an organizing principle of society. Many are veterans who learned pacification techniques while conducting the house-to-house searches that turned Afghanistan and Iraq into human catastrophes unreported in the US press. They even refer to themselves as "door kickers".

Their managers take a broader view and *study* the collective terror Israel dishes out to crush the Palestinian soul. At the highest levels of government, they wage the feudalistic "economic warfare" sieges that drive entire nations into poverty. Madeleine Albright as US Ambassador to the United Nations acknowledged that US sanctions on Iraq had led to the death of half-a-million children. "We think the price is worth it," she said.

Our monstrous rulers know how to justify their disastrous interventions by demonizing foreign leaders in the media. If fear of straw dogs like Saddam or Qaddafi or Kim doesn't win the hearts and minds of American citizens, they issue color-coded warnings of attacks that never occur. Network news reports that behind the scenes, without your knowledge, secret agents saved the day.

As Guy Debord famously said, "Yet the highest ambition of the integrated spectacle is still to turn secret agents into revolutionaries, and revolutionaries into secret agents."

The Homeland Security cadres are expert in implicit as well as explicit terror – of jack-booted Guardsman eyeballing travelers in airports, and Keystone Cops hanging onto armored vehicles, buffed up in bullet proof vests and swinging machine guns while searching cars and homes without probable cause in an entire city on lockdown after the Boston Marathon bombing, or after some deranged white kid on Prozac slaughters his suburban classmates.

Earlier I mentioned the manipulation of social forces to quell the type of protests Colin Kaepernick initiated when he refused to stand for the National Anthem. The same phenomena occurred in July 2016, when police arrested people for criticizing cops on Facebook and Twitter, after the shooting of Dallas cops.[12] In a similar assault on Constitutional rights, the chair of the Oklahoma's public safety committee introduced the bill that would make "it unlawful to wear a mask, hood or covering during the commission of a crime or to intentionally conceal a person's identity in a public place."[13]

The message is clear to the friends and families of the targeted and arrested people: you are free, up to the point you actually express your freedoms.

The purpose of such psyops is to make you believe the authorities know everything about you and will use that information to destroy you. To that end they have established in America the four programs that imbued the all-seeing Phoenix with omnipotence: surveillance and informant networks that identify suspects; interrogation centers that torture them; counterterror teams that kidnap and kill them; and administrative detention laws that make it all possible.

The domestic version of the CIA's Hamlet Informant Program in Vietnam began when Bush's attorney general John Ashcroft laid the groundwork for the Terrorism Information Program (TIP). Check it out online to see its many features of mass surveillance.

The counterterror teams created in Vietnam have been perfected and expanded; military veterans populate DHS and police SWAT teams. Many of these vets can't wait to relive their heroic experiences rousting Muslim families in their homes in Iraq and Afghanistan.

The PIC program is the model for the network of black sites, detention centers, prisons and jails America builds in every nation it occupies. At the Guantanamo facility in Cuba, the CIA has perfected torture and now punishes suspects by slowly driving them insane.

Same thing here. The DHS operates detention centers for illegal immigrants, but not their employers. Empty detention centers on military reservations await the sort of national crisis the CIA routinely provokes overseas to justify military intervention – at which point thousands of citizen suspects on dozens of blacklists shall be rounded up and interned.

Administrative detention is the legal nail upon which the pacification of America hangs. In Vietnam, suspects were carted between interrogation centers, detention centers and jails until they confessed, died or defected. Survivors were sent to a military tribunal or a CIA-advised, Stalinist security committee for disposition; for High Value convicts that meant imprisonment on Con Son Island, ninety miles off the southern tip of South Vietnam. Con Son with its tiger cages was the model for Gitmo.

In September 1969, the CIA formed the Central Security Committee (CSC) in Saigon to dispose of citizens arrested under the administrative detention laws. The Central Security Committee was chaired by the Prime Minister and included the Director of Corrections, the director general of the National Police, and five prison wardens. It reviewed cases of Communist offenders considered for conditional or early release. Unless a substantial bribe was paid, the Committee always recommended further detention. It is noteworthy that the National Assembly tried to abolish the CSC in December 1970 – without success.

If you don't think it can happen here, think again. Donald Bordenkircher headed the CORDS prison system in Vietnam and served as chief advisor to the Director of Corrections. Bordenkircher began his career in 1957 as a correctional officer at San Quentin State Prison. By 1967 he was an assistant warden. Recruited that year by the Agency for International Development's Office of Public Safety (a frequent cover for the CIA), he spent five years "improving" conditions in Vietnam's prisons and jails. "We were doing a magnificent job with the prisoners and the rest of the war," he claimed.[14]

The problem, he said, was that liberal politicians in Washington "handcuffed" the military.

After Bush invaded Iraq, Bordenkircher at age 69 volunteered to help bring that benighted nation under American rule. As with many Vietnam veterans, he was dying to win one. He became a contractor with the Department of Justice and, as National Director of Operations for all prisons in Iraq, got the job of shutting down Abu Ghraib. "I was in charge of a team that went into the prison often," he said. "After reading and looking at everything and talking to a hell of a lot of people, I came to the conclusion there wasn't a lot of brutality caused by American troops at Abu Ghraib."

Today, the penal system in America resembles the prison regimes it imposed upon Vietnam, Iraq and Afghanistan. The same jailers with the same Ultra attitudes are in charge here, and they are doing well; like the War on Terror, incarceration is a growth industry. Since Nixon declared war on drugs in 1970, the prison population has grown from several hundred thousand to several million, mostly blacks. According to the ACLU, one in 31 adults is in prison or jail, on parole or probation. With only 5% of the world's population, America has 25% of the world's prison population.

Ask yourself, how can we be the land of the free and simultaneously the world's largest jailer with its highest per capita incarceration rate?

Private as well as publicly-owned prisons are a cornerstone of the critical infrastructure industry of domestic repression, as well as a boundless source of wealth for investors in the legally criminal

Homeland Security apparatus. Seen from this pro-business perspective, administrative detention is the growth industry of the future; along with the plea-bargain boondoogle, it is how the National Security Establishment will keep jails packed with people who aren't guilty of any crime.

For a glimpse into the future look at Israel, which has had a leading role in teaching Americans "how to do it". There, administrative detention makes it okay to round up civilians, detain and torture them indefinitely, destroy their homes with bulldozers, cast them to the four winds, and steal everything they own simply because they are Palestinians.

Being a stateless Palestinian is a crime of status. In America, being a pacifist is a crime of status. The key is loosely defining what a terrorist suspect is.

The Patriot, Homeland Security, and Domestic Security Enhancement Acts set in place the elements of administration detention. Americans captured on foreign soil like John Lindh, or said to be involved in terrorist activities overseas, can be held indefinitely in a military prison and denied access to lawyers and family members. No federal court can review the reason for the detention. They can be executed if found guilty by the President. Meanwhile, America's version of the Central Security Committee at Guantanamo Bay is still conducting secret Stalinist tribunals in 2016, seven years after Obama bragged, in his Nobel Prize acceptance speech, that he had ordered the facility closed.

Detention laws apply domestically too. To say nothing of having the same name, if you even resemble someone on the "no-fly" list you can be detained. DHS routinely detains suspects without charge or having to disclose their names or location. DHS agents posing as cops can punish protestors and coerce them into becoming informants by holding them indefinitely as "material witnesses" when there is no basis to charge them with a crime.

Secret subpoenas used by DHS to obtain information can't be refused or disclosed, making it impossible to defend against false charges. People arrested for unknown crimes uncovered as a result of secret surveillance are not entitled to judicial review of the warrant or the evidence obtained as a result. Detentions, evidence, trials, deportations and executions are now conducted in secret.

Administrative detention is structural violence for the professionals. It works in tandem with informant and surveillance programs that identify "terrorist surrogates" at the grassroots level of society. In this manner the jerry-rigged justice system, always biased against the poor, becomes the ultimate form of Ultra terrorism. It is the greatest blackmail scheme ever invented: if you didn't do what the homeland gangsters want, your name appears on the blacklist and into the Black Hole you go.

Check out what happened to Jose Padilla.

Political and Psychological Warfare

Capitalism is America's ideology and business its dominant party, controlling both political parties. Its Democratic wing works with labor's management class and has been responsible for some of the recent key anti-labor policies, such as off-shoring; the Republican wing always supports business over labor, landlords over renters. The Business Party's strategic goal is the political control of people at home and abroad – and the subsequent acquisition of their property, wealth and resources – through the centralization of power in multinational corporations and giant financial institutions exempt from anyone's laws, as well as through psychological operations.

Myths about democracy are used along with Rotary Club-style front organizations to disguise the Business Party "infrastructure" in America, just as they were in Vietnam, where the only rule of the psyops game was post your own score. Blessed with limitless resources, and using sales techniques perfected by its private sector instructors in the advertising industry, the Americans distributed millions of leaflets stressing traditional Confucian values of obedience to authority, while portraying the Communists as a socially disruptive force that must be eliminated – the way Rudy Giuliani stigmatizes Black Lives Matter.

But the Americans were out of touch with the reality of life in rural villages and could only reach the people through "media" like leaflets. And while Americans relied on cartoon books to sell "democracy" and "free enterprise" to a largely illiterate people, VCI cadres went from person to person talking into ears, connecting on a human level.

Unable to sell its product through media, the CIA resorted to coercion, and drastically expanded the Hamlet Informant Program. Village chiefs were instructed to conduct classes on government ideology for villagers with revolutionary thoughts or relatives who had them. Attendance was mandatory. There was a one-week course "with extensions for problem individuals." Day care and lunch were made available in "vacated" homes. Creating defectors was emphasized, counseling was provided, and "the populace was encouraged to report the activities of the VCI by dropping a note addressed to the police in local mailboxes." This method was credited with approximately 40% of the information used in Phoenix operations in one province.

Psyops in support of Phoenix proved to be such a potent weapon in the attack on the VCI that in August 1970, the Pentagon's Special Assistant for Counterinsurgency and Special Activities described Phoenix as "the number one MACV PSYOPS priority."

At the same time, Congressional investigators revealed that the CIA used the Phoenix program as "an instrument of mass political murder" to neutralize politicians and activists who opposed the puppet regime or espoused peace.[15]

Five years later, the Church Committee revealed the extent of the FBI's similar attempts to suppress the Communist Party in the United States, which it claimed controlled the anti-war and civil rights movements. The FBI used the same kind of illegal operations Phoenix used in Vietnam: spreading lies and using forged documents to break up marriages and otherwise harass people into submission. FBI agents were able to persuade college administrators to prevent dissidents from giving public addresses. There was no evidence that any of them were Soviet agents fomenting armed rebellion; it was their ideas about a just society the FBI was trying to stamp out, along with the First Amendment.

The military was at the forefront of the repression of the anti-war movement, and is leading the charge again. As noted in Chapter 4, Sid Towle was a lieutenant with the 116th MIG in Washington, DC, in 1970. As chief of a counterintelligence team, Towle investigated the anti-war activities of army personnel and conducted "offensive counterintelligence operations" in the nation's capital. One job was disrupting antiwar demonstrations by building bonfires and inciting people to riot, so the capital police could be called in to bash heads.

As Ed Murphy recalled in the same chapter, the 116th MIG targeted specific leaders of the anti-war movement. Photos of the targets were posted at headquarters.

That's what DHS agents are prepared to do in the US. And with advances in technology and 40 years to learn from mistakes, political neutralizations are easier than ever. Consider the anthrax letters mailed to Democratic senators after 9/11, now recognized as an inside job.[16] It took only a few "black propaganda" terror operations to silence the political opposition's leadership and its resistance to the Patriot Act.

Information management – including official secrecy and false accusations – is the key to pacifying the people through implicit terror, while making the internal security apparatus appear legal, moral and popular. This is being done against American citizens through the most ambitious psywar campaign ever waged on planet Earth.

Another essential ingredient of psychological warfare is properly indoctrinating and organizing political cadres. As Michael Ledeen, former employee of the Pentagon, the State Department and the National Security Council (and involved in the transfer of arms to Iran during the Iran-Contra affair), stated in the days after 9/11, "New times require new people" with the will power to "stamp out" the "corrupt habits of mind" manifest in the thoughts or actions of anyone who can't be assimilated into the Business Party or opposes its aggression disguised as the War on Terror.

The military has a lot of experience training political cadres. Soldiers slated to participate in Phoenix were given the CIA's patented "motivational indoctrination" course at Fort Bragg. They were the first political cadres to infiltrate the American military. In return for adopting the Business Party line and violating the laws of warfare by targeting civilians, a successful career was guaranteed. As noted, several CIA and military Phoenix veterans have held important DHS posts. The first chief of DHS counter narcotic operations, CIA officer Roger Mackin, ran Special Police operations in Da Nang.

At Fort Bragg, CIA psywar experts taught Phoenix advisors how to wage political warfare. In the early 1980s CIA officer Duane Clarridge had the training manual translated into Spanish and reprinted for use in the Reagan régime's illegal Contra War. Titled "Psychological Operations in Guerrilla Warfare", it stated that "the human being should be considered the priority objective in a political war. And conceived as the military target of guerrilla war, the human being has his most critical point in his mind. Once his mind has been reached, the 'political animal' has been defeated, without necessarily receiving bullets."

DHS cadres pass through the same motivational indoctrination courses before they hit the streets. DHS cadres in turn instruct civilian "critical infrastructure" personnel on how to spy and report on colleagues who serve as "terrorist surrogates" by even inadvertently revealing information on infrastructure vulnerabilities. DHS spies monitor private sector terror suspects until it comes time to expose them in the media as being under investigation. The most intimate details of a person's private life, all of which are known through blanket surveillance, become his or her greatest liability. Extramarital affairs, medical marijuana use, or mental health care are revealed, leading to a target being neutralized.

In the absence of vulnerabilities, the CIA's Dark Army of computer hackers can create them.

Through highly refined motivational indoctrination methods, complacent Americans are converted into Ledeen's "new people" who idolize the CIA, FBI, NSA and DHS. People who aren't DHS cadres but wish to serve the Ultra cause join "front" organizations like the Citizen Corps, or the Office of Social Innovation and Civic Participation, or Community Emergency Response Teams. The ever popular Neighborhood Watch Program supplies overly-aggressive cops at fusion centers with the false rumors they need to detain activists as terrorist surrogates. The Medical Reserve Corps gives overpaid doctors working in hospital emergency rooms the chance to identify suspects among the masses of poor people falling through the safety net at the bottom of the jerry-rigged health care system.

The pressure to join the new legions is irresistible. When Bush announced the DHS on 6 June 2002, he stressed that its primary mission was to "mobilize and focus" the American people "to accomplish the mission of attacking the enemy where he hides and plans." By which he meant having Ledeen's "new people" root out the enemy within, just as the CIA roots out insurgents in the colonies.

The most highly motivated cadres are trained "in techniques of persuasion over control of target groups" as outlined in "Psychological Operations in Guerrilla Warfare". In the next national emergency, these cadres will be mobilized, attend mass meetings, carry placards, shout the proper slogans and, if necessary, grab ropes and form lynch mobs.

Theoretically, only five percent of the population needs to be organized in this fashion in order to wield control over the indifferent 90% and defeat the five percent that form the resistance.

Waging this type of psywar is the maximum danger posed by the Homeland Security apparatus. Blackmail is the key. Hundreds of businesses and institutions across the country have already been placed on the consolidated Terrorist Watch List. One Bush official said that merely being on the list "could destroy the livelihood of all those organizations

... without a bomb being thrown or a spore of anthrax being released."[17]

Blacklists abound: the TIPOFF blacklist; the No-Fly blacklist; the CAPPS II blacklist which uses credit card information and secret databases to assess a person's security risk level; and local blacklists like the one kept by the Denver police department.[18]

And the secret ones you don't know about.

Initially, the proliferation of blacklists had "the leaders of many federal departments and agencies scrambling to figure out how they could influence [Homeland Security] without appearing disloyal."[19]

Writing for *USA Today* in 2002, James Bamford cited a Knight Ridder report saying that, "A growing number of military officers, intelligence professionals and diplomats privately...charge that the administration squelches dissenting views and that intelligence analysts are under intense pressure to produce reports supporting the White House's argument that Saddam poses such an immediate threat to the United States that pre-emptive military action is necessary."[20]

If a dissident or resistant bureaucrat has no past indiscretions, forged documents are used. One political opponent jailed in Vietnam by President Thieu revealed the existence of "a systematic campaign of vilification by use of forged documents." Forged documents used to justify false arrests or conceal illegal operations often emerged as "captured documents." A legislative aide working for the Senate committee investigating Phoenix in 1970 wryly observed that, "There seems to be captured documents to prove any point or to support, retrospectively, almost any conclusion."[21]

If what's past is prologue, in the forthcoming national emergency, the paranoia that currently infects the Muslim American community will spread nationwide until no one is sure who is a spy for the Thought Police. Midnight arrests and disappearances into detention centers will be commonplace, as the definition of a terrorist surrogate expands to include people deemed dangerous to the Public Order. As Ambassador Ellsworth Bunker wrote in 1972 about a secret emergency decree issued by the GVN: "This means that virtually any person arrested can now be held on criminal instead of political charges."[22]

No specific charge is required: a DHS spy will accuse his neighbor, the one whose dog poops on his lawn, of disturbing the public order; off the unlucky fellow goes into the local Gitmo.

Last but not least, the crime of sedition will be resurrected and expanded to include disseminating information about government corruption and undermining the will of the State by challenging its authority. Calling for civil disobedience will be equated with threatening Homeland Security. Cadres in the Office of Cyberspace Security will expose you as a terrorist surrogate for sending sarcastic or satirical emails blaming Bush and Israel for 9/11. In the absence of actual "utterances", cadres will manufacture them.

Don't laugh. Anti-terror legislation passed by Congress allows for *secret* searches of the homes of people who meet the nebulous criteria of "suspected terrorist." Because these secret searches violate the Fourth Amendment, the government is devising "new tools that ease administrative burdens."[23]

Remember, CIA legal experts argued that Article 3 of the Geneva Conventions applies "only to sentencing for crimes, and does not prohibit a state from interning civilians or subjecting them to emergency detention when such measures are necessary for the security or safety of the state."

In this way indefinite detention, torture and summary execution, all carried out without previous judgment pronounced by a regularly constituted court, are perfectly legal in the criminal Homeland Security state, because they result from "administrative procedures."

This is Phoenix, and this is what the National Security Establishment has in store for America.

PART IV

MANUFACTURING COMPLICITY: SHAPING THE AMERICAN WORLDVIEW

"All experts serve the state and the media and only in that way do they achieve their status. Every expert follows his master, for all former possibilities for independence have been gradually reduced to nil by present society's mode of organization. The most useful expert, of course, is the one who can lie. With their different motives, those who need experts are falsifiers and fools. Whenever individuals lose the capacity to see things for themselves, the expert is there to offer an absolute reassurance."

Guy Debord, Comments on the Society of the Spectacle

Chapter 18

FRAGGING BOB KERREY: THE CIA AND THE NEED FOR A WAR CRIMES TRIBUNAL

This chapter is a compilation of two articles. One was published in December 2003 and titled "Preemptive Manhunting: The CIA's New Assassination Program" in response to an article by Seymour Hersh titled "Moving Targets: Will the counterinsurgency plan in Iraq repeat the mistakes of Vietnam."[1]

The other article, written two and a half years earlier, was titled "Fragging Bob Kerrey: CIA War Crimes and the Need for a War Crimes Trial." It tells how former Senator Kerrey led a team of Navy SEALs into a village in Vietnam and murdered 20 women and children in 1969. He lied about the operation and said the team killed 21 VC. He was given a medal as a reward.

Kerrey's career took off as a result of that war crime and cover-up. He moved from one important public sector job to another until May 2016, when he was appointed chair of the board of trustees of the Fulbright University in Vietnam.

One can only imagine what J. William Fulbright would have thought of that supreme act of arrogance. As Mark Ashwill has observed, "As Fulbright said in his book, *The Arrogance of Power:* 'One simply cannot engage in barbarous action without becoming a barbarian … one cannot defend human values by calculated and unprovoked violence without doing mortal damage to the values one is trying to defend.'"

The American media reacted as expected, with non-judgmental

accounts about the irony of appointing a mass murderer of Vietnamese to head a Vietnamese institution. Featured in most accounts were the comments of Vietnamese who supported the decision.

But what if the tables were turned? If the government of Vietnam sent a former revolutionary, known to have murdered American women and children, to head a Vietnamese university in America, the media would have flipped out and called for the renewed bombing of Hanoi.

The hypocrisy of the American media is a wonder to behold.

In my 2001 article about Kerrey, I argued that the CIA, which instigated the raid on Thanh Phong, should be tried for its policy of waging war crimes in Vietnam. I'm still hoping that will happen, especially since 9/11 and the resulting CIA horrors, many of which have been carefully documented. The only difference is that I would now put the media in the dock too.

Seymour Hersh's December 2003 article is an example of how the mainstream media dissembles when it can no longer conceal evidence that political assassinations are official US policy. In his article, Hersh revealed "a new Special Forces operation" in Iraq called "preemptive manhunting." He compared the operation to Phoenix and noted that "The new civilian Assistant Secretary for Special Operations in the Pentagon is Thomas O'Connell, an Army veteran who served in the Phoenix program in Vietnam, and who, in the early eighties, ran Grey Fox, the Army's secret commando unit."

An article by Julian Borger published the same day as Hersh's (8 December 2003) dealt with the same subject, minus the sensational rhetoric.[2] As Borger noted, and as *The New York Times* had reported a month earlier, Task Force 121 was the name of the unit conducting the Phoenix-style operation in Iraq. Trained by Israeli commandos, Task Force 121 was originally designed to capture and assassinate High Value targets within Saddam Hussein's Ba'athist Party.

However, the targeted Ba'athists tried to hide among family, friends and supporters, and soon Task Force 121 death squads were kicking down the doors to private homes and, as Hersh correctly observed, killing everyone within "the broad middle of the Ba'athist underground."

As CIA officer Frank Snepp had written 40 years earlier, "the Phoenix strike teams opted for a scattershot approach, picking up anyone who might be a suspect, and eventually, when the jails were packed to overflowing, they began simply taking the law, such as it was, into their own hands."

Hersh's article was billed as news, but it wasn't. CIA commandos had been in Iraq since 2002, preparing rebel Kurdish forces to guide the task forces that followed in 2003. These earlier CIA units assembled the blacklists that Task Force 121 later used to target Saddam and his senior staff. The military called this earlier adventure "decapitation" and credited it with degrading the Iraqi army's ability to resist the US invasion.

Prior to the invasion, CIA officers also squeezed key Iraqi army officers and civil officials into defecting and spreading CIA-scripted black propaganda in widely dispersed articles like the one Chris Hedges wrote for *The New York Times* on 8 November 2001, titled "Defectors Cite Iraqi Training for Terrorism".

Likewise, characterizing Phoenix as a Special Forces assassination program is a half-truth at best, akin to saying that baseball is only about throwing a ball, without mentioning the fielding and hitting. The CIA managed the entirety of the multi-faceted Phoenix program, just as it manages every "task force" sent into Iraq, Afghanistan, Pakistan, Yemen, etc. Some prominent left journalists have spread the fiction that the military is in charge, hopefully out of stupidity.[3]

Special Forces units participated in Phoenix operations, yes, but, as I'll show in this chapter, as one of the many elements the program coordinated, and always under the supervision of senior CIA officers.

Phoenix operations ranged from small units on snatch and snuff missions to My Lai-style cordon and search operations involving hundreds of American and Vietnamese soldiers, Special Police officials, and psychological warfare (psywar) teams. In their pursuit of Communist political cadres, senior Phoenix officials conducted operations in Cambodia, Laos and North Vietnam, as well as in South Vietnam. As Colonel Douglas Dillard revealed to me, they even had the authority to call in massive air strikes.

From mid-1968 until mid-1969, Dillard, under the guidance of Jim Ward, the CIA's region officer in charge, coordinated Phoenix operations in the Delta region of South Vietnam. Dillard told me that he and Ward had the authority to call in B-52 strikes on targeted groups and individuals. "The idea was that if we knew their pattern and if we could put the fear of God in them, then we could influence their movements so they could never assemble as a battalion," Dillard explained. "We continued to try to do that from the summer of 1968 on, and we started getting in some pretty good defectors because of that pressure. The overall coordination was working."

Indeed – and this is important in understanding Bob Kerrey's mission – coordination at every level of the Phoenix program was absolutely essential. For example, the CIA could not run a small unit operation in enemy territory without first consulting its military associates, because, as Dillard put it, "it's conceivable that the operations people have scheduled a B-52 strike in that area."

In a thesis he wrote for Air University in 1974, titled "The Future Applicability of the Phoenix Program," CIA officer Warren Milberg described a typical Phoenix operation involving several US army infantry companies. The operation was conducted in the village of Thuong Xa in Quang Tri Province in early 1968. As Milberg noted, Thuong Xa had served as a staging area for the Vietminh in the First Indochina War and its inhabitants still supported the Communists. However, according to Milberg, the villagers' support for the Communists had been coerced through atrocities and armed propaganda, and therefore the Americans had no choice but to save the villagers from themselves.

The decision to conduct a Phoenix operation of "massive proportions" against Thuong Xa was made by the Province Security Council at the direction of Milberg's boss, Bob Brewer, the CIA's province officer in charge. Brewer functioned like a warlord, and once permission was granted, "Only the barest essential information was given to the various Vietnamese agencies in Quang Tri," Milberg wrote.

Cutting out the Vietnamese was designed to prevent local officials on the VC payroll from interfering with the "planning process." To further ensure security, "The actual name of the targeted village was not released to the Vietnamese until the day before the operation."

In preparing the Thuong Xa operation, information from South Vietnamese Police Special Branch informers, along with information from Province Interrogation Center (PIC) reports, was fed into the Phoenix program's newly established District Intelligence and Operations Coordinating Centers (DIOCCs) near Thuong Xa. A blacklist of suspected VCI was compiled in Quang Tri's Province Intelligence and Operations Coordination Center (PIOCC), and then cross-checked "against master Phoenix lists" at the Phoenix Directorate in Saigon to ensure that high level CIA penetration agents were protected.

Before the operation, Provincial Reconnaissance Unit (PRU) teams, advised by US Marines detached to the CIA, were sent to locate and surveil targeted Communist cadres, known as members of the Viet Cong Infrastructure (VCI). Escape routes were studied for ambush sites and local US Army and Marine units were conscripted to act as a "blocking force" to seal off the village, just as happened at My Lai on 16 March 1968.[4] At dawn on the day of the Phoenix operation in Thuong Xa, US military aircraft dropped thousands of psywar leaflets on the village urging the targeted VCI to surrender, and offering rewards to defectors and informers. All that happened at My Lai too.

None of the villagers took advantage of the deal. Instead, the residents braced for the shock. In the early morning hours, the PRU "counterterror" teams accompanied by Special Branch interrogators and CIA advisors like Milberg started searching people's homes for weapons, documents, food caches and VCI suspects.

As Milberg noted, the Special Police and its CIA advisors "compared the names and descriptions on the blacklists with every man, woman, and child in Thuong Xa."

Suspects were sent to screening zones where they were interrogated, while people identified as innocent bystanders were fed and "entertained" by RD Cadre psywar teams. The VCI, meanwhile, were driven into the northeast corner of town, where they were killed or captured as they tried to escape through Milberg's "ring of steel."

The result was two VCI captured. One was the district party chief; the other was the chief of the local National Liberation Front farmers' association. Both were sent to the CIA's brutal interrogation center in Da Nang. Eight other targeted VCI were killed or escaped. Two psywar teams stayed behind to assert the puppet government's presence, but within a month they were driven out of town and Thuong Xa reverted to Communist control.

As a result of such costly failures, which depleted resources without producing spectacular body counts, the CIA turned to small, unilateral operations like the one Bob Kerrey conducted. The military initially resisted on moral and legal grounds. General Bruce Palmer, commander of the Ninth Infantry Division in the Mekong Delta, objected to the "involuntary assignment" of American soldiers to Phoenix. He did not believe that "people in uniform, who are pledged to abide by the Geneva Conventions, should be put in the position of having to break those laws of warfare."

Despite the hesitancy of conventional military commanders, US Special Forces, including Navy SEALs, have no compunctions about killing civilians. As Frank Snepp noted, as mentioned above, small unit Phoenix operations proliferated and took "the law, such as it was, into their own hands." They also proved to be the most efficient way of waging a counterinsurgency.

Today, under CIA guidance and coordination, US Special Forces and the military's legion of unaccountable mercenary contractors have become the de facto policemen of the American empire, and each branch of the military has created its own commandoes to conduct such "extra-legal" operations. It's the new wave.

But counter-subversion is a police responsibility, and as the American agency mandated to work with foreign special police forces, the CIA will always manage Phoenix-style assassination programs, with the military providing the manpower to staff them in America's colonies around the world.

Blaming the Victim

To his credit, Seymour Hersh was correct when he said the original "moving targets" were members of the Ba'ath Party.[5] But he studiously avoided putting either the Vietnam war or the Iraq War in its proper context. He ignored the overarching fact that the CIA's assassination programs in Iraq and Vietnam were both illegal precisely because they targeted civilians. He didn't mention the network of CIA interrogation centers and special police informant programs upon which pacification depends. Nor did he mention that American war managers, through administrative detention laws, denied targeted Iraqi and Vietnamese civilians due process in their own country, as part of the Phoenix model the CIA applies in every nation the US conquers and corrupts.

Hersh did focus on the problems caused by faulty information, but he omitted a significant gory detail: that based on the word of an anonymous informant, Ba'ath Party members who had never harmed a single American were detained indefinitely and tortured until they confessed or became double agents spreading CIA propaganda. Instead, Hersh focused on soldiers who escaped the dragnet.

He did not accuse US commander Stanley McChrystal of systematic war crimes related to the "political cleansing" that preceded the "reconstruction" of Iraq. Nor did he call the task force hit teams "death squads" or name the war criminals who ran the murder machine at McChrystal's headquarters 50 miles north of Baghdad.

Something else Hersh failed to mention: *anyone* who resisted the American invasion was put on the CIA's hit list, not just former Ba'ath Party members. Nor was the murder of those people a mistake arising from faulty intelligence, as Hersh suggested. It was and is policy. As the CIA learned in Vietnam, killing specific targets doesn't terrorize an entire population into submission; only indiscriminate mass murder can achieve that ghastly goal.

Phoenix, according to Hersh, was on everyone's minds in late 2003. He said that "many" of the anonymous officials he interviewed were afraid the pre-emptive manhunting strategy would turn into another Phoenix program. But that's not true. The officials planning the war within the Bush regime, including Phoenix-veteran John Negroponte, knew exactly what the consequences of pre-emptive manhunting would be. They had every intention of using the Phoenix model to permanently fracture Iraq society, rule it through a regime of corrupted collaborators, and then steal all its oil wealth. Hersh never characterizes American military aggression as a function of capitalism and imperialism.

The trick for journalists like Hersh was to cover up the plan, using cherry-picked interviews that follow the CIA script. For example, one anonymous Pentagon advisor Hersh interviewed justified pre-emptive manhunting by asserting that America's leaders had to stop the 9/11 "terrorists" from striking again. In other words, America had no choice. But, as Hersh strikingly neglected to mention, Iraq had nothing to do with 9/11. The Iraqis were "terrorists" only in the sense that they resisted the American occupation of their country. They hadn't even had WMDs.

Hersh never says anything about the CIA or Special Forces as instruments of an unstated but intentional policy of systematic and sustained war crimes. There is always, in his reporting, a justification for what Americans do. They can be misled. And sometimes they mislead. But only when the nation's survival is at stake.

In a final apologetics tour de force, Hersh exonerated his American sources for any mistakes that were made. "In choosing targets," he said in regard to Phoenix, "the Americans relied on information supplied by South Vietnamese Army officers and village chiefs. The operation got out of control."

Even for a craftsman like Hersh, this generalization was a nifty piece of disinformation. As Milberg noted above, the CIA excluded its Vietnamese counterparts from Phoenix planning, but the operations failed anyway – and not because the Communists had coerced the people, as Milberg claimed, but because the people supported them.

Hersh failed to note that the Americans were fully aware much of the incriminating information they were fed was false. But, as this book has shown, their system was geared to work that way. The CIA deliberately jerry-rigged the Phoenix program so it would overflow with false confessions and accusations, precisely so it could get away with mass murder and terrorizing the population.

What a writer doesn't say is often more important than what he or she does say. In this regard, Hersh did not mention that as soon as American soldiers started fighting and dying in Iraq, they cultivated grievances against the Iraqis who hated them for kicking down their doors, invading their homes, and carting off their men to torture chambers. American war managers always factor this inevitability into their schemes. Why don't journalists acknowledge it?

William Calley and his men blamed every Vietnamese man, woman and child for the deaths of their comrades, which is why the majority of Americans refused to condemn them for massacring hundreds of civilians in My Lai. This is what makes America exceptional: our lives have value, others' don't. It's that double standard that enables the American war machine to cut a swath of righteous savagery across the Muslim world, and for the media to characterize it as "protecting the American people from terror."

This places me among those who say it: some of America's top leaders do have evil intentions. Those who planned the war on Iraq knew that war crimes like the My Lai massacre would proliferate in Iraq just as they had in Vietnam, and for all the same reasons. The CIA is their increasingly not-so-secret instrument for carrying out many of those evil plans, including a long and well documented history of well concealed programs that result from the mass murdering of civilians whose beliefs the war managers hate and whose wealth they covet. And over the course of the CIA's criminal career, it has relied on journalists like Hersh to never tell that part of the story. In their corrupt world of anonymous sources and quid pro quos, Americans never have evil intentions.

Quoting one of his stable of anonymous sources – invariably tough guys who talk like John Wayne – Hersh perpetuated the myth that the Iraqis attacked us first. "The only way we can win is to go unconventional," Hersh quoted one of his patent heroic American sources as saying. "We're going to have to play their game. Guerrilla versus guerrilla. Terrorism versus terrorism. We've got to scare the Iraqis into submission."

All this BS served its intended purpose: it made Hersh's audience of pseudo-intellectuals, middle class liberals and Compatible Leftists feel good, thinking that America was a victim and had no choice but resort to terrorism.

Men in Black

In a concerted effort to "scare" an entire population into submission, the CIA went "unconventional" in Vietnam, establishing Phoenix centers and conducting "selective terrorism" in each of the country's 240 districts. The stated policy was to replace the bludgeon of B-52 bombings and My Lai-style search and destroy operations (which had alienated the people) with the scalpel of assassinations of selected VCI. Phoenix co-creator Robert Komer called this the "rifle shot" approach.

Much of this terrorism was the result of unilateral CIA counter-terror operations. As Dinh Tuong An noted in his series of articles in 1970 and 1971 about Phoenix for *Tin Sang*, Phoenix was "a series of big continuous operations which destroy the countryside and put innocent people to death. In the sky are armed helicopters, but on the ground are the black uniforms, doing what they want where the helicopters and B-52's do not reach."

"Americans in black uniforms," said An, "are the most terrible."[6]

An could have been writing about the SEAL team mission former Nebraska governor and senator Bob Kerrey led into Thanh Phong village on the night of 25 February 1969. During that mission, Kerrey and his seven-man squad murdered, in cold blood, more than a dozen women and children, as reported by Gregory Vistica 32 years later.[7]

To make matters worse, the SEALs lied about it when they got back to their Navy base. Kerrey reported that they had killed 21 Viet Cong guerrillas in a terrible battle, and received a Bronze Star in return.

The CIA's strategy of using systematic war crimes was christened Contre Coup by its creator, CIA officer Ralph Johnson, in South Vietnam. A veteran of the Flying Tigers and notorious ladies' man whose most famous liaison was with Nguyen Cao Ky's wife, Johnson was described by one colleague as "a good-looking, fast-talking snake-oil salesman." In his book *The Phoenix Program: Planned Assassination or Legitimate Conflict Management*, political warfare pioneer Johnson described Contre Coup as "Turning the Communist terrorist strategy, which had proven effective, into a US-Saigon pacification strategy."[8]

This is the same disingenuous argument Hersh made above, the idea that we have no choice but to adopt the enemy's use of "selective terrorism" and use it against them to protect ourselves. This strategy of being more terrifying than the Viet Cong was based on the belief that the war was essentially political and psychological in nature. The CIA misrepresented the war as being fought by opposing ideological factions, each side amounting to about five percent of the total population, while the remaining ninety percent were caught in the cross-fire and just wanted the war to go away.

On one side were Communists supported by comrades in Moscow and Peking. The Communists fought for land reform, to rid Vietnam of American militants, and to unite the north and south, which had been split apart at the end of World War Two. The other faction was composed of Americans and its GVN collaborators, many of whom were Catholics the CIA had relocated from North Vietnam in 1954. This faction was fighting to protect South Vietnam's rich political elite under the direction of Quiet American businessmen.

The object shared by both factions was to win the uncommitted ninety percent over to its side, by coercion if necessary.

The Contre Coup strategy was adopted and advanced by Peer DeSilva, who arrived in Saigon in December 1963 as the CIA's station chief. DeSilva claimed to have been shocked by what he saw. In his autobiography *SubRosa*, he described how the VC had "impaled a young boy, a village chief, and his pregnant wife on sharp poles. To make sure this horrible sight would remain with the villagers, one of the VC terror squad used his machete to disembowel the woman, spilling the fetus onto the ground."[9]

Several military and CIA veterans I spoke with had the same experience as DeSilva. Warren Milberg, for example, served his first tour in Vietnam as an air force security officer. He returned in 1967 as a CIA employee, at which point the scales fell from his eyes and he began to see "evidence of how the Vietcong were operating in the hamlets. And what will always stand out in my mind was the terror and torture they used to strike fear and get compliance from the villagers."

Milberg cited "an event where a particular village chief's wife, who was pregnant, was disemboweled and their unborn baby's head was smashed with a rifle butt. We stumbled on this incident quite by accident within hours of it happening. I'd never seen anything like it in my life."

The aforementioned Colonel Douglas Dillard had the same experience. Assigned as the senior Phoenix officer in the Mekong Delta in February 1968, Dillard, as he recalled, "arrived in Can Tho on a Friday afternoon. The two army sergeants that had come in to be my administrative assistants met me at the airport and took me over to the compound and settled me in the CIA's regional Embassy House."

The next day Dillard took a chopper to Chau Doc Province on the Cambodian border. "It was my first introduction to the real war," Dillard said. "It was right after Tet, and there was still a lot of activity. The young sergeant there, Drew Dix, had been in a little village early that morning. The VC had come in and got a couple out that were accused of collaborating with the government, and they'd shot them in the ears. Their bodies were lying out on a cart. We drove out there, and I looked at that, and I had my first awareness of what those natives were up against. Because during the night, the damn VC team would come in, gather all those villagers together, warn them about cooperating, and present an example of what happened to collaborators. They shot them in the ears on the spot.

"So I knew what my job was. I realized there was a tremendous psychological problem to overcome in getting that specific group of villagers to cooperate in the program. Because to me the Phoenix program required adequate, timely, and detailed information so we could intercept, make to defect, kill, maim, or capture the Vietcong guerrilla forces operating in our area. Or put a strike on them. If either through intercepting messages or capturing VCI, you could get information on some of the main force guerrilla battalion activity, you could put a B-52 strike on them, which we did in Four Corps."

It's debatable how random such introductions to VC terror actually were. As I mentioned in Chapter 6: "The Afghan 'Dirty War' Escalates", CIA officer Robert Haynes (who was serving as a deputy to Evan Parker in the Phoenix Directorate in February 1968) told Senator Brewster that CIA teams committed atrocities and made them look like the work of the VC.

Such "black propaganda" was not uncommon. In his auto-biography *Soldier,* Anthony Herbert told how he reported for duty with the CIA's Special Operations Group in Saigon in late 1965 and was asked to join a top secret psywar program. "What they wanted me to do was to take charge of execution teams that wiped out entire families and tried to make it look as though the VC themselves had done the killing. The rationale was that other Vietnamese would see that the VC had killed another VC and would be frightened away from becoming VC themselves. Of course, the villagers would then be inclined to some sort of allegiance to our side."[10]

Herbert refused to join the "black propaganda" SOG program. Not only that, he spilled the beans on one of the CIA's dirty tricks. As a result, Herbert was vilified in military circles. For above all, Americans can never be said to willfully do anything evil.

They can never be said to be hypocrites either, but station chief DeSilva, who said the VC "were monstrous" authorized the creation of small "counterterrorism teams" (later renamed the PRU) to do the exact same thing, and worse – to commit acts of selective terror and blame them on the VC. As DeSilva described the counterterrorism teams in the passage from his book cited above, they were designed "to bring danger and death to the Vietcong functionaries themselves, especially in areas where they felt secure."

Ever suspicious of their Vietnamese counterparts, the military branches organized their own counterterrorism teams to terrorize VC in territory they controlled. The Navy had responsibility for the Mekong Delta and gave the job of creating counterterrorism teams to its nascent SEAL program, which President Kennedy authorized in 1962 and was still experimental in the mid-1960s.

In *The Phoenix Program,* I featured my extensive interview with Navy Lieutenant John Wilbur. In 1967, Wilbur arrived in Vietnam as deputy commander of SEAL Team 2, a 12-man detachment with no combat veterans in its ranks. Wilbur's SEAL team was assigned to a naval riverine warfare group and quartered in a Quonset hut at the My Tho River dock facility in the middle of the Mekong Delta.

"Frankly," Wilbur told me, "the Navy didn't know what to do with us. They didn't know how to target us or how to operationally control us. So basically they said, "You guys are to go out and interdict supply lines and conduct harassing ambushes and create destruction upon the enemy however you can.""

"Mostly we were to be reactive to, and protective of, the Navy's PBRs (patrol boats, river)," Wilbur said. "That was our most understandable and direct mission. The PBR squadron leaders would bring us intelligence from the PBR patrols. They would report where they saw enemy troops or if there was an ambush of a PBR. Then we'd go out and get the guys who did it."

Knowing what to do and doing it were two vastly different things. Despite being highly trained and motivationally indoctrinated, the SEALs started out, in Wilbur's words, "with the typical disastrous screw-up operations. In our first operation we went out at low tide and ended up getting stuck in mud flats in broad daylight for six hours before we could be extracted. We didn't have any Vietnamese with us and we didn't understand very basic things. We didn't know whether it was a VC cadre or a guy trying to pick up a piece of ass late at night. The only things we had were curfews and free fire zones. And what a curfew was, and what a free fire zone was, became sort of an administrative-political decision. For all we knew, everybody there was terrible.

"We got lost. We got hurt. People were shooting back at us, and other times we never got to a place where we could find people to shoot at. There was a lot of frustration," Wilbur said, "of having no assurance that the information you got was at all reliable and timely."

Wilbur cited the time his team "raided an island across from where the US Ninth Infantry Division was based. We surrounded the settlement that morning and came in with guns blazing. I remember crawling into a hut – which in Vietnam was a sort of shed encompassing a mud pillbox where people would hide from attacks – looking for a VC field hospital. There I was with a hand grenade with the pin pulled, my hand on my automatic, guys running around, adrenaline going crazy, people screaming – and I didn't know who the hell was shooting at who. I can remember that I just wanted to throw the goddamned grenade in the hut and screw whoever was in it. And all of a sudden discovering there was nothing but women and children in there. It was a very poignant experience."

The CIA assigned Vietnamese scouts from its PRU program to Wilbur's SEAL teams as a way of improving its effectiveness. But the PRU were not trusted and, once acclimated, the SEALs worked unilaterally.

Which brings us to Bob Kerrey.

Phoenix Comes to Thanh Phong

The village of Thanh Phong was located in Kien Hoa Province in the Mekong Delta. It was one of the places the VCI were said to control in February 1969.

Crisscrossed with waterways and rice paddies, Kien Hoa Province was an important rice production area for both the insurgents and the GVN. It was close to Saigon, densely populated, and one of the eight most heavily infiltrated provinces in Vietnam. The estimated 4700 VCI in Kien Hoa Province accounted for more than five percent of the insurgency's total leadership.

In Operation Speedy Express, the US Army's Ninth Infantry Division spent the first six months of 1969 rampaging through the province, obliterating villages and killing an estimated 11,000 civilians, all supposedly VC or VC sympathizers.

Meanwhile, the US Navy was patrolling Kien Hoa's waterways, looking for guerrillas who had escaped the army's genocidal offensive. As the Navy's "unconventional" warriors, the SEALs had the task of mounting Phoenix-style "snatch and snuff" operations against targeted VCI in the Delta.[11] The Navy coordinated its anti-VCI with the Phoenix Directorate in Saigon, with Phoenix regional headquarters in Can Tho, and with the CIA's officer in charge in whatever province the operation was to occur. Coordination was necessary to make sure the SEALs were not targeting CIA double-agents in the villages, as Jim Ward and Doug Dillard explained earlier.

As Gregory Vistica noted in his book, *The Education of Lieutenant Kerrey*, "SEAL advisors were made available to the CIA's Phoenix program, and Langley used them to train Vietnamese Provincial Reconnaissance Units." Vistica added, "By 1968 it was common for complete SEAL platoons to operate with the PRU."[12]

Phoenix advisors in Kien Hoa Province did not report to individual military units, but were organized within MACV Advisory Team 88 as part of the CORDs program. Phoenix advisors in the province's District Intelligence and Operations Coordinating Centers (DIOCCs) wore the MACV patch and were often army counterintelligence officers like Sid Towle involuntarily assigned to the program (see Chapter 4). As Vistica noted in his book, the head of MACV Advisory Team 88 "had to coordinate the State Department's pacification program, and CIA and army intelligence."[13]

Based on information from the local Phoenix DIOCC, the

MACV Team 88 commander believed the tiny, coastal village of Thanh Phong was a VC stronghold and that an important VCI cadre was planning a visit there. This intelligence was passed to the CIA's Province Officer in Charge (POIC), who had cognizance over all "anti-infrastructure" operations in Kien Hoa, and from the POIC to the CIA's region officer in charge (Jim Ward or his replacement) and from the ROIC to Navy Seal commanders. The Seal commanders assigned Lt Bob Kerrey and his SEAL team the job of capturing or killing the targeted individual. It was Kerrey's maiden mission. He was 25.

In an article written for *The New York Times*, Vistica recounted how the operation unfolded.[14]

"Kerrey's group was called Delta Platoon, Seal Team One, Fire Team Bravo," Vistica said. "Unofficially, they would be dubbed Kerrey's Raiders, in honor of their enthusiastic commanding officer, who was ready to take on Hanoi, as he has said many times, with 'a knife in my teeth.' Only two of the men, Mike Ambrose and Gerhard Klann, had previous experience on SEAL teams in Vietnam. The others – William H. Tucker III, Gene Peterson, Rick Knepper, a medic named Lloyd Schreier and Kerrey himself – were flying into the unknown."

Kerrey's platoon was based at Cat Lo near Vung Tao, cite of the sprawling RD Cadre facility where the CIA trained its PRU teams. Kerrey's SEAL team launched their mission into the "Thanh Phong Secret Zone" from the joint CIA/Navy compound at Vung Tau. They were delivered on Swift boats.

Everything indicates Kerrey's SEAL Team was on a traditional Phoenix operation. The program was still under CIA control in February 1969, and the intelligence for the mission came from a DIOCC through the chain of command described above. Vistica interviewed Captain David Marion, the senior CORDS advisor in the district where Thanh Phong was located. Marion's GVN counterpart, Tiet Lun Du, was "a 45-year-old military officer trained at Fort Bragg in North Carolina." According to Vistica, Du designated Thanh Phu District "a "free-fire zone" which allowed combat pilots and Navy warships to attack "targets of opportunity," including people and villages, "without prior command authority."

Marion's intelligence, obtained from the Thanh Phu DIOCC, indicated that the VCI "village secretary" was planning a meeting in the area at some unknown point in time. Based on that sketchy information, the preemptive manhunt for a moving target commenced. Again, it followed Phoenix SOP.

Thanh Phong consisted of 75 to 150 people living in "groups of four or five hooches ... strung out over about a third of a mile of shoreline. On Feb. 13, 1969, according to the SEALs after-action reports, Kerrey's team entered a section of Thanh Phong, searched two hooches and 'interrogated 14 women and small children,' looking for the village secretary. They departed on a swift boat the next day, then returned to the general area later that night only to abort because of a malfunctioning radio."

Kerrey's team performed exactly as Warren Milberg and Dinh Tuong An described Phoenix operations earlier in this book: the CIA always sent a small unit (the PRU or "hunter" team) into a village the day before the operation to map out the village and capture people targeted for interrogation. The next day the CT/PRU team would return with the "killer" team to take out the larger target – the people in the village itself. The massacres were afforded plausible deniability back at headquarters, where – in so far as the only rule in psychological warfare is "post your own score" – the victims were identified as armed and dangerous VC guerrillas.

Some important details standard to such operations are missing from Kerrey's story. For example, how did the SEALs conduct their interrogations? Did they have a PRU interpreter with them? Did they chop off fingers? In any event, Kerrey knew how the village was laid out, how many people lived there, and where they lived. All that was needed was a provocation, generated through CIA "black propaganda" or otherwise, and such a provocation magically occurred a few days later when the VC allegedly committed an atrocity of some sort in the area, the "monstrous" kind Milberg, DeSilva and Dillard have described above.

Once the provocation had occurred, Captain Martin and District Chief Duc responded in the usual manner; they told the villagers an operation was going to be conducted and that anyone who wasn't gone would be considered VC and killed. And indeed, on the night of 25 February, a Swift boat brought Kerrey and his SEAL team back to Thanh Phong to finish their business. The marauders moved in around midnight and, by Kerrey's account, the killings were committed in self-defense.

According to Kerrey, his team stumbled on a home they hadn't noticed the first time they were in the village, even though it was on the pre-arranged path they had walked a few days earlier. The home was occupied, Kerrey said, by two lookouts. Kerrey ordered two SEALs to kill the lookouts using their knives, often Gerber Mark II daggers. American commandoes are taught how to put their hand over the sleeping victim's mouth, slip the dagger up under the second rib through the heart, and then give it a flick so it snaps the spinal cord. Or they just slice the throat from ear to ear.

Having done that, the team, according to Kerrey, worked their way along a dyke into a hamlet consisting of four hooches. Suddenly without warning someone opened fire on the SEALs, who, in a blind fury, responded with everything they had, expending 1,200 rounds of ammunition. When the dust settled, 14 people were clumped together, dead. Seven more were killed trying to flee.

That's Kerrey's version, as reported by Vistica. According to Gerhard Klann, the most experienced SEAL on the mission and later a member of SEAL Team 6 (credited with killing Osama bin Laden), the murders were not committed in response to an ambush, but were conducted systematically, in cold blood.

Klann told Vistica that Kerrey ordered him to kill an old man, an old woman, and three children in the first home – the one Kerrey said was occupied by armed VC guerrilla lookouts. When the old man resisted, Kerrey kneeled on him so Klann could slit his throat. Reminiscent of a scene out of Truman Capote's book *In Cold Blood*, a third SEAL came to their assistance and helped kill the old woman and kids, who were now fully awake and screaming.

A Vietnamese woman, Pham Tri Lanh, witnessed the murders and confirmed Klann's account. She added that the old folks – Bui Van Vat and his wife, Luu Thi Canh – were the children's grandparents. Vistica confirmed they existed by visiting their graves in the village (something the *New London Day* could have done, if it really wanted to know what really went on in the PIC Rob Simmons ran, as described in Chapter 15).

Having dispatched with those five yellow-skinned "Commie symps", the heroic SEALs abandoned their preemptive manhunt for the elusive, moving VCI cadre. They knew the other villagers had heard the murdered family's screams, so, according to Klann, they rounded up all the "women and children from a group of hooches on the fringes of the village." Having done that, they searched their homes. Finding no arms or evidence of the political cadre they were hunting, they massacred everyone else in an attempt to conceal the murder of the five people in the first home, and as a psychological warfare warning to villagers in surrounding villages. Klann said they were less than ten feet away from the people they cut down, and that Kerrey gave the order. Some were still crying and squirming after the first barrage, so they finished off the survivors, including a baby.

As CIA officer Peer DeSilva put it, the SEALs were monstrous in the application of murder to achieve the political and psychological impact they wanted. Then they went home and reported they had killed 21 VC.

"You spend half your life just covering up"[15]

It's ludicrous to think Kerrey and the SEALs didn't know what they were getting into and didn't intend to murder everyone in Thanh Phong.

While on contract with the CIA from early 1967 through early 1969, Marine Captain Robert Slater served as director of the PIC program and chief interrogation advisor to the Special Police. In a 1970 thesis for the Defense Intelligence Institute titled "The History, Organization and Modus Operandi of the Viet Cong Infrastructure," Slater described the District Party Secretary as the "indispensable link" in the VCI hierarchy.

As Slater explained, "The District Party Secretary usually does not sleep in the same house or even hamlet where his family lived, to preclude any injury to his family during assassination attempts." But he added, "the Allies have frequently found out where the District Party Secretaries live and raided their homes: in an ensuing fire fight the secretary's wife and children have been killed and injured."

Kerrey's SEAL team targeted a Village Party Secretary for assassination in Thanh Phong, and the same result occurred: even though they couldn't find the target, everyone present was killed, including children.

This is the intellectual context in which Kerrey's war crime took place: it was standard procedure to kill the target along with his family and friends. For purposes of plausible denial, you could say the others were unintended victims and collateral damage, but when you know it's going to happen and it happens every time, consistently, over years, that threadbare excuse doesn't hold water. Omerta, the Mafia's term for its sacred code of silence, alone enabled Kerrey and the SEAL team to get away with the premeditated murder and mutilation of 21 defenseless people, and then report it as a fierce battle with VC.[16]

That's American military idolatry in a nutshell. Convicted of murdering 22 unarmed civilians in My Lai, William Calley was venerated as a hero and served three years under house arrest until pardoned by Richard Nixon. Calley's defense was to say that massacring civilians happened all the time.

Bob Kerrey's friend and colleague, Secretary of State John Kerry, used the same "everyone else does it" grade school rationale to defend Kerrey. Along with senators Max Cleland and Chuck Hagel, Kerry (then a senator), issued a statement in 2001 stating their belief that an investigation into the Thanh Phong massacre would be counterproductive, in so far as it blamed "the warrior rather than the war."[17]

While "in effect conceding that the war as a whole was criminal in character...Kerry elaborated, in one television appearance, on the thesis that soldiers should not be held responsible for actions that were in accordance with the policies of the US government. The raid on Thanh Phong was part of Operation Phoenix, he said, and 'the Phoenix program was an assassination program run by the United States of America.'[18]

Kerrey's war crime was made worse by the fact that the unarmed civilians his SEAL team murdered were prisoners. But unrepentant Bob defended himself from that charge by claiming he was ordered not to take prisoners. He didn't want to kill those little kids; he was told to do it.

Where have we heard that before?

In any event, justice of a sort prevailed; on his next mission, a grenade exploded at Kerrey's feet. Who put it there is not known. Is it possible that he was fragged by his fellow SEALs for some unknown reason? However the grenade got there, it blew off the lower part of a leg. Kerrey's career as a killer came to a close and he went home to weep in his mother's arms.

After a few months of self-pity, Kerrey began his descent into the self-deception and revisionism that accompanies war crimes. It is a process of identity recreation he shares with many veterans of Vietnam and America's neo-colonial wars since 9/11. To a large extent, as I've noted throughout the text, the success of their collective cover-up defines America's exceptionalism.

Kerrey's rebirth as a certified hero began when he received the Medal of Honor on 14 May 1970, a mere ten days after the Ohio National Guard murdered four anti-war protestors at Kent State. The medal was a meal ticket not unlike being inducted into the Mafia as a "made man". One of the Protected Few, Kerrey was forever guaranteed fame and fortune. The only burden he carried was the grudge he held against the anti-war protestors who didn't appreciate his sacrifice.

Elected governor of Nebraska in 1982, he dated movie starlet Debra Winger, became a celebrity, and got elected to the US senate where he served as vice-chair of the intelligence committee. The picture of a neoliberal, he even ran for president in 1990, showering self-righteous criticism on draft dodger Bill Clinton for his penchant for lying.

Kerrey was no longer in government in 2001 when Klann revealed what had really happened in Thanh Phong. But the Ultras immediately and wholeheartedly rallied to his defense. His SEAL team, apart from Klann, closed ranks and backed his version of events. Kerrey accused Klann of having a personal grievance against him, and implied he was lying.

Colonel David Hackworth, representing the military establishment, defended Kerrey by saying "there were thousands of such atrocities." Hackworth said that his own unit committed "at least a dozen such horrors." He said it nonchalantly, as if he were mowing the lawn.[19]

Representing Hollywood and the propaganda industry's huge financial investment in the myth of the American war hero, Jack Valenti told the *LA Times* that, "all the normalities [sic] of a social contract are abandoned" in war. By the same token, this means it is perfectly okay for terrorists to attack Western civilians because CIA officers operate in secret and cannot be located.[20]

Kerrey also received support from veterans of the Vietnam press corps. Former *New York Times* correspondent David Halberstam, author of *The Best and the Brightest*, described the region around Thanh Phong as "the purest bandit country." He added that "by 1969 everyone who lived there would have been third-generation Vietcong."[21]

Clichés are the grist of revisionism at its sickest, and Halberstam's racist, anti-Communist rant exposed him as nothing more than a myth-maker for the rich political elite. Halberstam might just as well have said, "Kill them all!"

Two other journalists stand out as examples of the press corps' complicity in war crimes in Vietnam. Neil Sheehan, author of the aptly titled *Bright Shining Lie*, confessed that in 1966 he saw American GIs slaughter as many as 600 Vietnamese civilians in five fishing villages. He had been in Vietnam for three years by then and it didn't occur to him that he was witnessing a war crime. It was business as usual.

Morley Safer is next on the list of co-conspirators. Safer vented his personal hatred for me when he wrote the half page review in *The New York Times* that killed my book *The Phoenix Program* in its cradle.

I wasn't surprised that the *Times* employed Safer to assassinate my book. In it I'd said, "When it comes to the CIA and the press, one hand washes the other. In order to have access to informed officials, reporters frequently suppress or distort stories. In return, CIA officials leak stories to reporters to whom they owe favors. At its most incestuous, reporters and government officials are actually related, like Delta PRU commander Charles LeMoyne and his *New York Times* reporter brother James.[22] Likewise, if Ed Lansdale had not had Joseph Alsop to print his black propaganda in the US, there probably would have been no Vietnam War."

At the time of the review (October 1990), I thought Safer hated me primarily for accusing the press corps of covering up war crimes. I thought he did for pecuniary reasons too; Safer's self-congratulatory book on Vietnam had come out a few months before. It wasn't until 25 years later that I found out that Safer owed William Colby a favor. Safer revealed his incestuous relationship with Colby for the first time at the American Experience conference in 2010.[23]

"I got a call to come and see [Colby] in his office," Safer explained. "And I walked in – and I had met him; we had no strong relationship at all – but – and [Colby] said, 'Look, can you disappear for three days?' (Laughter.) And I said, 'I guess.' (Laughter.) And he said, 'Well, be at the airport – be at (inaudible) at the airport tomorrow morning at 5:30.'"

Bernard Kalb, the moderator, asked Safer if Colby wanted him to bring along a camera crew.

"No, no," Safer replied. "And I showed up and [Colby] said, 'Okay, here are the rules. You can see that I'm going on a tour of all the stations. You can't take notes and you can't report anything you hear.' And I spent three days first of all, down in the Delta and they were really, really revealing. There was only one meeting that he would ask me to leave the barracks. And it was fascinating because the stuff that these guys were reporting through whatever filters to you had been so doctored by the time it got to you – I mean, to this day, I still feel constrained in terms of talking about."

Colby introduced Safer to all the top CIA officers in Vietnam, and introduced him to the interrogation centers and counterterrorism teams. Safer got to see how the CIA crime syndicate was organized and operated. And like Don Corleone dispensing favors in *The Godfather*, Colby knew that one day Safer would be obligated to return it.

That is how the CIA, as the organized crime branch of the US government, functions like the Mafia through its old boy network of complicit media hacks.

Can Bob Kerrey Be Tried for Murder?

Kerrey says his actions at Thanh Phong were an atrocity, not a war crime. He feels remorse, not guilt. Totally rehabilitated, he has come to view Vietnam as a "just war."

"Was the war worth the effort and sacrifice, or was it a mistake?" Kerrey asked rhetorically in a 1999 column in the *Washington Post*. "When I came home in 1969 and for many years afterward, I did not believe it was worth it. Today, with the passage of time and the experience of seeing both the benefits of freedom won by our sacrifice and the human destruction done by dictatorships, I believe the cause was just and the sacrifice not in vain."

At the Democratic Party Convention in Los Angeles in 2000, Kerrey lectured the delegates not to be ashamed of war crimes and to treat Vietnam veterans, like him, as heroes, not terrorists. "I never felt more free than when I wore the uniform of our country," he said without irony, and without noting that wearing the uniform made him "free" to murder women and children.

Promulgating the militaristic Business Party line is the price Bob Kerrey pays for getting away with mass murder. As long as he promulgates it, he's one of the Protected Few, entrusted with the government's top secrets. Indeed, he is one of a handful of Americans who has read the secret 28 pages on Saudi Arabia's role in 9/11. He knows where all the bodies are buried.

Gregory Vistica traveled to Vietnam and visited the graves of Bui Van Vat, his wife Luu Thi Canh, and their three grandkids in Thanh Phong. And now that Kerrey knows where his victims are buried, he could pay his respects to the victims too. While he's in Vietnam running the Americans' Fulbright University, he could also pay a visit to the War Remnants Museum in Ho Chi Minh City. According to Wikipedia, the "War Remnants Museum features a display 'based on the (Thanh Phong) incident. It includes several photos and a drain pipe, which it describes as the place where three children hid before they were found and killed.'"

The display includes the following account: "(The SEALs) cut 66 year-old Bui Van Vat and 62 year-old Luu Thi Canh's necks and pulled their three grandchildren out from their hiding place in a drain and killed two, disembowelled one. Then, these rangers moved to dug-outs of other families, shot dead 15 civilians (including three pregnant women), disembowelled a girl. The only survivor was a 12-year-old girl named Bui Thi Luom who suffered a foot injury."

One wonders if Kerrey will visit the graves of the children his SEAL team disemboweled the next time he visits Vietnam. Perhaps he fears being arrested if he does?

As attorney Michael Ratner at the Center for Constitutional Rights told Counterpunch: "Kerrey should be tried as a war criminal. His actions on the night of February 24-25, 1969 when the seven man Navy SEAL unit which he headed killed approximately twenty unarmed Vietnamese civilians, eighteen of whom were women and children, was a war crime. Like those who murdered at My Lai, he too should be brought into the dock and tried for his crimes."

The Geneva Conventions, customary international law and the Uniform Code of Military Justice all prohibit the killing of noncombatant civilians. The brutality of others is no justification. That is why there is a moral imperative to expose the Phoenix program as the basis for the CIA's ongoing policy of committing war crimes. It is imperative to try the CIA officers who created it, as well as the people who participated in it, including the journalists who covered it up.

If America's policy of conducting war crimes is ever to end, people of conscience must expose the dark side of our national psyche, the part that allows us to employ terror to assure our world dominance. To accomplish this there must be a War Crimes Tribunal like the one Bertrand Russell and Jean Paul Sartre put together in 1966-1967. I've assembled enough evidence in this book alone to put the likes of Bruce Lawlor, Rob Simmons, Frank Scotton and Bob Kerrey in the dock.

The National Security Establishment will try to prevent it. The US government has gone to great lengths to shield itself and its cadres from international law, while corrupting international institutions like the United Nations to prosecute US enemies like Slobodan Milosevic.[24] But if the UN could free itself from US influence, it could establish an ad hoc tribunal, such as it did with the Rwanda ICTR and Yugoslavia ICTY.

Alas, according to Ratner, the legal avenues for bringing Kerrey and his cohorts to justice in the US are limited. A civil suit could be lodged against him by the families of the victims under the Alien Tort Claims Act. There is no statute of limitations for war crimes, and under 18 USC sec. 2441 War Crimes, Kerrey could be sentenced to death or life imprisonment. But at the time of his crime in Vietnam, US criminal law did not apply to what US citizens did overseas. Only military law applied, and now that Kerrey is no longer in the Navy, the military courts have no jurisdiction over him.

In yet another great irony, Kerrey as a senator voted for the war crimes law, allowing others to be prosecuted for crimes similar to those he committed.

Prosecution in Vietnam and extradition are also possibilities. "Universal jurisdiction does not require the presence of the defendant – he can be indicted and tried in some countries in absentia – or his extradition can be requested," Ratner said. "Some countries may have statutes permitting this. Kerrey should check his travel plans and hire a good lawyer before he gets on a plane. He can use Kissinger's lawyer."

But that's not going to happen. The rule of law ended with 9/11, when illegal invasions and occupations became stated policy, along with targeted assassinations and mass murder. And until the media stops glorifying "preemptive manhunting" of "moving targets" as necessary for our security, rather than fueling the terrorism that threatens the unprotected many, the war crimes will never stop.

Chapter 19

TOP SECRET AMERICA SHADOW REWARD SYSTEM

After Dana Priest and William M. Arkin's three-part series, "Top-Secret America," appeared in the *Washington Post*, pundits and academics began falling all over themselves in a rush to quantify the post-9/11 "counterterrorism" apparatus. Although few of them had seen fit to even notice the elephant in the room before, they all swooned at its $75 billion price tag, as well as the implications such a monstrous surveillance and covert action apparatus has for a "free" society.

There were, however, dimensions to the problem that Priest and Arkin didn't dare touch upon.

Let me tell you a story that fills in some of the blanks.

In 1985, I was contacted by a CIA officer. Larry had served as a deep-cover agent overseas for over 15 years. He'd had a breakdown and wanted to tell me his story. He'd read my book about my father, *The Hotel Tacloban,* and thought I'd understand.

Larry's story began in South Vietnam in 1966 where, as a gung-ho Marine, he came to the attention of a CIA "talent scout". The CIA officer ran a background check and discovered that Larry was an only child from a broken marriage. Larry was an emotional orphan, looking for something to latch onto. He chose the ultraconservative route. In high school his favorite activities were attending the local Lutheran church and participating in the Rotary Club debate team. His dream was to become a self-described "crusader" and follow in the footsteps of his hero, John Wayne.

Larry described himself as being "for freedom, the American way of life, and free enterprise." Plus he was avidly anti-Communist and a combat veteran, which made him even more attractive to the CIA.

Strange things began to happen. Although still a Marine, he was sent to Okinawa and given special training in scuba diving, skydiving, demolition and the martial arts. No one told him why he was being groomed; and being a good soldier, he didn't ask. But he soon learned that the CIA had decided to turn him into a "deep cover" agent.

At the time, the CIA's Central Cover Staff managed a worldwide network of deep cover agents and freestanding proprietary companies. It existed (and may still exist with some new name) outside the regular CIA bureaucracy, and was used by presidents to conduct the CIA's most sensitive operations.

The Central Cover Staff concocted an elaborate cover story. Only Larry's case officer knew what was fact and what was fiction.

The story went like this: Larry' father was an Australian soldier who, during a tour in the Philippines in the Second World War, had an affair with a woman whose maiden name was Velesco. His mother was half Spanish, half Filipino, from the upper class. The necessary documents were forged to prove that his mother had been a lawyer working in Samboaga.

Larry's mother and the Australian soldier were never legally married, but Larry was, by birth, a Philippine citizen.

Abandoned by the Australian soldier, Larry's mother succumbed to depression and never recovered. She was hospitalized, and Larry was put up for adoption. At the age of three, he was adopted by a loving foster family in America. His middle class parents raised him as their own son, never mentioning that he was not their natural child. He was (according to the "legend" the CIA created) popular and smart, with an aptitude for mechanics.

The CIA forged documents to show that he'd received a scholarship to the General Motors Institute for Automotive Engineering, and had attended the Sloan School of Management at MIT.

According to his cover story, Larry enlisted in the Marines and based on his mechanical aptitude was selected for helicopter pilot training. However, during the required security check, the Marines discovered that he was a Filipino citizen, not an American. This revelation came as a shock, but it also provided him with a pretext to visit the Philippines "to discover his past."

Larry made the trip immediately upon leaving the Marines in 1968. As outlined in the Central Cover Staff's script, and as actually happened, Larry learned to speak the language and settled in the land of his birth. He got a job as a manager and translator with a Japanese mining company. He did well but left that job to manage a Shell Oil service station franchise on the island of Leyte.

Over the next ten years, Larry held management positions with BF Goodrich, an American building and supply contractor to Clark Air Force Base, General Motors, VISA Card, and Westinghouse, which built the first nuclear reactor in the Philippines. As is true of most American multinationals, Larry's employers all knowingly provided cover for CIA agents, as a way of maintaining influence overseas as well as in Washington.

By 1980, Larry had established himself as an upright Filipino citizen. His cover was impeccable and, to make a long story short, he was elected to public office. While in that position, however, things went wrong. The US State Department became aware that he was a deep cover CIA officer serving in the Philippine legislature. A series of actions were taken to destroy all records of his existence, and he was whisked out of the Philippines.

After Larry's breakdown, the CIA got him a job as a manager of a Playboy club in Detroit. Later, they transferred him to Washington, DC, as manager of the posh Four Ways restaurant off DuPont Circle. When I met him there, his Filipino wife and entourage were working as the kitchen and wait staff. To make sure Larry behaved himself, the CIA had placed a former security officer in charge of finances.

This restaurant was the fanciest place I had ever been in my life. It was a place where striped pants State Department officials, foreign dignitaries and business tycoons met to make deals while sampling fine wines and haute cuisine. Each lavishly appointed room had its own dining table and waiter.

I was directed to a leather booth in the wood-paneled basement barroom, where Larry casually explained that each room was bugged by the CIA.

As we were talking, a group of well-dressed young men and women, chaperoned by an older man, took the booth next to us. The rest of the barroom was empty. They ordered drinks but remained silent and alert as Larry explained the ins and outs of his CIA experience to me.

At one point Larry nodded to the older man at the next booth, then informed me that the young people listening to our conversation were junior officer trainees from Langley.

Larry told me that the CIA manages a parallel society where deep-cover agents like him, as well as retired CIA officers and their agents, are provided with comfortable employment in their retirement years, or when they otherwise need sanctuary and recompense for their services.

Many of these agents have no applicable résumé, so they are folded into this parallel universe as managers of the local Ford dealership, or proprietors of a Chinese restaurant, or in hundreds of other jobs held in abeyance by cooperating businesses.

Think of it as a witness-protection program which, since 2001, has grown exponentially. It is the hidden geography of Top-Secret America, a subculture of highly trained operators with a dangerous set of skills that can be called upon at any moment. The one thing they have in common is that they are entirely dependent on the war criminals running the CIA.

As John Lennon said: "Imagine."

Chapter 20

HOW THE GOVERNMENT TRIES TO MESS WITH YOUR MIND

LEW ROCKWELL: Those of us who were interested in the Church Hearings, which we don't hear much about anymore, learned about Operation Mockingbird, the CIA's program to take control of the US media. Has Operation Mockingbird continued? Is the American mainstream media pretty much a PR operation for the CIA?

VALENTINE: Mockingbird, as you know, was a program the CIA launched in the early 1950s to influence the mass media. CIA officers Cord Meyer and Frank Wisner are credited with creating Mockingbird. Meyer, through his friendship with the owner of Random House, tried to suppress Al McCoy's book, *The Politics of Heroin in Southeast Asia,* in 1972. Wisner famously referred to the CIA's army of Morley Safer-style assets in the publishing and journalism world as the Mighty Wurlitzer, which he could turn on and off whenever he wished. Wisner's son, by the way, served in the Phoenix program.

    In her book, *Katherine the Great: Katharine Graham and the Washington Post,* Deborah Davis said that "By the early 1950s," according to Deborah Davis, "Wisner had implemented his plan and 'owned' respected members of the *New York Times, Newsweek,* CBS, and other communications vehicles, plus stringers, four to six hundred in all, according to a former CIA analyst."[1] Carl Bernstein, citing CIA documents, said basically the same thing in his famous 1977 expose for *Rolling Stone,* "The CIA and the Media: How America's Most Powerful

News media Worked Hand in Glove with the Central Intelligence Agency and Why the Church Committee Covered It Up."

The CIA established a strategic intelligence network of magazines and publishing houses, as well as student and cultural organizations, and used them as front organizations for covert operations, including political and psychological warfare operations directed against American citizens. In other nations, the program was aimed at what Cord Meyer called the Compatible Left, which in America translates into liberals and pseudo-intellectual status seekers who are easily influenced.

All of that is ongoing, despite being exposed in the late 1960s. Various technological advances, including the internet, have spread the network around the world, and many people don't even realize they are part of it, that they're promoting the CIA line. "Assad's a butcher," they say, or "Putin kills journalists," or "China is repressive." They have no idea what they're talking about, but they spout all this propaganda.

Nowadays it goes way beyond the CIA. Several government agencies are propagandizing not only the American people but the world. This includes the State Department and the military. The military is the nation's biggest advertiser, I believe, and the media depends on its revenue. Television, especially, isn't dependent on viewers, but on advertisers. So the media is probably more financially dependent on the military and the State Department than it is on the CIA. But the CIA laid the groundwork.

The question one has to ask, given all this propaganda, is what makes CIA propaganda different than State Department or military propaganda, or even the red white and blue advertisements being thrown at the American people every second of every day. Everywhere you look there are signs wrapped in American flags selling things, and that's propaganda too, it's just emanating from the Business Party. What makes CIA propaganda different?

ROCKWELL: You make an interesting point about advertising. Doesn't the DEA do a huge amount of advertising, too?

VALENTINE: Well, sure. The DEA is selling the notion that America is the victim in the War on Drugs. It spouts this kind of nonsense at Congressional hearings and through taxpayer-funded propaganda campaigns like DARE and Nancy Reagan's "Just Say No" idiocy. They coordinate their message with state and local law enforcement agencies and their civil offshoots. The DEA claims foreign countries like Mexico are push-ing drugs on us, and therefore the DEA needs $50 billion-a-year to police the world and stop these horrible people, most of whom don't look like "us". Meanwhile, the American demand for drugs persists and the war goes on and on. But the propaganda is convincing, and Americans feel good that it's not their demand that's fueling the problem; it's the fault of a couple of cartels in Mexico.

The FBI has a huge propaganda machine too. Gangbuster J Edgar Hoover understood how to promote FBI agents as heroic "crime stoppers", as the good guys who got John Dillinger. Like the DEA, Hoover knew how to manipulate statistics, and how to go after the proper criminals to promote the interests of his fiefdom. The government is composed of huge bureaucracies like the FBI and DEA, all competing for federal taxpayer dollars. They each have their own propaganda machine, which exist primarily for bureaucratic reasons, so that they can get a bigger piece of the federal budget.

There are all sorts of reasons for propaganda, and many types of propaganda, and the CIA is one of the agencies engaged in self-promotion to get more of your money. But the CIA also has operational reasons for using propaganda to target particular people or nations.

ROCKWELL: What is it that differentiates CIA propaganda from all the rest of these agencies?

VALENTINE: The CIA advances the *unstated* goals and policies of the United States government, as opposed to the State Department, whose propaganda is promoting its *stated* objectives – which of course are wrapped in the same kinds of circumlocutions and euphemisms the CIA and military use. The language is pretty much the same for whichever agency is propagandizing, which adds to the confusion about where it's coming from.

The purpose of CIA propaganda is to create plausible deniability: to hide or disguise the fact that it is the source of a particular piece of misinformation designed to mislead the American public. It has briefing officers who tell PR people in other government agencies what to say, to hide the fact that it is engaged in a particular covert action that is designed to start a war or that supports a terrorist group, or subverts a friendly government, or promotes a fascist political party in Ukraine or a military dictatorship in South America – the sorts of things that if the public was to find out that the US government is doing them, would cause the president and the government embarrassment, like the attempted Gülen coup in Turkey. Journalists, of course, report all these carefully scripted communiques as fact.

The CIA is in charge of doing the things that are illegal and anti-democratic. Its propaganda is generally referred to as "gray" or "black" propaganda. Black propaganda is used to completely disguise CIA operations and blame them on someone else, be they friends or enemies. Gray propaganda uses questionable sources, the sort of anonymous sources Seymour Hersh is famous for using.

I'll give some examples. The CIA introduced *New York Times* reporter Chris Hedges to two Iraqi defectors who claimed, in November 2001, that Saddam Hussein was training terrorists to attack America. That's black propaganda. It was completely untrue but the lies could be blamed on the Iraqi defectors.

The Ben Affleck film Argo, winner of multiple awards, told a fictionalized story of the CIA's successful rescue of several Embassy employees held Hostage in Tehran in 1979 and 1980. It was based on a book written by a CIA officer and the CIA helped produce the film through its old boy network and its "Entertainment Industry" liaison office. The CIA has an office that works with Hollywood. If a film is pro-CIA, it provides advisors. That's propaganda designed to rewrite history – in this case the Canadians had more to do with the rescue than the CIA – and to give the CIA a good name and portray its officers as happy-go-lucky heroes.

Journalists writing articles and authors of political books on current affairs tend to deliver CIA propaganda, some wittingly, others because they're stupid. There is an obscure discipline known as "the interpretation of intelligence literature" that involves studying these texts, like rabbis studying the Talmud for eschatological meaning, or English Lit majors wondering why Eliot said, "Madame Blavatsky will instruct me in the Seven Sacred Trances." There's an esoteric quality to propaganda that can drive some people crazy trying to figure it out. Some CIA officers spend their careers trying to unravel Russian propaganda. Some end up paranoid, seeing enemy agents everywhere. That's why Colby fired James Angleton – Angleton thought Colby was a Russian agent.

Sometimes, however, it is easy to identify and discern the meaning behind CIA propaganda.

Back in 2011, reporter Jeff Stein wrote an article about Fethullah

Gülen, the American-based Turkish exile I referenced above. Gülen was accused of trying to overthrow Prime Minister Erdoğan in July 2016. In his article, Stein referred to a memoir written by Osman Nuri Gundes, "a top former Turkish intelligence official" who alleged that the Gülen movement "has been providing cover for the CIA since the mid-1990s." Citing the Paris-based *Intelligence Online* newsletter, Stein reported that the movement "sheltered 130 CIA agents" at its schools in Kyrgyzstan and Uzbekistan alone."[2]

Having CIA agents operating out of schools in Kyrgyzstan and Uzbekistan sounds like something the CIA would do. It's a great way of manipulating a social and political movement. Case officers could easily place principal agents (PAs) in the schools. The PAs could run agent nets or even assassins into Russia as legal travelers. Maybe the schools are spreading CIA propaganda; it was certainly influencing political and social movements. It may even front for a drug smuggling apparatus, here and in Central Asia.

Journalists like Stein know they have to look to foreign magazines and sources to get the true story about what the CIA is doing. At the same time, they have to maintain their "credibility" here in the States, which means they have to report the CIA line. Being a responsible journalist, Stein contacted two former CIA officers who both said the allegations were untrue, that the CIA would never do anything like that. So whom do you believe; the CIA or your own lying eyes? Stein's is not an article one needs to pick apart for hours, trying to figure out if it's gray or black propaganda, or Russian disinformation.

The New York Times, however, functions as the CIA's protector and thus dutifully published a series of stories that did their best to bury under a mound of disinformation and overtly biased reporting any hint that Gülen is a CIA agent. One article, steeped in schmaltz, described Gülen as a "moderate" who "promotes interfaith dialogue, leads a worldwide network of charities and secular schools, favors good relations with Israel and opposes harder-line Islamist movements like the Muslim Brotherhood and Hamas."[3]

According to *The New York Times,* and as universally adopted as truth by its readers, someone who favors Israel and opposes Hamas is all right, even if, as it acknowledged, "a former C.I.A. official helped [Gülen] get a green card."

The *Times* reporters did not explain that the CIA routinely creates and manipulates social and political movements like Gülen's and keeps them in place for decades until the time is right to launch a coup. They didn't explain that the Gülen movement ran one of Turkey's largest, most anti-Erdoğan newspapers, or that the CIA uses such newspapers to spread propaganda before a coup. Instead, they cited Gülen's denials and his defenders, at length. One expert said the Gülen movement was a "golden generation of young people who are educated in science, but have Muslim ethics."

No one in the media will examine the network of schools the Gülen "movement" has planted in the US, to see if they are part of an elaborate CIA counter-espionage operation, like Operation Twofold (see Chapter 12), through which the CIA is hiding an operational unit that bumps off Gülen's political opponents. The fact that the mainstream media never looked too deeply into it proves it is a CIA operation.

Indeed, the media does exactly the opposite. Within days of the coup, the writers group PEN, which functions as a propaganda arm of the Israeli government and the CIA, sent all its members an urgent request to sign a petition to the Turkish government protesting the arrest of journalists involved in the coup. PEN never mentioned that many of the arrested journalists were, by virtue of their anti-Erdoğan work on behalf of Gülen, tacitly working for the CIA. The purpose of signing such a meaningless petition is not to put pressure on Turkey, but to shape the assumptions of PEN's deluded members, to make them hate Turkey, which is not Israel's best friend.

ROCKWELL: The CIA has always specialized in assassinations; the military, too. But now we have the president openly assassinating people and claiming he has the right to. In the earliest days, the CIA was allegedly prevented from operating within the US. I think that was always a myth. Now, the CIA is just openly and massively involved here. Do you think it is committing assassinations here as well?

VALENTINE: It's impossible to prove. You'll never find a document that says the president ordered the CIA to kill some critic like Senator Paul Wellstone when Wellstone died in a suspicious plane crash. You're never going to find any proof that can be used in a court of law that would show the CIA conducted that kind of a political assassination within the United States. The CIA doesn't conduct that kind of an operation unless it's deniable.

My inclination, based on everything I know about the CIA, is that, yes, they do. But I can't prove it because of the reasons I've just stated. They get the Mafia to pay some petty crook to kill Martin Luther King, Jr., and then work with what Fletcher Prouty called the "Secret Team" to cover it up.

ROCKWELL: What's your opinion of Philip Agee's book *Inside the Company: CIA Diary*? He was, of course, a former CIA agent who wrote about just how many people were on the payroll and how many people were controlled by the agency. Is that a persuasive book?

VALENTINE: Absolutely, it is. Modern history of the CIA begins with Agee and his revelations. Nothing Agee said has been disproved. His fatal mistake was telling the truth, naming over a hundred CIA officers and linking some of them to specific crimes. He was easily discredited on that basis alone. And anyone who reads Agee and responds rationally to his revelations is also, by association, a traitor. His revelations were akin to the collateral murder video Chelsea Manning gave to Wikileaks. Manning was tormented and imprisoned for revealing the truth about what the CIA and military really do, which is the equivalent of treason in America. Agee was never imprisoned, but he was threatened and forced to settle in Cuba.

     Agee and his publishers revealed the inner workings of the CIA. It's not a coincidence that the Church Hearings followed pretty much on the heels of his revelations. A lot of things were coming out in the late 1960s and early 1970s, but Agee and later John Stockwell were the only CIA officers ever to reveal the CIA's criminal deeds and, more importantly *criminal intentions*, in operational detail.

     That will never happen again. After Agee and Stockwell, the CIA placed one of its officers, Rob Simmons [see Chapter 15], in the Senate Intelligence Committee where Simmons shepherded the Agent Identities Act into law. It's now illegal to name CIA officers and if you do, you go to prison like John Kiriakou, who exposed the CIA's use of waterboarding. That repressive measure was the legal outcome of Agee's revelations.

ROCKWELL: We're finding out just now a lot more information about the *Paris Review*, a very influential literary publication, being, in effect, a CIA front. I've always been interested in *National Review*, one of my least-favorite publications, which was founded by Bill Buckley, a former

CIA agent – maybe I should put "former" in quotes. A number of other former CIA people were also involved. This is a magazine that set out as its goal to destroy any anti-war feelings on the so-called right. Do you think that the *National Review* was a CIA operation too, like the *Paris Review*?

VALENTINE: I'm glad that you asked that question, because there are CIA "agents" who work for a CIA case officer and are on the payroll; and then there are people, in this case media propagandists, who do it for "love". They inform on colleagues or otherwise help a spy agency for ideological reasons. Buckley is a perfect example of this. There are people who, by predilection, appear to be CIA officers, but are simply ideologically in sync with it and would do these things anyway. In Buckley's case, it isn't necessary to try to distinguish whether he was an agent of the CIA or just somebody doing it out of, like I say, love.

Where you need to focus is not on people whose ideology is the same as the CIA's, but on the left, which in my usage of the term include liberals. *The Nation*, for example, is a popular leftist/liberal magazine. Would *The Nation* promote the CIA line in a particular instance? Could it be infiltrated? Could the CIA be directing some of its efforts, in critical situations?

The CIA doesn't have to infiltrate and direct the Ultras. It directs its efforts at what Cord Meyer called the "Compatible Left." Cord Meyer was associated with Operation Mockingbird, which was a way of "courting" the Compatible Left. This is what the CIA does. It's not courting Bill Buckley or the *National Review*, because the Ultras already love the CIA and know exactly what to say about it. They say the same things as the CIA anyway. The CIA penetrates the media that pretend to be non-partisan or leftist. The further to the left a magazine or a media outlet is, that's where the CIA would be found.

ROCKWELL: For example, the Congress for Cultural Freedom in the early years, too.

VALENTINE: Yes. The CIA doesn't have to tell *The New York Times* what to say. Arthur Ochs Sulzberger, Jr and his staff know what to say. They're on the CIA's wavelength. They have the same interests and exist within the same stratospheric economic and political class.

The CIA wants to know what everyone is thinking and

planning, from Marine Le Pen to Benjamin Netanyahu to Bashar al-Assad. It is trying to influence everyone to as great an extent as possible. It's infiltrating Socialist parties and trying to bring them over to the freewheeling capitalist model. They're going to concentrate in areas that are thought to harbor enemies of the United States, like the Chinese and Russians. They're going to infiltrate troublesome domestic groups as well. They're going to try to move the Black Lives Matter people to moderate their positions on equality. They're commandeering emigre groups like Gülen's and redirecting them against foreign opponents within the United States. But mostly they are trying to adjust American public opinion to support intervention abroad; arming Israel and Saudi Arabia and Egypt, to keep the oil flowing.

ROCKWELL: You know, Doug, if somebody wanted to learn about the CIA, what would be the books that you would tell them to read?

VALENTINE: Regarding propaganda, people should read *Manufacturing Consent: The Political Economy of the Mass Media,* and *Counter-Revolutionary Violence: Bloodbaths in Fact and Propaganda,* both by Noam Chomsky and Edward S. Herman. For books about the CIA, I'd recommend Agee's and Stockwell's books, as well as Victor Marchetti's *The CIA and the Cult of Intelligence.* Another book from days gone by is Fletcher Prouty's *The Secret Team,* which does the best job explaining how the CIA hides itself in other agencies and how its briefing officers write the script for the rest of the government. I'd stay away from books written by anyone working for *The New York Times.* If you read books about the CIA by Evan Thomas or Tim Weiner, do so with a block of salt; they're basically advocating hero worship. I'd also stay away from academic books that rely on official documents, all of which (including the Pentagon Papers, as Prouty explains) have all the credibility of Bob Kerrey's after-action report, the one that said his SEAL team killed 21 VC, instead of 21 women and children.

Those early books are important, but the CIA has undergone significant organizational changes in the last 15 years. The clandestine services have been reorganized and are under new names. It's a shell game. So these older books refer to the CIA organizationally in ways that are outdated, although the policies and practices haven't changed.

It's important to read whatever information the CIA publishes about its organizational structure. It has a website that sketches its organizational structure, its different branches and divisions and what they do, in a straightforward way. Looking at its organizational chart is the first step, while keeping in mind that, as with any organization, channels of power flow off the organizational chart. An organization like the CIA has back channels and ways of doing things that defy any kind of structural analysis.

It's difficult to understand, like higher mathematics or the petro-chemical industry. It takes serious study and a lot of effort. You have to read a lot of books and you have to stay up to date. A serious student has to read a lot of translated foreign publications on the subject as well. You have to get into the details.

For example, in 1989 there was an article in *Marine Corps Gazette* talking about modern warfare. That was 27 years ago. The authors of this article said, "The new type of warfare will be widely dispersed and largely undefined. The distinction between war and peace will be blurred to the vanishing point. There will be no definable battlefields or fronts. The distinction between civilian and military will disappear. Success will depend heavily on effectiveness and joint operations, as the lines between responsibility and mission become blurred."[4]

The kicker in the article was when they said that, "This new type of warfare will depend on psychological operations manifested in the form of media information intervention."

All of this became standard operating procedure, at home and abroad, in terms of the military and CIA intervening in media information.

The article said, "One must be adept at manipulating the media to alter domestic and world opinion. On this new psychological battlefield, television news may become a more powerful operational weapon than armored divisions."

Twenty-seven years ago, before the Internet, the military was talking about how, in the global village, national boundary lines would vanish and the US would become the dominant power and influence events everywhere through the control of information. The article predicted that propaganda and psychological operations would become the defining factor in shaping political and social affairs.

This was before Facebook allowed people to talk to people in Brazil or the Philippines, or enemy nations like Russia or China. This was before we could read *Russia Today* and get information from sources that contradict the official US line. The military and State Department and CIA understood that this was evolving and were making plans to control it.

To become an individual who can look at all this information, and understand that the CIA is covertly trying to manipulate it – to make you think, feel and behave a certain way – well, that is a breathtakingly complex thing to do. It's almost impossible to try to figure out where a particular piece of information is coming from – is it from the State Department or the military or the CIA? As the *Marine Corps Gazette* said, the boundaries have vanished. The information is so rapid and overwhelming and mixed in with corporate messages, other kinds of messages that are coming at us. It's just like the person who wrote that article said: it's a blur. Guy Debord talks about it in *The Society of the Spectacle*.

How can people adapt themselves, and adjust their assumptions about reality, in order to be able to discern, within a media spectacle that produced Donald Trump as a viable presidential candidate, what is really happening and where messages are coming from? It's an incredible challenge. People are so overwhelmed and alienated, they tend to withdraw – which is how Trump could create and control a social and political movement through Tweets and symbolic messages. How can anyone begin to sort this out by reading a few books, if you see what I'm trying to say?

ROCKWELL: But it still is possible, isn't it? It's just a matter of a lot of work?

VALENTINE: Oh, it's possible, because all the information is there.

ROCKWELL: One last question. This is a huge question, so you may just want to sort of skip over it lightly. But since you're an expert on the DEA as well as the CIA, what about the story of CIA drug running? Is it true that, in the late 1940s, it began to get involved in the Golden Triangle and so forth, and maybe until recently, used drugs for political and maybe financial purposes?

VALENTINE: It's true. As I've explained elsewhere, the CIA made a point of infiltrating the DEA under the Nixon administration, as a result of rising addiction in the US being tied to the CIA's drug networks in the Far East. All that was being exposed. But prior to that, the CIA didn't have to tell the people who ran the DEA or its predecessor organizations that the drug wars were essentially political, and dependent on psychological warfare.

Starting in 1949, it was official US policy to blame Communist China for America's drug problem. It was not true. But the CIA didn't need to tell the old Bureau of Narcotics to do that. The commissioner of the Bureau of Narcotics, Harry Anslinger, was one of the great propagandists of all time. He associated pot smoking with Mexicans trying to seduce white women; he associated heroin addictions with black musicians. He manipulated statistics in order to aim his agents at a rogues' gallery of despised minorities and leftist organizations.

Anslinger taught the CIA how to propagandize. He helped form the OSS. One of his senior agents, Garland Williams, went to England in 1942 with a man named Millard Preston Goodfellow, who was a Hearst executive and owned the *Brooklyn Eagle*. Williams and newspaper magnate Goodfellow were members of the Office of the Coordinator of Information. They went to England and met with John Keswick, who ran England's Special Operations Executive. Keswick had been involved in the opium trade in China and, based on that knowledge and experience, was put in charge of England's Special Operations Executive, which conducted dirty tricks in World War Two. Williams and Goodfellow returned to Washington with the SOE's training manuals and set up the OSS.

In other words, the guys who created the CIA included a narcotics agent who taught OSS officers how to avoid the security forces of foreign nations, which is what the narcotics people had been doing for decades. Not surprisingly, it was a newspaper man who taught the OSS how to control the message.

This stuff is standard operating procedure. It doesn't matter whether it's the DEA, CIA, FBI or the military. These people all know what to do. They mostly do it for their own different bureaucratic reasons, but the CIA ultimately controls the final product.

ROCKWELL: Well, Doug Valentine, thank you for what you do. This is not the sort of career that leads to power and wealth. You've chosen the path of truth and of teaching truth, and we're all very much in your debt. Please come back on the show again. This has been terrific.

VALENTINE: You're very welcome. I would love to.

Chapter 21

DISGUISING OBAMA'S DIRTY WARS

In a speech to West Point cadets delivered in early December 2009, President Barack Obama declared, "We're in Afghanistan to prevent a cancer from once again spreading throughout that country. But this same cancer has also taken root in the border region of Pakistan. That's why we need a strategy that works on both sides of the border."[1]

The hackneyed phrasing and use of the buzzword "cancer" signaled that Obama's "troop surge" in Afghanistan, announced a week earlier in direct opposition to his campaign promises to reduce US military presence in Muslim nations, would adhere to the dictates of what the CIA calls political and psychological warfare, the cornerstones of any counterinsurgency.

As I've stressed throughout this text, political and psychological warfare depends on information management; in this case, the careful revising of history and official government communiques to conceal the fact that American covert actions and unstated policies, including its reliance on drug-trafficking warlords, were responsible for the so-called "cancer" in the first place.

Indeed, at a meeting a month before Obama announced the surge, the US Ambassador in Kabul advised against a large buildup of forces, according to one report, "as long as the Karzai government remained unreformed."[2] Regional commander General David Petraeus "told Mr. Obama to think of elements of the Karzai government like 'a crime syndicate.' Ambassador Eikenberry was suggesting, in effect, that America could not get in bed with the mob."

All of this rhetoric was completely disingenuous, given that America had installed the Karzai crime syndicate in the first place.

Let's review the actual history. America's ignoble defeat in Vietnam in 1975 did not end its militant anti-Communist jihad, which President Carter simply repackaged and sold as a policy of promoting "human rights." While Carter was preaching "human rights," his national security advisor, Zbigniew Brzezinski, was secretly subverting the pro-Soviet regime that had ascended in Afghanistan in 1978. The covert actions began immediately and consisted of CIA case officers recruiting, funding, arming and forming warlords from Afghanistan's non-Pashtun ethnic groups into the infamous Northern Alliance. Through allied Islamic nations like Saudi Arabia, the CIA also recruited mercenaries like Osama bin Laden and aimed them against the secular Communists.

Brzezinski's big idea was to provoke Soviet military intervention and drag the Russians into a debilitating Vietnam-style war through a carefully sustained insurgency. The "cancer" America was eradicating at the time was Communism, along with its goals of income equality and the liberation of Afghan women, who were encouraged to attend universities and get jobs.

Like Monsanto selling dioxin-laced herbicides to happy American suburbanites as the solution to their lawn problems, the CIA launched an information campaign to convince Muslims that communism was antithetical to Islam's basic tenets, such as the belief in God. To wipe out the commie weeds, the CIA created the mujahideen, paving the way for al Qaeda. It created the civil war that destroyed Afghanistan's emerging, modern society.

Just as mighty US corporations in search of profits produce the toxins that create actual cancer, the CIA created the conditions that prompted the traumatized Taliban to arise from the ashes of the CIA-provoked civil war in an attempt to restore law and some semblance of order to their nation.

If Obama really wanted to rid the world of cancer, maybe he should have bombed Monsanto, or sicced his death squads on the tobacco companies?

While we're on the subject of carcinogens, Obama borrowed a page from Carter and, while visiting Vietnam in the spring of 2016, chided the Hanoi government for "human rights" violations. He did so without acknowledging the horrific plague of cancers the US visited on Vietnam through the systematic spraying of some 20 million gallons of

Agent Orange over 12 % of Vietnam, adversely affecting over 3 million innocent people. And don't think this is Vietnam War history; it's a huge problem today.

As Marjorie Cohn noted in December 2015, "Those exposed to Agent Orange during the war often have children and grandchildren with serious illnesses and disabilities. The international scientific community has identified an association between exposure to Agent Orange and some forms of cancers, reproductive abnormalities, immune and endocrine deficiencies and nervous system damage. Second- and third-generation victims continue to be born in Vietnam as well as to U.S. veterans and Vietnamese-Americans in this country."[3]

Individual CIA officers made liberal use of poisons in Vietnam as early as 1961, when, according to Tom Ahern in his book *Vietnam Declassified*, CIA officer Ralph Johnson's Vietnamese counterpart "proposed deploying special teams to poison VC rice depots, booby trap VC munitions depots, kill or capture VC cadre in ambushes or in raids on Communist-controlled villages, and gather intelligence. Johnson endorsed this program, saying he expected it to tie down Viet Cong military forces and reduce Communist pressure on Montagnard villages."[4]

While stationed in Kien Hoa Province in 1964, Ahern proposed "the use of sophisticated booby traps, incendiaries, and materials toxic to livestock in areas considered to be under uncontested Communist control." Ahern encouraged this despite "the possibility of civilian casualties and suggested using leaflet drops to warn that persons using particular routes now incurred mortal danger."[5]

CIA officers like Ahern were well aware of the cancer they were spreading. The US government, along with its British allies, developed dioxin in the 1940s as a weapon of war ostensibly to destroy Nazi and Japanese crops. They had known since the 1950s that it (along with nuclear fallout) was a lethal cancer-causing agent. The US also knew what would happen to its own expendable soldiers, as well as the Vietnamese people, by saturating Vietnam with dioxin, just as it knew what would happen when it planted the mujahideen cancer in Afghanistan.

When asked if he regretted creating terrorists, Brzezinski replied: "What is most important to the history of the world; the Taliban or the collapse of the Soviet empire? Some stirred-up Moslems or the liberation of Central Europe and the end of the cold war?"[6]

When asked by Leslie Stahl if she regretted that US sanctions on Iraq had led to the death of half-a-million children, former Secretary of State Madeleine Albright said, "We think the price is worth it."

Albright's comment was made on 60 Minutes in 1996, but, as reported by Rahul Mahajan, "a Dow Jones search of mainstream news sources since September 11 turns up only one reference to the quote – in an op-ed in the *Orange County Register* (9/16/01). This omission is striking, given the major role that Iraq sanctions play in the ideology of archenemy Osama bin Laden; his recruitment video features pictures of Iraqi babies wasting away from malnutrition and lack of medicine (*New York Daily News*, 9/28/01). The inference that Albright and the terrorists may have shared a common rationale – a belief that the deaths of thousands of innocents are a price worth paying to achieve one's political ends – does not seem to be one that can be made in U.S. mass media."[7]

Commenting in October 2011 about her needless destruction of Libya and the ramming of a knife up Muammar Qaddafi's rectum, Hillary Clinton chortled majestically, "We came. We saw. He died."

Being an exceptional American means never having to say you're sorry. If you're a top American leader, it also means never going to prison.

Left as Right

Delivered a week after he addressed cadets at West Point, Obama's Nobel Prize acceptance speech (in which he boasted about ordering the Guantanamo torture center closed) marked an important juncture for him as he took on the job of selling more war in Afghanistan. It didn't matter that American hands had already been stained by the blood of thousands of innocents killed in bombing raids.

Never mind all that innocent blood; Obama's double-talk was hailed by neoconservatives who believed they had, surprisingly, found in the young bi-racial President a far more effective spokesman for their interventionist causes than the inarticulate, buffoonish George W. Bush.

"The shift in rhetoric at Oslo was striking," observed neocon theorist Robert Kagan in a *Washington Post* op-ed. "Gone was the vaguely left-revisionist language that flavored earlier speeches, highlighting the low points of American global leadership – the coups and ill-considered wars – and low-balling the highlights, such as the Cold War triumph."[8]

But then, those words were intended for the American public, with a view to winning an election. Indeed, in his Oslo speech, Obama shoved six decades of bloody "low points" behind one five-word clause, "whatever mistakes we have made." [9]

Obama more than willingly shouldered the job of arms salesman for the war in Afghanistan; he reveled in his role as custodian of the "Kill List" and boasted of his power to cross international borders to assassinate Taliban leaders in Pakistan and later, an American citizen in Yemen. Under Obama's stewardship, the role of the president evolved from moral leader to Predator drone orchestrator conducting surgical hits.

Being a tough guy who enjoys murder is also a popular stance in America: Obama leaves office in the summer of 2016 with a 51% approval rating.

But it was never necessary for Obama to win the support of the majority of the American public for the War on Terror; programmed Americans instinctively rally around the flag and support the troops. It is the knee-jerk reaction Obama and the National Security Establishment counted on when they sent 30,000 soldiers to Afghanistan. And even though the surge would eventually count among "mistakes we made," decades of political and psychological warfare have successfully shifted the responsibility for those mistakes from leaders with good intentions onto the general public, which has as its only obligation the moral imperative to support the troops.

The trick is to make the public feel, every day in every way, that there is an ongoing, urgent need for wars they must support. So Obama packaged his surge as a cure for cancer. He made it an involuntary matter of personal survival, like the radiation and chemotherapy treatments that take a terrible toll on a patient's body, but are necessary if the patient wants to live.

Fifteen years after Bush invaded Afghanistan and provoked its current civil war, the American public is still paying for some magical cure that will stop the fear and insecurity its leaders created; a condition of psychological dependence that makes the public incapable of shaking off its political oppressors here at home.

Beyond relying on alternating doses of medicinal fear and patriotism, Obama's incestuous war council (symbolized by the marriage of neo-con Robert Kagan and Obama's neo-liberal Assistant Secretary of State for European and Eurasian Affairs, Victoria Nuland) knows that public confusion is helpful. Most Americans don't have the time to learn what really happened in Afghanistan – in this case, that there was never an "insurgency" to counter, but rather a resistance movement to American military occupation by Afghan nationalists.

One could say that America's unstated policy of conquest through massive corruption was a mistake. Or one could say that the National Security Establishment wanted to control the drug trade and use the profits to train a new generation of special operations forces (who since 9/11 primarily invade private homes at midnight on targeted "snatch and snuff" missions, and thus refer to themselves as "door kickers") while colonizing Afghanistan and using it as a base to subvert Russia and China.

Either way you say it, that's what intentionally happened, and will continue to happen.

What Is Counterinsurgency?

In his speeches, President Obama defines America's objectives in Afghanistan as: 1) suppressing the Taliban resistance forces to American military occupation and the corrupt puppet regime the US installed in 2001; 2) eliminating several Arab terrorists; and 3) creating a stable, pro-American government and economic infrastructure.

David Galula, author of *Counterinsurgency Warfare: Theory and Practice* and a recognized authority on the matter, stressed that counterinsurgency includes "building or rebuilding a political apparatus within the population."[10]

In this sense any counterinsurgency is also an insurgency; it just depends on who is telling the story, and when the story begins. In Afghanistan, the Taliban ruled for several years until the CIA's Northern Alliance drove them out. Since the civil war, there have been two governments.

Obama's successor will continue to define the Taliban as the insurgents. But the Taliban, who by 2005 once again controlled many parts of Afghanistan, view the Americans as invaders backing a corrupt insurgency that undermines traditional Muslim law.

As every government propagandist knows, the essence of existence is no longer "to be or not to be," but to define or be defined. Thus, "military occupation" is not a phrase one hears when Americans tell the story of Afghanistan. One only hears the word "counterinsurgency." But the US military's strategy for defeating the Taliban has always been to "clear and hold" territory the corrupt warlords on its payroll covet for economic purposes.

To "clear and hold" means to drive the resistance out of their secure areas in the countryside through Phoenix-style operations perfected in Vietnam. Such operations range from small unit death squads like Bob Kerrey's, when his SEAL team slaughtered the women and children of Thanh Phong – just like the US commandoes did in Ghazi Khan 40 years later. The idea in either case is to terrorize the public into no longer supporting the resistance movement.

This terror strategy worked in Iraq. According to the story told by Washington's ruling National Security Establishment, President George W. Bush's 2007 "surge" and the "clear and hold" strategy "won" the war in Iraq – although it merely gave rise to ISIS, yet another "cancer."

As in Afghanistan in 2002, the reality in Iraq is diametrically opposed to the story we have been told. More important than the surge and the temporary drop in violence were the massive bribes (billions of Pentagon dollars are still unaccounted for) used to pay off Sunni tribes in 2006, along with Bush's agreement in 2008 to reduce the US military presence. But that is not what Bush and Obama wanted people to believe.

For instance, Establishment propagandists Evan Thomas and John Barry at *Newsweek* asserted that the "clear and hold" strategy worked because it protected the "friendly civilians" who provided the tips that enabled the CIA and its Special Forces sidekicks to find and kill people who were, as in Bob Kerrey's after-action report at Thanh Phong, said to be terrorists or members of the resistance.

"By ratcheting back the heavy use (and overuse) of firepower," they claimed, "[US military commander in Afghanistan Gen. Stanley] McChrystal has reduced civilian casualties, which alienate the locals and breed more jihadists."[11]

The reality, however, is far less humane and clinical.

1) It is false to assert that a counterinsurgency is gentler than the shock and awe of, say, the Iraq invasion. Such an assertion is propaganda intended to deceive its target population in the United States into thinking that innocents are not being intentionally killed and robbed of everything they own.

2) The assertion that only "jihadists" are targeted for assassination obscures the fact that thousands of people are fighting not for religious reasons, but for nationalist reasons – Afghans (or name your

target population) are simply opposed to American invaders and their corrupt collaborators.

3) The notion that civilians provide information because they are "friendly" to the Americans is misleading, since most intelligence is coerced or bought. Only in the world of illusion created by Barry and Thomas can a warlord like Gul Agha Sherzai, whose tips in 2001 led to the massacre of hundreds of his personal rivals and sparked the civil war, be said to be a "friend". As Anand Gopal revealed in *No Good Men Among the Living*, Sherzai supplied the CIA with a network of informants that targeted their business rivals, not the Taliban. In return Sherzai received the contract to build the first US military base in Afghanistan, along with a major drug franchise. In an effort to create an insurgency, and a pretext for eternal military occupation, the CIA methodically began torturing and killing Afghanistan's most revered leaders in a series of Phoenix-style raids that radicalized the Afghan people.

The *Newsweek* propagandists were correct only when they said that Obama's dirty war was modeled on the Phoenix program, whose goal was to "target and assassinate Viet Cong leaders." As usual, they only told the part of the story they wanted people to hear. They didn't add that waging a successful dirty war depends on spreading disinformation as to who is the enemy and why they and everyone around them are being killed.

Intelligence

Intelligence is gained primarily through informants, detainees, interrogations, defectors, electronic intercepts, and secret agents.

1) Voluntary informants like Sherzai typically work for money and vengeance. Ideology is a factor, but more often informants in a civil war are given no choice. Fracturing a society or culture into opposing factions (Sunni vs Shia) and then coercing rivals into becoming informants is the CIA's strong suit.

2) Detainees also provide coerced information in an effort to escape a jerry-rigged legal system in which due process is denied and spilling the beans is the only alternative to torture and death. Producing and coercing detainees is one of the CIA's major means of assuring that a society will remain divided and manageable. Sowing suspicion, fear and confusion keeps a subject population suppressed.

3) In the Afghan conflict, interrogations are conducted by

members of the Afghan National Army (ANA), the Afghan secret police (KHAD), or private militias operated by warlords like Sherzai. When not actually conducted under the supervision of CIA and military officers in jointly managed facilities, torture sessions are conducted unofficially by private militias acting as CIA mercenary forces. High Value targets captured in unilateral CIA operations are tortured in secure facilities off-limits to militiamen.

Not publicized by *Newsweek* is the fact that the CIA and US military purchased from members of the corrupt Afghan government the right to operate secret torture and detention centers, as well as the right to use unilateral paramilitary teams to target, capture and kill Afghans who pose security risks to its profitable drug network.

Based on "administrative detention" laws developed in Vietnam, the CIA's secret detention and torture centers were supposed to be handed over to the Afghan secret police. Suspects theoretically appear before "review boards" that afford them a fleeting chance to present evidence of their innocence. Reporters and international human rights officials are supposed to have access to the trials.

The reality is far different. As reported in the 28 November 2009 *Washington Post*: "Two Afghan teenagers held in U.S. detention north of Kabul this year said they were beaten by American guards, photographed naked, deprived of sleep and held in solitary confinement in concrete cells for at least two weeks while undergoing daily interrogation about their alleged links to the Taliban."[12]

4) The CIA's defector programs for Muslims evolved from the CIA's Chieu Hoi program for Communists in Vietnam. Defector programs are the essence of political and psychological warfare and rely totally on the control of information. A typical defector program consists of dropping leaflets on a targeted village in a secure enemy village; the leaflets promise mutilation and slow death to those who resist, and riches beyond one's wildest dreams to those who defect.

Immediately upon defecting, defectors are interrogated, often by former comrades who have defected and repented. Defectors are made to prove their loyalty by providing actionable intelligence so military operations can be mounted immediately. Having proven their worth, defectors are then taught the American "line" by other defectors; to further prove their sincerity, they are then conscripted into CIA-funded militias and sent back to contact other resistance members and recruit more defectors. Defectors are used as "pseudo-insurgents" in black propaganda operations, and as translators and interrogators in torture centers. The CIA's espionage operations are populated by defectors.

5) American electronic intercepts are entirely unilateral and directed mostly against the various agencies of the puppet Afghan government, as a way of detecting double agents and discovering information that can be used to bribe and coerce officials in the puppet regime.

6) The CIA and US military run agents in liaison with militia leaders like Sherzai, as well as with subservient police and military officials in the Afghan government. Often, however, the militias target police and military officials belonging to rival tribes. Thus, the CIA values most highly its unilateral agents within the various militias and government agencies, in order to keep in touch with real events, as opposed to the stories it tells to the press.

It is difficult recruiting agents within the Taliban leadership, which is composed of religious clerics who dispense justice, not social services, per se. Taliban leaders have not succumbed to the cash nexus and are not easily bribed. They do not have bookkeepers nor do they organize in Western-style corporate hierarchies. They do not issue press releases, broadcast their plans and strategies, or allow photography (which can confound CIA assassins).

These ideological precepts make them nearly impervious to blackmail, extortion and corruption – the CIA's standard means of penetrating the enemy infrastructure, and the means by which it controls top-ranking officials in the Afghani government.

The Taliban leadership does meet with foreigners to negotiate land and mineral rights, as well as to form alliances. But after being "preemptively man-hunted" for 15 years they are loath to deal with Americans, which further hampers the CIA's ability to penetrate their ranks. The Taliban's cultural practices make it hard to know if any intelligence gathered is reliable, but that does not much matter. The Taliban, according to Hillary Clinton, treat their women like animals, and that is reason enough to wipe them off the planet and steal everything they own.

The main function of intelligence in the Afghan dirty war is to create public support for US government policies. Intelligence managers skew intelligence to this political purpose, as happened with the bogus reports of WMD in Iraq. Any policy can find supporting intelligence, especially when the meaning of words is garbled by Afghan (or Iraqi or

Syrian) collaborators and US officials who are required to report what the CIA wants to hear, and which they disseminate, respectively, for their own survival and/or career advancement.

As Phoenix program veteran Stan Fulcher explained to me: "The Vietnamese lied to us; we lied to the Phoenix Directorate; and the Directorate made it into documented fact. It was a war that became distorted through our ability to create fiction."

Intelligence programs have two other functions in a dirty war. One is to map out the clandestine organizations that drive the resistance, so they can be destroyed. At the secret detention and torture centers it operates in Afghanistan, the CIA draws up blacklists of actual and fabricated Taliban cadres based on their social and family ties, position within the infrastructure, age, sex and profession, etc.

The idea is to send paramilitary teams out to capture them, make them inform on their comrades, turn them into double agents, or kill them and their families and friends. None have the right to due process.

Some of these death squad operations have surfaced during US military disciplinary proceedings. In one case, an Afghani, identified as suspected insurgent leader Nawab Buntangyar, was encountered on 13 October 2006 by an Afghan army patrol led by US Special Forces Captain Dave Staffel. Afraid that the suspected terrorist might be wearing a suicide vest, the Americans kept their distance while checking his description against the CIA's "kill-or-capture list." Concluding that the man was indeed Buntangyar, Staffel ordered American sniper Troy Anderson to fire from a distance of about 100 yards away, putting a bullet through the man's head and killing him instantly.[13]

The soldiers viewed the killing as "a textbook example of a classified mission completed in accordance with the American rules of engagement," the *International New York Times* reported. "The men said such rules allowed them to kill Buntangyar, whom the American military had designated a terrorist cell leader, once they positively identified him."

When Staffel's civilian lawyer said the Army's Criminal Investigation Command concluded that the shooting was "justifiable homicide," a two-star general in Afghanistan then initiated a murder charge against Staffel and Anderson. Both were released on technicalities.

An even more telling tale involved Sergeant Major Anthony Pryor, who in 2007 was awarded the Silver Star for gallantry in action. As Pryor said modestly at the award ceremony, "I just did what I had to do."[14]

Anand Gopal chronicled the actual event in *No Good Men Among the Living*. In his book, Gopal told how Pryor's Special Forces A-team attacked a schoolhouse where al Qaeda terrorists were said to be hiding. It was January 2002, only three months after the US launched its invasion of revenge for 9/11. The men in the schoolhouse were said to have defended themselves, but were overwhelmed.

As Pryor soon discovered, the men he attacked were part of a pro-American local government. Like Bob Kerrey after Thanh Phong, "Pryor claims he acted in self-defense," Gopal wrote, "but Khas Uruzgan residents point out that the bodies were found in their beds, handcuffed, and there were no signs of struggle. Either way, every official was killed."[15]

As Gopal noted, the massacre would have been controversial anyway, but the schoolhouse was within the governor's compound. The anti-Taliban police chief lived in the compound but he too was beaten and kidnapped. The governor, Tawildar Yunis, heard the commotion and escaped, but others were summarily shot in the head. The survivors were put in an AC-130 gunship (the kind featured in the Collateral Murder video Chelsea Manning was sent to prison for leaking) and flown to a CIA/military base. Pryor and his team left behind a sadistic card saying, "Have a nice day. From Damage, Inc."

Gopal said, "In a thirty-minute stretch, the United States had managed to eradicate both of Khas Uruzgan's potential governments, the core of any future anti-Taliban leadership – stalwarts who had outlasted the Russian invasion, the civil war, and the Taliban years but would not survive their own allies."

Weeks later the Americans realized their "mistake" and released the prisoners. Brutalized beyond belief, they were now eager to fight back. As usual, a series of such "mistakes," the kind Obama referenced in his Nobel Prize speech – and which the Pentagon claimed was the reason US and British forces killed and wounded dozens of Syrian soldiers who were fighting ISIS on 17-18 September 2016 – created the nationalist resistance that would "force" the United States to occupy Afghanistan for the next 15 years, and into the foreseeable future.

At some point one must ask, are they really mistakes based on faulty intelligence? Or are they the essential ingredients of colonization and military occupation?

In Afghanistan, the CIA aims its death squads at Taliban judicial officials operating "religious law" courts and assessing and collecting taxes; resistance members operating business fronts for purchasing, storing or distributing food and supplies, including farm products; public health officials distributing medicine; security officials targeting American collaborators and agents; officials in transportation, communication and postal services; military recruiters; and military leaders and forces. Or anyone said to be engaged in these activities.

The other major purpose of the intelligence programs is to understand how resistance leaders prepare Afghan civilians to cope with the violence the CIA and US military visited upon them for generations. Through opinion polls and surveys, the CIA tries to understand what drives people into the resistance or, conversely, into the arms of corrupt warlord regimes. Based on this attitudinal intelligence, the CIA seeks to establish the rationale for its own parallel government, which it portrays to the press as free of corruption and drug traffickers, and modeled on Afghan sensibilities.

The media admits the CIA occasionally makes mistakes, but minimizes the "mistakes" by insisting the Agency and its military adjuncts only have good intentions – guys like William Calley, Bob Kerrey, Rob Simmons, Frank Scotton, Dave Staffel, Troy Anderson and Tony Pryor.

It's enough to make you want to give the CIA a big medal.

How to Disguise a Dirty War

The CIA forms its parallel governments in foreign nations in conjunction with the US military and State Department. In Afghanistan it hides itself in consulates and secret compounds on military bases, as it does in most of the hundreds of military bases America has spread around the world.

After establishing itself on military bases, the CIA expands its operations under cover of the State Department's Agency for International Development (AID) "civic action" missions. Psywar is what makes it all possible; having collaborators like Thomas and Barry who are willing to tell the American public the approved version of the story – good guys doing good deeds who occasionally make mistakes.

The CIA follows in the tradition of the Christian "missions" that brought Bible classes to undeveloped nations around the world. In the process, the benighted natives were softened up for military conquest, bureaucratic colonization and economic exploitation, no matter how well-intentioned the missionary. Indeed, the more effective the missionary's message, the more malleable the natives became.

AID missions serve the same softening-up function today, though their gospel is "development" not the word of god. In either case – by accepting the outsider's medicines and message – the natives tacitly accept the outsider's authority. They are converted into a compliant workforce; recruited into the occupation army or as petty officials in the puppet government; and as special police in its homeland security apparatus.

As were Christian missionaries of old, the modern AID worker is a highly indoctrinated fanatic. As one aid worker in Afghanistan told me: "The ANA [the Afghan National Army] is really good: people trust them and share intelligence with them, something they are not willing to do with internationals."

This AID worker did not acknowledge the Taliban as being people; after all, one cannot become an AID worker unless one preaches the CIA gospel, chapter and verse. No heretics need apply.

As I've mentioned ad nauseam in this book, AID programs provide cover for the CIA and are symbolic of the evil intentions that lurk behind the righteous US façade. In the following paragraphs I'll outline an AID program that existed in Thailand during the Vietnam War, and which serves as an example of what is currently happening worldwide on a massive scale.

The CIA proprietary company Joseph Z. Taylor Associates was planted in Thailand as a community development counseling service. At the same time, it had a contract with the Thai Border Patrol Police (BPP). The BPP was a paramilitary force of 10,000 airborne rangers created by the CIA in the early 1950s and charged with "internal security," which meant killing Communists, guarding the King's opium fields, protecting CIA drug smuggling networks, and eliminating the competition.

Taylor Associates employed CIA contract officer Ray Coffey and his Green Beret assistants to oversee BPP intelligence collection, counterinsurgency, and border control operations in northern Thailand. As Coffey explained to me, in 1972, CIA-advised BPP operations in northern Thailand were redirected on narcotics intelligence collection. Coffey was not happy about the job; he recalled sitting on a mountain side in 1973 and watching a battalion of KMT soldiers with 200 mules moving a huge opium shipment.

"I had thirty men to stop a battalion," Coffey recalled, "so I said, 'Forget it.'"

According to Coffey the Thai military also moved drugs: "Ten tons of opium at a time on barges into Chiang Mai."

In the early 1980s, when author James Mills was in Chiang Mai writing about DEA operations, the BPP was still considered "totally corrupt and responsible for the transportation of narcotics."[16]

I was told the same story by Gordon Young, a CIA officer in Thailand since 1954. Originally a BPP advisor, Young in 1972, as part of Nixon's incipient war on drugs, was put under AID Public Safety cover and assigned to Houei Sai, Laos (which is mentioned elsewhere in this book as the epicenter of the CIA's drug operations in the Golden Triangle).

Young described the anti-narcotics effort between 1972 and 1974 as "a messy, uncoordinated affair" with "each outfit (CIA, DEA, USAID Public Safety, State, the military and Customs) all pulling in different directions – each looking jealously for the rewards!"

Like Coffey, Gordon had no illusions that he could overcome official corruption fueled by the CIA. As is true in Afghanistan today, "No one was there to be heroes," he said.

"It was like dealing with Mafia chiefs," Young added. He recalled a trip he took to meet a BPP captain in the jungle. The captain was sitting beside a huge pile of heroin, morphine and opium. Young asked if he would surrender it.

"You may have it," the captain said, "but by time you get through...."

Ray Coffey's area of expertise was not drug interdiction; it was conducting "civic action" operations in remote areas. To this end, through a facet of Taylor Associates called DEVCON, Coffey and his Special Forces assistants created the Hilltribe Research Center in Chiang Mai, Thailand in 1967.

As part of the CIA's parallel government in Thailand, the Hilltribe Research Center employed Thai nationals as teachers, agronomists, animal husbandry-men and engineers. Under the supervision of American case officers, these Thai nationals doubled as Principal Agents who recruited informants and ran agent nets. As a cover for its espionage activities (and to baptize the indigenous people in the holy Cash Nexus), the Center bought and marketed their handicrafts. Many of them were recruited and sent back into the local opium growing areas to gather intelligence on drug traffickers.

The Hilltribe Research Center famously employed Puttaporn

Khramkhruan, a CIA agent arrested for smuggling opium into the US. The case began in 1972, when Puttaporn sold opium to several Americans through a Peace Corps volunteer in Chiang Mai. The Americans packaged the opium in film canisters and sent it home. An initial shipment went through without any problems, but a second 59-pound package was spotted by Customs inspectors in Chicago. The receiver was arrested when he came to pick it up.

Upon closer examination, the inspectors found that Puttaporn had wrapped the opium in a magazine with his name and address on it. A Customs agent was sent to Thailand to investigate. Although snubbed by the CIA officer in Chiang Mai, the Customs agent learned that Puttaporn was, at that very moment, in the US as part of a business seminar sponsored by the Agency for International Development. AID, in fact, had given him $1600 for airfare.

Back in the US, Customs agents arrested Puttaporn and stuck him in the Cook County jail. When questioned, he confessed to everything. Not only did he name his US accomplices, he said he was an officer in General Li Mi's Kuomintang army in Burma. His job, he said, was to guard opium caravans traveling from Burma to Houei Sai, Laos. It was a CIA operation, he said, and he named his CIA case officer as the US consul in Chiang Mai, James Montgomery.

In 1973, the CIA under William Colby was looking at the Big Picture, meaning Nixon's overture to China, which included negotiations over the status of Taiwan. Many CIA senior officers had invested 20 years of their lives supporting the Kuomintang in Taiwan. They considered Taiwan a strategic military base and were violently opposed to rapprochement with China. As Rob Simmons was quoted as saying in an earlier chapter, they would do anything to eradicate Communism.

One thing they did was use opium caravans to detect Chinese troop movements. Despite Nixon's official presidential directives to the contrary, doing so was official policy. And in Afghanistan it still is, for all the same Russian and Chinese reasons.

DEVCON agents spied on Soviet and Chinese agents in Thailand, and Puttaporn was directly involved in the intrigues between the CIA, the KMT in Burma and Taiwan, and the Chinese. Nixon took a personal interest in his case after Puttaporn told DEA agents that he had led commando raids into China for the CIA. Puttaporn threatened to confess that he had smuggled the opium into Chicago at the request of the CIA. His lawyer stated his intention to call DEVCON boss Joseph

Taylor, as well as the CIA station chief in Bangkok, Louis Lapham, and the CIA base chief in Udorn, Thailand, Pat Landry, as witnesses. His defense team was also preparing to subpoena incriminating documents.

The CIA's reaction was predictable. It refused to provide the documents and witnesses, and directed the assistant US attorney in Chicago to dismiss the case in April 1974. The stated reason was to protect Joe Taylor, who was working with senior Thai police and political officials planning intelligence operations against Chinese agents in Malaysia and against Russian agents in North Vietnam.

On July 24, 1974, two weeks before his resignation, Nixon appointed Joseph Z. Taylor as Assistant Inspector General of Foreign Assistance.

At Congressional Hearings into the Puttaporn case, CIA Director William Colby said: "We requested the Justice Department not to try him for this reason. They agreed."

CIA lawyers told Senator Charles Percy that Puttaporn was hired only to report on narcotics trafficking in northern Thailand (not to attack and spy on China), and that his crime was a "controlled delivery" designed to counter narcotic trafficking.

Percy said with a heavy sigh, "CIA agents are untouchable — however serious their crime or however much harm is done to society."[17]

Fred Dick ran the DEA's office in Bangkok at the time and was involved in the Puttaporn operation. As he explained to me, "The Agency folks are masters at going behind the scenes in the US court system and convincing the judiciary an open exposure of this sort would jeopardize national security. To my knowledge they have never failed with this ploy."

DEA agents knew the CIA was lying and, at Dick's direction, told Senator Percy that Puttaporn had been employed by the CIA since 1969, "as a member of a multi-million dollar opium ring." They also told Percy that Puttaporn's close friend, Victor Tin-Sein, "had been killed while living in the United States by unnamed parties for his involvement in and knowledge of Puttaporn's smuggling ring."[18]

The murder dovetailed with a case CIA/DEA Agent Joe Lagattuta was working on. A member of Lou Conein's CIA-controlled special operations unit outlined earlier in this book, Lagattuta was sent to Amsterdam to recruit a specific Chinese asset – Victor Tin-Sein. Victor was not an informant but an agent and part of a CIA operation "for Conein and a significant figure who must remain nameless."

Lagattuta hinted that the significant figure was William Colby.

"We were very successful," Lagattuta said, "not just in heroin seized but the planning and execution of the sting leading to arrests and destruction of several significant trafficking rings."

Unfortunately, Victor Tin-Sein was sent to San Francisco against Lagattuta's wishes where, according to Lagattuta, he was assassinated (as opposed to being murdered).

For his part, Puttaporn was released and returned to Thailand.

CIA case officers and their agents in the puppet Afghan government are following the same script. And anyone who deviates from the script, even some stratospheric character like Ahmed Karzai, the former Afghan president's half-brother, is assassinated. Ahmed's assassination occurred, it should be noted, after mainstream reporters connected him to drug trafficking.

Anand Gopal summarized the situation in Afghanistan: "Bush administration officials had drawn up a list [in 2005] of the most wanted international drug barons who posed a threat to US interests. When Assistant Secretary of State Bobby Charles saw it, he asked, "Why don't we have any Afghan drug lords on the list?" This was, in fact, a thorny problem because some of the biggest Afghan narcotics kingpins –Gul Agha Sherzai and Ahmed Wali Karzai chief among them – were allied with Washington, and in some cases even paid by the Americans."[19]

Running the drug business in a foreign country is dangerous work. Afghanis who collaborate with the CIA in this criminal endeavor must inform on their countrymen or die. Likewise, Afghanis working in US AID programs as part of the CIA's parallel government must preach the party line: they must refer to the resistance as "insurgents" in exchange for their prosperity and survival. The CIA is just like al Qaeda and the Taliban in this regard: no heretics allowed.

As the AID worker in Afghanistan told me with all the histrionics of a Clinton or Trump campaign speech: "The wrath on informants [should the resistance prevail] will make the rape camps of Serbia look like picnics in the park."

How he knew this is not the point: his job is to propagandize – to terrorize – Americans.

The terror that accompanies institutionalized CIA corruption enables Civic Action teams to train rural villagers how to build perimeter defenses. When not administering medicine and forming militias, CIA-guided Special Forces units, having learned to dress and grow beards like Afghanis, slip into the countryside at night and, using intelligence from their assets, "snatch and snuff" the local resistance cadre. Urban units do likewise in cities.

Sometimes they engage in "black propaganda" activities designed to produce defectors by inflicting atrocities on the population that can be blamed on the enemy. When they function in this manner, they are terrorists.

Instilling terror, as their Jesuit forefathers knew, is how the CIA creates converts among the resistance. Any AID worker who helps the CIA in this mission is someone author Graham Greene would have described as "a dumb leper who has lost his bell, wandering the world, meaning no harm."

It doesn't matter that many Taliban men, women and children are pure in thought and deed, and are seeking only to defend their homes and culture from foreign invaders. Most do not participate in terrorism or even guerrilla action, and yet they are uniformly dehumanized as "cancer" by the likes of Hillary Clinton and Donald Trump, who must prove their willingness to stigmatize and kill innocent people in order to command the respect of the National Security Establishment.

Meanwhile, in the mainstream news media, the US government's intentions are always characterized as heroic, generous, cancer-curing. Which is how bad becomes good. Dependent on official government sources like addicts depend on heroin, the media's propagandists justify the policy of war crimes by covering up the existence of CIA parallel governments dependent on corruption and criminal collaborators, and by blurring distinctions between combatants and non-combatants.

Few reporters dare to report that in Afghanistan – as in Vietnam – the CIA offers bounties to anyone willing to identify the political leaders of the resistance, the shadow government of the people that exists apart from the CIA-imposed criminal conspiracy that is despised for its corruption and collaboration.

I'll give an example. Griff Witte wrote in the *Washington Post* on 8 December 2009 that the Taliban has "an elaborate shadow government of governors, police chiefs, district administrators and judges that in many cases already has more bearing on the lives of Afghans than the real government."[20]

Witte quoted Khalid Pashtoon, "a legislator from the southern province of Kandahar who has close ties to Karzai," as saying: "These people in the shadow government are running the country now."

Witte also cited the case of "the shadow governor, Maulvi Shaheed Khail," who "is regarded as fearsome but clean. A former minister in the Taliban government, he became the shadow governor here last year after being released from government custody. Residents said he spends most of his time in exile in Pakistan but occasionally crosses the border to discuss strategy with his lieutenants."

In many parts of Afghanistan, Witte continued, "Afghans have decided they prefer the severe but decisive authority of the Taliban to the corruption and inefficiency of Karzai's appointees. From Kunduz province in the north to Kandahar in the south, even government officials concede that their allies have lost the people's confidence and that, increasingly, residents are turning to shadow Taliban officials to solve their problems."

All of these statements are confirmed by my independent sources. And yet, while Witte spoke truth when interviewing Afghanis, he veered into propaganda when quoting US sources. Specifically, he claimed that all Taliban officials are combatants: "There are no clear lines between the Taliban's fighting force and its shadow administration. Insurgents double as police chiefs; judges may spend an afternoon hearing cases, then take up arms at dusk."

Although sprinkled with truth to achieve believability, Witte's article ultimately supported the notion that all Taliban, including civilians, are "legitimate" military targets to be subjected to murder and mutilation without due process.

Secret Government

The intelligence apparatus in Afghanistan is the foundation of the CIA's parallel government. Just as it operates under the cover of US and NATO AID missions, it lurks behind whatever group of professional criminals and warlords it installs in the official government in Kabul.

Obama, like every public official, struggles to present this criminal enterprise in the best terms possible, though in reality it is no different than the corrupt political apparatus the CIA imposed on South Vietnam.

In 1965, the CIA named Air Force General Nguyen Cao Ky as chief of national security. In exchange for a lucrative narcotic smuggling franchise, Ky then sold the CIA the right to extend its parallel government from Saigon into the countryside. Called the Revolutionary

Development Cadre program, it consisted of CIA covert action programs staffed by corrupt Vietnamese officials.

The CIA did the same thing in the 1980s, when it coerced US law enforcement agencies into "looking away" in regard to both cocaine smuggling by the Nicaraguan Contra terrorists and heroin trafficking by the Northern Alliance warlords fighting the Soviets in Afghanistan.

This history is not lost on Afghan bandits. A 2010 article by the McClatchy Newspapers noted that by blocking a diplomatic solution in Afghanistan in favor of Obama's surge, US militarists spared President Karzai from having to make meaningful reforms; he even refused to send his drug-dealing half-brother, Ahmed, into honorable exile.

After 15 years of US military occupation and misrule by its collaborators, the situation hasn't changed. Informants, interrogators, hit teams and corrupt politicians understand the evil they're doing, but their prosperity and lives depend on US patronage. As a result, the definition of "insurgent" gets skewed to mean anyone who is not compliant with the US occupation. Just like Rudy Giuliani and Ultra law and order fanatics petition Obama to label the Black Lives Matter organization as a terrorist group.

I would like to close this chapter by quoting from John Cook, an army officer assigned to the Phoenix program in Vietnam. CIA officers taught Phoenix advisors at the Vietnamese Central Intelligence School. As Cook recalled: "There were forty of us in the class, half American, half Vietnamese. The first day at the school was devoted to lectures by American experts in the insurgency business. Using a smooth, slick delivery, they reviewed all the popular theories concerning Communist-oriented revolutions. Like so many machines programmed to perform at a higher level than necessary, they dealt with platitudes and theories far above our dirty little war. They spoke in impersonal tones about what had to be done and how we should do it, as if we were in the business of selling life insurance, with a bonus going to the man who sold the most policies.[21]

"Those districts that were performing well with the quota system were praised; the poor performers were admonished. And it all fitted together nicely with all the charts and figures they offered as support of their ideas."

Like many of his colleagues, Cook resented "the pretentious men in high position" who gave him unattainable goals, then complained when he did not reach them.

Fifty years later, the US government has expanded Phoenix worldwide, with all the missionary zeal of Jesuits. Only now its cadres are more highly indoctrinated. There is little resentment anymore among the rank and file.

Former Delta Force Commander, General William Boykin, is a born-again Christian who casts the War on Terror as a Holy Crusade against Islam. As zealous as any jihadist, he believes an anthropomorphic god directs his personal actions. When asked about Phoenix and the War on Terror, Boykin said: "I think we're running that kind of program. We're going after these people. Killing or capturing these people is a legitimate mission for the department. I think we're doing what the Phoenix program was designed to do, without all of the secrecy."[22]

On July 16, 2012, Family Research Council president Tony Perkins announced that Boykin had been named the group's Executive Vice-President.

Like the terrible god Boykin believes in, with its savior crucified on a cross, the "cancer" Obama sought to destroy in Afghanistan was merely a projection of the dark side of the twisted American psyche, and more of a threat to the safety of the American people than to any Taliban or ISIS terrorist.

Whomever the Business Party, in the name of its one true god, Mammon, forces upon the American people in the 2016 elections and beyond, his or her job will be to preserve the myth of America as altruistic liberator.

The terrible truth is that a Cult of Death rules America and is hell-bent on world domination.

Chapter 22

PARALLELS OF CONQUEST, PAST AND PRESENT

After the bloody Battle of Hastings in 1066, William the Conqueror's army of Norman invaders buried its fallen comrades, but left the mangled corpses of the Anglo-Saxon defenders to rot in the fields. Wounded defenders were mutilated.

William's "Shock and Awe" invasion quickly turned into a brutal occupation. The pacification strategy, like America's today, was to eliminate the enemy's leadership and terrorize the civilian population into submission. Colonization is murderous work.

Anglo-Saxon lords had their eyes plucked out and their hands and feet cut off, and were left in chains in front of their castles for the peasants to behold. Others were castrated and thrown into the dungeon in one of the hundreds of castles William built across the countryside to defend Norman interests.

The pacification campaign took 20 years. During that period, an estimated 300,000 indigenous peoples were murdered and starved to death (one fifth of the population) and an equal number of French and Norman entrepreneurs and bureaucrats were planted in England in vacant positions of authority.

The entire Anglo-Saxon nobility was exterminated. William took all their property and gave it to the Norman upper class. By the time William repented his sins on his deathbed in 1087, England had been totally transformed.

Such is the beastly nature of colonial war: the victor inflicts all manner of suffering and humiliation on the vanquished, and steals everything they own.

Nearly a millennium later, the United States is doing the same thing in Iraq and Afghanistan. The only difference is that William the Conqueror bragged about his brutal theft of another nation and its wealth, while America's ruling class cloaks its barbarism and plunder under a veil of good intentions and self-defense.

When accepting his Nobel Peace Prize, President Obama put on the Don Vito act and said with a straight face: "I believe the United States of America must remain a standard bearer in the conduct of war. That is what makes us different from those whom we fight. That is a source of our strength. That is why I prohibited torture. That is why I ordered the prison at Guantanamo Bay closed. And that is why I have reaffirmed America's commitment to abide by the Geneva Conventions."

All lies. From Thanh Phong to Ghazi Khan and a thousand villages in between, American "boys" have been slaughtering Muslim civilians as part of vicious pacification campaigns in nations that pose no threat to the United States. Guantanamo remains open, and CIA officers continue to torture Muslims there and in dozens of dungeons around the globe, hidden in CIA compounds on military bases, in secret police safe houses, and on US Navy vessels. Boasting like William the Conqueror, Ultras in the United States trumpet their disdain for international laws, the United Nations, and the Geneva Conventions. Due process for citizens in American colonies is non-existent, and will soon evaporate in the US too.

While the US-led occupations of Iraq and Afghanistan are different in minor details, there are disturbing parallels in the extent of the carnage and the strategy of coercion, in the innocent blood that has flowed and the number of survivors who have been tormented, tortured and terrorized.

Just as William the Conqueror ignored the English battlefield dead, the US government has not publicly identified – nor even estimated – the number of Iraqis, Afghanis, Libyans and Syrians it has killed, or caused to be killed, during its invasions, occupations, and CIA-led insurgencies. Neither is anyone in the media publicly counting the number of Muslims the US has killed, crippled, rendered homeless, starved, driven into poverty and despair, and/or condemned to disease and insanity.

US government officials say they are "looking away" as a means of avoiding the "body count" mindset that incentivized ambitious CIA and military personnel to commit mass murder during the Vietnam War. But "looking away" also makes it impossible to quantitatively measure the amount of misery US policymakers are wreaking on civilian populations in nations they have ravaged since 9/11.

The lack of official numbers also enables the US government to cast doubt on unofficial estimates that put the number of Iraqi dead alone in the hundreds of thousands or possibly over one million. Most reports in the mainstream US news media cite much lower estimates, to avoid offending the powers-that-be in Washington.

Out of the Press

As much as possible, US leaders have sought to keep the ugliness of these wars – the mangled bodies, the burned-off faces, the squalid refugee camps, the abused captives – out of the press and away from the public's consciousness, in order to preserve the pretense of moral superiority that defines American "exceptionalism."

One advantage of having no official casualty estimates and few photos of atrocities in Muslim nations is that the American people aren't reminded of the horrendous consequences of the wars of aggression launched by Presidents Bush and Obama. Making Americans feel good about their wars is a top priority of American politicians. By suppressing the human toll and censoring the press, the Bush regime was able to sell the wars against Afghanistan and Iraq as benefiting the Afghani and Iraqi people.

That fiction has been thoroughly dispelled by the rise of ISIS from the heap of ashes that once was Iraqi and Syrian culture. Raised in America's gulag archipelago of detention and torture centers, many young Muslim men know nothing about the world they have inherited except oppression and injustice. No wonder they are filled with rage.

However manipulated or "protected" by the West insofar as its actions further unstated US goals, ISIS remains a manifestation of the intense suffering America has visited upon the Muslim peoples of North Africa, the Middle East and Central Asia. And yet the American media is able to shield our criminal leaders and allow them to avoid "residual responsibility" by blaming the rage of Muslim men on the nature of Islam, while always casting American methods and motives in a positive light.

That is one big difference between the slaughter of Englishmen by William the Conqueror and the carnage unleashed by Bush and Obama and Hillary Clinton, our modern-day conquistadors. William's cruelty was done in the light of day. Our brave leaders rely on prevarication, stealth, and manufacturing complicity.

Truth be told, the US government does keep tabs on those it kills, maims, and renders as orphans. It simply doesn't want the American people to know the quantity or the specifics, as a way of stripping the human dimensions from its actual war against Islam.

In Afghanistan, for example, the CIA and military have conducted a census of every village, town and city in the country – much like William's infamous Domesday Book, which assessed the property (including tenant farmers) of every English landowner for the purpose of levying taxes or confiscation. And don't forget the extensive corporate studies on profitable Afghan resources. As reported in the 14 June 2010 *New York Times*, "The previously unknown deposits — including huge veins of iron, copper, cobalt, gold and critical industrial metals like lithium — are so big and include so many minerals that are essential to modern industry that Afghanistan could eventually be transformed into one of the most important mining centers in the world, the United States officials believe.

"An internal Pentagon memo, for example, states that Afghanistan could become the 'Saudi Arabia of lithium,' a key raw material in the manufacture of batteries for laptops and BlackBerrys.

"The vast scale of Afghanistan's mineral wealth was discovered by a small team of Pentagon officials and American geologists. The Afghan government and President Hamid Karzai were recently briefed, American officials said."[1]

Likewise, the commanders of the US occupation armies know the name of every Afghan, Iraqi, Libyan, and Syrian property owner, so their analysts can decide who is a collaborator and might be spared, and who, in the vague vernacular favored by Hollywood-obsessed Americans, are the "bad guys." The bad guys are invariably robbed and their businesses plundered. US businessmen wait in the wings, like Joe Biden's son in Ukraine, to gobble up the spoils.

The facts are all there; but one needs to dig deeper than network news.

Tracking the Taliban

Through their ongoing surveys, American war managers determine where each man lives, how many people are in his family, who his wife and children and relatives are, where he works and where his property is. In places like Marjah, a Taliban stronghold in Afghanistan where a US-led offensive unfolded in 2010, the CIA and military obtain actionable intelligence through their dubious networks of spies, as well as via electronic surveillance, including satellites. This biographical information about Afghanis is entered into a computer at occupation headquarters, where the material is painstakingly monitored by the CIA and military special operations units for High Value targets and targets of opportunity, including business opportunity.

Within a separate folder for suspected Taliban, every man is categorized by his rank and position within the organization. His valuable possessions are also known.

Low-level fighters are left to the blue-collar Marines, while High Value targets are handled by CIA and military special operations forces, and their acquisitive collaborators in Afghanistan's warlord upper class. High Value targets get the kind of special attention William the Conqueror reserved for English noblemen, whose possessions the Normans coveted.

Make no mistake about it: High Value targets in Afghanistan own the property (intellectual as well as material, including opium fields) that America's colonial administrators wish to own and share with their collaborators. As a result, much more biographical information is gathered about property owners than non-property owners, and their movements are tracked 24 hours a day, seven days a week.

Through their spies and sophisticated electronic surveillance devices, CIA and military commanders have a very good idea when "High Value" targets are leaving one safe house and traveling to another. The jets are fueled, the drones are in the sky, and the black choppers are fueled and waiting.

This is how and why 27 Afghan civilians were slaughtered on 21 February 2010, while traveling between remote provinces in a caravan of minibuses. The CIA and military special operations forces were alerted that some "High Value" target was traveling with his family, and General Stanley McChrystal seized the opportunity to kill them all.

For despite their alleged disinterest in "body count", the CIA exists solely to start wars, and military commanders like McChrystal solely to kill in them, so American businessmen can steal everything they own. The only way for individual CIA and military officers to succeed, and become wealthy warlords, is to show piles of dead bodies, like the English corpses laid out at Hastings.

In dirty wars like the ones in Afghanistan, Iraq, Libya and Syria, killing "High Value" targets almost always means murdering them while they are at home or while traveling with their families. Despite the spin, it is official if unstated policy, for the killing of a nation's leaders, along with their entire families, has a devastating psychological-warfare impact on the rest of society.

The mainstream US news media plays along by never citing this central fact of US dirty wars. The killing of civilians is always dismissed as accidental, and is always accompanied by a routine apology from some anonymous US spokesperson whose facts cannot be challenged because they are classified, and, it is said, to release them might put Americans at risk (of being tried for war crimes).

Most of all, killing important leaders along with their families makes it easier to buy their vacated property at ten percent of its value – always a perk for American geologists and the US occupation army's corporate camp followers.

Savagery, Past and Present

Though US media propagandists treat CIA and military commanders as honorable "warriors" doing the hard work necessary to protect America, the truth is that they are no less savage than William the Conqueror or the ISIS militants demonized for atrocities. Both spread terror by killing their enemies, dismembering bodies and inflicting death and cruelty on non-combatants as well. One needs only to see the bodies mutilated by missiles fired from drones or helicopter gunships.

Rhode Island Senator Jack Reed, patron of Textron Systems and the senior Democrat on the Senate Armed Services and Intelligence committees, is a typical American businessman in his blue suit and red tie, with his manicured finger nails and distinguished white hair, selling 15,000 pound Daisy Cutters to Saudi Arabia for use in Yemen. Daisy Cutters were perfected in Vietnam and Afghanistan, and brought huge profits to many members of Reed's enterprising class.

The only difference between them and William the Conqueror,

is that the Norman leaders actually fought alongside their men, unlike American chicken-hawk politicians. William and his army did their killing up close with battle axes and swords for everyone to see, while American politicians and their high-tech killing machines inflict their carnage from far away with 2,000-pound bombs – and then cloak the horror behind censorship and propaganda.

These cover-ups are essential; otherwise the American public might resist Washington's imperial adventures, which often end up with working-class American soldiers dead or maimed while invisible US corporate bosses slither away with valuable resources from the conquered countries or otherwise use them for economic or geopolitical ends.

This strategy works because most Americans don't know – and many don't care to know – the names and biographies of their victims.

Chapter 23

PROPAGANDA
AS TERRORISM

Interviewer's Note: Author Douglas Valentine says that the United States does not abide by any of its international obligations and its calls for war against Syria violate international law and the UN Charter.

"The US has threatened about 50 nations with military attack. Warmongers on the left and right claim this right on the basis that America is an 'exceptional' nation. That means the US is an exception to all laws. It is the policeman of the world and policemen don't obey laws; they enforce them on others," said Douglas Valentine in an exclusive interview with the Fars News Agency.

What follows is the text of FNA's October 2013 interview with Mr. Valentine on the ongoing crisis in Syria and the US war threats against it. The interview has been updated, but is meant as a general overview, not a comprehensive review of all events.

KOUROSH ZIABARI: The US war rhetoric on Syria looms large these days, and despite the agreement between the United States and Russia to bring Syria's chemical weapons under the UN safeguards (as well as the ceasefire agreement arranged by Secretary of State John Kerry and Russian Foreign Minister Sergei Lavrov in September 2016), some extremist neo-cons in the US Congress and administration are continuing to call for a military strike against Syria. (Indeed, on 17-18 September, US and British military forces sought to undermine the ceasefire agreement by bombing Syrian army forcess against US and

Israeli-backed ISIS forces.) Why does the United States persist on its hawkish policies? Hasn't it learned a lesson from its previous military adventures in Afghanistan, Iraq and Libya?

VALENTINE: America's greatest strength is its vast military forces and intelligence services. This is what makes America the dominant world power, not its diplomatic corps, which serves primarily as a stalking horse. Americans identify with and celebrate their military prowess, their many wars, and their honored war dead. The extremist neo-cons were the group most associated with this militant ethic in America, but the Democratic Party under hawkish Hillary Clinton has adopted the same ethic. In order to win the support of the thoroughly brainwashed American public, this protected group of war profiteers portrays themselves as the guardians of America's prestige, which is symbolized by the military, which in turn is always viewed as heroic.

For its part, the military's inclination is to always call for action, in high hopes of accommodating its financial backers and prospective employers in the US arms industry, which needs to expend ammunition and constantly develop new weapons in order to make profits. There are always vocal exceptions, but the policy has been in place for generations and advances on a specific course like an aircraft carrier fleet, which can only be tweaked and never driven off course.

It is more complex than that, of course. There are also the dynamics of American culture to consider – the sense many Americans have that they are "exceptional" and destined to rule with an iron fist a world that is hostile to the "American Way." Donald Trump is the popular manifestation of this "America as victim" delusion. It is the "lie in the soul" that enables America to project its collective "shadow" on "the other."

This has been recognized for decades. On 4 April 1967, Dr. Martin Luther King, Jr. delivered his famous "Beyond Vietnam" speech at the Riverside Church. Citing a "very obvious and almost facile connection between the war in Vietnam and the struggle I and others have been waging in America," King said he had moved into "an even deeper level of awareness," through which he realized that he "could never again raise my voice against the violence of the oppressed in the ghettos without having first spoken clearly to the greatest purveyor of violence in the world today: my own government."

The speech was considered treachery by America's Ultras, and a year later King was dead – assassinated allegedly by a petty criminal, a "lone gunman" who had been paid by a cabal of Mafioso and Southern racists, while under 24 hour a day surveillance by the FBI, military intelligence and local police forces.

On 7 May 1970, the eminent British historian Arnold Toynbee put his life on the line when he said in *The New York Times*: "For the whole world, the CIA has now become the bogey that Communism has been for America. Wherever there is trouble, violence, suffering, tragedy, the rest of us are now quick to suspect the CIA had a hand in it." Toynbee was responding to Henry Kissinger's barbaric invasion of Cambodia. "In fact," Toynbee continued, "the roles of America and Russia have been reversed in the world's eye. Today America has become the world's nightmare."

For many years even the so-called left believed America was in a life and death struggle with the Soviet Union. This Cold War was fought largely in the Third World, though the Americans were conducting all manner of covert political actions in Europe as well, to assure that no industrial state would emerge as a threat to its economic interests there. Average Americans believed they were fighting "totalitarian" communism in Africa, for example, while in reality, the capitalist elite was suppressing nationalism and independent economic policies of emerging states that favored their domestic development. We were stealing their wealth and resources, but it had to be done in way that assuaged the public. So the job was given to the CIA. The CIA, covered by complicit media, still and in greater force operates in the shadows as a projection of the dark, rapacious side of the American psyche.

With the rise of the "fundamentalists" in Iran in 1979, and the demise of the Soviet Union ten years later, America's ruling elite has been able to redirect the energies of the American people away from Communist and Socialist nations toward Muslim nations – all of which are stigmatized as inscrutable, inferior and hostile.

The Holy Crusade against Islam, and the attendant wave of manufactured hatred sweeping America, began when Richard Perle and a cabal of pro-Israeli neo-cons in the Bush Administration's Office of Special Plans grabbed control of the Mighty Wurlitzer, the CIA's propaganda machine (see Chapter 20), after 9/11. They created the conditions for neo-colonial imperialism, in order to ensure Israel's ability to appropriate Palestinian land, and to prevent the Russians and Iranians from exerting any influence in the Middle East. Through a carefully orchestrated propaganda campaign, assisted by the Israeli Lobby and other ideologically attuned organizations, they trained the American people to love the song Trump is singing out loud: ban Muslims and Mexican immigrants. This nativist call to arms against "the Other" encompasses black Americans, whose struggles for equality are still resented by a large percentage of Americans. Sixty years after King brought the Civil Rights movement into mainstream American politics, blacks are still being gunned down by cops and confined to segregated communities.

The hatred is visceral and ubiquitous. Trump symbolizes the imbedded racism within America. Make America Great Again means make America white again. The racists are proud of it. In order for an individual to lead America, he or she must represent this supremacist "might is right" ethic. It is part of the irreversible strategic course I referred to early in my aircraft carrier fleet allusion; National Security in the United States is equated with white supremacy. It always will be.

The entire strategy is wrapped in lies and deceptions and double standards. During an address to Dartmouth College in May 2015, Hillary Clinton defined Iran as an "existential" threat to Israel and promised that as president she would happily "obliterate" Iran if Israel's protection required it. She made this statement despite the fact that Iran has no nuclear weapons and Israel has 200, all of which, as former secretary of state Colin Powell observed, are pointed at Iran. If that isn't an existential threat, nothing is.

Clinton has also expressed her willingness to use cluster bombs and toxic agents as well as nuclear weapons. She is also a proponent of Bush's "first-strike" policy. As Secretary of State she proved her militancy by destroying Libya and chiding Obama for not doing likewise to Syria. She is truly vicious, but that's what Americans want in a leader.

I'll give you an example. While having my teeth cleaned recently, I asked the hygienist how her son was doing. She said he was in the Air Force repairing fighter planes in Saudi Arabia. I asked her how she felt about that. With no compunctions or self-awareness, she said, "Better to kill them over there before they kill us here."

She represents the prevailing sentiment. Only a very few enlightened individuals are aware of the problem, and they are incapable of preventing the rich political elite from seeking a military solution to every problem the CIA provokes. As our strutting leaders love to proclaim, they rule the world and there's nothing anyone can do about it.

As President Putin said in an Op-Ed for *The New York Times*, America's elite increasingly relies on brute force to get what it wants. And what it wants is to assert its power and to control all other nations of the world. The political elite must also accommodate its financial backers in the Israeli Lobby and arms industry. There is certainly a lot of outside pressure on America from various nations. But most of the so-called left has been assimilated and is as dedicated to these supremacist ends as the Ultras are, as the achievement of these ends validates their sense of superiority and enables them to prosper.

Seen from this perspective, the wars in Iraq, Libya, Afghanistan, Somalia, Sudan and Syria are going just fine. America has destroyed any significant progress those nations had made in education, healthcare, infrastructure such as water treatment and electricity, postal services, courts. By degrading the standards of living for people in perceived "hostile" nations, America's ruling elite empowers itself, while claiming that it has ensured the safety and prestige of the American people. Sometimes it is even able to convince the public that its criminal actions are "humanitarian" and designed to liberate the people in nations it destroys.

ZIABARI: In recent days, and especially after the United States discarded its plans for attacking Syria following its agreement with Russia concerning chemical weapons (this occurred in September 2013), more attention has been paid to the role of Iran in resolving the crisis in Syria and bringing to an end the almost three-year civil war in the Arab country. The United States has so far refused to accept that Iran should be included in the comprehensive international talks about Syria, but a number of American newspapers and TV channels are suggesting that Iran needs to be part of the talks for finding a solution to the Syrian dilemma. What's your viewpoint about the role Iran can play in ending the violence and unrest in Syria?

VALENTINE: The US has not discarded its plans to destabilize Syria and oust Assad. It never will. The equation changed when Russia interceded and began attacking ISIS. That led to a tenuous ceasefire in early 2016, in which Iran and other regional players had a voice. But it was an exercise in futility, as Obama was by then a lame duck, and John Kerry was viewed as giving away the store by the entrenched National Security Establishment, which will never accept any Russian influence in the region. Russia still attacked ISIS, and the CIA and America's client Arab states still armed and supported anti-Assad forces. Ultimately the US military took matters into its own hands, as it tends to do when a new administration is waiting in the wings, and it bombed Syrian army forces, killing and wounding dozens.

As it always does, the US propaganda machine characterized this terrorist attack as "a mistake," but the results speak for themselves. The US National Security Establishment does not follow international law and reserves the right to kill as many people as it wants, without any consequences, and without acknowledging it is policy.

Having said that, I'm unaware of the plans and strategies of Iran's ruling elite. I assume there are conflicting forces in determining those plans and strategies. It's my understanding that Iran publicly backs Assad, as does Russia, and that Iran seeks to help Assad defeat the rebels, many of whom are foreign mercenaries trained and financed by the CIA, Israel, Jordan, Turkey and Saudi Arabia. I assume Iran will impose its will on the situation to whatever extent it can, whether through direct negotiations, indirect negotiations, or in the absence of negotiations.

In view of its having sabotaged Kerry's ceasefire, it is obvious that the National Security Establishment is unwilling to negotiate an end to the crisis. It created the crisis as part of a long term strategy to defend Israel and help effectuate its racist, expansionist policies, while gobbling up the region's resources and countering Russian influence. America does not recognize Syria's sovereignty, and has violated that sovereignty for years through covert action and its support for the mercenary armies attacking Syria.

Iran ought to be officially involved in negotiations around Syria's fate. But if history is any indicator, the US is an unreliable negotiating partner. Some American national security officials and politicians might accept Iranian participation in negotiations, but only as window dressing and a cover for more covert political actions. It's hard to know what Trump would do, but I suspect he would become a willing captive of the National Security Establishment.

We know Hillary Clinton won't deal honestly with Iran and will only accept a deal that leaves Syria in the same hellhole the Palestinians inhabit. Trump said he didn't want to create more refugees, but Clinton keeps calling for regime change in Syria. Her policies created the conditions that sent Syrian refugees pouring into Europe, with the result that certain European nations are destabilized and Syria no longer poses a threat to

Israel, which has pretty much annexed the Golan Heights. Obama and Secretary of State John Kerry are marginalized, and Syria has been totally destabilized as Hillary Clinton intended when she started the insurgency.

We have seen the US and Iran reach an agreement. Iran agreed to abandon its nuclear weapons program and the US agreed in return not to "obliterate" Iran as Clinton threatened. But Iran has still not agreed to the partition of Syria and that could sweep the old agreements away. To that end the US and its regional allies continue to engage in covert actions and maintain sanctions against Iran, in hopes of provoking a response that will give the Ultras, under Trump or Clinton, a "green light" to attack Iran in one way or another.

Remember, the US elites do not consider Iran to be a sovereign nation. It was an American colony from the CIA's 1953 coup d'état and installation of the Shah until 1979, when students, leftists and Islamists tossed him out. But the US National Security Establishment hasn't forgiven that blow to its prestige; and prestige, as I mentioned earlier, is the ambiguous measure for all policy decisions. It will never forgive Russia for the same reason. It still thinks Iran is a colony, like a slave that temporarily escaped into Mexico. The US won't negotiate honestly with a former colony, so what purpose would negotiations serve?

ZIABARI: There have been extensive reports indicating that Saudi Arabia, Israel, Jordan and Qatar were involved in supplying chemical weapons and illicit materials to the rebels in Damascus and other Syrian cities. With such weapons, the rebels would be able to destabilize Syria and sponsor insecurity and unrest there. Why don't the international organizations take action to stop them and their dangerous actions?

VALENTINE: By "international organizations," I assume you mean the UN and Human Rights Watch. I'm not sure why these organizations adhere to the American "line" that Assad's forces are responsible, when even Ultra pundits like Rush Limbaugh accused Obama of staging the chemical attacks as a provocation. The simple answer, I suppose, is that the CIA has suborned top officials in these international organizations. We know the NSA spies on everyone, and that the NSA passes information to the CIA. Perhaps these officials have been bribed or blackmailed. There is certainly enough corruption to go around. Others may have aligned with the US for ideological reasons. There is certainly no objectivity, or even a pretense of objectivity. The World Court and ICC don't do anything against the US for the same reasons. To look to international organizations for relief is ridiculous.

ZIABARI: According to the French Interior Minister Manuel Valls, in 2013 there were 110 French terrorists fighting the government of President Bashar al-Assad in Syria. This meant that half of the European combatants taking part in the civil war in Syria, at the time, came from France. Some commentators suggest that France is looking for ways to regain its colonial dominance over Syria, and that is why President Francois Hollande continually pushed for a war against Syria. What's your viewpoint on that?

VALENTINE: If history is any indicator, that is correct. A century ago, France persuaded the Czar to mobilize against Germany, after Germany had finally reached an agreement with Russia. It was this action taken with the consent of the British government that ultimately triggered the Great War.

France's elite are economically and ideologically aligned with the US and UK elites, against socialism anywhere, and against nationalism in other nations seeking sovereignty. And that includes the Socialist Party. It is a major colonial power. France wants its colonies (along with the wealth that colonialism entails) and prestige back. It has never given up control of the Algerian army, just like the US continues to control the South Korean military. The UK was the primary fighter in Libya.

Hollande is a socialist when he runs for office, but like every other French president, governs like an imperialist. On 17 July 2016, using CIA intelligence, France slaughtered 120 civilians in Syria.[1] It was a symbolic gesture done to avenge the killing of dozens of people in Nice by a non-practicing Muslim from Tunisia. There was no other reason to attack Syria.

The flood of Syrian refuges into Europe, the attack on the Charlie Hebdo cartoonists in Paris in 2015, the bombings in Brussels in 2016, and finally Nice, have been used by French and American propagandists as an excuse for imperial aggression. Islamophobia is reaching a crescendo in France. "French Minister Bernard Cazeneuve said they will start shutting down mosques that preach hate and violence. They will check all the mosques and imams in France."[2]

Trump and his nativist faction want to do the same thing in America.

ZIABARI: According to the UN Charter and the General Treaty for Renunciation of War as an Instrument of National Policy, to which the US is a signatory, the unilateral use of military force, or threatening to use force against a sovereign nation is illegal and a violation of international law. However, the US has repeatedly threatened Syria with a military strike, and no international organization has raised its voice to protest the US calls for war. What do you think in this regard?

VALENTINE: The US has threatened about 50 nations with military attack. American militants on the left and right claim this right on the basis that America is an "exceptional" nation. Meaning international laws don't apply to it. It is the policeman of the world and, as everyone knows, policemen don't obey laws; they enforce them on others.

There is nothing anyone can do about it. The US has a monopoly on force. Sovereignty is the key issue from the standpoint of international organizations and international law. But it is impossible for the UN to acknowledge that America engages in aggression within the meaning of the act because 1) the US can intimidate enough UN members and 2) the UN itself has a long history of intervention, going back to Korea and the Congo. The UN is largely an instrument of US foreign policy.

ZIABARI: If you look at what many former US officials and intelligence executives say, you'll find that many of them are opposed to a US military strike against Syria. They argue that the United States does not have the legal or political authority; that it's not Washington's business to do the tasks of an international policeman. Do you agree?

VALENTINE: What does it matter what I think, or they think, or what the laws say? If it wishes, the United States can rain death and destruction down on Syria, simply through its air and naval power. It can do to Syria what was done to Libya. It can do what Israel did in 2009 in Gaza, and did again in 2014.

Sure, the US regime has no legal authority to do anything in Syria. But it is already violating international law by giving weapons to the so-called rebels. The US military and the CIA will do what they are told to do. The job of CIA officers is to follow illegal orders, to provoke a crisis. I don't trust anything former military or intelligence officers say – even when I agree with them – because they tend to couch subtle deceptions and ulterior motives in their statements. They say one thing and secretly do another.

ZIABARI: Some analysts and critics of the US foreign policy say that the US is adopting a hypocritical attitude toward the concept of terrorism by supporting and arming the al Qaeda and ISIS-aligned mercenaries fighting in Syria, while it has launched its project of War on Terror with the purported aim of dismantling the same al Qaeda and ISIS organizations which the United States considers a threat to global peace. Why is the United States behaving in such an insincere manner?

VALENTINE: The "War on Terror" is a monumental fraud, the greatest covert operation ever. As recently reported in Russia Today, Obama waived America's own anti-terrorism provisions to arm its mercenaries in Syria, a process the CIA has been managing for five years anyway, the way it manages the international trade in illicit drugs. Reagan called CIA-backed terrorists in Nicaragua "Freedom Fighters." It just goes on and on.

Al Qaeda and ISIS provide America with a pretext to intervene in every Muslim nation in the world, and to wage preemptive wars, as promulgated on 20 September 2002 in the "National Security Strategy of the United States." That's the imperial "first strike" strategy Hillary Clinton has embraced.

Al Qaeda and ISIS also provide mercenaries to topple governments, like Syria's, that the US does not like.

The US has really never been "against" al Qaeda. The CIA created al Qaeda in Afghanistan as a force against the Soviets, and has used factions of al Qaeda to fight in Chechnya, Kosovo, Bosnia, and other places. The US has created a colonial army of mercenaries much like the British did with their Nepalese Gurkhas. The US mercenaries are from all over the Muslim world. They are fighting in Africa right now. This is the US proxy army worldwide, trained by US Special Forces under CIA control.

Ultimately, the term al Qaeda is an empty vessel used to tell whatever story the US government needs to tell to justify its wars to its own people. Orwell described the phenomenon very well: *1984* is full of war reporting where the allies and enemies are constantly changing from day to day. The terms friend and foe ceased to have any recognizable meaning for those watching the TV screen. That's where we are today.

ZIABARI: Iran and Russia say that diplomacy is the best way to deal with the crisis in Syria and eradicate extremism and fanaticism in the

Arab country, but the United States hasn't so far allowed diplomacy and dialogue to work. Why is it insisting on a military solution to the crisis in Syria while a negotiated solution through a comprehensive national dialogue can solve all the problems?

VALENTINE: The US does not negotiate unless a preponderance of compels it to do so. Consider the events at the US Embassy in Tehran in 1980. Reagan famously refused to negotiate with terrorists, even while secretly selling arms to Iran, as part of a policy to destabilize Iraq and Iran on behalf of Israel. The reality of CIA and MOSSAD support for SAVAK, or the fact that the Shah allowed the CIA to use Iranian nationals and territory to spy in Russia was never mentioned. All that mattered were the photographs of Americans bound and blindfolded and being held as hostages.

All that matters is that Americans have died in Iraq, Afghanistan and Libya. When pushed into a corner as to why she was instrumental in and celebrated the murder of Qaddafi, Hillary Clinton forgets all about the "humanitarian intervention" cover story. All that mattered was that Qaddafi, she said, had blood on his hands. As if she doesn't.

Reconciliation and negotiations are impossible when a nation is committed solely to dominance and vengeance. They are merely tactical maneuvers in a bigger game.

The American war against Syria and its covert actions against Iran are part of a larger strategy to weaken and encircle Russia. The US is insisting on a military solution because it believes that Iran and Russia will ultimately sacrifice Syria to avoid war with the US. Syria is just another domino about to fall.

The goal of the American elite is to make Syria, and then Iran, and then Russia join the ranks of Korea, Vietnam, Afghanistan, Libya and Iraq. The plan is to smash it into ethnic and religious lines, and to fuel fighting between these groups for many years.

Time will tell if I'm right.

Chapter 24

THE WAR ON TERROR AS THE GREATEST COVERT OP EVER

The War on Terror is the greatest covert operation ever. In explaining why, I'll begin by defining some terms, because, when discussing business, politics and terrorism, word management is all important.

The FBI defines terrorism as "the unlawful use of force and violence against persons or property to intimidate or coerce a government, the civilian population, or any segment thereof, in furtherance of political or social objectives."

Clearly, this ambiguous definition begs the question, when is terrorism lawful?

The US Government's stated policy regarding terrorism is well known. It always condemns terrorism, and accordingly, America is never a perpetrator of terrorism, but always a victim of it. The War on Terror is the ultimate expression of this stated policy: it is lawful violence in self-defense – not unlawful violence by a non-state actor – for a political or social purpose.

That is the stated policy, incessantly hammered into the dim American collective consciousness by Pentagon and State Department saturation ad campaigns. But if one looks behind the suffocating cloak of secrecy, censorship and propaganda that surrounds the government's unstated policies, an entirely different story emerges about deliberate war crimes against humanity, committed on a massive scale.

Like Diogenes with his lantern held high, I visited the FBI office in Springfield, Massachusetts on 21 November 2012. I didn't have an appointment, but one of the resident agents agreed to listen to me. My intent was to make him respond to evidence of the CIA's engagement in and support for terrorism in Syria. To that end, I cited a 21 June 2012 *New York Times* article stating that, "A small number of C.I.A. officers are operating secretly in southern Turkey, helping allies decide which Syrian opposition fighters across the border will receive arms to fight the Syrian government, according to American officials and Arab intelligence officers."[1]

I asked the FBI agent if the article wasn't proof that CIA officers were engaged in terrorism. Not only was CIA violence designed to overthrow the Syrian government, it was driving thousands of civilians into poverty, ruin, early graves, and the despair of exile. And while the President and Congress undoubtedly gave the CIA legal authority to overthrow the Syrian government, its violence against innocent Syrian civilians was certainly illegal, yes?

I added that, according to *The Times*, CIA officers arranged for tons of weapons to be smuggled across the Turkish border "by way of a shadowy network of intermediaries" that included "jihadists" the US government itself identified as terrorists. Apart from managing a criminal conspiracy within the illegal arms and drugs smuggling network, I said, the CIA's arming of al Qaeda constituted support for terrorism, even if the US media kindly refers to CIA-sponsored terrorists in Syria as "rebels".

The flabbergasted FBI agent referred me to FBI headquarters, and after a lot of artful dodging, FBI spokeswoman Kathleen Wright threw in the towel and said, "With regarding to questions about the CIA, or USG policy related to the CIA, that is not within *our lane* [my italics] to answer."

In other words, the nation's premier law enforcement entity has no legal authority over the CIA. And only within the context of this institutionalized double-standard can the profitable business of American terrorism be properly understood.

As I hope to show in this chapter, the CIA is the preferred weapon in this international criminal enterprise, because it conducts its terrorism secretly and you never know about it. And when revealed accidentally (like in the recent Gülen "flap", or for propaganda purposes), CIA terrorism is always equated with national security. When defined as extra-legal self-defense, it is called counterterrorism.

The CIA manages the international arms trade like it manages the drug trade, through a covert army of mercenaries from every nation, all of whom are homicidal maniacs with combat experience and a thirst for more of it. During the Vietnam War, the CIA paramilitary officers in charge of this army were called "knuckle-draggers." The mercenary army is supported by "deep cover" CIA finance officers operating offshore banks like Nugan Hand; "deep cover" logistics officers like Ed Wilson running proprietary and deniable shipping companies; and foreign intelligence staff officers within the CIA's back-channel counterterror network corrupting strategically placed military officers and special policemen (often trained at American schools) as well as politicians who then provide safe passage for drug traffickers and black sites for torture as needed – all compartmentalized and managed by the big bosses at CIA Central.

CIA officers and their political bosses are never punished for engaging in terrorism. As we recently learned, they even get away with planting plastic explosives in a Virginia school bus. It was a "training" exercise we are told. But why are CIA officers trained to plant explosives in school buses?[2]

Because once you enter the CIA, the rest of us, even school kids, are either lab rats or cannon fodder, as far as the CIA is concerned.

Psychological Warfare and Covert Operations

Politics is said to be the process by which people make collective decisions. But who really makes the overarching political decisions in America? Who makes terrorism policy?

America is ostensibly a nation of laws, but our elected officials in Congress, the nation's premier law making body, have exempted CIA officers engaged in terrorism from federal laws aimed at terrorists. When CIA officers are revealed to be engaged in terrorism, as in Syria, the media does its job and follows the script. It never reveals the contradictions that permit state-sponsored terrorism.

The continued existence of this Big Lie is truly phenomenal, given the mass of available evidence exposing it. Yet it is applied systematically, without exception, as the essential feature of spectacular domination, with the desired effect: a majority of Americans not only believe it, they applaud it. They believe that CIA officers engage in terrorism to protect *them*. Convincing them of this is the greatest covert operation ever.

As Carl Jung said, "Everyone carries a shadow, and the less it is embodied in the individual's conscious life, the blacker and denser it is."

The Business Party that rules America has helped to impose this mass psychosis on its customers and consumers. It is essential to perpetuating the capitalist system, in which one percent of the population possesses most of the nation's wealth. Should the people emerge from the shadows of self-deception, and stop projecting their irrationality onto others, the house of cards would collapse.

In order to maintain the fiction that America does not engage in terrorism, the government and media, on behalf of big business, deceive the public in a variety of practiced ways that can best be discerned and understood if viewed as a standard covert action program.

The CIA will only launch a covert action if it meets two criteria. First it must have "intelligence potential". It must be able to gain knowledge that allows it to shape events that advance its plans and objectives. For example, smuggling arms to terrorists in Syria allows CIA officers to gather intelligence on military and criminal activity in the region. Other times the "intelligence potential" involves knowing things that allow CIA officers to influence masses of people psychologically as a means of managing political and social movements at home and, like ISIS, abroad.

The second criterion of a covert action program is "plausible deniability". In 1975, during Senate hearings into CIA assassination plots against foreign leaders, "plausible denial" was defined by the CIA's deputy director of operations as the use of circumlocution and euphemism in discussions where precise definitions would expose covert actions and bring them to an end. Legalized double standards fall into this category, as does the entire range of government disinformation and propaganda.

A standard covert action program is buried in layers of cover stories. As Winston Churchill (and later Joe Pesci) famously said, "it's a mystery wrapped in a riddle inside an enigma." Churchill also said that, "In wartime, truth is so precious that she should always be attended by a bodyguard of lies."

As I've explained elsewhere, CIA operations are often disguised as "civic action programs" designed to help people, like the vaccination program in Pakistan that led to the assassination of Osama bin Laden, or the CIA's Phoenix program in Vietnam, which advertised itself as "protecting the people from terrorism."

Covert actions directed against the American people also

meet these two criteria: they advance the government's unstated plans and can be plausibly denied. They are largely psychological, although "accidental" deaths have been known to occur. They occur in the realm of consciousness, and are simultaneously abstract and determinant.

The government wages psywar against the American public in various ways for various purposes. The CIA plants deceptive articles in foreign newspapers, like the recent Panama Papers leak. Domestic media are notified and dutifully report the stories. Such disinformation, or "black propaganda" when the stories are false, creates false perceptions that generate public support for military actions or economic sanctions against foreign governments the US government wishes to subvert. Other times, it assures Americans that abusive regimes like Israel, Egypt and Saudi Arabia are worthy of massive tax-funded aid programs. In either case, language is the key to creating perceptions and assumptions that justify immoral or illegal policies the American public would otherwise repudiate as state terrorism.

Through language that deceives, intimidates and coerces, the US government's covert action programs are ultimately designed to terrorize Americans – to make them feel inferior, infantile and powerless. This is the shadow side of the propaganda that makes them feel exceptional, of their vicarious enjoyment of being Number One; they are also made to feel victimized, and the resulting confusion makes them governable in detrimental ways they would not choose, if they knew the truth."

The CIA, of course, is not the only branch of government that engages in disinformation. It happens across the board. What is important is to be able to recognize the modus operandi and, in particular, the language used to conceal bad intent. What is not said is often more telling than what is said.

The war on Iraq is the premier example. Needing a pretext to launch a war of aggression to seize Iraq's oil and destabilize the region on behalf of Israel, the Bush regime launched a disinformation campaign to convince Americans that Iraq posed an existential threat. To this end it planted false stories such as the one that Iraq possessed a stockpile of "yellow cake" uranium that would result in an imminent "mushroom cloud" in America.

The Bush administration's "mushroom cloud" descriptor terrorized the public, as did a *New York Times* article by Chris Hedges citing claims by defectors that Iraq was training terrorists to attack America. The defectors were fabricating, of course, on behalf of their

CIA masters, just as there was no "yellow cake" being made into nuclear weapons for use against America.

What actually happened was that a group of corrupt officials used the covert mechanisms of government to conduct a massive war of aggression, the ultimate form of terrorism, for personal gain, while throwing the world into chaos and the American public into debt and confusion. And even when the public does intermittently discern and understand that it was fooled, the social and bureaucratic systems put in place since World War Two guarantee that the public is powerless to resist or effect any meaningful change.

This is no secret. Especially since 9/11, the invisible hands guiding our official rulers boast about their ability to shape perceptions of reality. Ron Suskind reported about this problem in a 17 October 2004 article for *The New York Times Magazine* titled "Faith, Certainty and the Presidency of George W. Bush". In the article, Suskind quoted Bush political advisor Karl Rove as saying, "We're an empire now, and when we act, we create our own reality. And while you're studying that reality – judiciously, as you will – we'll act again, creating other new realities, which you can study too, and that's how things will sort out. We're history's actors ... and you, all of you, will be left to just study what we do."[3]

This imperial arrogance has been the nation's driving force since 1945, when America emerged unscathed from the ashes of World War Two as the world's only superpower. Since then, those who secretly rule the US have ruthlessly used the nation's military might and economic clout to punish foreign nations that impede its plans for global hegemony. They have succeeded in this business venture by waging the greatest covert operation ever, one that has thoroughly conditioned the American public to believe it is a perpetual victim of foreign powers, when in fact it is victimized by its unnamed rulers with their own secret interests.

The plan for world hegemony is rooted in language. The anti-Communist discourse put in place after World War Two evolved through the collapse of the Soviet Union and the rise of Islamic fundamentalism into the current discourse of terrorism, the new bête noire. Anyone operating outside the realm of pseudo-critique could discern this sea change in stated policy after the terror attacks of 11 September 2001. It was explicitly articulated in the days after 9/11. Republican Party stalwart Kenneth W. Starr, who served as President Bill Clinton's impeachment inquisitor, said the danger of terrorism required "deference to the judgments of the political branches with respect to matters of national security."[4]

In other words, national security, which had been non-partisan, would henceforth be controlled by the Ultra conservative business branch of American politics. According to Richard Thornburgh, who served as attorney general under Presidents Reagan and George W. H. Bush, America should also henceforth stop abiding by the law. Thornburgh said that due process sometimes "strangles us." When it comes to counter-terrorism, the former attorney general said, legally admissible evidence "may not be the be-all and end-all."[5]

It is no coincidence that, when Thornburgh and Starr made these carefully choreographed pronouncements, government officials had already drafted administrative detention laws aimed at Americans while establishing the torture chamber at Guantanamo.

In the wake of 9/11, America's reactionary Ultra clique claimed ownership of the national security apparatus, which it used to impose its ideology on the America people. Anyone who did not adopt their doctrine was considered an enemy of the state. "This is time for the old motto, 'Kill them all, let God sort 'em out'," purported terrorism expert Michael Ledeen asserted. "The entire political world will understand it and applaud it. And it will give us a chance to prevail."[6]

This is where the symbolic meaning of words prevails. By the "political world" Ledeen meant those who really understand the deep underside of how the whole war process works: the owners of the burgeoning terrorism business, the secret rulers and capitalist looters who've been manipulating American political and social movements since its inception. Taken together, Starr, Thornburg and Ledeen's rhetoric is emblematic of the false perceptions that Americans traditionally embrace about their victimhood and exceptionalism. The rhetoric of the Ultras paved the way for the reorganization of American society to fight an eternal one-size-fits-whatever War on Terror, which in turn was used to justify disastrous, neo-colonial wars against Afghanistan, Iraq, Libya and Syria. And it was all a Big Lie designed to enrich a few protected individuals.

It doesn't matter that an American is more likely to be killed by a bee sting than a terrorist attack. It doesn't matter that, in comparison, 30,000 people die every year in automobile accidents. They climb into their SUVs and hurtle down the highway at 80 MPH, heedless of the danger. But it's terrorism they fear. A survey conducted in December

2015 "found that about 79 percent of respondents believe a terrorist attack is somewhat likely or very likely in the next few months. Around 19 percent of respondents said they believe terrorism is the most important national issue – up from the 4 percent last month."[7]

This irrational fear is both the instigator and result of the War on Terror, the greatest covert operation ever devised, in which America's secret rulers manipulate the information industry to enrich themselves and enslave the nation's citizens while cutting a swath of righteous savagery around the world.

Which begs the question: Who are these secret rulers?

The National Security Establishment

Through their control of the media, political and bureaucratic systems, America's secret rulers engage in terrorism abroad and at home for economic purposes. This foreign-domestic symmetry was articulated by Marx and Engels, when they demonstrated how capitalists wage imperial wars abroad for the exact same reasons they create systems to oppress labor at home. The objective is to maximize profits and concentrate wealth and political power in fewer and fewer hands.

The global War on Terror and its domestic homeland security counterpart are flip sides of the same counterfeit coin. They are the capitalist ideology applied to foreign and domestic security policy. And like the capitalist system it serves, an unstated national security policy is consolidated in fewer and fewer ideologically correct hands as the empire expands and its contradictions become more apparent.

This consolidation of power is antithetical to democratic institutions and results not in greater security for American citizens, but in the loss of legal protections like due process. The consolidation of national security policy also means the deterioration of the two-party electoral system.

In theory, America's two major political parties represent opposing ideologies. Democrats are pro-labor but divided into a Socialist Left which wishes to smash the big banks, and the Compatible Left of Hillary Clinton, which is aligned to Goldman Sachs, Israel, and the imperial war machine. Joe Biden's evolution illustrates how a labor boss was co-opted, but continues to serve as a spectacular representation of what he no longer is. If one believes Biden's rhetoric, the Democratic Party elite seek to end income inequality and racial injustice, and to enfranchise minorities rather than subvert Ukraine, take over its government and civic institutions, and steal its wealth. The Republican Party is openly racist, militant and business-oriented. Trump's populist appeal seemed like a departure from Reagan elitism, but that was a result of shifting demographics, not establishment policies. The Republican base voted for Trump because of his outspoken racism. Trump didn't use code words like the Party leadership.

Either party may control the government for a period of time but, in theory, their open and honest dialectic resolves their ideological conflicts and pulls them inexorably to the center, thus creating the democracy that benefits everyone. Meanwhile, behind the scenes, "the state" endures and, in times of crisis, prevails without debate. Leaders in both political parties champion the state's preeminence. They rally round the flag and claim to do what's best for the country.

The problem is that, with the War on Terror, America is constantly in crisis. When the state is revealed (sometimes accidentally, more often by the state itself for propaganda purposes) to have created the crisis, it is more important than ever for elected politicians to affirm that the state transcends politics and represents the nation's enduring interests. That's why, during the campaign, Clinton studiously avoided her role in destroying Iraq, Libya, and Syria, and instead presented herself as a dispassionate bureaucrat who understands the intricacies of the system and can make the tough decisions as the first female chair of what can be understood as the national Phoenix Committee.

In Europe, the state is acknowledged as "industry" and is comprised of the people with the largest financial stake in any particular nation. Given their wealth and influence, these industrial elites, like the ancient nobility, are understood to have the experience and independence to engage in politics. Industry is ownership; it excludes wage earners, immigrants, refugees and disenfranchised minorities.

In America the state is referred to as the Establishment. As defined in the American Heritage dictionary, an Establishment with a capital E is "An exclusive group of powerful people who rule a government or society by means of private agreements and decisions."

The Establishment owns, equips and operates the instruments of state, and conspires to use them to its advantage, to keep wages low and maximize profits.[8] The CIA is the organized crime branch of this criminal conspiracy to "rule a government or society by means of private agreements and decisions."

The state's private, commercial interests are protected by its military, judicial, law enforcement, intelligence and security services – a.k.a., the National Security Establishment. We are taught that the bureaucrats and technocrats who administer these services are non-partisan and dedicated solely to protecting all the citizens of the United States. Ensconced in top management jobs in the private and public sectors, these apparatchiks claim they can only serve "the sacred trust" by placing themselves above the law. Cops, as everyone knows, do not follow the law, they enforce it.

The state's terrorism – the needless destruction of Iraq, Libya and Syria, and before them Vietnam and dozens of other nations – is based upon the premise that its National Security Establishment is above politics. But that's just a cover story for the greatest covert operation ever.

Here's how it works. Members of each party's hierarchy cultivate ideologically qualified candidates to run for public office. When elected, these officials appoint members of their party to top management jobs in the various bureaucracies. But when it comes to national security, no actual leftists are allowed. This is the determinant factor in the War on Terror. After generations of propaganda – from the Red Terror through the loyalty oaths of the McCarthy Era, up until the "eternal present" of the War on Terror – being a leftist automatically disqualifies a candidate from serving in the National Security Establishment, which is dedicated to capitalism.

Since 9/11, the commitment to fight Islamic terrorism, and absolve America of any hint of engaging in terrorism, is as stringent a requirement as anti-communism.

No one who writes a book like this one will ever belong. One cannot belong if one understands and disapproves of the reality that the state conducts terrorism, as its unstated policy, against working people at home, as well as foreign nations sitting on coveted natural resources. One cannot seek to hold office while denying the existence of an anthropomorphic god, America's righteousness, or the prevailing assumptions about the blessings of capitalism, for these myths describe the philosophical and psychological context in which the state's illegal operations are possible. They are the ultimate cover story, embodied in and embraced by the true believer.

Conversely, the state's covert operations can only be discerned and understood by transcending these beliefs and assumptions.

Transcending these self-destructive beliefs and assumptions is the most difficult challenge facing Americans. It is also the first step in an objective analysis of the components of the National Security Establishment. Such an analysis is not easily achieved, however, for the National Security Establishment is not accountable to the citizenry. One cannot make a citizen's arrest of a CIA officer, an FBI agent, or a cop for criminal activity, let alone a corporate executive or American president.

Apart from the deliberately confusing "pseudo-critiques" that define the spectacle in which we flounder, the National Security Establishment has built a labyrinth of thoroughly anti-democratic moats around itself (just as Rove, Starr, Thornburgh and Ledeen advocated) precisely to keep enquiring citizens out of its dirty business. They've destroyed as much evidence as possible.

The military is the most obvious example. Barricaded on bases at home and around the world, and fortified with its own judicial system, the military is divided into an upper class of highly indoctrinated officers who do not fraternize with the lower ranks. Officers are trained to send the lower ranks into battle to be maimed and killed. The lower ranks are trained to obey without question; and when they lose limbs and die, they are glorified as heroes who died for their country, not to advance the interests of the likes of Dick Cheney and Halliburton – what we loosely identify today as the One Percent.

The US military machine is the world's biggest consumer of energy and its biggest polluter. It manages the foreign policy mechanisms of the government for self-serving purposes, gobbling up the nation's tax dollars in order to maintain a global protection racket that exists solely to keep shipping lanes open so American businesses can exploit foreign markets. Dominated by fascists, the military is the pillar of the state and is never said to be connected to business or politics. And that illusion is the Establishment's greatest achievement.

Unlike the military, the CIA operates under cover, provoking conflicts in Russia and China, in nations surrounding them, and in Muslim nations surrounding Israel, so the military has a pretext to intervene. Military intervention and intimidation assure that the military's corporate sponsors control the resources the military needs to maintain the empire.

The FBI, as noted, has no legal mandate or ideological inclination to interfere in the CIA's illegal actions. Its "lane" is to infiltrate Muslim groups in America and sometimes prevent and other times provoke terror incidents here, while blurring "the lanes" between organized crime and the Establishment.

Based on the Phoenix program model developed in Vietnam and perfected in Latin America, the Department of Homeland Security (which is totally dependent on the War on Terror) coordinates the lower tier members of the National Security Establishment for the purpose of suppressing dissent in America. It does so through implicit violence.

Top bureaucrats and technocrats like Nelson Brickham, who created the Phoenix program, coordinate the systems of repression from within invisible "intelligence and operations centers" like the National Security Council, in league with trusted senators and congressmen, as well as representatives of big business, the media and academia. The bureaucrats and technocrats organize the chains of command to focus power in certain areas for specific goals. The primary goal is to assure that the CIA enjoys plausible deniability in its criminal pursuit of the Establishment's unstated policies. It's a shell game that allows elected representatives to claim they didn't know. The system is structured so that true power flows off the organizational charts presented to the public; all evidence leading back to the Establishment is concealed, and no one is ever held accountable.

To be invited into the National Security Establishment, and to rise to a position to organize and manage American society, one must be to the manor born, make billions of dollars like Trump, or submit to years of indoctrination calibrated to a series of increasingly restrictive security clearances designed to reject anyone who can't be ideologically assimilated. Endlessly proving one has embraced doctrine on various issues (Israel, Islam, terrorism, Black Lives, Mexican immigrants, etc.), is the drawbridge an individual like Hillary Clinton must cross to enter the self-regulating National Security Establishment. The capacity to recite doctrine and engage in massive war crimes is what enables a person to rise to a position of authority within the ruling Cult of Death.

The National Security Establishment's stated job is to defend the nation from foreign and domestic enemies, while expanding its economic and military influence abroad and preserving its freedoms at home. Its unstated job, conducted clandestinely, is to keep the lower classes from exerting any political control, publicly or privately, that might possibly result in the just and equitable redistribution of the Establishment's wealth. It is to this unstated end that the ruling Cult of Death covertly engages in massive terrorism against the people it pretends to protect.

Capitalism and State Terrorism

The disenfranchised have no voice in making policy in America. Wolf Blizter avoids acknowledging them and their viewpoints as assiduously as he stigmatizes Palestinians. They are Galeano's "Nobodies". They are not quoted in *The New York Times*. They have no access and cannot change conventions or alter basic assumptions about America, all of which are perpetuated in well-designed symbolic ways.

But when the Establishment exerts its overarching influence on government, the media does not define it as politics; it is the neutral, non-partisan status quo.

As with the financial crisis of 2008, Big Bankers were said to be "too big to fail." They were credited with creating jobs and dutifully accommodated with trillion dollar bailouts, paid for by workers losing pension funds and furloughs. No questions asked. No need for Trump to release his tax returns or Clinton to release her speeches to Goldman Sachs.

Politicians representing liberal causes must accommodate the Establishment and keep the system afloat in times of state manufactured crises, such as the invasion of Iraq in 2003. If they don't, they are labeled un-American – which is how ownership is equated with national security.

It has been this way since the wealthy landowners and merchants who organized the American Revolution raised and paid for armies out of their pockets. The Founding Fathers wrote the Constitution to preserve the prerogatives they purchased. That is why the media never identifies, let alone exposes or even investigates, wealthy individuals who benefit from tax breaks and offshore tax havens. The rich are never said to play the business card the way blacks are said to play the race card.

According to conventional American assumptions, capitalism is not based on political power, but on ideologically neutral profits and the economic "growth" that provides for the common good. And even when the scandal of tax breaks and tax havens affects some unscrupulous politician or industrialist, there is no legal penalty imposed on the offender. Obscene wealth is not illegal or, increasingly, immoral.

As part of the greatest covert operation ever, the National Security Establishment's unstated job is to preserve the systems that ensure inequality and obscene wealth in the face of needless poverty and suffering. Similar to the class divisions in the military, which is held aloft as the model of free American society, the lower classes cannot be allowed to enjoy the same degree of privilege and security as the upper classes. Workers are forced to live from paycheck to paycheck, on minimum wages, in perpetual fear of losing their jobs, homes and medical benefits.

The rich are not said to be sadistic for enjoying their lavish lifestyles while the poor are paralyzed by the fear that their children will be condemned to the hopelessness of eternal indebtedness, or, if they're a despised minority or immigrant, to rot in prison. The rich could easily share their wealth and power, and relieve the suffering of the poor, but they don't, because instilling terror in the poor keeps them politically suppressed. Some of the lower classes have given up hope entirely; some cling to rainmakers like Donald Trump and Hillary Clinton, and others are content to live in the fantasy world of potential and limitless commodities. In either case, voter turnout in the land of the free is kept around 54 percent – whether through complacency, curtailment of voter lists, incarceration, or the lack of candidates who inspire hope of change.

Feelings of alienation and desperation, on the one hand, and beliefs in popular myths on the other, are so pervasive that political disenfranchisement has become the reality Karl Rove chortled about above.

Terrorism as Business as Usual

State-sponsored terrorism – colonization abroad and repression at home – is the Establishment's primary means of extracting profits and maintaining ownership. It has been this way since slave owner and serial rapist Thomas Jefferson declared "all men are created equal," except Africans, women, and, as he wrote in the Declaration of Independence, the "merciless Indian savages, whose known rule of warfare, is undistinguished destruction of all ages, sexes and conditions."

Not surprisingly, Jefferson and his co-conspirators soon came to own all the Indians' land. The Founding Fathers built the nation on stolen land and the free labor of African slaves. Likewise, the prospect of free land propelled settlers from sea to shining sea, culminating in the Horatio Alger myth of the exceptional American, pulling himself up by his bootstraps.

The greatest covert operation ever symbolically transforms these traditional values into the myth of the great, exceptional American. It does so through the telling, retelling and selling of its cover story; the

John Wayne cowboys and Indians movie morphing into good American snipers fighting bad Muslim terrorists.

The purpose of the story is not just to create and glorify American heroes; it is intended to make you afraid of not embracing the story. This is the terrorism part. As every security company knows, the fear of surveillance is as effective as surveillance itself. They have only to suggest that the burglar is waiting to break into your house to sell you an ADT system. Likewise, fear of massive internet surveillance suppresses people from expressing their true feelings. There is no fear of Big Brother watching you, unless you believe that he is watching.

Once they make you afraid – which, as I've explained in this book, is achieved through an endless series of CIA provocations abroad, which in turn enables an endless series of FBI, DHS, and police provocations at home – they sell you the things that make you feel safe. Suggestion and salesmanship are all it takes. Trump's wall will protect you from Mexican rapists and drug-crazed black teenagers, and Hillary's regime change wars will protect you from demons like Saddam and Qaddafi and Assad. Forget that her regime-change wars created ISIS; she has proved she's capable of killing Muslims and she will again. She'll be glad to slay the demons she creates for you.

Selling the great American myth is as easy as selling the war on Iraq, or candidate Clinton, or Pepsi Cola. It's the same bill of goods in every case, the promise of something better. It is capitalism.

Capitalism tells us to be optimistic, to believe in a brighter future through things you can buy. The orgiastic future can be yours for no money down. It tells you to forget that Clinton sent your jobs overseas so her corporate sponsors could pay lower wages; if you vote for her, she'll bring those jobs home, and you'll have more money to buy more things. Forget that your austerity is her prosperity. Vote for Hillary!

The Bill of Goods

I've explained the CIA's role in the process, but I want to explain why the process exists.

The greatest covert operation ever is illustrated by the sweetheart scam in which the Pentagon bribed the billionaire owners of a dozen professional football teams with up to one million dollars each of your federal taxpayer money, to glorify their city's "hometown heroes" who serve in the military and wage the War on Terror.

You are taught to believe the War on Terror is waged by people like you, for you. But the greatest covert operation ever, aka the War on Terror, is a business enterprise that exploits people like you, especially if you are poor.

Telling the Homeric cover story not only enables this criminal enterprise, it is indistinguishable from it. It is the immensely profitable icing on the cake of the world's greatest weapon of mass destruction ever; it disenfranchises workers and then channels them into an army that is all too happy to brutalize entire nations. In return, they are glorified at football games.

Go Team! Number One!

Selling the story of the American hero is a profitable business not just for the Pentagon and its business partners in network news, it is a boondoggle for the National Security Establishment's strategic intelligence network of corrupted Hollywood and TV production companies that shape our spectacular dreams.

Advertising executives, public relations experts, spooks and generals, TV news and movie producers, and politicians read from the same script. They conduct surveys and map out demographics. Like highly indoctrinated Phoenix coordinators motivated to meet sales quotas, they target selected groups of consumers and sell them commodities that reinforce the myths they believe about themselves.

Trump the billionaire sold himself as an anti-establishment agent of change to a precariat convinced by Fox News that immigrants and minorities were stealing their jobs. Clinton labeled that message, as well as its messenger and its audience, as "deplorable." But her political supporters at MSNBC also skew the reality of our common predicament in order to deliver messages and commodities that its target audience of liberals wants. The messages may seem different, but they are both selling a bill of goods.

That's capitalism. Whether it's Tucker Carlson at Fox News or Chris Matthews at MSNBC, the person delivering the news is a salesman making a pitch. They cut to a commercial break, and you are sold a product that appeals to your demographic.

While the Republican Party and Democratic Party elites keep the lower classes at each other's throats, they are sharing drinks at the Country Club. It's a game for them. It's fun. When they get together, like the Clintons and Trumps do occasionally at high society charity events, they laugh at the working classes, which are locked out. The people they exploit have no alternatives. There is no third way.

The Clintons and Trumps, and the talking heads at Fox News and MSNBC, think the Green Party exists to mow their lawns for pennies.

Every minute of every day, through the national security mechanisms outlined in this book, the oligarchs that own America and through it seek to own the world symbolically transform themselves from murderous beasts into a force for good that protects us from them.

They call it "America", but what does that word represent: a shining city on a hill above a fruited plain, or a segregated oligarchy with a murderous dark side?

The answer is obvious. You are the victim of a massive criminal enterprise, and the key to its success is its ability to keep its crimes and corruption secret. The secret rulers have made it illegal to blow the whistle on what they are up to. There is no freedom of speech or public right to know.

The billionaire owners of professional football teams, and the talking heads they and their network news partners hire to shape the story and sell their merchandise, are appalled when a black player like Colin Kaepernick kneels during the National Anthem. They try to make the spectators feel that such behavior is "disrespectful" of America. They try to make the spectators feel like they should not sympathize with the endless series of black kids shot dead by a cop for selling cigarettes outside grocery stores. They reinforce their message like a candidate running for office, by wrapping themselves and their product – a football game – with the trappings of militarism and law enforcement.

It doesn't matter that the top cops have an accommodation with the bosses of organized crime, or that the CIA runs the world's illicit arms-for-drug business, or that the Pentagon illegally invades and destroys foreign nations so corporations can steal everything the people in those nations own. It doesn't matter that the corporate crime bosses get away with savaging your environment for profit.

As Guy Debord said, "The Mafia is not an outsider in this world; it is perfectly at home. Indeed, in the integrated spectacle it stands as the model of all advanced commercial enterprises."

You'll never hear a media buttonman like Wolf Blitzer speak honestly about Palestinians as outlawed victims of oppression in their homeland. You'll never hear him criticize ReMax for selling and renting homes on stolen Palestinian land. Criticizing Israel, like criticizing "America" is not in the script. It's a story told in a foreign language, if at all.

You'll never hear Blitzer portray America's financial policies as state sponsored terrorism designed to prevent people from making a decent living, so they have no choice but to become soldiers or cops. You won't hear this because state sponsored censorship – especially in regard to the CIA's illegal deeds – is indistinguishable from state sponsored terrorism.

Only the "selective" style of terrorism employed by the poor and dispossessed "non-state actor" is ever portrayed as terrorism. The state's systematic and extra-legal terrorism is simply regarded as business as usual, which it is.

Wolf Blitzer is free to say that America has no political prisoners, because the war on drugs provides profits as well as security for elites like him. Disenfranchising and imprisoning blacks is good business that helps keeps wages low for all workers. It's not a problem, it's business. Women earn less than men and the minimum wage is kept below poverty levels, we are told, for reasons that have nothing to do politics. And that is true: it is business as usual.

The Establishment and its security chiefs know what they are doing. It is worth repeating, as Johan Galtung said, that "The legal criminality of the social system and its institutions, of government, and of individuals at the interpersonal level, is tacit violence. Structural violence is a structure of exploitation and social injustice."

Politics and business are said to be mutually exclusive, and that Big Lie enables the greatest covert operation ever. Business people manipulate political and social movements, including terrorists and counterterrorists, through instruments like the CIA, so they can make more money. The police keep resistant poor and black neighborhoods in lockdown. The FBI manipulates lost, insecure, and even intellectually disabled individuals into attempting acts of terrorism, which they then jump in to prevent. The CIA conducts false flag operations all over the world to enhance public fear of terrorists, even as they arm and train them in Syria, Iraq and elsewhere to overthrow elected governments.

Having been implemented covertly over decades, the War on Terror defines the contours of America's legally criminal social structure, which, in the name of protecting the people from terrorism, steals from the poor and gives to the rich.

Underlying the "structural violence" of state-sponsored terrorism is an ever-expanding National Security Establishment comprised of nearly a million cadres, all of whom profit from the structural violence they maintain. At the lower tier, cops and soldiers get to be heroes. The oligarchs get to laugh. In the middle, at Homeland Security, they get jobs.

Emanating from the super-secret CIA, which informs every other government bureaucracy, this criminal enterprise corrupts every social and political movement in America, forming consumers of myths and commodities into a moat of true believers that surrounds the Establishment elite that oppresses them. It's a perfect system, stabilized by manufactured crises du jour, and ineluctably heading in a predictable direction.

In the next national emergency – the next financial meltdown or environmental catastrophe – cadres will be mobilized, shout slogans, and appeal to our traditional values or diversity. Their managers will review reports about the suspicious activities of terrorist surrogates. The definition of a terrorist will be expanded to include people deemed dangerous to the Public Order, at which point the non-believers will be arrested on criminal charges for political offenses, like protesting climate change.

It's not hard to imagine a few of the most highly motivated cadres grabbing ropes and forming lynch mobs, and going after those who refused to stand for the National Anthem.

Only five percent of the people need to be organized in this fashion to install a fascist dictator in the United States. That is the ultimate objective of the greatest covert operation ever, the one in which the oligarchs steal everything you own.

The five percent who resist will be subject to "compromise and discredit" operations like the letter the FBI sent to Martin Luther King, Jr. encouraging him to commit suicide. Forged documents, like the ones the Bush regime used to justify the illegal invasion of Iraq, will become indistinguishable from real ones.

Did the Russians hack the DNC, or was it a disgruntled DNC cadre? You'll never know.

False rumors will proliferate and ruin the reputation of anyone who refuses to comply. People will become more terrified than ever. They will grab their precious guns and start shooting. Midnight arrests and disappearances into administrative detention centers will become commonplace.

Amid the confusion, the CIA will activate assassination units within the front organizations it has placed around the country, and plant plastic explosives in school buses, not as training exercises, but as provocations to call in the militarized police.

Property values will plummet, blood will run in the streets, and 10,000 Trumps and Clintons, safely ensconced in their pre-secure Israeli-style Bantustans, will buy everything on the cheap.

This is the Phoenix future, the ultimate goal of the greatest covert operation ever.

ENDNOTES

INTRODUCTION

Chapter 1

1   Phoenix is Phụng Hoàng in Vietnamese.

2   <http://www.cryptocomb.org/Phoenix%20Tapes.html>

3   See David Kilcullen, "Countering Global Insurgency", *Small Wars Journal*, September-November 2004.

4   Tom Hayden, "Reviving Vietnam War Tactics", *The Nation*, 13 March 2008.

5   Seymour Hersh, "Moving Targets: Will the counter-insurgency plan in Iraq repeat the mistakes of Vietnam?", *The New Yorker*, 15 December 2003. Hersh said, "According to official South Vietnamese statistics, Phoenix claimed nearly forty-one thousand victims between 1968 and 1972; the US counted more than twenty thousand in the same time span."

6   <https://www.youtube.com/watch?v=5rXPrfnU3G0>

7   Lansdale is known as the father of US counterinsurgency strategies and tactics. He is famous for putting down the Communist insurrection in the Philippines (1950-1953), and for installing the repressive Catholic regime under President Ngo Dinh Diem in South Vietnam, where he managed the counter-insurgency from 1954-1957. He was the Assistant Secretary of Defense for Special Operations from 1957 until November 1963.

8   To be discussed at greater length in Chapter 9: The CIA in Ukraine.

9   "The Clash of the Icons", *Lobster* #40 (Winter 2000/1).

10   The aforementioned Church Committee noted in its report on page 336 that Lansdale was instrumental in the CIA's attempts to assassinate Fidel Castro and subvert Cuba, and that in 1962, he proposed the introduction of cheap marijuana into Cuba's underground economy, and falsely accusing Cuba of drug trafficking. In a memo to his staff, Lansdale said: "Gangster elements might prove the best recruitment potential for actions [murders] against police G-2 [intelligence] officials." Lansdale added that, "CW [Chemical Warfare] agents should be fully considered."

11   "Will the Real Daniel Ellsberg Please Stand Up!", Counterpunch, 2003.

12   Michael Levine, *The Big White Lie: The Deep Cover Operation That Exposed the CIA Sabotage of the Drug War*, 1990.

Chapter 2

1   Douglas Valentine, "The True Relationship between Crime and Law Enforcement", Counterpunch, 2 January 2015.

2   *The Hotel Tacloban* was published by Lawernce Hill & Company in 1984, Angus & Robertson Publishers in Australia in 1985, and Avon Books in 1986. It is now available through iUniverse.

3   Verso published *Wolf* in 2004 and TrineDay published *Pack* in 2009.

4   <https://nsarchive.wordpress.com/2011/10/03/no-foia-request-needed-the-douglas-valentine-u-s-government-drug-enforcement-collection/

5   Alfred W. McCoy, *The Politics of Heroin: CIA Complicity in the Global Drug Trade*, Lawrence Hill Books, 1991, p. 211.

6   Douglas Valentine, "The CIA and Drugs: A Covert History", Counterpunch, 7 November 2014.

7   See Douglas Valentine, "The French Connection Revisited: The CIA, Irving Brown, and Drug Smuggling as Political Warfare", *Covert Action Quarterly*, 1999.   <https://www.scribd.com/document/212247684/Valentine-Douglas-The-French-Connection-Revisited-The-CIA-Irving-Brown-And-Drug-Smuggling-as-Political-Warfare-1999>

8   Compton Affidavit given to US Attorney John E. Clark in Texas in August 1975.

9   Douglas Valentine, "Operation Twofold", Counterpunch, 25 January 2008.

Chapter 3

1   *The Toledo Blade*, 1 January 1987, p. 27. The commander of US forces in Central America in the mid-1980s, General Paul Gorman, described it as "a form of warfare repugnant to Americans, a conflict which involves innocents, in which non-combatant casualties may be an explicit object."

2   Frank Snepp, *Decent Interval*, Random House, New York, 1978, p. 12.

3   "US Assistance Programs in Vietnam", (Foreign Operations and Government Information Subcommittee, Committee on Government Operations, July 15, 16, 19, 21 and August 2, 1971), p. 206.

4   Dinh Tuong An, *The Truth About Phoenix*, Tin Sang, Saigon, 1970-71,

available at Widener Library.

5   See Douglas Valentine, "Fragging Bob: Bob Kerrey, CIA War Crimes, and the Need for a War Crimes Trial", Counterpunch, 17 May 2001, republished here.

6   Warren H. Milberg, "The Future Applicability of the Phoenix Program", Research Study, Report #1835-74, Air Command and Staff College, Air University, Maxwell Air Force Base, Ala., May 1974.

7   Dana Priest, "U.S. military teams, intelligence deeply involved in aiding Yemen on strikes", *Washington Post*, 27 January 2010.

8   John Swaine, "Barack Obama 'has authority to use drone strikes to kill Americans on US soil'", *The Telegraph*, 6 March 2013.

Chapter 4

1   David Galula, *Counter-Insurgency Warfare: Theory and Practice*, Praeger, 1964, p. 117.

2   Robert Slater, "The History, Organization and Modus Operandi of the Viet Cong Infrastructure", p. 21.

3   Galula, p. 124.

4   John Marks, *The Search for the Manchurian Candidate: The CIA and Mind Control*, Time Books, 1979, p. 131.

5   Ibid. 132.

6   Ibid. 132.

7   From 1967-1969, Colonel Douglas Dillard managed Phoenix operations in IV Corps. Dillard said, "I became a major construction tycoon in the Delta as a sideline to my Phoenix business." As well as giving $15,000 to every district chief to build a DIOCC, he worked with the CIA in building "those little jails, as I call them, which really were interrogation centers." As Dillard recalled: "The agency sent down an elderly gentleman from Maryland who was a contractor. His job in the Delta... was to get these interrogation centers constructed. Pacific Architects and Engineers did the work, but this guy was an agency employee. I remember going into one we'd built in Chau Duc that had several monks inside. They had a steel chain chained to their legs so they wouldn't run off."

8   The US State Department's Agency for International Development (AID) had an Office of Public Safety formed mostly by former cops and corrections officers who advised foreign police departments.

9   See Chapter 15: The Spook Who Would Be a Congressman.

10   Major General Joseph McChristian, *The Role of Military Intelligence 1965-1967*, Department of the Army, Washington, DC, 1974.

11   Ibid, p. 71.

12   Ibid, p. 26.

13   David Pallister, "How the US sent $12bn in cash to Iraq. And watched it vanish", *Guardian*, 7 February 2007.

14   As Anand Gopal says in *No Good Men Among the Living*: "A military base in a country like Afghanistan is also a web of relationships, a hub for the local economy, and a key player in the political ecosystem. Unravel how (the US base in Kandahar) came to be, and you'll begin to understand how the war returned to Maiwand." p. 107. Maiwand is a district and village in Kandahar province.

15   PRU (for Provincial Reconnaissance Unit) was the new name given in 1966 to the CIA's Counterterrorism Teams.

16   Abbie Hoffman et al were leaders of the anti-Vietnam War movement.

17   The MOS numerical designation for army counterintelligence officers was 9666.

18   Phoenix was also referred to by its Vietnamese sobriquet, Phung Hoang.

19   Phoenix personnel staffed province (PIOCC) and district (DIOCC) Intelligence and Operations Coordinating Centers.

20   CORDS, the Civil Operations and Revolutionary Development division at MACV, managed "pacification."

21   While posing as the State Department's Narcotics Control Officer in Iran, Ahern, who was actually the CIA's station chief, was one of 52 Americans taken hostage in Teheran in 1979.

22   Loved by William Colby, Vann was exposed as a rapist in Neil Sheehan's book *A Bright Shining Lie*.

Chapter 5

1   John Barry, "The Defector's Secrets", *Newsweek*, 2 March 2003.

2   As a grad student at Harvard, Moyar wrote to me in 1992. He said my Phoenix book was "very informative" and begged me to refer him to the CIA officers I'd interviewed. Sensing a scam, I agreed, but only on condition that he acknowledge that he'd based his research on mine. Moyar then went to my sources and said – as one of them later told me – "Now is your chance to screw Valentine." Not satisfied with ripping me off, he smeared me in his thesis. He graduated first in Harvard's history department; Harvard is, after all, a pillar of the imperial war machine.

3   Richard Oppel Jr and Abdul Waheed Wafa, "Afghan Investigators Say U.S. Troops Tried to Cover Up Evidence in Botched Raid", April 5, 2010.

4   Anand Gopal, *No Good Men Among The Living: America, the Taliban, and the War Through Afghan Eyes,* Metropolitan Books/Henry Holt & Company, 2013, pp. 110-117.

5   John Barry and Michael Hersh, "The Pentagon May Put Special Forces Led Assassination and Kidnapping Teams in Iraq", 7 January 2005.

6   Jason Ditz, "Pentagon Report: Afghan Civilian Casualties at 'Record Highs,' Warns Congress Security Situation 'Dominated' by Resilient Taliban", Antiwar.com, 17 June 2016.

7   David Galula, *Counter-Insurgency Warfare: Theory and Practice*, p. 124.

8   <http://watson.brown.edu/costsofwar/costs/human/civilians/afghan.

9   Nadia Khomami, "Afghan president: I have no issue with Cameron corruption remark", *Guardian*, 12 May 2016.

10   Craig Murray, "How a Torture Protest Killed a Career", Consortium News, 26 October 2009.

11   "U.S. Denies Entry to former British Ambassador Craig Murray", Global Research, 12 September 2016.

12   Nguyen Ngoc Huy and Stephen B Young, Understanding Vietnam, The DPC Information Service, The Netherlands, 1982, p. 168-70.

Chapter 6

1   J. Max Robins, "Military Interns Booted From CNN, NPR: How Did Army Officers Get Into The News Business?", TV Guide, April 15-21, 2000.

2   Daniel Nasaw, "Taliban suicide attack kills CIA agents at US outpost in Afghanistan", *Guardian*, 31 December 2009.

3   Joby Warrick and Pamela Constable, "CIA base attacked in Afghanistan supported airstrikes against al-Qaeda, Taliban", *Washington Post*, 1 January 2010.

4   Jerome Starkey, "Western troops accused of executing 10 Afghan civilians, including children", *The Times*, December 31, 2009.

5   Robert Parry, "Bush's Global Dirty War",, Consortium News, 1 October 2007.

6   See previous article for Vietnamese teachers falsely accused and placed on the Phoenix blacklist.

7   "Deadly suicide blast strikes Afghan compound", Al Jazeera Afghanistan, 16 January 2016.

8   The acronyms are confusing, I know, but I didn't create them. Just to clarify, RD teams were part of the overall RDC program that trained the CIA's PRU and Census Grievance (yet to be explained) personnel as well.

9   *The Herald Tribune*, October 21, 1965

10   Tom Ahern, *Vietnam Declassified: The CIA and Counterinsurgency*, The University Press of Kentucky, 2009.

11   The insurgents referred to themselves as Viet Minh, but in the early 1950s, in an attempt to stigmatize them in the Western mind, CIA officer Ed Lansdale renamed them the Viet Cong (Cong for Communist). Just as the US press uniformly referred to the Peoples Republic of China as "Red China", it thereafter referred to the Vietnamese insurgents pejoratively as the VC, as a form of psychological warfare directed against the American public.

12   Census Grievance Teams were the primary way a principal agent contacted sub-agents in the village – by ostensibly setting up a secret means (usually a portable shack) for civilians to complain about the government. The PRTs have this Census Grievance element within their intelligence unit.

13   Chieu Hoi is discussed at length in the next chapter.

14   Thomas Thayer, *A Systems Analysis of the Vietnam War 1965-1972, Vol. 10: Pacification and Civil Affairs* (Washington D.C.: Office of the Assistant Secretary of Defense, 1975), pp. 40-43

15   Philip Rucker and Robert Costa, "Trump questions need for NATO, outlines noninterventionist foreign policy", *Washington Post*, 21 March 2016.

16   Dahr Jamail's *Beyond the Green Zone: Dispatches from an Unembedded Journalist in Occupied Iraq*, Haymarket Books, 2008.

Chapter 7

1   Elisabeth Bumiller, "Gates Says Taliban Must Take Legitimate Afghan Role", *International New York Times*, 22 January 2010.

2   Kristen Chick, "General McChrystal: Taliban could be part of solution in Afghanistan", *Christian Science Monitor*, 25 January 2010.

3   "No decision yet on offer of talks: Taliban", *The Jakarta Post*, 30 January 2010.

4   See Douglas Valentine, "The Afghan 'Dirty War' Escalates".

5   Rod Nordland, "Lacking Money and Leadership, Push for Taliban Defectors Stalls", *International New York Times*, 6 September 2010.

6   <http://www.af.undp.org/content/afghanistan/en/home/operations/projects/crisis_prevention_and_recovery/aprp.html>

7   In 1999, when the world went seriously digital, the USIA was renamed the Broadcasting Board of Governors.

8   September 7, 2010 <https://www.atu.edu/research/Professional DevelopmentGrants/09-10/Woods_Final_Report.pdf>

9   Ibid.

10   Chris Hedges, "Defectors Cite Iraqi Training For Terrorism", *The New York Times*, 8 November 2001.

Chapter 8

1   Manny Fernandez, Richard Perez-Pena and Jonah Engel Bromwich, "Five Dallas Officers Were Killed as Payback, Police Chief Says", July 8, 2016.

2   John King and Brian Todd, "Armitage admits leaking Plame's identity", CNN, 8 September 2006.

3   "Afghan Opium Production 40 Times Higher Since US-NATO Invasion", teleSUR, 31 August 2016: see <https://www.mintpressnews.com/afghan-opium-production-40-times-higher-since-us-nato-invasion/219974/>

4   Jessica Donati, "Afghan civilian deaths up in 2013 as war intensifies: U.N.", Reuters, 8 February 2014.

5   Robert Burns, "Pentagon report says Afghans feel less secure", Associated Press, 17 June 2016.

Chapter 9

1   Retrieved February 10, 2016, from <http://centreua.org/en/team/445/>, as cited in Chris dePloeg, *Ukraine in the Crossfire*, Clarity Press, Inc., 2017.

2   R. Olearchyk, (2013, December 14). Ukraine: Inside the pro-EU protest camp. Retrieved from <http://blogs.ft.com/beyond-brics/2013/12/14/ukraine-inside-the-pro-eu-protest-camp/?Authorised=false>, cited in dePloeg, *Ukraine in the Crossfire*.

3   Cited in dePloeg, *Ukraine in the Crossfire*.

4   Stephen Lendman, ed., *Flashpoint in Ukraine: How the US Drive for Hegemony Risks World War III*S, Atlanta, Clarity Press, 2014.

5   Eamon Javers, "Why Twitter chose to do battle with the CIA", CNBC, 13 May 2016.

6   See Chapter 4: The Systematic Gathering of Intelligence.

7   <http://fas.org/irp/dni/icd/icd-304-2008.pdf>

8   Joshua Cook, "Exclusive: FBI Whistleblower and Teacher Expose Islamic Gülen Movement Infiltrating U.S. Through Charter Schools", Truth in Media, 28 July 2014.

9   <http://www.ancreport.com/documentary/decades-of-deception/>

Chapter 10

1   Douglas Valentine, "The Spook Who Would Be a Congressman", Counterpunch.

2   Interview in documentary film: The War on Democracy (2007),

directed by John Pilger. View online at: <http://johnpilger.com/videos/the-war-on-democracy>

3   "SWORD deals in 'Repugnant' Warfare", *The Toledo Blade*, 1 January 1987, p. 27.

4   See *The Phoenix Program* for my complete interview with Gregg.

5   David Corn and Michael Isikoff, *Hubris: The Inside Story of Spin, Scandal, and the Selling of the Iraq War.*

6   Barry, "The Pentagon may put Special Forces led assassination tearms", 7 January 2005.

7   Tom Lasseter and Yasser Salihee, "Sunni men in Baghdad targeted by attackers in police uniforms", Knight Ridder Newspapers, 27 June 2005.

8   <http://brusselstribunal.org/IraqUNHRC.htm>

Chapter 11

1   Michael Calderone, "CNN Removes Reporter Diana Magnay From Israel-Gaza After 'Scum' Tweet, The Huffington Post, <http://www.huffingtonpost.com/2014/07/18/cnn-diana-magnay-israel-gaza_n_5598866.html>

2   The SOD is now known as the Special Activities Division.

3   Ahern was working undercover as the Embassy's Narcotics Control Officer.

4   Interview with David Whipple

5   Peter Dale Scott, "North, Iran-Contra, and the Doomsday Project: The Original Congressional Cover Up of Continuity-of-Government Planning", *The Asia-Pacific Journal*, 21 February 2011, citing a quote from the 5 July 1987 *Miami Herald*. Scott originally published the article in 1989 as "Northwards without North: Bush, Counterterrorism, and the Continuation of Secret Power." <http://apjjf.org/2011/9/8/Peter-Dale-Scott/3491/article.html>

6   Ibid. *Miami Herald*, July 5, 1987.

7   Ibid.

8   Ibid.

9   Ibid.

10   Ibid.

11   Michael McClintock, *Instruments of Statecraft: U.S. Guerilla Warfare, Counter-Insurgency, Counter-Terrorism, 1940-1990*, p 306.

12   Guy Taylor, "CIA goes live with new cyber directorate, massive internal reorganization" *Washington Times*, 1 October 2015.

13   Ibid.

Chapter 12

1   Douglas Clark Kinder and William O. Walker III, "Stable Force in a Storm: Harry J. Anslinger and United States Narcotic Policy, 1930-1962."

2   See my article "Sex and Drugs and the CIA" for the intimate details of the MKULTRA Program; see *The Strength of the Wolf* for how the impending exposure of the FBN's role in providing safe houses for the CIA's illegal domestic operations contributed to the dismantling of the FBN and its rebirth as the BNDD.

3   Charlie Siragusa with Robert Wiedrich, *On The Trail of the Poppy: Behind The Mask of the Mafia*, Prentice Hall Inc., New Jersey, p. 108.

4   30 January 1967 Memorandum for the Record, by Dr. Sidney Gottlieb, available at the Douglas Valentine Collection at the National Security Archive.

5   Report to the President by the Commission on CIA Activities within the United States, GPO, Washington, DC, June 1975, pp. 232-4.

6   Adrian Swain, *The Time of My Life: Memoirs Of A Government Agent From Pearl Harbor To The Golden Triangle*, Axelrod Publishing, Tampa, 1995, p. 465.

7   Ibid, p. 467.

8   Tom Tripodi with Joseph P. DeSario, *Crusade: Undercover Against the Mafia & KGB*, Brassey's, Washington, DC, 1993, p. 179.

9   Alfred W. McCoy, *The Politics of Heroin: CIA Complicity in the Global Drug Trade*, Lawrence Hill Books, Brooklyn, 1991, p. 249.

10   Conein letter to Harper Row President Winthrop Knowlton, October 10, 1972. See Douglas Valentine, "Will The Real Daniel Ellsberg Please Stand Up."

11   Special Agents William Logay and Robert Medell to Andrew Tartaglino, Deputy Director for Operations, "Project BUNCIN — Operational Plan", November 2, 1972, p. 2.

12   Ibid, p. 3.

13   Lou Conein referred me to Medell, while Tully Acampora referred me to Logay.

14   Phillip R Smith Acting Deputy Assistant Administrator for Intelligence to George M Belk, Acting Assistant Administrator for Intelligence, July 19, 1973, "DEACON I: Drug Enforcement Administration Clandestine Operations Network (SEC-SI-73-2506)", p. 2.

15   See Cockburn and St. Clair, "The CIA's Secret Killers", Counterpunch, 19 December 2014. <http://www.counterpunch.org/2014/12/19/the-cias-secret-killers/>

16   Interview with DEA Inspector Mortimer Benjamin.

17   Jack Anderson and L. Whitten, *Boston Globe*, 3 October 1977.
18   Daniel P. Casey, Assistant Administrator for Enforcement, to Peter B. Bensinger, Administrator, re: Central Intelligence Agency.
19   Peter Dale Scott & Jonathan Marshall, *Cocaine Politics: Drugs, Armies, and the CIA in Central America*, Berkeley: U. of CA Press, 1991, pp. x-xi.
20   *Cocaine Politics*, p. 28.
21   Senate Committee on Foreign Operations, Subcommittee on Terrorism, Narcotics and International Operations, Drugs, Law Enforcement and Foreign Policy, 100th Congress, 2nd Session, GPO, Washington, DC, 1989, p. 135.
22   Interview with Robert Bonner.
23   John Shiffman and Kristina Cooke, "U.S. directs agents to cover up program used to investigate Americans", Reuters, 5 August 2013.

Chapter 13

1   Allan Nairn, "Confessions of a Death Squad Officer", *The Progressive*, March 1986.
2   See also the "War Crimes as Policy" article.
3   TDY means temporary duty.
4   Meos is another name for the Hmong.
5   Carl Rowan column "Pressure Builds For Exposing Viet Nam Graft" was quoted and cited in 21 November 1966 letter from Senator Stuart Symington to Secretary of the Army Stanley Resor.
6   Alfred W. McCoy, *The Politics of Heroin: CIA Complicity in the Global Drug Trade*, Lawrence Hill Books, Brooklyn, 1991, p. 226.
7   Nguyen Ngoc Huy and Stephen B Young, *Understanding Vietnam*, The DPC Information Service, The Netherlands, 1982, p. 139, 148.
8   The Illicit Traffic in Weapons and Drugs Across the United States-Mexican Border, 95th Cong., 1st session, January 12, 1977 , GPO, Washington, DC, 1977.
9   Henrik Kruger, *The Great Heroin Coup*, South End Press, Bosston, 1980, p. 178. See also James Mills, *The Underground Empire: Where Crime and Governments Embrace*.
10   *The Phoenix Program*, p. 424.
11   John Shiffman and Kristina Cooke, "U.S. directs agents to cover up program used to investigate Americans", Reuters, 5 August 2013.
12   <http://www.boilingfrogspost.com/2013/06/19/podcast-show-112-nsa-whistleblower-goes-on-record-reveals-new-information-names-culprits/>

Chapter 14

1   Michael B Kelley, "CONFIRMED: The DEA Struck A Deal With Mexico's Most Notorious Drug Cartel", *Business Insider*, 13 January 2014.

2   Kinder, "Stable Force" p. 916. See also Jonathan Marshall, "Opium and the Politics of Gangsterism in Nationalist China, 1927-1945".

3   Marshall, "Gangsterism", *Bulletin of Concerned Asian Scholars*, July-September 1976, p. 29.

4   William O. Walker III, *Opium and Foreign Policy: The Angle-American Search for Order in Asia, 1912-1954*The University of North Carolina Press, Chapel Hill and London, p. 78.

5   Keswick in World War Two ran the British Special Operations Executive (SOE) and provided former FBN Agent Garland Williams with the training manuals used to train OSS officers.

6   Jill Jonnes, *Hep Cats, Narcs and Pipe Dream*, New York: Scribner, 1996, p. 95.

7   As explained on the National Archives website, "In January of 1917, British cryptographers deciphered a telegram from German Foreign Minister Arthur Zimmermann to the German Minister to Mexico,von Eckhardt, offering United States territory to Mexico in return for joining the German cause. This message helped draw the United States into the war and thus changed the course of history." <https://www.archives.gov/education/lessons/zimmermann/>

8   Ed Reid, *The Mistress and the Mafia*, Bantam, New York, 1972, p. 42.

9   Ibid., p. 90.

10   Ibid. p. 90.

11   Ibid. p. 123.

12   Ibid. p. 129.

13   Peter Dale Scott, *Deep Politics and the Death of JFK*, University of California Press, Berkeley 1993, p. 142.

14   William Howard Moore, *The Kefauver Committee and the Politics of Crime 1950-1952*, University of Missouri Press, 1974, p. 105.

Chapter 15

1   Chavez v. Martinez, 538 US 760 (2003).

2   "John McCain, Prisoner of War: A First-Person Account", *US News and World Report*, 28 January 2008.

3   Agence France-Presse, "US on Defensive as Reports of 'Secret Torture Flights' Pile Up", 2 December 2005.

4   Sydney H. Schanberg, "Why Has John McCain Blocked Info on

MIAs?" *The Nation*, 18 September 2008.

5   MACV Teams were part of CORDS.

6   CORDS had eleven divisions: Public Safety; Pacification and Security Coordination; Regional and Popular Forces; Phoenix; Chieu Hoi; Psyops; Refugees; Public Health; Management Support; Political; and New Life Development.

7   Don Luce, *Hostages of War*, Indochina Resource Center, 1973. Luce did what the US press corps didn't dare to do; he investigated GVN's prison system. In April 1970 he broke the Tiger Cage story. Luce called the GVN a "Prison Regime" and said Phoenix was a "microcosm" of the omnipotent and perverse US influence on Vietnamese society. He blamed the CIA for the deterioration of values that permitted torture, political repression, and assassination. For Luce, abuses were not accidental but an integral part of the system. "The widespread use of torture... can be explained by the admissibility of confession as evidence in court", he said, and noted that "Phoenix was named after the all-seeing mythical bird which selectively snatches its prey - but the techniques of this operation are anything but selective. For many Vietnamese, the Phung Hoang program is a constant menace to their lives."

8   David Morales, a trusted associate of Station Chief Ted Shackley.

9   In 1971, George Weisz managed the station's Viet Cong Branch that reviewed Phoenix and Special Branch reports and absconded with their best penetration agents.

10   Ralph Johnson, *The Phoenix Program: Planned Assassination or Legitimate Conflict Management,* American University, Washington, DC, 1982).

11   Thomas Gaist, "US Defense Department announces deployment of troops in Yemen", World Socialist Website, 9 May 2016.

12   "Sure we got involved in assassinations", said Charlie Yothers, the CIA's chief of operations in I Corps in 1970. "That's what PRU were set up for - assassination. I'm sure the word never appeared in any outlines or policy directives, but what else do you call a targeted kill?"

13   Dinh Tuong An, "The Truth About Phoenix" (see *The Phoenix Program*, pages 217-220).

14   US Assistance Programs in Vietnam" (Foreign Operations and Government Information Subcommittee, Committee on Government Operations, July 15, 16, 19, 21 and August 2, 1971); passim.

15   "Vietnam Policy and Prospects 1970" (Hearings before the Committee on Foreign Relations, US Senate, February 17-20 and March 3, 14, 17, 19, 1970); passim.

16   Colby's strategy was outlined in State Dept. Telegram 024391 (17

February 1970) which says: "We believe the line of questioning attempting to establish the Phoenix program as an assassination program [can be] successfully blunted by repeated assertions regarding US/GVN policies, coupled with admissions of incidents of abuses."

17   Lydia DePillis, "How it feels to torture", *Washington Post*, 11 December 2014.

18   Recall the photograph of a hooded man standing Christ-like on a box with his arms outstretched and wires attached to his genitals and fingers at Abu Ghraib Prison.

19   "US Assistance Programs in Vietnam"; passim.

20   Jennifer Van Bergen and Douglas Valentine, "The Dangerous World of Administrative Detention", *Case Western Reserve Journal of International Law*, Volume 37, Issue 2, 2006.

21   Ibid.

22   Bob Woodward, *Veil: The Secret Wars of the CIA, 1981-1987*.

23   Joseph Persico, *Casey: The Lives and Secrets of William J. Casey: from the OSS to the CIA*, p 276.

24   Ibid, p. 276.

25   Ibid,, p. 277.

26   "The Secret Wars of the CIA", excerpts from a talk by John Stockwell. <http://www.serendipity.li/cia/stock1.html>

27   Ibid.

28   Bob Woodward, *Veil: The Secret Wars of the CIA, 1981-1987*, p. 171.

29   On The Issues Website (2010) <http://www.ontheissues.org/International/Rob_Simmons_Homeland_Security.htm>

30   Smith/Dixon interview: <http://www.democraticunderground.com/discuss/duboard.php?az=view_all&address=143x3992>

Chapter 16

1   "Afghanistan: Crisis of Impunity: The Role of Pakistan, Russia, and Iran in Fueling the Civil War", Human Rights Watch, July 2001.

2   I quoted from this source in my Counterpunch article, "An Open Letter to Maj. Gen. Bruce Lawlor."

3   Matthew Harwood and Jan Stanley, "American military technology has come home to your local police force", *The Nation*, 19 May 2016.

4   <http://www.dkv.columbia.edu/demo/ethics-in-america/site/war_stories/participants.html>

5   Al Santoli, *Everything We Had: An Oral History of the Vietnam War*, 1985.

6   Seymour M. Hersh, "The Qaddafi Connection", *The New York Times*, 14 June 1981. Loomis in 1976 went to work under cover of an aircraft

company in the Far East as part of the CIA's off-the-shelf counter-terror network.

7   Georgie-Ann Geyer, "The CIA's Hired Killers", *True magazine*, 1970.

8   Robin Moore referenced this card trick in his 1966 book *The Country Team*. The book features Mike Forrester, a privateer who'd been chased out of Cuba and then purchased a rubber plantation in mythic Mituyan. The CIA asks Forrester to buy the local poppy crop before the Communists can grab it and sell it to the Mafia. Forrester takes the job after the CIA promises to sell the opium to US pharmaceutical companies. He keeps half the profits to keep his private army "oiled." Forrester buys the harvest from a tribal chief, who resembled the real one in Houei Sai, Laos, near where the CIA had its 118A base I referenced in Chapter 2. He brings along a CIA-supplied press to squeeze the opium into bricks. The vengeful MitComs descend on his plantation, but waiting for them is a hit team managed by a CIA officer named "Scott" working undercover for the USIS. When Scott(on) meets Forrester, he produces a deck of cards. Each card is black "with a hideous white eye in the center." As Scott explains, the USIS printed 20,000 of them in Vietnam. "When we discovered who the Communist agents in a city or village were, we assassinated them and put this eye on the body", Scott cheerfully explains.

9   Michael Ledeen, *The National Review Online,* 1 October 2001 .

10   Casper Weinberger, Robert McFarlane, Elliott Abrams, Clair E. George, Duane R. Clarridge, and Alan D. Fiers Jr.

11   David Johnston, "Bush Pardons 6 in Iran Affair, Aborting a Weinberger Trial; Prosecutor Assails 'Cover-Up', Bush Diary At Issue", *The New York Times*, 25 December 1992.

12   *Washington Post*, "Homeland Security struggles toward goals", 7 September, 2003.

Chapter 17

1   On the Homeland Security website, the threat of terrorism is said to be "a permanent condition."

2   Trevor Aaronson, "The Sting", The Intercept, 16 March 2015.

3   Since October 2012, the Director of National Intelligence has responsibility for neutralizing whistleblowers.

4   Timothy B. Lee, "Here's everything we know about PRISM to date", *Washington Post*, June 12, 2013.

5   Jay Stanley, "The Surveillance Industrial Complex: How the American Government Is Conscripting Businesses and Individuals in the Construction of a Surveillance Society", ACLU, August 2004.

6 See the previous essay for how Bruce Lawlor's résumé conceals his CIA service.

7 Matt Apuzzo and Adam Goldman, "How A Former CIA Official Turned the NYPD Into A Spying Powerhouse", Business Insider, 6 September 2013.

8 Ibid.

9 In July 2016 a hotel desk clerk in Ohio accused a Muslim man of pledging allegiance to ISIS. The cops arrested him. But he'd never said anything. He was in the US for medical attention. "U.S. apologizes for Arab man's 'unfortunate incident'" in Ohio" CBS News, 4 July 2016.

10 Herb Brown, "California's Terrorism Liaison Officer Program Modeled Nationwide", California Peace Officers Association, 27 October, 2014.

11 Beau Hodai,"Dissent or Terror: How the Nation's Counter Terrorism Apparatus, In Partnership With Corporate America, Turned on Occupy Wall Street", *Center for Media and Democracy*, May 2013. Darwin Bond Graham, "Counter-Terrorism Officials Helped Track Black Lives Matter Protesters", *East Bay Express,* 15 April 2015.

12 Naomi LaChance, "After Dallas Shootings, Police Arrest People for Criticizing Cops on Facebook and Twitter", 12 July 2016.

13 Counter Current News Editorial Team, "Opposition Grows To Bill That Would Jail and Fine Protesters Who Wear Masks and 'Hoodies'", 4 February 2015.

14 Don Moore, "The man who closed down Abu Ghraib Prison talks about conditions in Iraq", War Tales online.

15 Vietnam Policy and Prospects 1970 (Hearings Before The Committee On Foreign Relations, U.S. Senate, February 17-20, March 3, 14, 17, 19, 970), Statement for the Record On The Security Aspects of Pacification And Development by Ambassador William E. Colby.

16 Graeme MacQueen, *The 2001 Anthrax Attacks*, Clarity Press, 2014.

17 Bob Woodward, "CIA Told to Do 'Whatever Necessary' to Kill Bin Laden", *Washington Post*, 21 October 2001.

18 Matthew Rothschild, "More Anti-War Activists Snagged by 'No Fly' List," *The Progressive*, 16 October 2002. See also Unisys News Report, Blue Bell, Pa., August 19, 2002

19 David Firestone and Elizabeth Becker, "Traces of Terror: The Reorganization Plan; House Leadership Bows to President on Security Dept.", *The New York Times*, 19 January 2002.

20 Bamford, James, "Maintain CIA's Independence", 24 October 2002, *USA Today.*

21 Senate Committee on Foreign Relations: Cambodia, May 1970 Staff Report, p. 5.

22 "Presidential Decree Law on Administrative Detention and An Tri

Proceedings" (State Department Telegram 050556Z, January 1973, Ambassador Ellsworth Bunker).

23   Attorney General John Ashcroft, Prepared Remarks for the US Mayors Conference, October 25, 2001.

Chapter 18

1   Seymour Hersh, "Moving Targets: Will the counter-insurgency plan in Iraq repeat the mistakes of Vietnam?", *The New Yorker*, 15 December 2003. The Ba'athist Party, notably, went "underground" only after the US invasion, specifically to avoid assassination.

2   Julian Borger, "Israel trains US assassination squads in Iraq", 8 December 2003, *Guardian*.

3   Douglas Valentine, "Antiwar Reporting On the National Security State", 8 February 2010, Lew Rockwell.com.

4   See "The Phoenix Program, My Lai and the "Tiger Cages"" at <http://whale.to/b/ph2.html> and relevant passages from my book *The Phoenix Program*.

5   As it had with the Communist VCI in South Vietnam, the US conferred upon itself the divine right to exterminate Ba'athist Party leaders, along with their families and friends. This seemed unfair to members of the Ba'athist Party, the vast majority of whom had no American blood on their hands. Like their Vietnamese counterparts in the village of Thuong Xa, Iraqis who survived the US "shock and awe" campaign, and weren't terrorized into submission by the massive CIA-police repression that followed, continue to resist. Some have reportedly formed alliances with or even joined ISIS. See Dina al-Shibeeb, "Where is Iraq's Baath party today?" Al Arabiya News, Friday, 21 August 2015.

6   ISIS reportedly dresses its forces in black.

7   Gregory L. Vistica, "One Awful Night in Thanh Phong", *The New York Times,* April 25, 2001.

8   Phoenix Phung Hoang: Planned Assassination or Legitimate Conflict Management?, American University, 1Washington D.C., 1982, p. 5.

9   Peer DeSilva, *Sub Rosa*, New York Times Books, New York, 1978, p. 249.

10   Anthony Herbert, *Soldier,* Holt Rinehart & Winston, New York, 1973, pp. 105-106.

11   Generally speaking, the Marines supported Phoenix in I Corps, the Special Forces in II Corps, and the US Army in II Corps.

12   Gregory Vistica, *The Education of Lieutenant Kerrey*, Thomas Dunne Books, 2003, p. 71.

13   Ibid, p. 75.

14   Gregory L. Vistica, "One Awful Night in Thanh Phong", *The New York Times*, April 25, 2001.

15   From the song "Born in the USA" by Bruce Springfield.

16   Omerta applies as well when dealing with CIA secrecy. It literally means "manhood" and refers to the idea of a man dealing with his own problems without the help of a lawful entity.

17   Patrick Martin, "New School students demand ouster of Kerrey over Vietnam War atrocity", World Socialist Website, 14 may 2001.

18   Ibid.

19   David Hackworth, "The Horror that Will Never Go Away", King Features Syndicate, 1 May 2001.

20   Jack Valenti, "Killing Civilians Goes With the Duty of War", *LA Times*, 8 May 2001.

21   Patrick Martin, "New School students demand ouster of Kerrey over Vietnam War atrocity", *World Socialist Web Site*, 14 May 2001.

22   LeMoyne commanded the Delta PRU at the time of the Kerrey mission into Thanh Phong.

23   US Department of State, Media Roundtable Discussion, The American Experience in Southeast Asia, 1946-1975, 29 September 2010.

24   It is worth noting that the ICTY exonerated Slobodan Milosevic in its ruling that convicted former Bosnian-Serb president Radovan Karadzic of war crimes. See Alex Wilcoxson, "The Exoneration of Milosovic: The CTY's Surprise Ruling," Counterpunch, August 1, 2016, < http://www.counterpunch.org/2016/08/01/the-exoneration-of-milosevic-the-ictys-surprise-ruling/>

Chapter 20

1   Deborah Davis, *Katharine the Great: Katharine Graham and the Washington Post* (1979).

2   Jeff Stein, "Islamic group is CIA front, ex-Turkish intel chief says", *Washington Post*, 5 January 2011.

3   Tim Arango and Ben Hubbard, "Turkey Pursues Cleric Living in U.S., Blamed as Coup Mastermind", *The New York Times*, 19 July 2016.

4   William S. Lind, Colonel Keith Nightengale (USA), Captain John F. Schmitt (USMC), Colonel Joseph W. Sutton (USA), and Lieutenant Colonel Gary I. Wilson (USMCR), "The Changing Face of War: Into the Fourth Generation", *Marine Corps Gazette*, 1989.

Chapter 21

1   Remarks by the President in Address to the Nation on the Way Forward

in Afghanistan and Pakistan, 1 December 2009.

2   Peter Baker, "How Obama Came to Plan for 'Surge' in Afghanistan", *International New York Times*, 5 December 2009.

3   Marjorie Cohn, "40 Years On, the Vietnam War Continues for Victims of Agent Orange", Counterpunch, 17 December 2015.

4   T. Ahern, *Vietnam Declassified: The CIA and Counterinsurgency*, University Press of Kentucky, 2010, p. 64.

5   Ibid, p. 132.

6   *Le Nouvel Observateur*, Paris, 15-21 January 1998.

7   Rahul Mahajan, *FAIR*, I November 2001.

8   Robert Kagan, "Obama shows he has learned from the early world resistance", *Washington Post*, 13 December 2009.

9   "Remarks by the President at the Acceptance of the Nobel Peace Prize", The White House, Office of the Press Secretary, 10 December 2009.

10   Galula, p. 95.

11   Thomas and Barry, "Rethinking", *Newsweek*, 6 November 2009.

12   Joshua Partlow and Julie Tate, "2 Afghans allege abuse at U.S. site", *Washington Post*, 28 November 2009.

13   Paul Von Zielbauer, "Army will examine Special Forces killing", *The International New York Times*, 17 September 2007.

14   Kyle J. Cosner, "SF Soldier gets Silver Star for heroism in Afghanistan", 2 February 2007, <http://www.army.mil>

15   Anand Gopal, *No Good Men Among the Living: America, the Taliban, and the War Through Afghan Eyes*, Metropolitan Books/Henry Holt & Company, 2013, p. 122.

16   James Mills, *The Underground Empire: Where Crime and Governments Embrace*, Doubleday, 1986, p. 780.

17   Christopher Robbins, *Air America*, Avon Books, New York, 1985, p. 242.

18   David Corn, *The Blond Ghost: Ted Shackley and the CIA's Crusades*, Simon & Schuster, New York, 1994, p. 300.

19   *No Good Men*, pp. 113-114.

20   Griff Witte, "Taliban establishes elaborate shadow government in Afghanistan", *Washington Post*, 8 December 2009.

21   John Cook, *The Advisor*, Dorrance, Philadelphia, Pa., 1973, p. 208.

22   Sami Ramadani, "Iraq invasion deception increasingly shapes coverage of occupation", *Guardian*, 8 February 8, 2006.

Chapter 22

1   Michel Chossudovsky, "The War on Afghanistan is a Profit driven 'Resource War'", GlobalResearch, 25 July 2015.

Chapter 24

1   Eric Schmidt, "C.I.A. Said to Aid in Steering Arms to Syrian Opposition", *The New York Times*, 21 June 2012.

2   Clarence Williams and Moriah Balingit, "CIA left explosive material on Loudoun school bus after training exercise", *Washington Post*, 31 March 2016.

3   Ron Suskind, "Faith, Certainty and the Presidency of George W. Bush", *The New York Times Magazine*, 17 October 2004.

4   Walter Pincus, "Silence of 4 Terror Probe Suspects Poses Dilemma for FBI", *Washington Post*, 21 October 2001.

5   Ibid.

6   Michael Ledeen, *The National Review Online*, 1 October 2001.

7   Jackie Salo, "American's Fear of Terrorism at Its Peak Since 9/11, New Poll Says" *International Business Times*, 10 December 2015.

8   For the estimated dimensions of the Establishment 35+ years ago, see Bertram Gross, *Friendly Fascism: The New Face of Power in America*, South End Press, 1980.

ACRONYMS

ACLU: American Civil Liberties Union

BPP: Border Patrol Police (Thailand)

CNC: Counter-Narcotics Center

AFIO: Association of Former Intelligence Officers

ARVN: Army of the Republic of Vietnam

ARPANET: Advanced Research Projects Agency Network

CI: Counterinsurgency or Counterintelligence

BNDD: Bureau of Narcotics and Dangerous Drugs (1968-1973)

BUNCIN: Bureau of Narcotics Covert Intelligence Network

CIA: Central Intelligence Agency

CORDS: Civil Operations and Revolutionary Development

CT: Counterterrorism or Counterterrorist

CTC: Counterterrorism Center

CTT: Counterterror Team

DEACON: Drug Enforcement Administration Clandestine Operations Network

DEASOG: Drug Enforcement Administration Special Operations Group

DHS: Department of Homeland Security

DIOCC: District Intelligence and Operations Coordination Center

FEMA: Federal Emergency Management Agency

FBI: Federal Bureau of Investigations

FBN: Federal Bureau of Narcotics

FI: Foreign Intelligence

GVN: Government of Vietnam

HUMINT: Human Intelligence

ICEX-SIDE: Intelligence Coordination and Exploitation –

            Screening Interrogation and Detention of the Enemy

IDIU: Interdepartmental Intelligence Unit

IGO: Intelligence Group - Operations

IOCC: Intelligence and Operations Coordination Center

ITG: International Terrorism Group

JTF-CS: Joint Task Force-Civil Support

KMT: Kuomintang

MACV: Military Assistance Command Vietnam

MIG: Military Intelligence Group

MSS: Military Security Service

NATO: North Atlantic Treaty Organization

NED: National Endowment for Democracy

NIC: National Interrogation Center

NIO: Narcotics Intelligence Officer

NLF: National Liberation Front

NSA: National Security Agency

NSC: National Security Council

NVA: North Vietnamese Army

OSS: Office of Strategic Services

PA: Principal Agent

PA&E: Pacific Architects and Engineers

PAT: Political Action Team

PHMIS: Phung Hoang Management Information System

PIC: Province Interrogation Center

PICC: Province Intelligence Coordination Center

PIOCC: Province Intelligence and Operations Coordination Center

PRT: Provincial Reconstruction Team

PRU: Provincial Reconnaissance Unit

RD: Revolutionary Development

RDC: Revolutionary Development Cadre

RIU: Regional Intelligence Unit

SAD: Special Activities Division

SIO: Strategic Intelligence Office

SOA: School of the Americas

SOD: Special Operations Division

SIFU: Special Intelligence Field Unit

TIPS: Terrorism Information and Prevention System

TLO: Terrorism Liaison Officer

USAID: United States Agency for International Development

USIS: United States Information Service

VC: Vietcong

VCI: Vietcong Infrastructure

INDEX